VANILLA

Vanilla

The History of an Extraordinary Bean

Eric T. Jennings

Yale
UNIVERSITY PRESS
NEW HAVEN & LONDON

Published with assistance from the Mary Cady Tew Memorial Fund.

Copyright © 2025 by Eric T. Jennings.
All rights reserved.

This book may not be reproduced, in whole or in part, including illustrations, in any form (beyond that copying permitted by Sections 107 and 108 of the U.S. Copyright Law and except by reviewers for the public press), without written permission from the publishers.

Yale University Press books may be purchased in quantity for educational, business, or promotional use. For information, please email sales.press@yale.edu (U.S. office) or sales@yaleup.co.uk (U.K. office).

Set in Spectral by Westchester Publishing Services.
Printed in the United States of America.

Library of Congress Control Number: 2025934093
ISBN 978-0-300-26453-1 (hardcover)

A catalogue record for this book is available from the British Library.

Authorized Representative in the EU: Easy Access System Europe, Mustamäe tee 50, 10621 Tallinn, Estonia, gpsr.requests@easproject.com

10 9 8 7 6 5 4 3 2 1

Contents

AUTHOR'S NOTE vii

Introduction 1
ONE. New Spain's Near Monopoly 17
TWO. A Belgian Wins the Race 39
THREE. An Enslaved Teen Cracks the Case . . . 63
FOUR. Queen of Vanilla: Réunion
Surpasses Mexico 89
FIVE. Madagascar's Mr. Vanilla 107
SIX. Tahiti's Black Gold 133
SEVEN. Vanillamania. 159
EIGHT. Revenge of the Orchid 186
NINE. Toward Bland and White? 212
Conclusion 227

NOTES 235
ACKNOWLEDGMENTS 283
INDEX 287

Author's Note

Edmond Albius, the enslaved person at the heart of chapter 3, received his surname upon emancipation in 1848, the same year that Bourbon Island changed its name to Réunion. I shall observe these distinctions in the text, referring to him only by his first name and to the isle of Bourbon prior to 1848. Even this does not fully capture the changing nomenclature of Bourbon/Réunion. The island was first named Diva Morgabin by Arab navigators. It subsequently became known as Santa Appolinia (1506), then Mascarin, then Bourbon (1649), later Réunion (1793), then briefly Île Bonaparte (1806–10), and Bourbon once more after 1810, before Réunion finally stuck in 1848. To avoid confusion, I have used only two designations: Bourbon before 1848, and Réunion after 1848. Similarly, New Spain became Mexico in 1821, and Isle of France (Île de France or Isle de France) became Mauritius in 1814.

Additionally, I have provided conversions from metric measurements throughout, except for tons, which I have kept in their original form because of their proximity to US tons.

Introduction

VANILLA PRODUCTION REQUIRES INFINITE CARE. ITS FLOWER blooms, then fades and falls within a single morning. If it isn't manually pollinated over the course of those few hours, it is lost and along with it, the potential for a precious vanilla bean to grow.[1] Today, every single vanilla bean in stores comes from an orchid flower that has been hand-pollinated, a delicate operation undertaken with a toothpick or needlelike implement. Vanilla *marieuses*—the French term for a matchmaker—set off before dawn to pollinate thousands of flowers per morning. They stretch upward to reach vanilla vines that have climbed up their host trees; they squat to achieve the same result on flowers near the ground. The seemingly low-tech process is actually the product of an agrobotanical revolution that occurred in the late 1830s and early 1840s; prior to then, only bees had generated vanilla beans.

The exacting operation just described results in what botanists term a capsule, commonly known as a bean or pod. It takes some nine months to mature on the vine. Then another flurry of activity begins. The pod must be picked at precisely the right moment. No machine can undertake the task, which necessitates experience and sound judgment, much like pollination. Picked too early, a bean won't develop full flavors; picked too late, it will crack, and its prized seeds will spill out. Next comes a short scalding or boiling process. Trade secrets are tied to each phase, and different preparers swear by varying scalding times and temperatures. Then vanilla is made to sweat in wool blankets. The pod gradually darkens, and its water content is reduced through sun drying, another delicate balancing act. Finally, vanilla needs to be conditioned in a wooden crate. Things can go wrong at every stage, as I discovered with several dozen green vanilla pods I had been offered by Polynesian producers, which I tried sun drying on baking sheets in my Toronto backyard over many weeks in August 2022 (all the while fending off curious squirrels and raccoons). The resulting pods were either too dry to use or hopelessly molded. And all of this does not even begin to account for the care vanilla vines require: looping, maintaining proper shade and sun levels, limiting the number of vines on a single host, and avoiding pest damage, to name only a few.

When properly undertaken, the final result is glorious. Take the time to slice a supple and fragrant vanilla bean carefully down its length. With a knife blade, gently scrape out its hundreds of tiny black seeds, where the flavors are most concentrated. Allow them to infuse, stir into milk, and simmer to make a crème anglaise or homemade ice cream. Or add them to white wine and use the mixture to poach pears. Like a pod, this history is composed of a multitude of individual seeds. Together, they tell the story of a commodity that runs against the grain of most others, clustering to form four central themes that run through the book.

The first has to do with the many stages of competition that made vanilla go global. Competition in the early modern period involved first piracy, then botanical espionage, and finally attempts to set up alternate production sites to the Spanish colonies, which held an early pod monopoly. None of these strategies ultimately yielded the desired results, at least not on a scale that could break the Spanish stranglehold over supply. Then, in the early nineteenth century, as orchidology gained sway, botanists both amateur and professional began scrambling to crack the secret of vanilla's manual pollination. That discovery, for which many claimed credit, finally allowed the relocation of vanilla to new regions, where the plant's natural pollinators were absent. The only restrictions on vanilla thereafter were climatic. Even then, some fancied that they could grow it in colder climes, under greenhouses. Thus, vanilla's globalization began with rival attempts to break the Spanish pod monopoly in the seventeenth and eighteenth centuries and culminated in the race to bypass vanilla's natural insect pollinators altogether in the nineteenth century.

A second and connected element, then, involves patterns and networks of diffusion and appropriation. After having been a Mesoamerican and then a Spanish monopoly, vanilla went global through French colonial circuits in the second half of the nineteenth century. Its patterns of movement and

INTRODUCTION

models of consumption followed colonial lines, to be sure. I show how vanilla knowledge radiated from Réunion to Madagascar, Tahiti, and beyond in a very short span, transmitted by naval and other state authorities. But modes of dispersion and trade were also supra- and interimperial. Prior to 1914, German buyers scoured the Pacific and Indian Oceans for French colonial vanilla. US firms set up offices in coastal Madagascar. Réunionese and Mauritian planters continued pod exchanges long after Mauritius split away from the French empire. French settlers in Mexico imported methods developed on Réunion. As this last case suggests, specific communities learned to embrace vanilla and make it their own. Vanilla has also empowered Chinese immigrants in Madagascar and Tahiti, as well as formerly indentured South Asian workers in Réunion. These communities were part of what Corey Ross terms a colonial "franchise venture."[2] Vanilla became stratified, featuring a host of disparate actors operating in isolation from one another. I attempt to stir them together across these pages.

A third key layer to this book has to do with natural vanilla's gradual replacement by artificial flavors. I show that vanilla proved resistant to what David Goodman, Bernardo Sorj, and John Wilkinson call appropriationism, which involves piecemeal encroachments of industry on agriculture. There simply is no way to mechanize most stages of vanilla production, be it the orchid's manual pollination or the picking and preparation of pods. In other words, attempts to "weaken the constraints of nature" on vanilla have failed, with the notable exception of manual pollination itself, which can hardly be considered an act of mechanization. Again, every vanilla bean on store shelves has been deftly pollinated by human hands. Conversely, by the twentieth century, vanilla emerged as a perfect candidate for what the same authors term substitutionism, in which real vanilla has been replaced by synthetic vanillin. Margarine's challenge to butter constitutes a classic example of substitution. As with synthetic vanillin, the emergence of margarine involved a multistaged process starting with a nineteenth-century discovery, followed by a quest for cheaper raw materials with which to generate the synthetic version (vegetable oils in the case of margarine, cloves or pulp paper waste in the case of vanillin), and finally the progressive "gaining of acceptance" of the new product as "a close substitute for the purer, original rural product." Indigo provides another, albeit nonedible, example. Advocates of synthetic indigo, which was developed in the nineteenth century, not only vaunted their product's homogeneity but also convinced the garment sector that this synthetic substance was "purer" than the natural dye. In each of these cases, gradual replacement has not resulted in the original product's eradication. Similarly, the meat and mining sectors are fighting back today against laboratory-grown substitutes for beef and diamonds. This reaction, as well, falls in line with Goodman, Sorj, and Wilkinson's framework, in which stakeholders in a "specific agricultural, marketing and primary processing system" tend to defend their rank.[3] In the case of vanilla, however, the defense better resembles a protracted, uphill campaign, waged by a particular configuration of the Global South.

The fourth ingredient in this confection centers on tensions between vanilla's natural features and different readings of them. I will analyze the extent to which vanilla's many properties have conditioned its modes of cultivation, which in turn have affected specific communities, promoting sustainability and empowerment for some while exacerbating coercion for others. Beyond that, much as Sven Beckert's study of cotton illuminates "the unity of the diverse," so do vanilla pods reveal a paradoxical alikeness and plurality.[4] There are three types of edible vanillas, as we will see. Curing techniques, vanillin levels, and a host of other factors contribute to diverse flavor palates and noses. Some swear by Tahitian vanilla, others belittle it. In other words, vanilla is as subtle and nuanced as it is varied and contested. And yet, since the late nineteenth century, vanilla has also often been increasingly flattened, to the point that it has come to connote bland. That shift, I posit, has much to do with the substitution process. These four themes run through this book, reflecting in part natural vanilla's fractured status as a luxury commodity. They swirl across chapters, which, by the very nature of vanilla's slender archival imprint, must constitute *mignardises* rather than full-fledged desserts.

As food shoppers know, vanilla is one of the world's most expensive "spices," rivaled only by saffron. *Spice* might not the best term for the exquisite orchid pod, but at least it conveys vanilla's commercial value, which is a direct result of its labor-intensiveness. (Spices have been defined as "aromatic items of commerce with a high unit cost" that travel dried, unlike herbs; vanilla fits each of these criteria, although it is not fully desiccated.)[5] Vanilla pods were and remain to a large extent a luxury good, one that requires considerable expertise to grow. Their preparation process is so intense, individualized, and specialized that they present parallels with haute couture. And just like elite fashion, vanilla stands out at market. It is often prestigiously displayed near the front of gourmet specialty stores, where shopkeepers can keep an eye on it. It is typically preserved in its own showcase: a glass, cylindrical tube.

Throughout this book, I follow vanilla from its points of production to its patterns of consumption and varied cultural meanings to produce a global history of the only edible orchid. Geographically, it connects Atlantic, Indian, and Pacific Ocean worlds that are seldom drawn into dialogue by commodity chain histories. Global commodity histories have been in vogue for many decades now. Vanilla tells a rather different story from existing ones. Unlike cotton, it does not epitomize the "remaking of global capitalism" in the modern era. Nor did it drive slavery, although an enslaved teenager did transform the sector in 1841.

The timing of that breakthrough meant that vanilla's mass, multicontinental production waited until the era of abolition in the second half of the nineteenth-century, long after the sugar, cotton, tobacco, and indigo plantation systems emerged in the seventeenth century.[6] With the notable exception of Madagascar, vanilla did not generally rely on other types of forced labor, and it certainly did not contribute to the rise of an industrial proletariat (although the labor practices around vanilla in seventeenth-century New Spain were extractive in the extreme). Perhaps because it never made an affordability turn, becoming a cheap mass commodity in the manner of cotton, sugar, or even rubber, natural vanilla has followed a different trajectory.[7] Its path is more fractured and contingent, which reflects the fragmentary nature of available sources. Vanilla therefore lends itself to an approach that blends miniature portraits with botanical-commercial flashpoints.

This is not to say that pods were a fleeting commodity, like the high-price ostrich feathers in fashion for women's hats between 1870 and 1914. Nor is it to suggest that vanilla was somehow spared the effects of the two industrial revolutions or globalization, quite the contrary. In fact, its dispersion from the Americas to other continents calls to mind those of rubber and cochineal, a much sought-after red dye derived from insects that thrived on cacti. It presents additional parallels with the British and Dutch challenge to the French colonial monopoly over West African gum arabic, a binding agent with many uses, whose export to rival European countries France expressly prohibited in 1752. The French breaking of the Spanish monopoly over vanilla also resembles the Dutch and French undoing of the Arabian coffee monopoly. Vanilla's boom even mirrors those of far less "noble" commodities such as tropical West African palm oil, initially used as an industrial lubricant. Vanilla can further be likened to tea, in the way that an upstart, multicontinental empire challenged an established producer—the French empire and New Spain/Mexico in the first instance, the British empire and China in the second. However, unlike vanilla, tea rapidly outgrew its luxury status. Even the fashion analogy I drew above proves imperfect. Contrary to vanilla, changes in production techniques were not at the heart of that sector's transformation but instead "the value added by design" and the "relationship of cloth-selling to clothing."[8] In other words, each of these comparisons quickly runs its course.

Vanilla's intrinsic characteristics partly account for its bucking of these trends. They have also determined some of the benefits vanilla has historically offered humans. To this day, thanks to the high price it fetches, and because it requires a host tree and therefore forests or undergrowth, vanilla offers considerable potential for empowerment and sustainability. At least this is true outside the context of early extractive colonialism. Concerning sustainability, anthropologist Sarah Osterhoudt refers to "agroforests" to describe vanilla cultivation, because these are, in her words, "cultivated systems that include trees." She adds that "mature agroforests" where vanilla grows in northeastern Madagascar feature pronounced "species richness," including a significant presence of endemic trees. They are seldom converted to make way for rice farming. Similarly, on nearby Réunion Island, geographer Judith Klein points to the "close links" that bind the protection of forests with the cultivation of vanilla.[9] Forest vanilla, whose vines climb a range of trees, is far less environmentally harmful than rice but also cacao, which often involves initial clear-cutting. Vanilla vines are hemiepiphytes and require a trunk or host of some kind to thrive. They build on existing woodlands and strengthen them. In that sense, vanilla represents the opposite of the banana, which has "thrown the entire Central American ecosystem out of balance."[10]

In terms of empowerment, vanilla continues to offer an astonishingly high value-to-weight ratio. This allows vanilla harvesters, like some wild rubber collectors, to "connect themselves to global networks of wealth."[11] Little wonder that vanilla was once "the diamond in Mexico's plant economy," to cite Emilio Kourí. Admittedly, in the second half of the nineteenth century property grabs dispossessed once relatively prosperous vanilla cultivators in that country, marking the end of communal landholding practices.[12] Yet, in

INTRODUCTION

Madagascar some local people quickly made themselves vanilla experts and were among the first planters in Sava, the island's famous vanilla coast.

The vanilla orchid and pod constitute full-fledged actors in this story, but ones with well-defined roles. The case of vanilla is entangled in a broader debate over plant agency. Vanilla's many traits, starting with how much it has relied on humans as pollinators and the multiple stages required to cure and condition its beans, have determined in large part how, where, and when it has been produced and prepared. Vanilla features an unusual type of propagation, rarely spreading through its actual seeds. (Although recent research led by Adam Karremans does confirm vanilla dispersion by specific mammals that eat and pass the seeds.)[13] Long before the manual pollination turn, humans had been disseminating it through cuttings, which are readily able to root. As for the pollination of its flower, the process that produces the precious pod, it was previously undertaken entirely by bees. However, after the 1836 and 1841 breakthroughs described in this book, humans gradually replaced insects and today constitute practically the flower's sole pollinator.

A central point to keep in mind is the global collapse in the share of edible vanilla pollinated by bees—which stood at 100 percent prior to 1836 but is now almost nonexistent. This suggests, in line with what Michael Pollan has advanced for other crops, that humans have become part of vanilla's "coevolutionary bargain." However, contrary to what Pollan contends, I would stress that it was humans, starting with those who mastered vanilla's manual pollination, Charles Morren and Edmond Albius, who were responsible for manipulating vanilla into this deal, and then of course for sustaining it, rather than vice versa. Human ingenuity, trade, colonial and intercolonial networks, along with contingency, lie at the heart of this book. They explain how vanilla went from being Mexican to Bourbon, Malagasy, Polynesian, Indonesian, and perhaps one day Floridian. If anything, vanilla's particularities, its needs in shade and light, its proneness to fungal diseases, its requirement of a host plant, its pollination limitations, its peculiar propagation, all constitute features that human minds and hands either overcame or are trying to overcome. In other words, this is a very uneven bargain. Retrieving plant agency has limits, and vanilla highlights them.[14]

This is not intended to turn the clock back to the "dualism" critiqued by Bruno Latour—the separating of the human from the nonhuman in the name of "efficiency and profitability." On the contrary, vanilla illustrates what Latour himself called "internalized ecology." He defined the concept as follows: "where so many animals, plants and materials are submitted to such an intense socialization, re-education and reconfiguration, that they change shapes, functions and even genetic makeup."[15] Certainly, via manual pollination and mass relocation, humans have shaped both vanilla's genetic similitude and geographic range. But although we have changed its reproductive partners (bees no longer) and altered where it grows, we remain bound by the inherent constraints of the orchid's propagation. And so, even though vanilla undoubtedly represents a complex botanical agent, throughout these pages it interacts first and foremost with the many people who have grown, pollinated, spread, dried, studied, prepared, shipped, sold, distributed, insured, and promoted it. In that sense, this book is fundamentally about entanglements between vanilla and people.[16]

I should add another point about the scope of my analysis. Only a few histories have explored vanilla. Most of those have concentrated on Mexico either as the plant's birthplace or, as in the case of Kourí's pathbreaking work, as a site of contested landholding in the nineteenth century. As for the handful of general overviews available, they rely largely on printed sources.[17] This book is rooted in archival material collected across six continents and is primarily concerned with what happened to vanilla as and after it went global, a process that began with the first manual pollinations in the 1830s and 1840s, which I examine in detail.

Vanilla's history can be divided into several broad periods: the pre-1836 epoch during which it was produced nearly exclusively in New Spain / Mexico and remained a rarefied luxury, used mainly as a flavoring for chocolate drinks; the 1836 and 1841 dual discovery of its artificial pollination by a Belgian botanist and an enslaved teen on Île Bourbon and the subsequent global vanilla boom, which saw its sites of production shift from Central America to the Indian and Pacific Oceans; and finally, the rise of synthetics starting in the late nineteenth century and the vanilla lobby's ensuing campaigns to fight back.

There are three kinds of edible vanilla. The native range of the vanilla most people know, *Vanilla planifolia*, extends from Mexico to Guatemala, Belize, and Honduras. (Technically, the varietal on our plates is known as *Vanilla planifolia* Andrews, but I have abbreviated the name for the sake of convenience.) Many gourmets regard it as the finest. It is known under several other designations, including Bourbon vanilla, which initially referred to *planifolia* grown in the Indian Ocean isles. *Planifolia* plants are easily recognized by the zigzag pattern their vines form as they climb and loop back down on host trees. Because it is manually pollinated, *planifolia* presents a high degree of genetic similitude the world over. *Vanilla tahitensis*, the varietal found in the French South Pacific, initially hailed from the Americas as well. Evidence suggests that it emerged naturally as a hybrid in the Americas prior to its transfer to the Pacific islands. Finally, *Vanilla pompona*, sometimes known as *vainilla grande* or *vainilla bania* in Spanish, *vanillons* in French, and "Guadeloupe vanilla" in English, features a considerably larger pod. Its natural range extended much farther south than *planifolia*, across large swaths of South America. To this day, it is both consumed as a food item and used in the perfume sector.[18]

Until the manual pollination revolution, *planifolia* production was monopolized by New Spain / Mexico, while *pompona*, on the other hand, was grown in Colombia, Venezuela, Peru, Suriname, Guiana, and French Guiana. Forms of knowledge about the best supporting plants, preparation techniques, and curing methods both competed and circulated widely, with many variations still enduring to this day (like pod scarring with fish teeth in lieu of scalding on the island of Guadeloupe).[19]

Due mostly to limited supply, until 1836–41 vanilla remained a luxury, largely restricted to elites. It was long seen as the ultimate refinement: Queen Marie-Antoinette's Trianon perfume, prepared by Jean-Louis Fargeon, contained lily, vanilla, and sandalwood. So rare and dear were the pods that they were subject to piracy, inquiries, larceny, and contraband. Some of the first samples to arrive in London did so through buccaneering on the high seas. In 1697, English corsair William Dampier recounted how his fellow pirates disposed of vanilla after seizing it from Spanish vessels, as they had no idea of its purpose. Other pirates mistook it for tobacco and puzzled over its drying method. Then, in 1704, the British navy captured a French man-of-war carrying vanilla, cochineal, and other goods. By this time, the pod's function had become clear. That vanilla was found on board a French vessel was no coincidence. France was emerging by then as the world's top consumer of the rare "beans," and would remain so until 1906. In 1706, the French consul in Cádiz reported a significant theft of vanilla pods that his staff were acquiring from ships arriving from New Spain. In 1729, the consul's successor disclosed that a recent delivery was severely dried out and weighed far less than expected. Half of it was lost. The very fact that losses were discussed in detail points to how valuable pods were. As a result, many entrepreneurs and bootleggers alike smelled an opportunity for profits. Vanilla contraband became so widespread that in 1822, ambitious young liberal French politician Adolphe Thiers used "ladies hiding vanilla in their purses in port" as a baseline to measure all smuggling across the Pyrenees.[20]

Before 1836, vanilla was consumed for different purposes but nearly always by elites. Louis XV's mistress Madame de Pompadour incorporated vanilla into a "heating diet" aimed at offsetting her "cold temperament" and retaining the king's favor. This function as an aphrodisiac endured. US author Solon Robinson's 1854 book of short stories evoked vanilla as a threat to morality: "'Tis here that mothers suffer young daughters to come at this untimely midnight hour to drink 'light wines,' or eat ice cream, drugged with passion-exciting vanilla." To be clear, the "drugging" had nothing to do with any spiked substance; it referenced vanilla's inherent properties. An 1885 medical manual still insisted that vanilla's role as a sexual stimulant "can leave no doubt."[21]

Others used vanilla to make themselves cold, rather than hot. In the 1780s, Thomas Jefferson first encountered vanilla ice cream in Paris. He famously transcribed a recipe for it. It called for "a stick of vanilla" to simmer in a pot full of "good cream." Jefferson was so captivated that in Philadelphia in 1791 he experienced vanilla withdrawal. He therefore ordered from France "a packet of 50 pods (batons) which may come very well in the middle of a packet of newspapers."[22] Was Jefferson trying to avoid paying customs duty, merely thinking of conservation, or both? Regardless, the era of vanilla ice cream was underway.

By the 1830s, women in New Orleans were adapting Jefferson's recipe, manually whirling the vanilla-infused cream in an ice tub for roughly an hour.[23] This American infatuation undoubtedly contributed to demand. There are other signs of mounting desire for vanilla in the United States in the 1830s, on the eve of the pod's globalization in the 1840s. The fictional Mrs. Marsden in Eliza Leslie's 1832 short story "Mrs. Washington Potts" is left unsettled by an absence of vanilla, as she wishes to impress her nouveau riche guest with homemade vanilla ice cream. When her servant reports that the local shopkeeper has never even heard of vanilla, Marsden declares that "a man who keeps so large a store has no right to be so ignorant." Left with no alternative, Mrs. Marsden ends up substituting lemon for vanilla, which, as Claire Bunschoten notes, sets off a chain reaction that ultimately leads to a culinary and social fiasco.²⁴ Prior to 1841, vanilla supply remained modest. Yet, as these two examples suggest, demand was intensifying.

The hankerings of Thomas Jefferson and the fictional Mrs. Marsden aside, nobody *needed* vanilla. Or did they? Consumer desire is complex, and many certainly *craved* it. Furthermore, food "necessities" are inherently subjective, informed by cultural, geographical, and chronological factors. For instance, their contours expanded significantly in the eighteenth century. Contrary to received wisdom, the 1792 food protests in Paris were more about demanding sugar and candles than they were about bread (and should therefore be termed "grocery riots"). In a time of restrictions, the revolutionary authorities soon came to recognize sausages, butter, cheese, honey, and wine, in addition to bread, as "articles of prime necessity," thereby reflecting changing norms of what constituted "necessities"—and all this on the heels of vigorous debates over whether luxury itself was corrosive or, conversely, progress-generating.²⁵ Still, the point remains that vanilla did not appear on such lists, at least not yet.

Much as porcelain allowed the nobility to erect an additional barrier dividing it from the rest of society that relied on earthenware, so did vanilla set elite tables apart, prior to the mid-nineteenth century.²⁶ Contemporary economic historians have tended to reject emulation as the sole driving force behind increased eighteenth-century demand. Yet vanilla was evidently a "positional good" that helped define rank. In that sense, parallels emerge with Champagne, truffles, caviar, and silk. All, vanilla included, eventually experienced some measure of "democratization" in the twentieth century—in part a sign that promoters of these goods managed to integrate critiques of luxury to better sell them.²⁷ Even caviar became a "mass market food" of sorts while remaining decidedly upscale. Indeed, much as Champagne did, vanilla succeeded in retaining aristocratic ties while gaining in popularity in the new bourgeois, even mass consumer culture of the second half of the nineteenth century. Like Champagne, vanilla pods both fostered affinities and forged divides—unlike sugar, whose "spread downward and outward meant that it lost some of its power to distinguish those who consumed it."²⁸ This luxury connection makes vanilla an exemplar of "Champagne capitalism," a category that encompasses everything from silk fashion to Roquefort cheese. In the wake of World War II, an official for Marseille's chamber of commerce put it plainly: "Before the war [. . .] vanilla was one of the flagships of French exports, on a par with luxury items, *haute couture*, fashion and perfumes."[29] Vanilla's globalization in the second half of the nineteenth century is clearly part of this same luxury "empire of taste." As we shall see, France relied on colonial and paracolonial networks to achieve a near monopoly over vanilla production by the dawn of the twentieth century—and this at a time when the nation faced stiffer competition across other luxury sectors.[30]

Truffles, too, offer some interesting points of comparison with vanilla. Both are priced as indulgences, the two were once considered aphrodisiacs, and each presents significant obstacles to cultivation. But major differences appear as well. For one thing, truffles are more profoundly tied to place, with different regions defending their distinct varietals—numbered in the hundreds. Although vanilla features localized preparation secrets, and there are three types of vanilla, *Vanilla planifolia* nonetheless holds the lion's share of the market and spans large parts of the globe. It features remarkable unity. To be sure, a prestigious "vanilla cellar" in Paris highlights variations in nose between *planifolia* pods, but those differences can result as much from modes of preparation as from terroir. On balance, then, vanilla and truffles share some of the characteristics of fractured luxury commodities but little more.[31]

Vanilla behaves strangely for a seemingly superfluous foodstuff. It bucked the trend of the French commercial slowdown after 1870, and its consumption in both the United States and France increased during the Great Depression. Admittedly, its price tumbled but not enough to pull it out of luxury status.[32]

Before 1841, nearly all the world's vanilla left the Atlantic port of Veracruz in central Mexico. Even so, New Spain / Mexico never exported more than five metric tons of vanilla per annum until 1830, except for the year 1802, an anomaly resulting from a break in the French Revolutionary Wars that had created a vanilla glut. These figures were completely incommensurate with tonnage of coffee or cacao: In the late eighteenth century, for example, Europeans consumed some 120 million pounds, or 5,443 metric tons, of coffee a year. Of course, vanilla was much costlier by the gram.[33] Indeed, vanilla was valuable enough that at its point of departure, it might warrant being placed in safe deposit boxes. It could even pass as currency. The few attempts to smuggle it out of New Spain involved elaborate subterfuge. Yet, in its sites of consumption, prior to 1841 it was usually bought and sold in such small quantities as to be nearly invisible within the historical record.

INTRODUCTION

Vanilla's manual pollination, the necessary condition for its global boom, lies at the heart of this book. Until now, the stories of its two creators have never been told in detail from original sources. In 1836, Belgian botanist Charles Morren first achieved vanilla's manual pollination. This made it possible, in principle, to cultivate vanilla beyond the Americas, where local bees served as its natural pollinators (one set of bees for *Vanilla planifolia*, and another for *Vanilla pompona*). Soon, Morren asked his wife, Marie, to present the Belgian vanilla, grown atop mounds of coal in a Liège greenhouse, at international competitions as Europe's only specimen. However, despite the novelty effect, Morren's technique proved cumbersome, confusing, and time-consuming. His greenhouse vanilla project turned out to be a mirage. Morren is a strikingly paradoxical figure: first to the finish line yet unable to monetize his finding or even to share it by transforming it into a method, for reasons I expose in chapter 1.

Instead, an enslaved teenager should be credited with the main artificial pollination method still used today the world over. In 1841, just a few years after Morren's breakthrough, and in complete isolation from it, young Edmond on Île Bourbon transformed the vanilla sector. Thomas Jefferson and Madame de Pompadour may be household names; Edmond is not, although he undoubtedly should be. Like many brilliant inventions, his seems disarmingly simple after the fact. He discovered a straightforward and efficient way of artificially pollinating the vanilla orchid in a matter of seconds with a toothpick or needle. Even more astonishing is the fact that he received credit for his method, despite several other botanists trying to rob him of it. We know his story in detail, interestingly, thanks to the rebuttal of his former owner against rival claimants. Records reveal that the enslaved twelve-year-old was an avid and accomplished botanist, a "specialized slave," who grew up on a modestly sized estate. Archival evidence suggests that he mastered the reproduction of other plants before applying that know-how to the vanilla orchid. In so doing, he established the first clear, easy-to-replicate method of manual pollination. Thanks to his discovery, his native isle rocketed to the top global pod producer in just a few decades.

Edmond's 1841 discovery changed everything. *Vanilla planifolia* could now be grown outside the range of vanilla's natural pollinators, the Central American Meliponini family of bees. French settlers introduced Edmond's technique to Mexico. The world soon experienced a vanilla craze. Réunion planters next sought out cheaper labor on nearby Madagascar, which became by far the top producer of vanilla in the twentieth century, after falling under French control in 1895. The British tried in vain to keep pace by producing vanilla in Mauritius, the Seychelles Islands, and Ceylon; the United States attempted to do the same in Puerto Rico; and the Dutch in the East Indies, modern-day Indonesia. Yet no region ever caught up to Madagascar, at least not for long. From 1860 to 1960, the Central American pod became increasingly associated with the French colonial empire and the Indian and Pacific Oceans.

After 1841, vanilla fever raged, with France and the United States its largest markets by far, and the French empire steeply gaining in its production share. Already in 1895, tiny Réunion Island exported 100 metric tons of vanilla, compared to Mexico's 8.1. In 1908, French colonies (Madagascar, Tahiti, the Comoros, the French Caribbean, and Réunion combined) generated 397 metric tons of vanilla, compared to Mexico's 141.5 tons and a mere 35 metric tons from all other parts of the world combined.[34] By the 1920s, French colonies, starting with Madagascar, produced 75 percent of the world's vanilla, with estimates reaching 85 percent the following decade. After surpassing French consumption in 1906, the United States alone absorbed five hundred metric tons of vanilla per year in the 1920s.[35] Both nations were awash in vanilla.

Previously, vanilla's rarity had meant that the public was largely ignorant of its sourcing and properties. A French dictionary from 1750 defined vanilla as follows: It was indigenous to the Americas and had been so named by the Spaniards. It should properly be termed a "pod" (*gousse*). European consumers could purchase it dried in packets of fifty, one hundred, or one hundred fifty units. It was a regular ingredient in hot chocolate. As for the plant itself, the entry specified that it "climbs and is cultivated like green beans, as on a trellis."[36] That comparison would prove to be especially enduring even as vanilla grew familiar. With more Europeans encountering not just disembodied extracts or powders but actual pods, in 1909, a Bordeaux trader expressed surprise at the extravagant cost of what he called a dead ringer for the common green bean (*haricot vert*). An indignant expert set about educating the merchant. Vanilla, he explained, had to be pollinated by hand, it required airy soil, three years' lead time prior to flowering, a host plant on which to grow, infinite care, pest control, sufficient yet not excessive sunlight, pruning and looping, picking, then, depending on the type of preparation, boiling or oven curing, sun drying, and finally preparation for

INTRODUCTION

market. The expert concluded, "And that's why vanilla is more expensive than *haricots verts!*"[37] Vanilla is certainly no ordinary bean.

Vanilla's broader cultural meanings have shifted constantly. As Madame de Pompadour's usage suggests, it was often tied to sex. Indeed, the very name derives from the Latin term for vagina. In 1783, the Marquis de Sade wrote his wife from a cell in the dungeon at Vincennes. The notorious libertine's letter about masturbation and ejaculation was titled *La Vanille et la Manille* (Of vanilla and Manila). Vanilla was one of several stimulants used by the jailed marquis. Yet, by the twentieth century, the word had become synonymous with "plain" or "unoriginal," decidedly unsexy—a usage popularized by the phrase *vanilla sex*.[38] One of the reasons for this alleged "blandness" probably has to do with the rise of muted synthetics at the expense of actual vanilla pods.

I like to tell students in my empires class that unless they see any of the following words on a label—natural, pods, beans, Madagascar, Mexican, Tahitian, Réunion, Indonesian—there's a good chance the "vanilla" they are ingesting is a substance composed of cloves and alcohol in the best of cases. Whether that matters is another question. If flavor is the main criterion, it may not.[39] Vanillin, the molecule contained in authentic vanilla, is very effectively synthesized. In fact, few instruments, let alone palates, can measure or even distinguish between chemical and real vanilla. Over time, a host of replacement materials, ranging from beaver secretions (castoreum) to lignin, were employed in lieu of the expensive orchid pod. The 1920s saw the advent of a new, more potent synthetic, ethylvanillin. The following decade, a Canadian chemist helped perfect a way of extracting vanillin from paper mill waste. By 1981, a company in Thorold, Ontario, was producing a staggering 60 percent of the world's vanillin in this manner. In the twenty-first century, Japanese chemist Mayu Yamamoto has succeeded in producing vanillin from cow dung.[40] As vanilla flavor shifted from inelastic to elastic—meaning it could be readily substituted—it became truly democratized but at a terrible cost to the real vanilla sector. Faced with an onslaught of cheap synthetics, the natural vanilla lobby began counterattacking in the 1960s. This led to an ongoing battle between real and synthetic vanillin. Consumer groups regularly take food corporations to court for introducing black flecks into yogurts and ice creams to mimic actual vanilla beans, or simply for falsely claiming vanilla as an ingredient. For instance, in 2019, a lawsuit alleged that Wegmans brand vanilla ice cream contained no actual vanilla, thereby misleading consumers. In general, only select premium ice cream makers still use real vanilla in their products.[41]

Becoming bland or being replaced by beaver excretions, paper pulp waste, and cow dung are not the only bizarre vanilla twists of the last two hundred years. Another has to do with race. Vanilla is sold in the form of a dark brown or black pod, distinguishable to consumers as black flecks, and its artificial pollination method was discovered by an enslaved Black teen, yet vanilla has somehow become white. That transformation was probably tied to the ascendancy of vanilla ice cream and the association of vanilla with the white orchid, which is the flower, not the fruit that produces actual vanilla. The link proved so powerful that Maya Angelou famously related how under Jim Crow, African Americans in Stamps, Arkansas, were barred from eating vanilla ice cream except on July 4—"other days [they] had to be satisfied with chocolate." Vanilla became an enduring marker of whiteness.[42]

Vanilla is a fractured, polyvalent, revealing symbol of the modern global village, and, as this last example suggests, a potent sign of the times. It has been freeze-dried and powdered in astronaut meals. Austrian scientists recently tapped vanillin as an ecological source of battery power.[43] The story of vanilla connects Totonac curing specialists, Betsimisaraka pollinators in Madagascar, Chinese middlemen in Tahiti, an American revolutionary, an ambitious Belgian botanist, and an enslaved teen on Île Bourbon. Vanilla serves as an ingredient in everything from sweet treats like crème brûlée and ice cream floats, to savory dishes, including seafood recipes, and even beverages like Coca-Cola. It is remarkably mutable. From Icelandic vínarterta torte to Japanese purin, Austrian vanillekipferl, Italian panettone, and French madeleines, vanilla provides a key flavoring component to iconic national and regional dishes.[44] Consumers tell of its comforting, even nostalgia-inducing effects. Let's dig in.

CHAPTER 1

New Spain's Near Monopoly

WHILE "VANILLA LOGICALLY FOLLOWS CHOCOLATE," AS Sophie Coe once contended, it has left far less of a trail. Although we know a great deal about cacao and its Indigenous uses, the story of the vanilla that flavored the famous Aztec drink *chocolatl* remains far murkier. Emilio Kourí suggests that only in the 1760s did vanilla begin to be cultivated by Totonac people in the hills around Papantla, in the sense that it "habitually obtain[ed] improvements from labor."[1] Prior to that, vanilla was picked in the humid forests of Mesoamerica. Indigenous people also spread vanilla vine cuttings. However, bees, as its natural pollinators, continued to generate the pods and dictate vanilla's range as a productive plant.

The vanilla orchid family probably dates back some sixty-five million years. As with palm oil, one should treat critically claims of human vanilla use around the Fertile Crescent in antiquity and earlier. A 2018 discovery of some trace components of vanilla in a Bronze Age grave in Israel has led some to speculate that actual pods reached the site via the Indian Ocean. However, vanilla specialists and some archeologists have reacted with "caution" to this hypothesis, as there is no corroborating evidence for a theory that would move vanilla's departure from the Americas up by some three millennia. It seems far more likely that this is a "false past" and that the chemical residues the archeologists found derived from other substances.[2] Until the sixteenth century, then, vanilla was unknown outside the Americas.

Although long confined to those two continents, pods were certainly not circumscribed to small regions. In fact, one important feature of early vanilla gathering in the Americas involves its substantial range. Whereas by the nineteenth century, *Vanilla planifolia* became intensely produced in the

FIGURE 1. New Spain, circa 1800. Map by Isabelle Lewis.

Veracruz and Oaxaca provinces of what is now Mexico, in pre-Columbian times it had been collected first by Maya people farther south. Scholars have deduced that the earliest human uses of vanilla for cacao flavoring occurred with the Maya, in what is now Guatemala, Belize, and southern Mexico. That does not even begin to cover *Vanilla pompona*, whose early history remains obscure. Only much later did Totonac people gather *Vanilla planifolia*, supplying the Aztecs with pods. Vanilla harvesting moved north first to satisfy Aztec demand, and then, after the arrival of the conquistadors in 1519, the Spanish. Thereafter, Mayan-produced vanilla started to suffer from a geographical disadvantage. Under Spanish rule, vanilla export routes followed silver, cochineal, and other commodities that streamed out of the port of Veracruz, first to Seville, then, after 1650, to Cádiz. Veracruz held a monopoly within the monopoly, so to speak, because 99.9 percent of New Spain's exports to Spain between 1520 and 1650 passed through its port. And so Papantla's proximity to this sole transatlantic outlet rendered it a more practical production site.[3]

We know that the Aztecs relished vanilla in their *chocolatl*. Like other Mesoamerican societies, the Aztecs attributed multiple functions to their cacao-based drink: it served as tribute, a medium between the human and

FIGURE 2. *Tlilxochitl* or vanilla as represented in Francisco Hernández's *Nova plantarum, animalium et Mineralium Mexicanorum historia*, 1651, p. 38. Courtesy of the John Carter Brown Library.

the divine, and a sacred force in its own right.[4] However, they appear not to have harvested the vanilla in the drink themselves, at least not routinely. Here is another leitmotif of vanilla: for much of its history, the pod was most appreciated outside its sites of cultivation. This may explain why the Aztecs called it the black flower (*tlilxochitl*) despite the fact that the orchid's blossom is actually white with yellow tones, the first of many color misnomers. The Spanish physician Francisco Hernández perpetuated the confusion in the massive tome he researched in New Spain in the 1570s by calling it *flore nigro araco aromatico* (the black fragrant flower).[5] In fact, the orchid's flower is odorless, unlike its pod. The volume was not published until the mid-seventeenth century. Its woodcut depicting *tlilxochitl* shows two splendid pods and four leaves zigzagging along a *planifolia* vine.

Franciscan friar Bernardino de Sahagún proved arguably more meticulous in his research, in no small part because he relied on a team of Nahua former students as well as local elders to compile his monumental *Historia General de las Cosas de Nueva España* in the 1570s.[6] The resulting chronicle of Aztec culture and history is known today as the *Florentine Codex*. One plate depicts vanilla vines, leaves, and two clusters of three pods. They are rendered with graphic flair and accurate detail compared to other contemporaneous representations of vanilla.

The earliest written descriptions of Indigenous uses of vanilla come primarily from Spanish clergymen and are not confined to eating or drinking. In 1696, Franciscan friar Andrés de Avendaño drew an ethnographic portrait of the "Itzá Indians," a Mayan ethnic group. Their sleeveless clothes were multicolored, and they often had pierced ears and noses. Crucially, according to the friar, they "usually" affixed "vanillas to their noses." Other sources suggest that the Aztecs used vanilla as a fragrant component of amulets they wore around their necks. Like the cacao with which it was commonly linked, vanilla fulfilled sacred functions in several Indigenous traditions.[7]

The lands that today comprise Mexico and Guatemala were not the only part of the Spanish empire to produce and export vanilla to elite European tables. The larger *Vanilla pompona* was harvested in what is today Colombia. A 1668 ordinance set the price at which prepared vanilla pods could be purchased from Indigenous people in the Popayán district.[8] Although global consumption of vanilla pods remained modest, they nevertheless generated considerable wealth at sites of production. Some middlemen began to find ways around emerging vanilla regulation. Fraud, larceny, and evasion of regulations would all become central characteristics of the vanilla trade for centuries.

As the Colombian regulatory example suggests, vanilla also surfaces in the historical record in cases of grievances or infractions. The latter occurred in 1653, in the Zapotec Sierra. There, the viceroy investigated the activities

FIGURE 3. Vanilla represented and described in the *Florentine Codex*, 1570s. The History Collection / Alamy Stock Photo.

of one André de Aramburu, accused of excessively exploiting Indigenous people who were forced to bring vanilla to him as tribute. The problem was not limited to how Aramburu got hold of the vanilla. The authorities also charged him with attempted fraud. Indeed, the eighty thousand vanilla beans taken from the Indigenous people were about to be sold outside the rules, and indeed outside the continent, to China. The document adds that there was "usually a demand" for vanilla in that land. This constitutes by far the earliest evidence of vanilla exports to China and hints at budding global demand in the mid-seventeenth century.[9] Yet the entire chain of production was tightly controlled by Spain, as evidenced by this attempt to curtail sales to Asia. Just as Ferdinand Magellan had once been tasked with breaking Portugal's monopoly over cloves, so would vanilla's lure fuel many an attempt to undo Spain's pod monopoly.

The accusations of corruption leveled against Aramburu should not obscure the fact that straightforward extraction and coercion lay at the heart of New Spain's vanilla sector. In seventeenth-century Verapaz (Guatemala), Itzá (Maya) people were compelled to bring vanilla to the authorities as part of "compulsory trade practices." Similarly, in eighteenth-century Oaxaca province, the *alcaldes mayores* (the civil officials who ran the region) practiced *repartimiento*. This procedure involved *mayores* issuing "cash or basic equipment or commodities to the Indians on the account of [. . .] merchants." In practice, in Teutila (Oaxaca province) this meant that merchants and civil authorities received vanilla and cotton from Indigenous peoples in exchange for cloth.[10]

Unfortunately, early sources remain mostly silent about vanilla preparation methods and producers. In what is now Mexico, one must leap forward to 1803-4 to German naturalist and geographer Alexander von Humboldt's impressions of the process and its social implications:

> The natives who remain eight successive days in the forests of Quilate, sell the vanilla fresh and yellow to the *gente de razon*, i.e. the whites, mestizoes and mulattos, who alone know the *beneficio de la baynilla*, namely, the manner of drying it with care, giving it a silvery luster, and sorting it for transportation into Europe. The yellow fruits are spread out on cloths, and kept exposed to the sun for several hours. When sufficiently heated, they are wrapped up in woolen cloths for evaporation, when the vanilla blackens, and they conclude with exposing it to be dried from the morning to the evening in the heat of the sun. The method of preparing the vanilla at Colipa is much superior to the *beneficio* employed at Misantla.[11]

Humboldt goes on to refer to the vanilla acquirers as monopolists. Although laden with a range of judgments, Humboldt's observations nevertheless provide much insight. They betray significant regional variations in pod preparation and suggest that Europeans and mestizos appeared to have dominated the curing and export business by acquiring pods cheaply from Indigenous peoples and reselling them prepared at a large profit. Other accounts flesh out Humboldt's portrait. One mid-nineteenth century source explains that Mexican vanilla was produced primarily by "Indians, Mulatoes and Zambos"—the last term being the contemporaneous designation for people of both African and Indigenous ancestry.[12]

A great many more records concern vanilla exports, which, although rare for the sixteenth century, are legion starting in the seventeenth. Like all trade from New Spain, vanilla exports were tightly controlled. In 1503, the Spanish crown founded the Casa de Contratación or House of Trade in the port city of Seville. The near monopoly Spain held over vanilla and the complete monopoly it held over cochineal meant that the Casa de Contratación and its agents became inescapable intermediaries for anyone wanting to procure those luxury goods. The House of Trade went through ups and downs in both the seventeenth and eighteenth centuries, including a pronounced decline in both vessels and tonnage from New Spain between 1600 and 1650. Then, in 1650, the Casa, and with it the hub for goods from the

Americas, left Seville for Cádiz, where the vast majority of exported vanilla pods flowed for the next two hundred years. Cádiz became the antechamber of the Americas.[13] Tapping into the Casa de Contratación monopoly to supply the rest of Europe required teams of people. Like remoras tied to an ever-moving shark, in Ana Crespo Solana's words these "foreign traders were not alien to the Spanish monopoly; instead, they fed off it and were its most important supporters." She adds that these merchant "nations," as they called themselves within Cádiz, constituted "micro-societies integrated in the real Spanish society of the Ancien Regime."[14]

Although foreign buyers were undeniably part of a broader system, the fact remains that they competed with one another, scrounging for vanilla in Cádiz. On March 6, 1685, Louis XIV's consul explained that he could not fulfil Versailles's most recent order for vanilla "because the season has already passed."[15] A fortnight later, the same official in Cádiz promised that the requested vanilla would be dispatched with great "punctuality" as soon as the New Spain fleet arrived. This shipment included not only vanilla but also tobacco and delicate fans. The arrival of the fleet from Veracruz via Havana was a much anticipated and celebrated event. On September 29, 1698, the French consul in Cádiz reported that the ships had reached port at last and were being unloaded. Word was awaited from Madrid regarding the portion to be allotted to the crown. The treasure included gold and silver, as well as cochineal, indigo from Guatemala, cacao, vanilla, sugar, as well as "other items."[16]

By the early eighteenth century, vanilla trade networks stretched into the Pacific. Archival evidence points to large quantities of vanilla leaving Acapulco to the Philippines aboard Spanish galleons in 1708.[17] Volumes exported to Spain were also expanding. All this trade, however, remained tightly controlled by Spain (enriching royal coffers), and most of it followed the route from Veracruz to Cádiz.[18] The vessels always traveled in herds to better fend off pirates and because this system allowed an expert pilot to guide several ships at once through the perils of the Gulf of Mexico.[19] From the archives in Seville, we can trace a 1756 shipment of vanilla from New Spain to Cádiz: The *Santiago* carried "a decorated box containing 15,000 pieces of vanilla," which was expensive enough to be insured, tracked, and placed in intricate containers. Careful packaging was essential because the risks were many. One batch of pods aboard the same ship arrived "damaged and chopped," having lost "a quarter of its value."[20] Vanilla's fragility in the hold of ships only enhanced its luxury status. Due to its susceptibility to rotting, spoilage, and singeing by seawater, as well as damage caused by excess humidity and exposure to temperature changes, vanilla was highly vulnerable.

Despite serving as headquarters of the Casa de Contratación, Cádiz was not the only Spanish port to receive American vanilla. In July 1749, the "India flotilla," an armada of nine merchant ships escorted by five war vessels, coming from Veracruz, docked at the Galician port of Ferrol. The French naval attaché to Spain reported that King Charles IV of Spain was cracking down on crew members who were secretly selling some of the "fruit" on board. The term *fruit* designated all nonprecious-metal merchandise, specified the attaché. He added that the Spanish monarch ordered that anyone caught conducting fraud or smuggling with the shipments should be fired on the spot, while their superiors should be held accountable for their actions. It was in that tense context that the merchant ships brought an impressive 828,350 vanilla beans to land. Fraud aimed at circumventing the House of Trade had been rampant for decades. A document from 1698 described how foreign traders at Cádiz illicitly loaded their ships under the cover of darkness, immediately after unloading their own cargo.[21] The French naval attaché at Ferrol was one of many foreigners trying to get his hands on vanilla. The case therefore also highlights how the House of Trade system was coming under strain, with buyers seeking to stretch purchasing points beyond Cádiz.

In the seventeenth and eighteenth centuries, non-Spanish European buyers competed for pods with ever greater urgency. One of vanilla's many paradoxes is that it held greater appeal in early modern France, Italy, and northern Europe than in Spain, where it first reached European shores. The logical next steps for those other European companies and crowns involved securing a reliable supply of vanilla by sidestepping the Spanish monopoly. A first scramble was underway, and it took many forms: the type of fraud we just encountered, buccaneering on the high seas, and "biopiracy" in Mexico itself, with the goal of stealing vanilla's cultivation secrets.[22] Last but not least, rival European empires started growing vanilla in their American holdings. Each of these approaches achieved limited results. Only in the nineteenth century would the race commence that finally doomed the Spanish/Mexican monopoly: the competition to replace vanilla's natural pollinators, Central American bees, with a manual technique.

Piracy achieved some modest success in breaking the Spanish monopoly. It largely explains the staggering difference in losses between ships bound for New Spain—a ninety-one-day journey in itself—and those returning. Between 1560 and 1650, the westbound passage resembled a clean sheet, whereas the return to Europe was nothing short of a gauntlet. The archives are dotted with cases of intercepted eastbound galleons with pods on board. However, vanilla was never the sole cargo. It shared the hold with cochineal, silver, coffee, indigo, and cacao.[23]

English privateers kept surprisingly detailed records of their deeds. These included complete registers of goods taken, thorough translations of correspondence seized, and comprehensive information about the captured ships themselves. This diligence aimed both to better handle court cases from passengers from nonaligned countries and to legitimize the practice of capturing, reflagging, and renaming vessels. Vanilla appears in several recorded cases. One spectacular seizure, with both vanilla and vanilla experts on board, occurred with the 1746 capture of *El Fuerte* or *Fort de Nantes*, captained by Jean le Depancier. The thirty-two-gun ship was sailing from Veracruz to Cádiz via Havana when it was captured off of Madeira by two English vessels. The many goods seized included cochineal, vanilla, indigo, sugar, tobacco, jalap, hides, and snuff. Each was duly inventoried in Portsmouth, including several "boxes of vanynillias." More interesting than the lists themselves is a curious French calligraphy manual from the seventeenth century discovered on board. It had been used as an improvised notepad by some of the Spanish and New Spanish travelers. One page includes jottings about two containers of vanilla beans, including a list of consigners. Here is a useful reminder that within the vast tide of transatlantic commerce, modest transactions connected individual vanilla acquirers—though not harvesters—in Veracruz and Oaxaca provinces with individual overseas customers.[24]

However, most European vanilla consumers resided far from Spain. After reaching Cádiz, some pods sailed to the top of the Italian boot. Already in the early eighteenth century, Genoa constituted a major vanilla import and reexport hub to the Balkans and the Middle East. And in 1769, King Charles III of Spain offered as a gift to Pope Clement XIV "12 lb. of vanilla in a golden casket."[25] Vanilla was expensive enough to warrant an ostentatious case, especially when given to the pontiff. Other pods were bound for the

North Sea. In 1806, 111,930 vanilla beans from New Spain were reexported from Cádiz to the port of Hamburg.[26]

An even larger portion headed to France. The Roux brothers of Marseille, whose acquisition radius was truly global at this point, were regular eighteenth-century vanilla purchasers. Their representatives in Cádiz monitored the arrival, availability, price, and quality of vanilla from Veracruz. Remittance documents for their individual vanilla shipments provide details about gradations of quality. On October 2, 1729, for example, the Roux representative in Cádiz loaded exactly 4,331½ vanilla beans on a boat bound for Marseille. The pods were described as Mexican and subdivided into seven categories, according to size and desirability.[27]

After it was weighed and ranked, most of the vanilla that reached Roux headquarters in Marseille then transited inland. Some headed to Paris, as occurred in August 1729. The following month, the brothers again acquired vanilla pods in Cádiz by the thousands. They purchased another four thousand vanilla beans in March 1730. July 1731 correspondence shows the Roux brothers making a very handsome 72 percent profit on their latest vanilla transaction. The Roux team sometimes opted to stockpile vanilla until prices reached their peak. Selling high has always been tricky, and the vanilla business is not for the fainthearted. On several occasions, the Roux brothers struggled to secure inventory. For instance, in November 1731, with demand soaring, the company's representatives in Cádiz complained of not being able to find vanilla at a favorable price. Yet the Rouxs' deep pockets and extensive reach allowed them to manage risk and uncertainty of this sort. They often served as insurance brokers, invested in the operations of select business partners, and sometimes even paid for those partners' legal fees.[28]

Unfortunately, the proliferation of purchasers in Cádiz alone, not to mention the small percentage of surviving records from them, render regular statistics elusive in this era. It is possible, however, to catch occasional glimpses of the overall scale of the transatlantic vanilla trade. One source indicates that five tons of New Spanish vanilla reached Spain between 1748 and 1753. Interestingly, over the course of that same half decade, another three tons of vanilla sailed to Spain from Colombia's port of Cartagena. This suggests that *Vanilla pompona*, the varietal native to South America rather than Central America, represented a much higher percentage of global supply than it has in the contemporary era.[29] As we shall see, *pompona*'s range, which extended past Colombia into Dutch, Portuguese, and French South

American colonies, also presented an opportunity for each of those powers to secure some supply.

It is also clear from the 1748–53 statistics that in Europe, vanilla consumption was no longer restricted to the royal courts or the Vatican. Perhaps more than the aristocracy, merchants and other bourgeois had acquired a taste for the remarkable bean. This squares with some recent arguments by historians of consumption: Michael Kwass suggests that merchants in the era in question sometimes developed "more refined habits of consumption than higher-status rural nobles." Meanwhile, Rebecca Spang and Colin Jones underline that French society underwent a more thorough consumer transformation in the eighteenth century than was previously acknowledged. As proof, they invoke demand for goods that on the surface might seem frivolous: "papier mâché chinoiserie" and faux beaver hats, both of which attest to the rise of "middling urban consumers" and exemplify the concept of substitionism.[30]

Admittedly, in eighteenth-century Europe, vanilla was far from "democratized."[31] It was consumed in modest quantities but by deceptively large segments of specific populations. In fact, it gained appeal beyond urban centers. Proof of this includes the word for vanilla finding its way into so-called regional languages, some of them inching toward extinction, others proving more resilient in regions remote from the centralizing impulses of European capitals. A 1744 French-Breton dictionary included an entry for *vanille*, spelled the same way in both languages. The pod appearing there is not altogether surprising, given Brittany's seafaring tradition, and the fact that Breton ports enjoyed close ties with Cádiz.[32] Overall, it is safe to deduce that vanilla bucked the pattern of an eastbound lag in the so-called Columbian Exchange. (Tomatoes did not find their way into European cuisines until the late nineteenth century, much as potatoes took time to grow on Europeans.)[33]

But where and in what form was vanilla being ingested? Evidence certainly points to vanilla being consumed in cacao drinks by elite colonists in seventeenth-century New Spain. There, European settlers and officials adopted chocolate drinks that, according to Marcy Norton, "closely resembled Indian concoctions."[34] In 1647, Alonso de Montoia and Don Martín de Aeta exchanged letters about a vanilla transaction that had gone sour. The latter was a clergyman and legal commissioner for the Inquisition, operating out of Durango in Nueva Vizcaya. Alonso de Montoia apologized for not having sent enough vanilla to the inquisitor. Instead of 240 pods, the clergyman had only received eighty-four, and eagerly sought the remainder "for his chocolate."[35] However, this rare example notwithstanding, vanilla's traces in this era remain ephemeral and spotty. A sampling of three Mexican cookbooks, from the late seventeenth to the mid-eighteenth century, reveals no trace of vanilla.[36] This suggests that in Mexico, vanilla was primarily used in drinks, which rarely find their way into cookery manuals.

On the other side of the Atlantic, one can identify a gradual shift toward eating vanilla. A handwritten Italian dessert manual from the late seventeenth or early eighteenth century is brimming with the stuff. Vanilla appears as one flavoring option in a chocolate parfait, the other being cinnamon. In this manuscript, vanilla sometimes steals the show, as in a *pan lauato di vainigli*. It further materializes in "vanilla water." And it pops up in surprising places, such as a soft-boiled egg recipe known as *œuf mollet*. It also flavors several creams, including a *spuma di panna*.[37]

The appetite for vanilla was growing even stronger in neighboring France. The great early nineteenth-century French pâtissier and chef Marie-Antoine Carême helped define both professions while serving the nobility, the Russian czar, the Rothschild family, and the British aristocracy alike. Among his extravagant *pièces montées*, one finds a *charlotte à la polonaise* with vanilla cream. The chef, whose remarkable social ascension out of poverty meant he would certainly not have encountered vanilla in his own childhood, also provided recipes for somewhat more modest *génoises à la vanille*. Those called for half a pod. Vanilla waffles, meanwhile, contained a whole "stick," and vanilla fanchonettes required "infusing one good vanilla pod in three glasses of milk, then simmer." The use of the adjective *good* reminds us of the vast quality range in the era before vanilla standardization, not to mention the demands of Carême's well-heeled "clientele" (his employers, to be more precise). Similarly, Carême's Bavarian cheese with vanilla required a "plump and well-*givred* pod," two characteristics that have endured as indicators of quality. Also known as vanilla rime or vanilla frost, *givre* is an efflorescence on pods formed by vanillin crystals that is highly prized by connoisseurs. Among Carême's other vanilla desserts—this is not an exhaustive list—one finds small vanilla soufflés, which again called for a whole pod.[38]

Vanilla was also widely employed in early nineteenth-century confectionery. In 1828, Parisian chocolatiers Debauve et Gallais—still in existence today at the same boutique on the rue des Saints-Pères—sold a range of chocolates containing one and two pods, in addition to elaborate vanilla-flavored chocolate sculptures of clocks, porcelain, bells, and calendars. A half-hour walk across the Seine led to the rival Marquis chocolate shop located in the trendy Passage des Panoramas, which also offered a wide assortment of chocolates. In 1838, the second and third most expensive on its impressive list were vanilla-flavored varietals bearing the lavish titles "Royal au Soconusco" (a locale in southern Mexico) and "Superfin, 2 vanilles au caraque" (ultrafine, two sailboat vanillas). Both Debauve et Gallais and the Marquis employed the designations "one" or "two vanillas" as markers of excellence and cost. The Marquis even branched out into vanilla-flavored pistachios.[39]

On balance, however, it would seem that vanilla was still drunk more than it was eaten in pre-1841 Europe. And in beverage form, vanilla was paired with cacao far more than with sugar. This explains in part why Britain, whose sucrose consumption surged in the nineteenth century, never became a top pod consumer.

Given its cost, cheating on vanilla content in drinks was widespread. Emma Spary has traced some of the adulteration taking place in expensive cacao drinks in prerevolutionary Paris and the reactions that followed. (This confirms that anxieties around food tampering were not born in the modern era; as Jack Goody reminds us, they go back at least as far back as ancient Greece.) Cheap beans and chestnut flour were being added to the drink. As a result, in 1765 one preparer or *limonadier* set about reassuring his clientele that he cut no corners and still included vanilla in his hot chocolate. However, some customers preferred their chocolate without any vanilla, an unembellished type of drink called *chocolat de santé* (health chocolate). *Chocolat de santé* was not restricted to France. In 1830, Brossat, a shop at the corner of Bourbon and Main Streets in New Orleans, was advertising it, alongside chocolate containing vanilla.

In fact, Spary discerns a trend toward "unflavored chocolate" in 1760s Paris. However, she makes the case that two ingredients, vanilla and sugar, were spared this decluttering vogue. Doctors proved more than pleased to endorse certain products. One of them pronounced confidently in 1773 in the *Gazette de Santé*, "An excess of vanilla is dangerous, but it is necessary to have a little in chocolate, otherwise weak stomachs [...] would find themselves overburdened by the weight of cacao butter. So-called health chocolate is thus improperly named; it should rather be called sickness chocolate."[40] And so, in small quantities, vanilla was considered not so much a spice as an enhancing flavor that enabled balance. In this sense, I would resist inscribing vanilla into the early modern "psychoactive revolution" tied to caffeine. To be sure, vanilla-flavored cacao may well have been the first caffeinated drink many Europeans consumed. And chocolate retained a sophisticated connotation well after coffee was enjoyed by the masses.[41] The point remains, however, that to eighteenth-century doctors at least, the vanilla in that cacao offset the effects of caffeine—the opposite of vanilla as aphrodisiac or stimulant. The contradiction should not come as a surprise, for vanilla was the subject of countless conflicting and meandering meanings.

France was certainly not the only European country to enjoy vanilla-flavored cacao beverages. Austrians in the era of Mozart were also fond of them. Again, the trail of evidence is unfortunately thin, but vanilla does show up in some legal records. In 1775, the authorities in Vienna investigated chocolatier Mathias Schöber. He stood accused of evading a duty on cacao and surreptitiously shipping vanilla to the town of St. Pölten, reminding us of the early modern state's regulation of the two luxury components of chocolate-vanilla drinks.[42]

Vanilla wasn't just savored in hot chocolate and desserts; its medicinal virtues were also lauded, especially prior to 1800. A 1721 French manual on how best to avoid the bubonic plague proposed vanilla as an ingredient for plague masks—at least, it added, "for the ladies."[43] Vanilla was already tagged as a feminine fragrance. Its reputed medicinal qualities varied from one country to another. A 1769 French description of Dutch Surinamese *Vanilla pompona* claimed that it induced periods in women, fortified and warmed the stomach, attenuated "viscous humors," and aided in childbirth. The text added that "the English consider it useful in dissipating melancholy."[44] This speaks to differing medicinal uses of vanilla across cultures, including a calming, even depression-fighting quality that some still perceive in vanilla's bouquet.

The example of Surinamese vanilla also holds the key to why this chapter's title refers to New Spain's "near monopoly." Across the Guianas—what would later become British, Dutch, and French Guiana—*Vanilla pompona* harvesting and, crucially, cultivation can be documented beginning in the seventeenth century. The varietal features vanilla's familiar fragrance, of course, but offers a different taste range, with smoky sweet accents. At market, it can be identified visually by its larger size compared to *planifolia*. Its range extends across vast swaths of South America, including Peru, Colombia, and the Guianas. *Pompona* therefore presented a unique opportunity to other European powers that had gained a foothold in South America. *Pompona* harvesting around the Guiana Basin betrays a concerted effort by several colonial rivals to break Spain's vanilla monopoly.

In the Pomeroon area of what later became British Guiana, then occupied by the Dutch, we see evidence of seventeenth-century vanilla commerce. The Dutch National Archives contain a March 31, 1684, report that reads as follows:

> The Jew Salomon de la Roche having died some 8 or 9 months ago, the trade in vanilla has come to an end since no one here knows how to prepare it so as to develop the proper aroma and keep it from spoiling. I have not heard of any this whole year. [...] Most of it is to be found in Pomeroon, whither this Jew frequently traveled, and he sometimes used to make me a present of little. In navigating along the river, too, I have sometimes seen some on the trees and picked with my own hands, and it was prepared by the Jew, although I was never before acquainted with the virtues and value of this fruit which grows wild and after the fashion of the banana. I shall do my best to obtain from the Company, in Pomeroon or elsewhere, as much as shall be feasible, but I am afraid it will spoil since I do not know how to prepare it.[45]

This invites several remarks. One concerns the existence of a sizeable Portuguese Sephardic Jewish community in Dutch colonial Suriname in the seventeenth century. As Natalie Zemon Davis has pointed out, it represented a third of Suriname's settler population circa 1700. These settlers acquired rights on location that made them "nearly citizens." Some ventured into neighboring Pomeroon, in a zone the Dutch claimed as a "commercial outlet."[46] More pertinent to us is what this passage reveals about the circulation of vanilla knowledge. It suggests that much was kept tightly secret, especially precise provenance and preparation methods. So much so that upon the death of a vanilla specialist and trader, key knowledge, including curing expertise, departed with him. Furthermore, the text implies that while de la Roche prepared and sold vanilla, he first obtained or at least located it thanks to Indigenous people.[47]

As was the case with North American ginseng, which French missionary Joseph-François Lafitau learned about from Mohawk informants in

1716, the pods were brought to de la Roche by Indigenous harvesters. He, in turn, became proficient in preparation thanks to them.[48] De la Roche and a handful of other Europeans then attempted to keep harvesting locations and preparation techniques confidential. Secrecy and sharing of knowledge were double-edged swords. Dutch and French representatives tried to break Spain's grip on pods without tipping their hands or inviting others in. Yet they needed to impart knowhow to a small circle of their compatriots in this specialized line of work, lest that knowledge fade, as it did with de la Roche.

De la Roche appears to have learned from Indigenous people how to find, pick, and cure vanilla. But mastering vanilla propagation was quite another matter. The first documented proof of rival Europeans setting about cultivating vanilla to break the Spanish monopoly comes from neighboring French Guiana, then known by the name of its main town, Cayenne. Just as de la Roche did in Suriname, the French acquired some of their knowledge from Indigenous groups. A French travel narrative from the 1680s tells of Arawak people trading cacao, vanilla, and cinnamon to Europeans near what is today Kourou.[49]

One key colonial official transformed vanilla from a traded commodity to one that the colonizers sought to cultivate. In the late 1680s, vanilla emerged as a major preoccupation in Cayenne. King Louis XIV's intendant for the nascent colony, the marquis Pierre-Eléonore de La Ville de Férolles, had first cut his teeth serving as a colonel in Newfoundland, where a peninsula still bears his name. Having left the iceberg coast for the tropics, Férolles governed French Guiana (first on an interim basis, then formally) from 1674 to 1698, with several interruptions. The doctor and eighteenth-century historian Jacques François Artur tells us that Férolles had petitioned the Vatican in 1690 for an exemption to wed his niece. Their family tree was not the cause for calling off the engagement nine years later; instead, the couple "recognized incompatibilities in one another's temperament." Férolles was also known for his lavish banquets at which he showed off his wealth, acquired at least in part from his large sugar-producing estate named Montsinéry, after the Indigenous Galibi word *seneri*, meaning drinking (after the river that ran through the land). The estate, which was the envy of other planters, ran on slave labor. In addition to slave quarters, it featured one of French Guiana's two water mills, a manor, and extensive gardens.[50]

When Férolles first set foot in Guiana, the region generated very few export crops: chiefly sugar and a plant pigment known as achiote pods (*roucou* in French). In fact, royal instructions to Férolles as late as 1685 had still insisted on clearing forests and increasing sugar output as twin agricultural imperatives.[51] Things quickly changed. In 1687, the secretary of state to the navy (tasked with colonial affairs) at Versailles alerted Férolles that Dutch traders were trespassing on French Guianese land, going up the Maroni River to acquire vanilla from Indigenous peoples. Férolles received clear instructions to encourage local French settlers to take up this commerce themselves, "so as to send [pods] to France and profit thereby from the advantages that the Dutch have been drawing by then exporting the vanilla to us."[52]

Férolles must have swiftly set about acquiring local pods, for in September 1691 Versailles thanked him for a vanilla bean he had just sent, pronouncing it of "very good quality." Now, the crown expressly ordered Férolles to have the inhabitants of the colony plant—not trade for—vanilla and cacao, to set in motion an "advantageous flow of it to Europe." The September 24, 1691, instructions added that the two crops represented the best path toward "making the colony flourish and bringing it prosperity."[53] Férolles, who had come under royal scrutiny over the previous decade for several interpersonal conflicts and therefore found himself on the hot seat, was keen to deliver. He also had little choice in the matter. On September 6, 1692, almost exactly a year after the first instructions to Cayenne to plant vanilla, Versailles followed up, indicating that the minister was "very impatient" to know whether the marquis had been able to grow vanilla in Guiana. (The wish list also included cinnamon, pepper, and cloves.)[54] Unsurprisingly, Férolles became consumed by the stuff. In a broader perspective, vanilla production in French Guiana fell in line with the goals established by Jean-Baptiste Colbert, the Sun King's long-standing minister of the navy who had passed away in 1683, to decrease France's imports while also "increase[ing] its production of luxury goods for export" and relying on teams of technicians and specialists.[55]

In May 1693, Férolles duly sent more "Amazonian" vanilla back to France. The marquis underscored all the difficulties the modest shipment had entailed. His accompanying letter dwelled on his uphill battle to persuade local planters to grow vanilla. The marquis explained that the planter class tended to possess small sugar plantations with relatively few slaves. Consequently, they preferred "a prompt culture," one that would bear fruit immediately—whereas vanilla takes three years to do so. Férolles further recommended studying how the pods were prepared in New Spain, because French planters currently lost "two-thirds of what they harvested." This accounted for why he was sending so little back to Versailles.[56] The secretary of state to the navy responded in July 1693, urging Férolles tirelessly to encourage the inhabitants of his colony to plant more vanilla.[57]

The following February, Férolles multiplied his grievances against local planters. Their "negligence toward the culture of vanilla" had led him to draft an ordinance against any planters who had not begun growing the orchid at the time of the next census. He now attributed their reluctance to several more causes: the influence of Indigenous people, which "makes them neglect their plantations," as well as the tropical climate. All this supposedly rendered settlers "lazy," charged the intendant, notwithstanding their claim that "nobody wishes to work more in the Americas than the people of Cayenne."[58]

The Guianese case betrays the importance Versailles attached to creating alternate production points for vanilla, beyond Spain's reach. And to some extent, the scheme worked, although clouds soon appeared on his horizon. In September 1694, Férolles explained that the "vanilla he had planted upon arriving [in Guiana] had not yet born fruit." With hindsight, this is unsurprising, given that specific bee pollinators had to track down the flowers. He added, "This plant enjoys being in the woods, in humid spots, and it requires trees on which it can climb that are old and worm-eaten." In May 1695, the marquis was still trying to make sense of why some vanilla produced pods and other vines did not. He inferred that the cuttings he had introduced to the intendant's garden only produced fruit when placed at the foot of nonprecious, old-growth trees.[59] Here he posed the question of the optimal host plant for vanilla, which would remain a topic of debate among botanists and horticulturalists for centuries.

In addition to contemplating why some vanilla plants bore fruit while others did not, Férolles took on the tricky matters of conservation and transport. Correspondence from 1684 reveals that the marquis sent his prepared vanilla back to France in tin boxes, a packaging method that endured well into the twentieth century.[60]

Férolles's vanilla quest followed him. By 1697, on the Sun King's orders, he attempted to expand French Guiana's boundaries to the southeast, at the expense of Portuguese-controlled Brazil. Upon capturing the Amazonian coastal fort of Macapa, the marquis noted that the Portuguese had profited from cacao production and trade at the site. However, Férolles only had eyes for the vanilla he saw growing around him: "In the places where I camped, half the trees had vanilla climbing up them."[61] To the single-minded Férolles, his border raid could serve to expand France's vanilla-producing domain. Thanks in part to his determination, Versailles could count on a modest but regular supply chain that circumvented Spanish control.

Early modern French attempts to diversify production sites did not stop there. From French Guiana, *Vanilla pompona* radiated out to other Caribbean lands, where its pollinators may or may not have been present. (Scientists are still studying *pompona*'s pollinators, which include but are not restricted to the *Eulaema cingulata* and *Eulaema meriana* bees.)[62] The Dominican missionary, botanist, and slave owner Jean-Baptiste Labat recounts how Guianese vanilla, presumably *pompona*, first reached Martinique from Cayenne in 1697. In the absence of competing narratives, we are largely bound to his. That year, two visiting Dominicans were about to return to Martinique when they saw vanilla cuttings that had not been taken by the previous ship headed to France. They asked for and received permission to bring the precious cuttings to Martinique instead. Upon arrival in Saint-Pierre, they handed the cuttings to their superior, Father Labat. He planted them at the foot of a coconut tree and watered them regularly. They flourished and soon climbed along several more hosts. Although most of the plants died during his subsequent absence, he recounts having managed to save a small vine. It flourished to such an extent that Labat even brought some cuttings to Guadeloupe in 1701. A short-lived British invasion of Guadeloupe in 1703 brought an end to that part of the botanist-missionary's experiment: He claimed that the English forces either stole or wantonly destroyed his vanilla plants.

Back in Martinique, to his amazement, Labat found other varietals of indigenous vanilla growing in the woods. He noted a set of differences with the cutting he had obtained from Guiana. Intendant François Roger Robert corroborated this in a report back to Versailles in 1701, revealing the presence of local pods that "greatly resembled vanilla," but were entirely odorless. Labat soon grew convinced that local vanilla was a false lead. Indigenous vanilla pods were altogether distinct and far less tasty than his Guianese ones, he concluded. He would have to wait for his *Vanilla pompona* to produce fruit, which had not happened by 1705. *Vanilla pompona* had definitely left Spain's orbit but to mixed results.

We know now that Labat was driven to succeed, not least because, like Férolles, his vanilla quest had been ordered by Versailles. And so Labat next sought out a "Jewish traveler" who had arrived from Latin America and "boasted" of knowing how to prepare both vanilla and cochineal. The clergyman arranged a meeting, during which the visitor obliged and told him how and when Indigenous peoples picked the pods, boiled them, placed them in the shade, covered them in oil, and wrapped them in canna lily leaves to dry them. Through this traveler, local planters, and his Dominican brothers, Labat proved gifted at extracting and gathering specimens as well as information.[63] Still, despite these elaborate intelligence-gathering operations, Martinican *pompona* appears not to have yielded fruit.

Farther afield, the first signs of vanilla on Saint-Domingue (modern-day Haiti) in 1732 suggest that the pods were not locally produced but rather "seized by buccaneers" off of Spanish ships. Just over a decade later, though, a 1743 treatise on medicinal plants sang the praises of the vanilla growing on the island. But the source pointed to differences between insular pods and Mexican ones, specifically related to the orchid's color and the beans' lack of odor. In other words, this was without a doubt a type of vanilla now considered inedible (the "odorless Haitian vanilla" type described by botanist Michel Etienne Descourtilz). This seems confirmed by Marie Armande Jeanne Gacon-Dufour's 1825 perfumery manual, which recommended avoiding "vanilla harvested in Saint-Domingue, [as it] is much less fragrant."[64] Spain's European rivals encountered obstacles when trying to build their own vanilla supply. Privateering could only go so far, and some rival vanilla varietals either proved to be sterile outside their land of origin or failed to match the quality of *planifolia*.

None of these schemes to compete with Spain amounted to much, although they did grow bolder over time. In 1777, a French agent set about shattering two Spanish monopolies in a single stroke: one on cochineal, the other on vanilla. He proved more successful with the first. Nicolas-Joseph Thiéry de Menonville was born in 1739 to a family of jurists from Lorraine. He broke family ranks and expectations when he moved to Paris to become a botanist. Amy Butler Greenfield describes him as "passionate, patriotic and more than a little vain," intent on attaining personal and national glory. He received the support of the French navy, which provided "covert backing" for his operation and promised to pay him handsomely once he brought his booty to Saint-Domingue.[65]

Menonville left France in 1776 with all the instruments his epic larceny would require: cases, flasks, and crates. He was aware of several impediments from the start. Chief among them was his mediocre Spanish, which he tried to overcome by posing as someone from the Franco-Spanish borderlands. On location in Mexico, the French "biopirate" ensured that the specimens he procured in Oaxaca were "real vanilla"—no doubt meaning *planifolia*— just like the ones he had seen in Veracruz. Menonville's operation involved quick botanical thinking, bluff, bribery, and subterfuge, including concealing vanilla cuttings before entering a Mexican inn while incognito. Later that night, in his room, he consigned the vanillas to two special travel cases. Then, before the hair-raising exfiltration from Veracruz, he carefully redistributed the cuttings across several barrels "so well masked amongst other plants that one would have to be a botanist to distinguish what was precious from what was not." His gamble paid off, and he reached Saint-Domingue with the vanilla cuttings and insects he had set out to capture. Yet even the preface to Menonville's self-serving treatise recognized that vanilla already existed on Saint-Domingue prior to his introduction—although the text did not specify that it was a different varietal. (The parallelism with cochineal is striking, as Menonville discovered to his amazement that another species of wild cochineal also existed on Saint-Domingue.) Menonville added that, once planted in Saint-Domingue, his vanilla cuttings only managed to grow a few extra "twigs." He made no mention of pods.[66]

Evidence suggests that the stolen *Vanilla planifolia* floundered in Saint-Domingue. This makes sense because *planifolia*'s insect pollinator was almost certainly lacking on the island, so Menonville's cuttings could not have borne fruit. His daring raid had fallen flat, at least in terms of vanilla. Spain's complete *planifolia* monopoly remained intact, and its *pompona* near monopoly centered on Colombia and Peru was barely dented by French, Dutch, and Portuguese competition across the Guianese basin and Brazil.[67] As for the Caribbean islands, they never emerged as large-scale vanilla producers. Curiously, they were and remained so in the French imagination. Already, Denis Diderot and Jean le Rond d'Alembert's titanic *Encyclopedia*, whose writing and publication stretched from 1751 to 1772, referred to vanilla as "growing in the warm isles of the Americas."[68] Vanilla would later become predominantly insular, but it certainly was not in the eighteenth century. In the end, none of these insular schemes, not even Menonville's covert *planifolia* mission, spelled serious competition for the vanilla juggernaut that was the Spanish colonies in the Americas. Admittedly, in times of war with Spain, powers with their own colonial vanilla could still access some precious pods. And, of course, piracy remained another option to secure limited supply.

As the seventeenth century drew to a close, however, Spain's grip over the vanilla trade showed signs of strain. The Casa de Contratación closed shop in 1790. Next, the Napoleonic Wars profoundly disrupted networks. And then Mexican independence in 1821 meant that the new country could export its vanilla wherever it wanted. Pods started directly reaching destinations other than Spain and the Philippines.[69] While the Veracruz-to-Cádiz transport monopoly had been undone, pod production was another matter altogether. It would take the breakthrough of manual pollination, untethering vanilla from its American bee pollinators, to globalize vanilla cultivation.

CHAPTER 2

A Belgian Wins the Race

VANILLA WAS AND REMAINS NOTORIOUSLY EXPENSIVE. AN 1831 local interest piece in a Brussels newspaper told how a gourmet had recently traveled to the port city of Antwerp. Initially he had set out to order coffee but then, in a "flight of fancy," decided to request vanilla instead. "Ignorant of how this ingredient is used in modest quantities," he ordered eight pounds of it from a middleman. His contact proceeded to scour the bustling city's shops, docks, and warehouses, gathering all the vanilla he could, which amounted to four pounds and three ounces. The price tag proved to be astronomical. So substantial was the purchase that word spread that the gourmet must have been up to something. Perhaps commodity speculation?[1]

This vignette points in two directions. On the one hand, even foodies in northern Europe did not fully grasp how to use vanilla or in what amounts. (Belgian chocolates, many of which incorporated vanilla, only took off in the 1840s and 1850s.) On the other hand, there was already an appetite for the pods. It may have been tied to a taste for novelty—note the "flight of fancy" of the opening vignette—or a long-standing Low Country craving for exotic substances, enabled by Dutch and Flemish firms in seventeenth-century Cádiz. It is also tempting to see this as an example of "innovative consumers" or "consumers actively engaged in a process of discovery," to borrow Jan de Vries's phrases.[2]

And yet, so long as vanilla could only be imported from Central America by sailing vessels, its price tag remained high and its exports were limited to only a few tons. Prior to 1830, New Spain / Mexico seldom exported more than three thousand kilograms (6,614 pounds) of vanilla a year.[3] This is why all of Antwerp could only muster four pounds of it. However, the two conditions were about to change: Mexico's *Vanilla planifolia* monopoly would soon be broken, and in a matter of decades, steam and propellers transformed ocean shipping, making it faster, more reliable, and therefore cheaper. A Belgian scientist would first challenge Mexico's vanilla dominance, winning the sprint to discover the orchid's pollination technique.

A short detour through Belgian history is required at this point. Belgium was a new country when the Antwerp vanilla story went to press. In 1789, taking their cue from Paris, revolutionaries had risen up in Liège against the Hapsburg empire. A brief experiment ensued in the form of the United States of Belgium, which barely got off the ground. Still, Belgium, a land of Catholic heritage, had succeeded in separating from the Protestant Netherlands. However, two waves of invasions quickly brought this first Belgian independence to an end. The Austrian emperor launched a reconquest in 1790. Two years later, the French army under General Charles-François Dumouriez poured into Belgium. Three years after that, revolutionary France annexed Belgium outright. In the wake of Napoleon's defeat at Waterloo, a United Kingdom of the Netherlands was established, encompassing all the Low Countries. Many Belgians felt occupied once more, this time by Protestant Holland, despite the nominal establishment of two separate capitals, one in The Hague and the other in Brussels. After decades of French-language dominance, in September 1819, Flemish became the language of reference within the new state. Flemish speakers now occupied the lion's share of diplomatic, cabinet, and high-ranking civil service and military command positions. In 1830, opposition to Dutch control erupted in the form of unrest in Brussels. Revolutionaries attacked symbols of Dutch power. Soon, the fervor spread to other cities, especially Liège. Both francophone Walloons and Flemish speakers participated in this revolution that ushered in the birth of Belgium. In 1831, Leopold I, Duke of Saxe-Coburg, became the compromise choice for king of the small, multilingual state.[4]

Technological and economic change matched the breakneck pace of these political upheavals. Between 1800 and 1850, the Low Countries underwent rapid industrialization. That being said, the process was uneven, with francophone areas emerging as the new nation's industrial heartland. Consequently, inequalities deepened between increasingly wealthy French-speaking regions and poorer Flemish ones. Provinces such as Liège, which had already been relatively prosperous circa 1820, grew more so over the following decades. Until roughly 1880, the "Walloon industrial belt" around Liège attracted significant internal economic migration. North of it, the Ghent region, where this chapter's protagonist was born, had achieved a more modest breakthrough in the cotton textile industry following the end of the continental blockade in 1814, despite fierce competition from British textiles.[5]

Charles-François Antoine Morren, who won the race to pollinate vanilla, was born in Ghent on March 3, 1807, in the heart of Napoleonic Belgium. He had Irish roots, his family having immigrated to the continent at the time of King Henry VIII's break with the Catholic Church. Morren attended high school in Brussels and university in Ghent. Between 1825 and 1829, the government of the United Kingdom of the Netherlands entrusted him with a vast cartography project, which saw him "travel the entire realm" to map what was still a joint state, comprising both the Netherlands and Belgium. Morren's doctoral thesis in biology and mathematics, successfully defended at the University of Ghent in 1829, dealt with the "spontaneous" sexual reproduction of living organisms. Morren was already grappling with a problem similar to vanilla's mysterious replication. The thesis was drafted in Latin. Morren was proficient in English, Latin, German, Dutch/ Flemish, and of course his mother tongue, French.[6] In 1830, he obtained scholarships to study in Berlin, Göttingen, and Paris. Much of Morren's tool kit that enabled his breakthrough was already in place: his interest in reproduction, his language skills, and his international networks. Like any recently minted doctoral graduate, he set out to find an academic position.

As it happens, the Belgian Revolution of 1830 opened an unexpected path for the budding botanist. He was in Paris at the time, on yet another mission for the United Kingdom of the Netherlands. Morren explained to his benefactor, the influential Goswin, Baron de Stassart, that as soon as revolution broke out in Belgium, he "felt it his duty to abandon the rights that [he] had enjoyed with the Dutch government and promptly returned to Brussels."[7] Upon coming home, the seas parted for Morren, who now draped himself in the new black, yellow, and red national flag. As a direct result of the revolution, Morren's former mentor, the distinguished Dutch physicist and physician Jacob Gijsbertus Samuël van Breda, was forced out of his position at the University of Ghent. Dutch faculty were being ousted in favor of francophone Belgians. Morren seized the opportunity and gladly took van Breda's place. In 1835, he obtained a second doctorate, this one in medicine.

It remains unclear whether he intended to change careers or simply expand his field of knowledge by embarking on a second degree.[8]

On June 4, 1833, twice doctor Morren wed Marie-Henriette-Caroline Verrassel. She was born in 1812 in Breda, which, after the divorce between the Netherlands and Belgium, ended up on the Dutch side of the border. Her father, Henri, had been a member of the elite Papal Order of the Golden Spur. A scandalous six months after their wedding, Marie gave birth to the couple's first of five children, Charles-Jacques Edouard Morren.[9] The apple did not fall far from the tree, and Charles-Jacques Edouard went on to become a prominent botanist in his own right.

Like many of his contemporaries, Charles-François Morren's range of interests was encyclopedic. He came to prominence shortly before the rise of intense specialization that characterizes present-day science. His son predicted that the vastness of Morren's expertise would prove "intimidating" to any historian who might one day take it on. Less charitably, the entry on Charles-François Morren in an 1899 encyclopedia of Belgium celebrities observed, "Had [Morren] specialized, he might have been able to concentrate his efforts on a smaller number of cases and objects, and would thereby certainly have rendered greater services to science."[10] It is true that Morren dabbled in paleontology, geology, geography, cartography, botany, zoology, horticulture, agronomy, anatomy, and other medical fields.

Although he cannot be faulted for being a product of his time, in hindsight, his lack of specialization presented obvious drawbacks. In 1827, Morren seemed consumed above all with fossils found in Wallonia.[11] But the following year, he and van Breda clashed with zoologist Pierre Léonard van der Linden and local surgeon J. Dubar over a putrefying whale that fishermen had towed to the budding resort town of Ostende. This was a surprisingly frequent occurrence: in the Low Countries, beached whales had attracted curious onlookers, artists, and anatomists alike since the sixteenth century. Such events had sometimes been interpreted as augurs, in other cases as metaphors of resilience or decline. Back on the beach, van Breda and his team, comprising junior colleagues and upper-year students including Morren, began dissecting the beast. However, the group soon quarreled with both Dubar, the local doctor, and the fisherman who towed the whale in, regarding ownership of the Leviathan. Things turned ugly. The surgeon accused van Breda's party of mistaking a muscle from the whale for a fetus, one of a litany of alleged displays of incompetence. Insults swirled between the two camps, warnings were issued in the press, and duels were narrowly avoided.[12] In addition to demonstrating Morren's encyclopedic interests, the episode points to a mercurial streak in the young scientist. The scandal may also have heightened his propensity for secrecy, which manifested itself after his vanilla breakthrough.

In 1835, Morren sought a position at the University of Liège, which had been created by the United Kingdom of the Netherlands in 1817 following Napoleon's defeat. To obtain this post, he wrote to his powerful patron Goswin, Baron de Stassart, a poet, freemason, former Napoleonic prefect, and leading proponent of tightening Belgium's ties to France. Stassart was familiar with various halls of power, and he also frequented both literary and scientific salons. Between 1803 and 1819, for example, Stassart exchanged letters with the leading French naturalist and early evolutionary theorist Bernard Germain de Lacépède. Indeed, Stassart's range of interests proved even more capacious than Morren's. He belonged to dozens of learned societies, across a vast range of fields that encompassed mineralogy, medicine, antiques and antiquities, education, archeology, agriculture, trade and commerce, history, fine arts, and philosophy. Most importantly for our purposes, the baron stood at the helm of Belgium's influential Royal Academy.[13] Morren asked him plainly to pull strings to land him the position of "professor of botany and plant physiology, or of zoology and comparative anatomy, preferably at the University of Liège."[14] This came to pass, no doubt thanks to Stassart's powerful reach.

Morren's reasons for moving to Liège were counterintuitive. He had contracted fevers, probably malaria, while collecting specimens in Flanders's swamps. He believed that a change of air would prove beneficial. Ironically, he headed to a city blanketed by thick industrial smog. The lifespan of his predecessors did not bode well, either. At Liège, Morren inherited the botanical gardens that had been directed by Richard-Joseph Courtois, who died tragically at tender age of twenty-nine in April 1835 from an "inflammatory disease." He had replaced the previous director, Henri Gaëde, who had perished prematurely in 1834 at age thirty-nine from an "organic lesion."[15] Liège certainly did not cure Morren's condition. In 1836, he was bedridden with fevers for nearly a month.[16]

In the early nineteenth century, Liège became the site where Britain's Industrial Revolution gained a foothold on the continent. In fact, the very term "Industrial Revolution" was first used to describe Belgium, rather than

Britain.[17] In 1829, Liège counted just under sixty thousand inhabitants. The period from 1800 to 1880 witnessed phenomenal economic growth and wealth produced in and around Liège, with disposable income rising significantly among the middle class. However, inequalities grew commensurably. New industries quickly made up for the impact of the Dutch-Belgian divorce and the sudden removal of protected trade outlets such as the Dutch East Indies (modern-day Indonesia).

A star visitor captured the changes in the local landscape. As he approached Liège in 1840, Victor Hugo wrote, "The entire valley seems to be dotted with erupting craters [. . .]. One would think that an enemy army has been through the area, as the sacked [. . .] towns in this dark night present all the stages of fire: some glowing, others smoking, others ardent. This spectacle of war is offered in a time of peace; this terrifying copy of devastation is in fact produced by industry." As for the sounds of the factories and smelting plants, he likened them to "hydras and dragons tormented by demons in a kind of hell." The city core was likewise undergoing a metamorphosis. Old facades were dismantled, and slate roofs were torn down. Modern "steeples" in the form of "Mr. Cockerill's factory" replaced the old medieval cathedral, destroyed in 1785. The novelist observed with a mix of fascination and dread that "ancient cities produced sounds, modern ones spit out smoke."[18]

At the end of their drawn-out shifts, Liège's laborers returned home to modest dwellings in the industrial outskirts. These workers toiled in machine works, coal plants, and foundries, producing everything from tools to lampposts, nails, guns, cannons, and wheels. Others crafted soap, sheets, beer, glasses, buttons, glasses, and playing cards. In 1825, British-born industrialist John Cockerill had founded a steel and iron production plant at nearby Seraing. The Liège region was renowned above all for its steelworks and metallurgy, but it produced nearly anything one could imagine in this era. Prior to 1836, however, vanilla might have seemed a stretch, even to those familiar with Liège's impressive range of output.[19]

Liège's *Vanilla planifolia* was descended from a large vanilla plant in Antwerp, itself the offshoot of a vine in London that had originated in Mexico. Botanist Parmentier d'Enghien had brought it to Antwerp in 1812 and donated it to the city's botanical garden. It soon reached massive proportions, and the garden's director decided to have it pruned. Over the following decade, offshoots were dispatched to botanical gardens in Paris, Brussels, Louvain, Ghent, and Liège.[20] There, in 1829, six years before his untimely demise, Courtois sent samples and drawings of the flowering vanilla at Liège's small botanical garden to his colleague Alexandre Louis Simon Lejeune in Verviers. From a single Antwerp plant, vanilla radiated across Europe and beyond.[21]

Liège's vanilla flowered regularly but never bore fruit. One desiccated branch, featuring three large flowers and Courtois's inscription *Vanilla planifolia*, as well as a note indicating that it had flowered on location, is still present in Liège's Herbarium library collection. Thanks to the tendril-like roots opposite its leaves, the vanilla had climbed some thirty feet on Canary Islands dragon trees (*Draecoena draco*), creeping along the greenhouse's glass ceiling by the time Morren reached Liège in 1835. Three years later, Morren estimated that his tallest vanilla plant had grown to one hundred feet. He owed a debt to his Liège predecessors Gaëde and Courtois, who had contributed to the extensive flowering of the vanilla. Gaëde and Courtois had taken to looping the vanilla vine, a technique still used today. However, according to Morren, his predecessors had resorted to this practice out of necessity because Liège's greenhouses were rather small, and its vanilla vines needed to be tamed.[22]

The question of flower and specifically orchid reproduction had only just begun to be tackled by scientists. Some continued to think of the matter as unseemly. Nevertheless, a race to pollinate vanilla without the help of insects had now begun, which presented Morren with a golden opportunity. Cracking the reasons for vanilla's "sterility" constituted a rare practical benefit in the new branch that was orchidology. The Liège professor was well aware of the growing fascination with orchids, a fashion that some have likened to the famous Dutch tulip mania of the seventeenth century.[23] In 1835, Morren described orchid enthusiasm as "a vogue." He added that nearly every horticulturalist now boasted a "dedicated greenhouse" reserved for orchids. He attributed this trend in part to novelty and to their "singular, sometimes bizarre appearance," which could resemble a helmet, a butterfly, or even a monkey.[24]

As the only orchid with uses beyond the purely ornamental—"bourgeois by virtue of being utilitarian," mooted a twentieth-century Swiss travel writer—vanilla's reproduction conundrum offered an additional commercial opportunity.[25] And Charles Morren was nothing if not enterprising. By the time Morren turned to the thorny question, vanilla plants were flowering in various locations across the Indian Ocean, much of Latin America and the Caribbean, in the Philippines, and in select botanical gardens in Europe. There seemed to be little rhyme or reason as to when the plants flowered and, outside of Central and South America, no edible vanilla of either varietal had yet borne fruit.[26]

By 1835, Morren was experimenting on the artificial reproduction of non-vanilla orchids in Ghent. The breakthrough with vanilla happened the very next year. Morren applied a new "peculiar horticultural treatment" to fifty-four of Liège's vanilla flowers.[27] A single line in a Liège newspaper on February 17, 1836, informed the public, "Vanilla is currently flowering in one of the university's greenhouses. Enthusiasts are welcome to come and see this rare event."[28] Slow botanical science was being consumed as instant spectacle.[29] A rival newspaper told how Morren had almost biblically predicted success the previous day, upon seeing Liège's vanilla flowers fully open. Witnesses were present, for he had undertaken the "artificial pollination procedure in the presence of the students in his class."[30] It took a full year for the pods to grow and flourish. Morren appears to have waited for the pods to ripen and actually fall, which was and remains anathema among vanilla cultivators.[31] He remarked that vanilla featured "one of the longest gestations known in the plant world."[32]

Morren later boasted, "Having been fecundated by me, [the plants] produced the same number of pods [as flowers]." *Vanilla planifolia*, previously barren outside of Central America, bore fruit in Liège. Morren explained that he focused on the vanilla vines draped around a single Canary Islands dragon tree. In February 1837, a full year after fertilization, this vanilla yielded fifty-four "ripe fruit." The year following, the same operation on a second vine entwined around another dragon tree produced some one hundred pods. Morren described his cracking of the orchid's secret as nothing short of a step forward for humankind. Given the "absence of the species of insect" that pollinated vanilla in Mexico, he noted, fecundation beyond Central America was only possible by "man alone, by a study of the organs."[33] But precisely because the process was now beyond nature's purview, it could become less haphazard. Morren explained that henceforth, thanks to his discovery, "when a [vanilla] flower was produced, a fruit would be too."[34] The Belgian grasped that he had set in motion a kind of automatization and efficiency in vanilla pollination.

Morren had little time to rest on his laurels. In 1838, a French journal downplayed Morren's accomplishment, suggesting without proof that the

Belgian had merely applied the same gestures that French botanists had previously used on other orchid varietals.[35] Given that Morren's breakthrough was likely not subject to any patent, national pride and competition between scientists loomed as some of the largest stakes. However, precisely because of this fear of having his discovery stolen, Morren remained discrete about his method.

What exactly had Morren done to the flowers to pollinate them? The Belgian enlisted tortured and telling colonial metaphors to describe the operation. While they betray racial prejudices and colonial attitudes, they hardly pin down the sequence and details of his fertilization process. He explained, "The presence of a veil on the vanilla orchid's column reminds me of the genitalia of the Boschimans [Bushmen] of the Cape of Good Hope. Vanilla is the Hottentot Venus of the plant world. She is a tender flower that only undertakes the work of the hymen very reluctantly. She requires the help of man, if she is refused the insects or birds which play the role of love's messengers in her native land."[36]

Here Morren anthropomorphized, sexualized, and racialized vanilla, likening the orchid to Sarah Baartman, the "Hottentot Venus." Baartman was a Khoikhoi (South African) woman "considered an oddity," who was subjected to a series of demeaning displays—some in cages—first in Britain in 1810 and 1811 and later in France in 1814. In his discussion of vanilla's "veil," Morren was specifically alluding to the fascination of his onetime professor, French biologist Georges Cuvier, with Baartman's genitalia, specifically her "apron" or supposedly elongated labia that purportedly distinguished her and "her people" from other Africans and Europeans. "Her people" were tellingly vague, as Morren wrongly conflated her with South African San people (Bushmen). This was a peculiar reading even for the time, for Cuvier and others believed that Baartman's genitals revealed "unrepressed sexuality," while Morren saw in them sexual "reluctance." On the basis of Morren's connections with the famous Cuvier, who had tried to inspect Baartman's genitals while she was still alive (but was rebuffed), and then dissected them after her death in 1815, the Belgian deduced that she, like vanilla, possessed unique sexual organs.[37]

Although Morren's passage reminds us that racial and gender hierarchies were being recast in this era, it provides frustratingly scant evidence of what the Belgian actually did to the vanilla flowers in his greenhouse. He did specify that there were two ways to make the vanilla flower pollinate: one could either "remove" or "lift the veil" on the orchid. Next, "one places the stigma in contact with either a whole pollen mass, or part of one."[38] To the Academy of Science in Paris, Morren explained, "One must lift the fleshy veil [separating male and female parts of the orchid] or cut it in order for fecundation to occur, although if the operculum is covered by a droplet of water, so that [...] the masses of pollen can bridge the veil in question, then natural pollination can occur."[39] If this were a sex-ed manual, it would not be a very helpful one ...

As Emilio Kourí has underscored, Morren had elaborated a method but not a technique.[40] Readers of Morren's cryptic reports on the artificial reproduction of vanilla could not have begun to fathom his steps based on his descriptions alone. His presentations were also frustratingly devoid of diagrams and practical details. And so, a reader was left to wonder, should one cut or lift the interfering "veil"? Cutting presented risks of its own. Too great a cut and the flower would be damaged. Too little and pollination could not occur. Should one water the plant copiously? How precisely should the pollen be applied to the exposed stigma? Was the procedure to be conducted entirely by hand, or were implements involved? If so, which? The amount of pollen transferred also remained subjective, as did the precise method of application and the amount of pressure required.

Morren's artificial pollination method was not only vague but also potentially time-consuming and finicky.[41] I would suggest that its vagueness was deliberate. While Morren certainly sent samples of his first harvest left, right, and center, he did not want his technique easily replicated by competitors. He therefore remained as unspecific as possible about the details of his discovery. Despite all these precautions, a major challenger emerged in Paris. In 1838, Parisian botanist Joseph Neumann, who had just been promoted to the post of lead gardener of the tropical greenhouse department of the Jardin du Roi, achieved vanilla's pollination. Some then claimed that he had reached the finish line first. It took Gilbert Bouriquet's 1954 study to set the record straight: Morren had in fact beaten Neumann by two years.[42] Whether Neumann copied the Belgian, (re)invented the same method, or came up with an alternate method is unfortunately impossible to determine from available sources.

In 1837, shortly after Morren's first vanilla harvest, Alire Raffeneau Delile, vice president of a small agricultural society in southern France, visited Liège and published his impressions of Morren's greenhouse. The Frenchman was immediately struck by Liège's industry, wealth, and bustle. He then remarked, "Mr. Morren has succeeded in giving fruit to vanilla by artificial pollination. The less pure air of this city, filled as it is with factories, has not had a deleterious impact on the excellence or the aroma of the fruit." He noted that the largest vanilla vine grew out of a pile of coal and coke. Morren himself boasted of this arrangement to the Academy of Science in Paris in 1838. He even attributed his vanilla's prolific flowering to the coal residue. Another of Morren's visitors added a detail relating to coal: the greenhouse in which vanilla had flowered was heated not only by the sun but also by a coal-powered energy source.[43] In short, *Vanilla planifolia* had borne fruit for the first time outside of Central America in one of the most industrialized settings on earth. Yet the method used to pollinate it was anything but industrial.

Morren's vanilla moment was as dependent on the small-scale advertising strategies of the era as it was on the Industrial Revolution. The botanist wasted little time spreading word of his achievement. On May 5, 1837, he wrote to his patron, Goswin, baron de Stassart, and enclosed with his letter a gift of one and a half beans of "his vanilla." In retrospect, this underwhelming quantity seems an unwitting admission of the limits of his experiment. The botanist offered the pod and a half to Stassart "as a national rarity," in hopes that the baron's chef might prepare it during a banquet scheduled four days later. Mostly, Morren admitted that he wished the gesture would earn the favor of the Belgian Royal Academy, thereby "improving his standing with them" (his "odor with them" reads the French, in an untranslatable metaphor) and demonstrating "through palate and nose that he [was] good at something."[44] Then, on the eve of the banquet, invoking an unexpected and unspecified botanical emergency, Morren sent his excuses to the baron and his wife for not being able to attend in person.[45]

On May 9, 1837, Stassart hosted the lavish banquet, which Morren attended vicariously through his vanilla. In addition to leading members of Belgium's Royal Academy and Brussels's Academy of Science, the nobleman invited parliamentarians and judges. The baroness was a member of the royal court, so between his masonic and her palace contacts, the couple's influence was arguably near its zenith at this point.[46] On the menu were "ice creams perfumed with indigenous vanilla, cultivated in Liège by Mr. Morren."[47] Morren's vanilla had become the stuff of one elite parlor and table. "Indigenous" here meant Belgian, a concept arguably more warranted than

"Belgian chocolate," given that unlike Morren's vanilla pods, cocoa beans were entirely imported from the tropics—at the time, largely from Latin America.[48] To Stassart, at least, the novelty of this "local" vanilla was well worth celebrating, partly due to snobbery, partly to help his protégé, and partly out of budding Belgian pride.

Morren's rapport with his patron was in some ways typical, albeit excessive. He dedicated and autographed articles and books to him, drew his phrenological portrait, and wrote poems for him, all the while requesting favors for himself and his friends. The relationship also featured revealing twists. The botanist repeatedly alluded to enemies or even conspiracies against him. Thus, in May 1838, Morren apologized for not attending the Royal Academy proceedings in Brussels, so as not to "open the door to those who dislike me." He then pivoted, referencing the enclosure of two more "indigenous"—again, read Liège—"vanilla pods for [the baron] to enjoy."[49] A few days later, Morren thanked Stassart for "his generous efforts which have done more than my constant publications to vanquish my adversaries [within the Royal Academy]."[50] Political battle lines were being drawn in 1830s Belgium around the new monarchy, the place of the Church, and the baron's liberal brand of politics. However, none of these directly involved Morren's Belgian vanilla, which would have served as a source of national pride across all those divides. It is therefore unclear whether Morren was tilting at windmills or actually counted columns of foes within the Belgian Royal Academy. To thank the baron for his backing against foes real or imagined, Morren continued making vanilla offerings.

Stassart's May 1837 soirée provided limited vanilla advertising in elite circles. But Morren did not stop there. That same year, before the Medical Association of his old haunt in Ghent, he touted that his discovery would bring down the price of vanilla. He argued that vanilla had previously been prohibitively expensive because of natural constraints: up to now, the orchid could only be pollinated by "insects or hummingbirds." Nature, he explained, was fundamentally unselfish. In the natural world, these two sets of creatures served as "love's messengers," yet in Liège's greenhouse, he himself had become vanilla's Cupid.[51]

In addition to promoting Liège vanilla himself, Charles Morren enlisted his spouse, who played a central role in this story. According to the couple's eldest son, Marie Morren not only translated most of Charles Morren's publications into foreign languages, but she also rendered many of "his" botanical sketches without receiving recognition for her work. She, too, enjoyed a wide range of interests, in keeping with her Catholic faith and noble origins. In 1833, Marie translated into French a British morality tale, *First Impressions, or the History of Emma Nesbit*. Then, in 1839, she translated and released a French edition of a British heraldry manual.[52]

On top of these translations in her own areas of interest, Marie Morren took on many translations for her spouse. On April 27, 1837, he wrote to his fellow orchidologist John Lindley of the prestigious Kew Gardens outside London. He sent along a French translation of Lindley's principles of horticulture, which was likely Marie Morren's doing, as she was the more accomplished translator. He also enclosed several of his articles, as well as his seed catalog. Next, Charles Morren asked if he could visit Kew to study its greenhouses. He explained that he had just secured a seven-hectare space from the city of Liège to construct a new botanical garden and sought inspiration from the best.[53] By 1840, the two botanists had become fast friends, as had their spouses. Charles Morren sent him more publications and offered to have Marie translate them into English for Lindley if he wished.[54] In so doing, Charles Morren betrayed his willingness to enroll his wife's labor to further his career ends. (The letter contains an implied quid pro quo of Marie's translation work in exchange for Lindley's greenhouse insights.)[55]

That said, the collaboration within the Morren couple speaks to other patterns of knowledge sharing. Marie and Charles evidently exchanged ideas on how exactly to translate passages and render drawings, thereby engaging in domestic professional dialogue. In turn, the slew of specialized periodicals in which they published these translations and drawings—all under Charles' name—were consumed both by full-time horticulturalists and botanists and by a segment of the public, of all genders, who were keen for new varietals and the latest floral findings. Belgium alone produced an impressive number of such publications in this era.[56] In other words, Charles Morren's vanilla moment was actually a team effort, facilitated by a growing popular fascination at this time for botany and especially orchids, as well as by his wife's unrecognized efforts.

Marie Morren was one of many women who played an important, although unremunerated, role in the field of botany. For well over a century, women botanists in Britain, France, Italy, the Netherlands, and the lands that would become Germany had served as patrons, practitioners, connoisseurs, correspondents, and collectors. A few received recognition as bona fide scientists and authors in the field of botany and beyond. Natalie Zemon Davis has described the late seventeenth- and early eighteenth-century German Maria Sibylla Merian as an "artist-naturalist" as well as an overseas colonial prospector.[57] However, the nineteenth century witnessed a powerful Victorian backlash beginning in the 1830s, led by none other than Charles Morren's British friend John Lindley. In part to demonstrate that botany need not be the privilege of an aristocratic elite, Lindley heaped scorn on previous Linnean botanists for viewing the field as "amusement for ladies." He sought to distinguish the work of "men of enlightened minds" from female amateur botany.[58] This was more than rhetoric: across Europe, women were gradually squeezed out of the discipline, outside their roles as collectors, patrons, and, in the case of Marie Morren, unpaid spousal collaborators. Indeed, by the 1860s, when he turned to the study of orchids, Charles Darwin assumed that the default way to reference female scientists in academic papers was to name their husbands.[59] Little wonder, then, that during this Victorian backlash, Marie Morren did not sign her botanical drawings or even credit herself with her publications.

Yet among gardeners, Marie Morren's name probably holds greater currency today than her husband's. In 1841, Liège horticulturalist and friend of the Morrens, Hyacinthe Haquin, succeeded in creating a new rose by crossing *Camellia japonica var. punctata* with another varietal. He declined to indicate the other flower, keeping it a trade secret. This secrecy was unsurprising, given that plants were Haquin's business. He named the new rose *Camellia japonica var. Maria Morren* in recognition of "the Belgian lady who honors horticulture by her talent at painting flowers from nature with remarkable perfection."[60]

In addition to her illustration and translation work, Marie Morren emerged as the prime presenter of Liège vanilla at Belgium's many fairs. It would seem that this was partly a maneuver devised to circumvent conflict of interest conventions: with Charles Morren highly placed in both selection committees and scientific societies, he must have realized that he could not present his own vanilla in competition. (Spousal conflict of interest obviously never occurred to him.) And so, Marie Morren began showing Liège vanilla at the Ghent and Antwerp agricultural, horticultural and botanical fairs in 1837, the year of its first harvest. She did so again at the 1848 Brussels agricultural and horticultural fair.[61] As handlers would a few decades later with dogs at the Westminster Kennel Club's annual show, she accompanied, primed, showcased, and proudly displayed the prize specimens. In so doing, she became the face associated with Liège vanilla. According to Charles Morren, crowds assembled around her stand. The pods Marie Morren presented were varied, reflecting the different stages of vanilla preparation: some were still green, some had ripened, and some were "ready for selling, coated in their powdery *givre*, which avid enthusiasts seek above all else."[62] This suggests that one or both Morrens had successfully prepared the Liège vanilla.

However, the grand agricultural fair held in Brussels in 1848 proved to be the spousal scheme's undoing. There, the jury panel decided that Charles Morren could not serve on the committee to judge his wife's vanilla and disallowed their entry. This came as a shock to Charles Morren. After all, he reasoned, he had clearly spelled out that the pods on display were the fruit of "Marie Morren's vanilla plantation," not his.[63] This statement lends itself to two readings: either Charles Morren was being especially cynical, or he was finally recognizing Marie's substantial participation in his professional activities.

Given her son's observation, and Hyacinthe Haquin's confirmation that Marie Morren was the author of many of the drawings that adorned her husband's works, I am tempted to see her hand behind a splendid 1849 color illustration (fig. 4). It shows the vanilla the Morrens presented at the 1848 Brussels fair. The chromolithograph bears the signature of G. Severeyns, a Belgian engraving firm, but this does not rule out the possibility of Marie Morren as the sketcher. It is titled "Vanilla produced in greenhouses." The accompanying text reads, "The illustration shows fruit around a stalk, in different forms and sizes: some green, others in the yellow hue that precedes maturity, another brown, this color always starting at the terminal point and moving forward every day [. . .]. On the side, one sees two large prepared pods."[64] The bulk of the "green" unprepared vanilla to the left is rendered in a bunch formation, reminiscent of bananas. The lithograph certainly highlights the ripening process. It also showcases the appearance of prepared pods, distinctly arranged on the right, ready for market, and presenting specks of white *givre*.

Morren's efforts to commercialize his greenhouse vanilla stand out, if for nothing else but their lofty ambitions. In March 1837, the Belgian press reported that the Russian consul in Hamburg had been impressed by Morren's discovery and had invited him to introduce vanilla to Russia.[65] Yet

FIGURE 4. "Vanilla produced in greenhouses" plate in Charles Morren's article in the *Annales de la société royale d'agriculture et de botanique de Gand*, vol. 5, 1849. Thanks to Wageningen University and Research Library, The Netherlands, for the reproduction.

the story quietly died, and vanilla's pollination secret did not find its way to Saint Petersburg or Moscow. Then, in April 1837, Morren sent a sample of his vanilla to King of Prussia Frederick William III. That same year, he offered some of his vanilla to the emperor of Austria, by way of the Austrian legation in Brussels. Finally, almost as an afterthought in 1840, he dispatched a sample to his own king, Leopold II. The monarch had an assistant politely thank the scientist for the gift and ask him to keep His Majesty appraised of "his progress in naturalizing this precious production."[66] The message was clear: Morren's initial success needed to be parlayed into mass local production. This never happened. At best, by 1840 we see evidence of small-scale emulation of Morren's technique in greenhouses in Leiden, Utrecht, Brussels, and Antwerp.[67]

Morren's objectives were grand, but he turned out to be a better inventor than an entrepreneur. In 1848, Morren still vowed to "establish vanilla plantations" in greenhouses while expressing "certainty" that he could turn a profit from it.[68] Three years later, Morren took stock of the situation. He regretted that the Belgian government had rejected his scheme to establish vanilla greenhouse production as a side business. The authorities invoked a conflict-of-interest law that forbade academics from holding secondary positions or pursuing other careers. Morren applied for an exemption and was promptly rejected. And so, Morren bemoaned, his vanilla remained a mere "curiosity."[69] A pattern emerges here, in which Morren believed he had been hindered by overzealous regulators and assorted adversaries, both at the Belgian fair of 1848 and in the halls of power in Brussels.

In reality, the crown bore no particular grudge against Morren. For instance, in 1838, at the very time Leopold II was rejecting the scientist's proposal to practice large-scale vanilla cultivation, the king disbursed some 10,000 Belgian francs for Morren's "fire machine." This product of the Industrial Revolution was used to pump water and distribute it as the botanist wished on the grounds of his seven-hectare botanical garden on the outskirts of town. That said, the city of Liège absorbed the costs of the new garden itself, spending 300,000 francs on installations and another 8,000 on plant purchases.[70] It seems likely that Morren's newfound vanilla fame accounts in part for this wave of generosity.

So, if his vanilla schemes were not actually hindered by kings and regulators, why did they wilt? The question is all the more puzzling because Morren's timing was impeccable. (Whether he anticipated or reflected demand is a chicken-and-egg question.) In the late 1830s, the confluence of the Industrial Revolution and the widespread embracing of liberal free trade especially in Belgium, combined with transformations in transport, an appetite for new flavors as revealed in this chapter's opening vignette, and a wave of orchidmania, should have spelled success for Morren's undertaking.[71] Specifically, his idea of dropping vanilla's prices by generating greenhouse competition for Central American pods was ingenious and timely.

There were many reasons that Morren's vanilla project ultimately withered. We have seen that the Liège botanist was highly secretive in his methods, only providing the vaguest indication of how he had pollinated vanilla. Unless one of Morren's students in attendance at the 1836 pollination decided to perpetuate his method, it was unlikely to be copied. Given that they depended on him for patronage, none of them dared to do so.

Another cause of Morren's failure seems ironic, given how much effort he and his wife invested in promoting Belgian vanilla. While King Leopold II did not block Morren, in the end, despite the botanist's outreach to potentates the world over, no czar, emperor, or king ever responded with anything more than polite encouragement.

A third, more profound factor that accounts for the failure of Morren's vanilla venture involves consumer habits. He explained that he had successfully exported cuttings of his Liège vanilla to the neighboring Netherlands, without mentioning the middlemen who by this time had established close relations with scientists.[72] From there, Belgian vanilla vines were sent on an epic voyage to Java in the Dutch East Indies, which they miraculously survived. In other words, Morren dispatched samples left and right, to importers, governments, and traders alike. He even dared to mail pods of his Liège vanilla to Mexico, a bit like sending rice or tea to China, or wine to France. This might have been a bridge too far. According to the Belgian scientist, a backlash ensued. In Morren's own words, Liège vanilla was soon "hindered by ridiculous prejudice."[73] Evidently, some consumers stubbornly continued to associate vanilla with the Gulf of Mexico rather than the coal mounds of Liège. Here was a challenge that many a vanilla producer would face: Vanilla was often nostalgically associated with previous geographies that were out of keeping with global trends. Still, Morren did not back down. In 1839, he published an article in the *Annals of Natural History*, in which he argued that his Liège vanilla was "of as good a quality (if not better) than that which is exported from Mexico."[74]

That said, who am I today to judge the flavor of Morren's Liège vanilla? And would today's vanilla expectations match those of the 1830s?[75] I was unfortunately unable to taste the descendants of Morren's Liège pods to detect possible flavor variations. But even had I been able to sample some of Morren's vanilla progeny, I still would not have been able to duplicate the Morrens' preparation, which remains a mystery, as we are about to see. Suffice it to suggest at this point that provenance and terroir have always mattered to consumers.

Another potential drawback to Belgian vanilla involves pod preparation. Indigenous people in Mexico had chosen, picked, sorted, and cured the pods for centuries, whereas Morren appears to have waited for the pods to fall from the vanilla vine. Early on, even when he did occasionally pick one from the vine, as in 1838 when he produced a single bean before the Academy of Science in Paris, he "presented it in its naïve purity," refusing to "subject it to any preparation whatsoever."[76] Was this scientific rigor or commercial laziness?

More crucially, when Charles Morren finally did deign to undertake pod preparation, did he master the complicated process? We saw that he or Marie had managed to make *givre* appear on their pods. We know, moreover, that Charles Morren had read Jean-Baptiste Christophe Fusée-Aublet's 1773 treatise on Guianese plants, which laid out "modes of [vanilla] preparation."[77] This also implies, interestingly, that Morren bypassed Mexican and Spanish sources in favor of French ones, perhaps simply because of his language skill set. Consequently, French Guiana and its *pompona* varietal served as the vanilla knowledge bridge from the Americas to francophone Europe. Fusée-Aublet's 1773 tome outlined how to prepare the three types of vanilla he claimed existed in Guiana.[78] The eighteenth-century botanist explained that the preparation bore similarities to the manner in which prunes were preserved in the cities of Tours and Digne, and raisins in Naples. First, the beans were boiled; next, a feather was used to cover them in oil; they were then suspended for drying; lastly, they were pressed. Fusée-Aublet attributed this method to the Galibis and Carib peoples of Guiana and the Garipon natives of neighboring territories.[79] Available sources do not reveal whether Morren followed Fusée-Aublet's instructions to a tee. If he did, then the pods he produced must have tasted different from the ones with which we are familiar, since the Mexican or Bourbon preparation methods that are commonly used today do not include the oiling or pressing stages.

Unfortunately, Charles Morren was terse in his description of the vanilla Marie presented in Brussels in 1848: "These pods are prepared for conservation, covered in *givre*, in a state completely analogous to the vanilla available in stores."[80] Had the couple properly boiled and sun dried the pods, then massaged them, to ensure they achieved the right luster and suppleness? Had they perhaps oiled them? *Givre* was a good sign, as it is usually associated with prolonged cellaring and superior quality.

The vagueness of his language opens the possibility that Morren's vanilla failed to impress, and therefore to compete, because it was poorly prepared and consequently sour, bitter, or rancid. We do know that its odor was overpowering. In 1851, Charles Morren explained his choice to have Marie show Belgian vanilla in a glass bell jar at the 1848 Brussels fair. The Morrens had noticed that their maturing vanilla let off a potent, "penetrating" smell that "some in attendance could not bear." At an earlier showing without the bell jar, some bystanders experienced headaches, others nausea.[81] However, this sensory reaction might not necessarily be a reflection on the Morrens' preparation; one has to factor in the novelty of vanilla to nineteenth-century Belgian noses.[82]

However, the primary reason for the failure of Belgian vanilla likely has to do with supply. After all, Morren could only spare one bean for the Academy of Science in Paris and one and a half for his mentor. The Morren story underscores the limits of greenhouses for large-scale commercial vanilla cultivation. We now know that Morren's dream of producing vanilla outside the tropics in the 1830s faced daunting odds. In 2012, scientists at Wageningen University launched a costly venture to grow greenhouse vanilla in Holland. They were motivated by the sky-high prices of vanilla, steady demand, as well as by Dutch expertise in growing other crops, such as tomatoes, on a massive scale under greenhouses. They were also armed with another 176 years in orchid research and backed by investors. Like Morren before them, they reveled in the jarring prospect of exotic vanilla flowering in the northern Low Countries. A 2016 article about the project reads, "In the middle of potato fields in a central Dutch rural town, scientists from Wageningen University have for the past four years been nurturing vanilla orchids." Indeed, the project's goal was to introduce vanilla as a cash crop alongside tulips and potatoes: "The aim was to increase the variety of crops grown by Dutch farmers as they search for improved profits." Another objective was to create a protected harvest by using greenhouses to solve the bane of producers the world over—vanilla theft. However, in 2019, lead researcher Filip van Noort conceded that the project had failed from a business perspective and announced that the team was giving up. A February 2019 article in *Dutch News* bore the unambiguous title "Dutch Efforts to Grow Vanilla Commercially Flop." Even at vanilla's exorbitant prices, intensive greenhouse production in a country with cold winters and high salaries did not yield sufficient profit margins for a crop that requires constant care, years for maturation, appropriate heat, sunlight and humidity, insider knowledge, manual pollination, and an intensive curing and preparation process.[83] Vanilla remains far easier to grow in the Global South—or, as was said in Morren's time, the tropics.

Tropicality was on Morren's mind as well. It therefore makes sense to apply a colonial lens to Morren's "acclimatizing" vanilla. This acclimatization framework was powerful in Morren's era. At the time, the concept meant "the rationally forced adaptation" of plants and animals to new environments.[84] But the colonial story revealed by this failure to fully acclimatize is complex. Belgium was not a colonial power when Morren made his discovery; it had split from the Netherlands and its multicontinental empire in 1830. Belgium's murderous involvement in Congo would only begin in 1885. In effect, by seeking to acclimatize vanilla, Morren had brought the tropics to Liège rather than the other way around. His greenhouses and coke were part of an attempt to harness, appropriate, and even re-create the fertility and plenty of the tropics. In 1776, a colonial official setting foot in Saint-Domingue had exclaimed, "Oh prodigy of industry! A space of earth equal to that of [. . .] the park in Versailles, produces more riches than half the Russian empire!"[85] However, for all his ambitions to acclimatize and master vanilla, Morren was never able to match these bountiful tropics in his industrial greenhouse.

There is an interesting parallel with Saint-Domingue's crystalline gold of the time, sugar. Long refined in Europe but produced in the tropics, overseas cane sugar faced a new challenge from European beet sugar by 1800. During the Napoleonic Wars, France imported and adapted Silesian beet sugar to satisfy European markets at the height of the British continental blockade. Sugar beet production then took off in the second half of the nineteenth century. But the comparison ends there. Contrary to beet sugar, cold-climate vanilla remained a mirage. And while on a smaller scale vanilla followed sugar's prodigious upward production curve in the nineteenth century, it did not mirror sugar's stunning "democratization." Indeed, in Britain especially, thanks in part to the confluence of beet production in cold climes and cane output in warm ones, sucrose went from being the preserve of the rich to the staple of the poor in the span of a century, from 1750 to 1850.[86] Vanilla, conversely, remained a luxury, or at least real vanilla did. The failure of Morren's project to cultivate vanilla in cold climes is not the only reason for this, naturally. Coffee cultivation remains exclusive to the Global South, for instance, without being a luxury product per se, as it is not nearly as costly as vanilla.[87]

So where does this leave Morren's vanilla in the colonial equation? A year after Morren's breakthrough, the Belgian press foretold that his discovery would render "Europe less dependent on Latin America and the East Indies."[88] Morren agreed. In addition to aiming to bring about a scientific transformation, he wished for his discovery to set in motion a commercial one: "May the consequences be felt in a few years' time on the relations between old Europe and a new world to which we pay a hefty tribute and from which we must liberate ourselves."[89] Here was a reverse emancipation from the wave of colonial independence spearheaded by Simón Bolívar a little over a decade prior. Thanks to his 1836 discovery, Morren added, "the cultivation of vanilla is now ensured to Europe."[90] If anything, and for all of his colonial references, Morren's goal was anticolonial: It was to make vanilla Belgian. The idea was conceived by a scientist whose youth had been marked by the British blockade of Napoleonic Europe and the resulting continental autarky.[91]

This is an important feature of Morren's adventure. It was more of a protectionist reaction, an equivalent to beet sugar, than the fruit of some long-range "European colonial science complex."[92] In this case, we witness not so much empires seeking to stymie free trade or early globalization but rather a failed protectionist experiment at the height of the Industrial Revolution.[93] Morren himself claimed to have ushered in "the industrial cultivation of vanilla."[94] Yet the Belgian never set foot in the tropics, his country possessed no empire, and he claimed no colonial expertise. Although he exchanged botanical knowledge with colleagues all over Europe, he never imagined contributing to a colonial project, nor did he appear to know much about Mexico, vanilla's point of origin. He certainly never sought insight from Mexican vanilla insiders. Nor do we have any evidence that Morren's scientific publications were widely read in regions that produced vanilla or were on the cusp of doing so. While some speculate that Edmond Albius somehow gained knowledge of Morren's breakthrough on faraway Réunion Island in 1841, I argue that he achieved a second manual pollination of vanilla without ever having heard of Morren.[95]

So what are we to make of Charles Morren's legacy? For all of his perceived enemies, he was certainly well-connected. He boasted in 1841 that French botanist and silk expert Matthieu Bonafous had copied his model for Liège's botanical garden in faraway Sardinia.[96] For many decades, Morren's name continued to resonate with naturalists, especially those interested in orchids.

Most notably, in 1860, two years after Charles Morren's death, none other than Charles Darwin responded to Oxford curator John Westwood, "I do not know of Morren's paper about orchids and insects," asking his colleague to kindly send it to him.[97] Darwin was fast becoming an international celebrity, thanks to *On the Origin of the Species*, published in November of the previous year. In 1861, Darwin posted an announcement in the *Gardener's Chronicle*. He asked the public to send him "exotic orchids"—"a few flowers and buds, of any member of the group, packed in a small tin canister." He then requested bibliographic assistance from the public: "Would you have the kindness to inform me, if in your power, whether the late Professor Morren has published anything (and where) on the fertilization of orchids by insect agency?"[98] It is not surprising that he received no answer, for Morren had been interested in replacing insects—and hummingbirds, whom he imagined as possible vanilla pollinators—rather than identifying the genus responsible for pollinating vanilla in its natural habitat.

In 1862, after having it proofread by his daughter Henrietta, who pruned some of the driest bits, Darwin published a book titled *On the Various Contrivances by Which British and Foreign Orchids Are Fertilized by Insects*.[99] The evolution theorist noted, "[Vanilla] is cultivated for its aromatic pods in Tahiti, Bourbon, and the East Indies; but does not fruit without artificial aid. This fact shows that some insect in its own American home is specially adapted for its fertilization; and that the insects of the above-named tropical regions, where the vanilla flourishes, either do not visit the flowers, though they secrete an abundance of nectar, or do not visit them in the proper method."[100] Darwin correctly deduced that only a specific type of insect, which turned out to be Central American bees (Meliponini) for *Vanilla planifolia*, was able to pollinate vanilla. The question had shifted from how to pollinate vanilla artificially to why such an artificial pollination was required in the first place. Morren had understood that either insects or hummingbirds were the answer but was not particularly interested in determining which genus. And so, in tackling this question, and despite his correspondence with Westwood two years prior, Darwin did not express any recognition of Morren's discovery.

In Belgium today, a few descendants of Morren's vanilla still populate a laboratory at the University of Liège. They are not harvested on a commercial scale. Yet I was able to set eye on them when I visited in 2018. Jarred in aseptic conditions that control for temperature and humidity and visible behind glass, they serve at once as tangible legacies of Morren's success and as enduring proof of its limits. Vanilla remains fragile and fickle, and it does not thrive in cold climes. Unlike marijuana, for example, it has proven impractical and unaffordable to produce in greenhouses. In other words, the University of Liège's jarred vanilla is the exception that proves the rule.[101]

CHAPTER 3

An Enslaved Teen Cracks the Case

WHY ARE SOME OF THE FINEST VANILLAS "BOURBON" AND some of the best chocolates "Belgian," and not vice versa? The reverse could just as easily have happened. Morren's vanilla greenhouse gambit was well-timed, and cocoa thrived on Bourbon Island prior to 1815. Of course, vanilla and cocoa both originated in the Americas. In hindsight, the Mascarene island in the southwestern Indian Ocean and the small European kingdom seem like strange brand associations for both vanilla and chocolate. There was certainly nothing predetermined about these food links. The successful experiments carried out by an enslaved twelve-year-old named Edmond, seven years before emancipation in the French colonies, lie at the heart of how vanilla became "Bourbon." In turn, vanilla's fractured yet united nature as a commodity is highlighted by these various labels. "Bourbon vanilla" is a widespread term, yet it is simply another name for *Vanilla planifolia*. The contingency in these designations has everything to do with diffusion, competition, and human ingenuity.

I first need to explain how and why vanilla from the Americas reached the isle of Bourbon in the southern Indian Ocean in the first place and how an enslaved youth gained botanical expertise. Plants circulated at an unprecedented pace between continents from the seventeenth to the nineteenth centuries. Shortly before the French Revolution of 1789, the Jardin du Roi drew up plans for French colonies to establish extensive botanical catalogs and exchange seeds with Paris as well as other colonies. In 1810, the head of Paris's botanical gardens issued strict instructions on the packaging of seeds. They were to be dried to avoid mildew, carefully wrapped in paper with their names and provenance indicated, and then packaged in specially designed crates. Moss, straw, and other protective matters were used to preserve seedlings.[1] Several decades later, an improved transport box, known as the Wardian case (after Dr. Nathaniel Bagshaw Ward), featuring a glass top and resembling a miniature greenhouse, markedly improved the odds of survival for saplings and other small plants on sea voyages. Still, many a plant was damaged or even lost in transit even after this transformation.[2]

Plant mobility was the order of the day. Bourbon was on the giving and receiving end of this flowering trade. A magnificent mountainous island of 970 square miles, renowned for its deep gorges, sheer cliffs—known locally as ramparts—and unrivaled natural beauty, Bourbon had long been considered a tropical Eden, uninhabited prior to European exploration. This stature, which was well established by the seventeenth century, collided with the reality that some of the island's lush forests were suffering from deforestation. A more pronounced version of this paradox was at work on Bourbon's sister island, the Isle of France (Île de France, later Mauritius). There, the king's representative Pierre Poivre emerged as a leading ecologist, determined to stem deforestation. This colonial environmentalism did not yet consider the mass transfer of outside vegetation to unique ecosystems a problem, although it did recognize the risk posed by "feral" animals, including rats, pigs, and dogs. Such animal introductions, deliberate or not, had contributed to the extinction of the flightless dodo bird on that very island around 1662. As intendant, Poivre oversaw the acclimatization of a wide range of varietals on Isle of France, especially luxury spice plants, including cinnamon and pepper.[3] Island gardens and garden islands emerged by the eighteenth century as key experimentation hubs, replete with intrigue.[4]

On Bourbon in August 1783, the head of the local botanical garden authorities listed thousands of recently imported plants for distribution on the colony's estates. Inhabitants were invited to submit their requests in writing. On the list were thirty-eight African baobabs, five hundred coconut trees, 178 cacao trees, one thousand clove plants, two thousand Ceylon cinnamon trees, and 340 Filipino nutmeg trees, to name only a small sample.[5] Vanilla did not figure in the impressive catalog. The question of who first brought it to the island, under what circumstances, and why elicited a surprising controversy decades later, once vanilla had become synonymous with Bourbon.[6]

Ensuring the success of Bourbon's botanical garden and supplying it with new varietals were the twin obsessions of local official and botanist Mézières Lépervanche. In 1815, the year of Napoleon's final defeat, he wrote

AN ENSLAVED TEEN CRACKS THE CASE

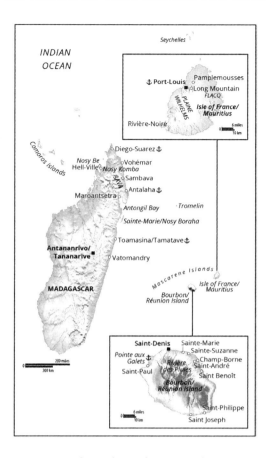

FIGURE 5. The insular southwestern Indian Ocean.
Map by Isabelle Lewis.

to the director of Paris's botanical gardens, enclosing sixty local Bourbon island seeds. In exchange, he hoped that Paris might send specimens that could thrive on Bourbon and expand the island's botanical garden. After all, Isle of France and its splendid garden of Pamplemousses had just fallen into British hands.[7] In other words, the dispatching of vanilla to Bourbon can be attributed, at least in part, to compensation and exchanges.

On New-Year's Day 1819, Swiss botanist Guerard Samuel Perrottet boarded the vessel of Bourbon-born Captain Pierre-Henri Philibert, setting sail from Rochefort. Four years earlier, France had suffered a global defeat, resulting in its overseas realm being reduced to mere crumbs of an empire already decimated in 1763: all that remained were Martinique, Guadeloupe, French Guiana, Saint-Pierre and Miquelon, Bourbon, and tiny outposts in southern India and West Africa. The incredible planetary voyage on which the two men and their crews embarked had one main objective: to travel to Asia to recruit between two hundred and three hundred "Chinese people trained in exotic plants" to bring back to French Guiana.[8] However, as with space missions today, the endeavor soon became multipurposed: a botanic agenda was added to the mission to help France's empire reverse its fortunes.

As it happens, the governor of French Guiana, Napoleonic General Claude Carra Saint-Cyr, had developed a passion for vanilla.[9] He now grafted vanilla onto Philibert's expedition. Saint-Cyr explained in a February 1819 report to Paris, "Commandant Philibert brings with him all of the plants and seeds from Guiana which he expects will successfully adapt to Bourbon, especially vanilla, a crop which I have been propagating as much as possible since my arrival here [two years ago]." Philibert himself specified that the Guianese vanilla had been carefully selected "from several *habitations* [. . .] on different types of land."[10] According to the Ministry of the Navy and the Colonies in Paris, the expedition's chief purpose was to bring "Chinese cultivators" to Guiana. However, the organizers found a way of making the voyage "profitable to the isle of Bourbon as well."[11] Two birds would be killed with one stone. People and vanilla vines would be uprooted and "acclimatized" in the process, traveling half a world away aboard two ships, the longest of which measured a mere forty-three meters (141 feet).

After an epic voyage across the South Atlantic and past the Cape of Good Hope, in June 1819, Philibert and Perrottet's two sailing vessels, the *Rhône* and the *Durance*, reached Bourbon. Philibert wrote the island's governor that he hoped "vanilla's introduction to the colony could offer it a source of prosperity," perhaps as an export commodity to Asia.[12] The botanist and the captain then promptly set about allocating vanilla to islanders in a more rational manner than the 1783 free-for-all. Philibert explained, "We distributed the plants to different inhabitants of the isle, located in sites distanced from one another, where one finds different temperatures and soil of various qualities; through this method, I hoped to acclimate this plant on Bourbon."[13] Philibert would have to justify this choice, as he was chastised by the island's governor for not handing over all his vanilla to the island's botanical garden. In his own defense, Philibert pleaded in July 1819, "Here are my reasons: given that these different types of vanilla were collected on remote and varied lands, far from one another, I am convinced that in order to achieve the success of this plant, it is prudent to spread it across different parts of the island, featuring different temperatures; this way, if it does not take in one area, we can suppose that it might in others."[14] Decades later, Perrottet corroborated this account: "Commandant Philibert was born in [Bourbon], his entire family lived there, and [. . .] he deemed it imprudent, and I concurred, to deposit our precious parcel in the hands of only one person." Instead of placing all his eggs in one basket, wrote the Swiss botanist, "he believed that distributing it to different parts of the island, to only the most accredited inhabitants, would better ensure its conservation and would thus bring greater odds of seeing it expand across the colony." And so, Philibert apportioned vanilla to Mrs. Fréon of Sainte-Marie and to Hubert de Monfleuris at Saint-Benoit. In fact, Perrottet paid follow-up visits to each of the planters, dispensing cultivation and placement advice for their precious charges.[15]

The vanilla voyagers proceeded eastward to the regions that now compose Indonesia and the Philippines. In the Philippines, Perrottet collected "a great many vanilla plants" for transport to Bourbon; he also brought vanilla from Java.[16] There are several nonedible varietals of indigenous vanillas in the Philippines. However, it is also possible that this sample originated from the Americas, as testimony from 1837 mentions "Guatemala vanilla" already present in the Philippines.[17] Perrottet described the vanillas he collected in the Philippines and Java as different from the varietal he had transported from Guiana: their stems were finer, their leaves smaller, their fruit slenderer and more fragrant. In other words, the vanilla Perrottet and Philibert introduced to Bourbon from French Guiana must have been *Vanilla pompona*.[18]

The expedition's two vessels were now laden with vanilla and other plants collected on the islands, as well as far more weighty trophies: eleven water buffalo deemed useful for farming in Guiana. This made for cramped quarters on board. However, the main mission of bringing back several hundred Chinese experts in tropical agriculture failed, after the ships' own crews hinted to those preparing to sign contracts that they would be replacing slaves. Only twenty-seven Chinese workers reached Guiana. Candid crew members were not the mission's only challenge. Biotransfer campaigns suffered high plant casualty rates before the advent of the Wardian case. On August 20, 1820, the same governor of Guiana who had sent vanilla to Bourbon in the first place complained that the many plants harvested in Asia had been "battered" by the return voyage. A slim list of plant survivors was drawn up. The water buffalo fared no better.[19]

In the end, who won the race to introduce vanilla to Bourbon? Did the Bourbon vanilla that Edmond pollinated originate from Guiana, the Philippines, Java, or elsewhere? In January 1821, naturalist Joseph Hubert noted that eight months after Philibert brought five vanilla cuttings from Asia, only one was showing any signs of life.[20] An 1823 article proclaimed that the "vanilla cuttings brought by Captain Philibert" from Guiana were thriving in Bourbon's botanical garden, a facility dedicated to "naturalizing" or acclimating the "most precious plants" to the isle.[21] It would seem that the *Vanilla pompona* from Guiana had successfully adapted, whereas the types introduced from Southeast Asia had not.

However, a botanical enthusiast and official by the name of Marchant undertook yet another vanilla introduction to Bourbon in 1822. In correspondence with Joseph Hubert from September of that year, Marchant raved of having secured "real Mexican vanilla" (read *planifolia*) via the Jardin du Roi in Paris. He transported it to Bourbon, where he claimed that only "Cayenne" (read *pompona*) vanilla existed. Marchant left one batch of *planifolia* with Saint-Denis's botanical garden, which died. But he brought another to his estate at Belle-Eau, which thrived.[22] It seems safe to conclude that Philibert and Perrottet crossed the finish line first, initially introducing *Vanilla pompona* to Bourbon from Guiana in 1819 and then other varietals from Asia, which fared poorly on location. And yet, given that Edmond pollinated *Vanilla planifolia*, which then became the dominant varietal on location, the vine on which he undertook the operation was likely introduced by Marchant in 1822. Of course, prior to Edmond's discovery, all these vanillas were mere curiosities on Bourbon. Until 1841, they sometimes flowered but never bore fruit.

Vanilla is one complex actor in this story; Edmond, the enslaved child who provided the practical solution to vanilla's sterility outside the Americas, is the other. As with most enslaved people, the only surviving contemporaneous sources concerning Edmond are those produced by others, be it reports on his remarkable 1841 discovery or representations of him. There are no equivalents to the English-language slave autobiographies that British and US abolitionists eagerly enlisted. At best, historians of Bourbon can retrieve the voices of a tiny minority of enslaved people who stood or testified at trial. Even those are often filtered through a translator or clerk, and sometimes reveal as much about defense strategies as they do about lives in bondage.[23] While still enslaved, Edmond never testified before a court. And so, a set of eleven nineteenth-century letters concerning him, produced in the 1860s by his former owner and others, constitute nearly the entire body of written knowledge about him from his lifetime. Although they need to be examined critically, these records do provide far more detail than we have for most other enslaved people.

Edmond was born in 1829, the son of Pamphile and Mélise, who died giving birth to him. His parents were the property of Madame de Bellier-Beaumont, who owned an estate at Bellevue, in the district of Sainte-Suzanne on Bourbon. Sainte-Suzanne rests on the isle's lush northeastern coast, which is visited by winds that cross the Indian Ocean and soaked by precipitation when clouds collide with the island's mountainous barrier chain. Culminating at a staggering 3,070 meters (10,072 feet), this magnificent massif is the result of ongoing volcanic activity. The island's eastern half, with its plentiful rains and rich volcanic earth, turns out to be perfect for vanilla.

The Indian Ocean brought more than trade winds and plants to the shores of the Mascarenes. Although not on the same scale as the Atlantic, it too served as a major slave trading route, one that featured its share of unimaginable tragedies. In 1761, the *Utile*, outfitted in Bayonne, ran ashore on the tiny, remote, and uninhabited Île de Sable while en route to sell its human cargo of 160 enslaved Malagasy to the Isle of France. The shipwreck island, later renamed Tromelin, has a summit of twenty-six feet and measures 765 yards in width and one mile in length. Accounts suggest that seventy-two of the enslaved Malagasy drowned in the initial shipwreck. Survivors, crew, and enslaved alike scrambled to dig wells. The crew soon succeeded in building a raft from the *Utile*'s debris, with which they alone reached Madagascar. As for the former slaves, they were left behind to fend for themselves. As the years passed, the castaways languished and then perished one by one. Freed from shackles but reenslaved by their new environment, they waged heroic struggles to survive. Only seven remaining women and an eight-month-old infant were found alive an astonishing fifteen years after the initial shipwreck and taken to Isle of France, where they were pronounced free. Archeological evidence reveals that they survived the ordeal by drinking from a well and eating birds, eggs, sea turtles, roots, oysters, and fish.[24]

On Bourbon, 366 miles to the south of Tromelin, place names to this day reflect Malagasy origins. Bourbon was exceptionally diverse, with multiple languages, cultures, and faiths represented. Enslaved people were brought there predominantly from Africa and Madagascar (the percentage from Madagascar has long been underestimated). A number of enslaved South Asians were also brought to Bourbon in the first decades of the eighteenth century; then, beginning in the 1820s, waves of Indian and subsequently Chinese migrants began arriving as indentured laborers. (There were 3,102 such Indian laborers on Bourbon by 1830.) Pamphile and Mélise almost certainly claimed both Malagasy and continental African ancestry, and possibly South Asian roots as well. Paradoxically, Bourbon's multiculturalism had the effect of reinforcing servile hierarchies, with plantation owners pitting groups against one another and encouraging the reporting of potential uprisings and escapes. Bondage workers on Bourbon undertook many forms of labor. Among them, a minority (16 percent in 1826) worked as domestic servants, while others toiled in a vast array of manual tasks including digging, road paving, planting, fishing, farming, and harvest work. In Edmond's rural district of Sainte-Suzanne, the percentage of the enslaved who served as domestics was lower, 9.8 percent in 1834. Enslaved people born on the island, known as Creoles, tended to occupy the top rungs of the ladder, serving as commanders of other slaves, skilled laborers, or heads of workshops. In 1834, when Edmond was five years old, his district of Sainte-Suzanne counted 4,542 enslaved individuals, 48.7 percent of them Creole. While France's Caribbean sugar islands relied on gradations of phenotypes to determine the price of enslaved individuals, Bourbon's human auction markets based their rates on expertise, strength, skill, and Creole status.[25]

The island's rugged, inaccessible interior, with sheer cliffs forming natural ramparts, enabled scores of intrepid women and men to escape enslavement; in some cases, they even established self-sufficient, parallel upland societies of maroons. This did not stop slave owners from counting "maroon slaves" in their registers or even selling them in absentia—a sign that owners regarded *marronnage* as a transient state. (Although authorities tended to distinguish between short-term *petit marronnage* and long-term *grand marronnage*.)[26] Tragically, as elsewhere, including the Middle Passage itself, suicide constituted another frequent form of servile resistance. Arson was another.[27] That said, Sue Peabody suggests that extreme cruelty toward the enslaved (torture, mutilation, staking in the sun) proved less frequent on

Bourbon than in the Atlantic colonies.[28] Between 1818 and 1848, Bourbon slaves considered "dangerous" were sometimes deported to the Île Sainte-Marie, a former pirate base and French holding off the northeastern coast of Madagascar. This strategy was largely a colonial overreaction to the revolution in Saint-Domingue.[29]

In some ways, then, Bourbon calls to mind the Caribbean context. For instance, Bourbon was not merely divided into free white people and unfree Black people: In 1815, it counted 49,369 enslaved Africans and Malagasy, 14,481 whites, and 4,459 free people of color who had achieved manumission. The young Edmond would certainly have encountered Black people who were not enslaved.[30]

Edmond's parents witnessed profound transformations in their lifetimes. The British occupation of Bourbon from 1810 to 1815 briefly halted the slave trade. Under French rule, it resumed, but after the 1817 abolition of the trade (but not slavery itself) in French colonies, most sales involved Creoles instead of new captives. That said, between 1817 and the French Revolution of 1830, an illicit slave trade to Bourbon endured, largely operated out of Nantes.[31]

Mélise and Pamphille also experienced climate-related disasters and epidemics. Successive droughts followed by terrible cyclones devastated the island in 1806 and 1807, triggering famine, revolts, rioting, and repression. In Sainte-Suzanne, the mortality rate increased by 130 percent in 1807. One source related that the majority of islanders, slave and free alike, were reduced to eating fern roots and grasses. In March 1807, Sainte-Suzanne's municipal council reported that six hundred whites and fifteen hundred slaves in the district were suffering from famine and that guards murdered slaves desperate for food. Several waves of cholera ravaged Bourbon starting in 1815; as a result, in 1821, slave mortality spiked spectacularly in Sainte-Suzanne. Two more hurricanes in 1816 and 1829 accelerated soil erosion. Local officials reported the loss of cacao, coffee, nutmeg, and clove trees, while a new plague, boll weevil, afflicted cotton plants.[32]

Dramatic international shifts also shaped Bourbon at this time. First came the British-led continental blockade of France in 1806, which crippled trade, then the British occupation of Bourbon between 1810 and 1815. Economically, exorbitant interest rates hampered the issuing of recovery loans after the 1806 and 1807 hurricanes. The solution to both the international transformations and the climate catastrophes was the creation of larger estates dedicated to sugar. France had recently lost the world's top sugar producer, Saint-Domingue, to revolution, and now Mauritius and the Seychelles Islands to British annexation. The metropole needed sugar.[33] Thus, after 1815, sugar planting began on a large scale, along with its monocrop protoindustrialism. Sugar production factories sprang up seemingly overnight in 1815, accompanied by a "frenzy of mechanization." Cocoa, coffee, wheat, nutmeg, and cloves never fully recovered from the hurricanes of 1806 and 1807. Coffee was definitively outpaced by sugar in the 1830s, and cotton lost even greater ground, in the wake of two more hurricanes in 1829 and 1830. Cocoa was nearly wiped out by the shift to sugar. Once renowned for its smaller plantations and crop diversity, indeed for its early environmental protectionism, Bourbon turned to intensive sugar monoculture.[34] However, ominous clouds appeared on the horizon in the 1830s. In that sense, Edmond's discovery proved timely. In 1841, in fact, a local newspaper had predicted the "inevitable collapse of our poor Bourbon's sugar industry," calling for a return to subsistence crops to avert ruin and famine.[35]

That very year, 1841, Edmond made the discovery that bucked the monoculture trend; the vanilla he manually pollinated requires undergrowth or forests to thrive, not a landscape of cane fields. Nor does it exact cacao's toll on tropical woodlands, especially when cacao becomes an intensive monoculture.[36] One nineteenth-century source suggests that vanilla's advent saved the island's soil. Prior to the orchid's cultivation, "thirty years of soil-depleting" monoculture had so deteriorated the land that sugar planters had come to rely heavily on South American guano and other imported fertilizers.[37] This line of thinking was not entirely new: several Enlightenment-era thinkers had warned of the unsustainability—morally, environmentally, and economically—of the servile sugar and coffee plantation complex.[38]

Where did Edmond fit within the elaborate hierarchies typical of servile societies? He was a gardener, a tiny subcategory of the "specialized" enslaved group (a problematic category but a term that avoids another even more troubling one, "talented slave," used in sources since the eighteenth century).[39] Historian Prosper Eve compellingly argues that those enslaved on Bourbon acquired wide-ranging agricultural knowledge of multiple crops, by virtue of the isle's diverse output prior to 1810. He adds that even those usually protected from the harshest forms of labor, the women and men he refers to as "talented slaves," occasionally had to help in the fields, "when the need arose." Thus, although it is safe to deduce that on most days the young gardener probably enjoyed greater latitude than enslaved people who regularly toiled in the fields, he was nonetheless exposed to occasional field labor of this sort. Just as importantly, he likely discussed agriculture with enslaved adults, thereby adding practical knowhow to his own botanical learning. For make no mistake: agricultural work was by far the main activity on Bourbon. In 1842, the year following Edmond's discovery, 52,086 of the island's 65,915 enslaved workers toiled in agriculture, while the remaining 13,859 worked as domestics or in industry.[40]

Despite rubbing shoulders with enslaved people toiling in the fields, Edmond benefited from the relatively better material conditions of "specialized" enslaved workers.[41] This was no homogenous group. In addition to gardeners, it included carpenters, shoemakers, bakers, blacksmiths, sugar and coffee technicians, wigmakers, butchers, shopkeepers, millers, nannies, nurses, midwives, and translators.[42] Literate and multilingual, slaves in this last category translated for missionaries and converted fellow slaves. Some such bondage workers of missionaries on Bourbon even became the first writers and readers of Malagasy in the Latin alphabet.[43]

It appears that Edmond could not read, unlike these enslaved translators. While slave literacy was forbidden in much of the Southern United States, it was not prohibited under French law. And Edmond certainly knew the technical names of plants, not to mention the science behind them. But the main piece of evidence suggesting that Edmond could not read or write comes from later in his life. In 1871, he married Marie Pauline Bassana, a twenty-year-old woman of partially Indian background. He and his bride both signed the register with an *X*.[44]

Many mysteries surround Edmond's childhood. One is how he became the gardener for Mrs. Bellier-Beaumont's brother, Ferréol. If the latter is to be believed, Edmond was Ferréol's "favorite." Yet it would seem that he technically remained Mrs. Bellier-Beaumont's property until France's 1848 emancipation proclamation. Uncertainty over ownership was surprisingly widespread. There are numerous cases of enslaved people across the French empire who were unclear about who owned them. Others were the "common property" of private companies or religious orders, and a few even belonged to the colony.[45]

A rare snapshot of the Bellier-Beaumont estate in 1844 shows that the siblings owned twenty enslaved workers. Their lands, estimated at four hundred by four hundred meters (roughly 1312 by 1312 feet), grew sugarcane and manioc. Comparatively speaking, this was a modest estate; nearby plantations listed hundreds of enslaved workers. The survey names Edmond last on the Bellier estate register, perhaps a sign that he was achieving some measure of celebrity. Columns record with jarring concision the data that mattered to colonial authorities. They record Edmond as aged fifteen, male, Black, Creole, his hair "curly," and his height a very specific 1.618 meters tall (5.308 feet).[46]

Other sources help flesh out Edmond's portrait. A letter from Mézières Lépervanche, a Sainte-Suzanne botanist and justice of the peace in 1853, suggests that although Edmond received no "formal" education, he quickly "became involved with [Ferréol's] horticultural work, and learned from his master [...] to recognize flowers and their technical names."[47] Ferréol provides additional details: Edmond assisted him in artificially pollinating several plants, most notably one called "jolifia," of the pumpkin family, as well as *Cassia alata*, commonly known in English as candle bush.[48]

Ferréol Bellier-Beaumont recounts the 1841 eureka moment as follows:

> One day as I walked with my faithful companion, I noticed that my only vanilla plant had produced a [...] bean. I expressed surprise and brought it to his attention. He told me he had pollinated the flower. I refused to believe him and walked on. But two or three days later, I saw a second pod growing near the first. He then repeated his assertion. I asked him how he had done it. He proceeded to execute the operation that everyone now does. The intelligent child had been able to discern, in a same flower, the male and female organs, and put them properly in contact with one another.[49]

Using a needle or a toothpick, Edmond had successfully placed the two organs in contact, in a gesture that has since become second nature to vanilla growers around the world. If the withered flower stayed attached to the extremity of the "embryo," added Bellier-Beaumont, the operation had succeeded and ten months to a year later pods would grow.[50] Subsequently, Edmond's technique was rendered in simple sketches. Here was a transparent and simple method, rapidly achieved with the help of only a needle.

This relation of Edmond's breakthrough elicits several observations. For one thing, Edmond had gone from Ferréol's "favorite" to his "faithful companion." What exactly did this mean? Megan Vaughan has suggested that on neighboring Isle of France, "small-scale slave ownership sometimes necessitated a degree of identification, even intimacy between master and

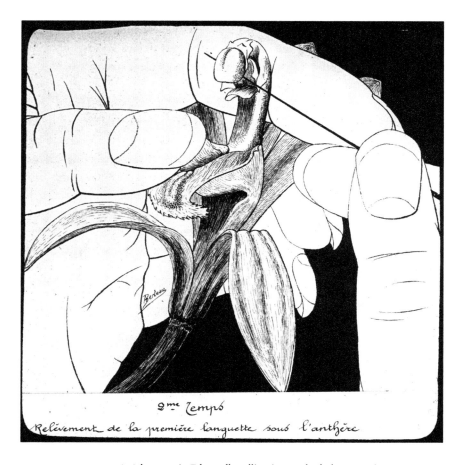

FIGURE 6. A key step in Edmond's pollination method, the retracting of the membrane. Armand Berteau, 1915 © CIRAD.

slave." The Beaumont estate met these conditions, with its modest number of bondage workers. However, as Vaughan goes on to show, "identification" did not necessarily foster compassion; if anything, it could be self-interested. And so, it should come as no surprise that the Bellier-Beaumont family never freed Edmond via manumission.[51]

Next, Bellier-Beaumont's testimony shows that Edmond's method was in many respects the antithesis of Morren's. Straightforward, transparent, and stage-based, it presented none of the Belgian's elliptical, secretive language. Third, the power inversion contained in this moment was palpable: try as Ferréol Bellier-Beaumont might to suggest his pumpkins and candle bush had served as inspiration, Edmond's discovery was not the fruit of Socratic dialogue. After all, Ferréol had initially refused to believe Edmond's claim. In a moment of revelation, the enslaved student used clear instructional tools to proudly show the technique to his master.

Thereafter, Ferréol is said to have placed an announcement in a local newspaper explaining the method. However, his description proved too vague, and local planters came calling for greater details. Demand was such that Edmond went on tour, achieving something close to celebrity status. Bellier-Beaumont mentions that planters arranged for Edmond to visit their estates using "very comfortable" means of locomotion "to which he was not accustomed."[52] This was likely a horse-drawn carriage, or perhaps a sedan chair carried by fellow slaves.[53] Edmond presented his pollination technique in person at several plantations, including those of Patu de Rosemond at Saint-Benoît, David de Floris at Saint-André, Joseph Desbassayns at Sainte-Suzanne, and Mr. Vinet at Sainte-Marie.[54] One can imagine the reactions of audience members and especially enslaved onlookers, overhearing one of their own arriving by carriage before delivering a lecture on how to pollinate a recently introduced flower before local dignitaries and gardeners alike. They must have been transfixed. This was more than breaking a glass ceiling; it was straining the shackles of slavery, shaking its very foundations.

Although Edmond's story is unique, for enslaved people to possess botanical knowledge was not. On Bourbon, maroons discovered the medicinal properties of many highland plants, some of which retain Malagasy names today, and shared their knowledge with those still enslaved.[55] In the Americas, many a plant varietal was introduced by enslaved Africans, and some of them managed to continue independent production of such crops. Also in the Western Hemisphere, enslaved Africans' proficiency at herbalism fused with Indigenous American knowledge to generate rich homeopathic cultures. The enslaved both prospected for remedies and conducted experimentation. Forms of slave knowledge, overlaid on Indigenous ones, were influential in treating dysentery and elaborating antidotes for poisonings. Such treatments, in turn, circulated between islands and continents, including between rival colonial empires. Enslaved women were often their carriers.[56]

Some enslaved people not only made medical-botanical breakthroughs but also received recognition for their work. Such was the case with Quassie in eighteenth-century Suriname. Informed in part by dialogue with Indigenous healers, he discovered the fever-reducing properties of a local tree. By the 1740s, he was healing fellow slaves with a decoction derived from its bark. Over time, whites began adopting the remedy, and in 1753, the eminent Swedish naturalist Carl Linnaeus named the tree *Quassia amara*. Quassie eventually gained freedom not on the basis of his discovery but for helping the colonial authorities track down maroons.[57]

Back in the Indian Ocean, on Isle of France in the 1770s, the king's intendant Pierre Poivre entrusted the enslaved Bengali Charles Rama with the post of head gardener at his *jardin d'acclimatation*. Poivre especially appreciated Rama's mastery of nutmeg, which he considered to be unrivaled among Europeans. According to Dorit Brixius, this reflected a growing "creolization of expertise" in the Mascarenes.[58]

Even closer to home, on Bourbon, one finds other examples of specialized enslaved botanists. Thus, in 1791, planter Joseph Hubert assigned the task of protecting a clove tree to one of his enslaved gardeners, Jean-Louis. Seeing the commitment Jean-Louis showed defending the tree in the middle of a hurricane, Hubert decided to free him. The speech he delivered for Jean-Louis's manumission on March 27, 1791, is worth quoting. He offered him a wage, adding, "I know you wish to stay in my garden. I, too, hope that you won't abandon the care of the precious plantations that you and I have raised together, and which are our children." He then credited Pierre Poivre and Poivre's spouse with his decision to manumit. To Pierre Poivre he owed the cloves and other spices he cultivated, which the famed intendant had brought to Isle of France. To his widow, he owed a portrait of said Pierre Poivre, "a gift which prompted my decision to move forward the moment of your manumission."[59] Rarely are motivations so clearly attributed in such cases. Poivre's philosophy, merging Enlightenment ideals with an environmental sensibility and a commitment to ending slavery, had been the main movers in this case. So, too, was a kind of botanical fraternity.

Edmond's story does not exactly match those of Rama, Quassie, or Jean-Louis. His discovery was not strictly medical, although vanilla was used for some treatments. He did not bring knowhow to Bourbon from afar, nor did he benefit from Indigenous knowledge, nor was he freed for his achievement. The vine he pollinated was exogenous to Bourbon, as were people for that matter, as the previously uninhabited island was first visited only in 1613 and the initial French settlement attempts occurred in 1638, only two centuries before Edmond's discovery. Yet Edmond's invention helped transform the vanilla economy, taking it from a niche Mexican spice to a global commodity. Still, the concept of the creolization of expertise is useful for thinking about Edmond. Based on the available evidence, it would seem that he combined the botanical skills he learned from Ferréol Bellier-Beaumont with practical experiments on his estate and supplemented this with herbal and agricultural knowledge he gained through oral transmission.

Unlike Joseph Hubert with Jean-Louis, neither Ferréol Bellier-Beaumont nor his sister ever freed Edmond. One can speculate that they did not want to lose one of the small number of enslaved laborers they had or that they may have turned a profit off of Edmond's local notoriety, perhaps charging a fee for his presentations to other planters. But this is little more than an educated guess. What we know for certain is that Edmond gained liberty through the second and final abolition of slavery pronounced in Paris by the Second Republic in 1848. The renamed isle of Réunion, definitively shedding its royal connection to the Bourbons, received a new lead official, General Commissioner to the Republic Joseph Sarda Garriga. On October 18, 1848, he published the earlier decrees of April 27, 1848, abolishing slavery once and for all in French colonies. One local newspaper that ran the proclamation still featured a suddenly obsolete ad to rent out fifteen enslaved workers.[60]

Surnames constituted potent symbols of freedom. Réunion's main newspaper in the early 1840s ran lists of the manumitted, providing their age, profession, and, rather solemnly, "the surname he/she is taking." Even the phrasing leaves unclear the agency of the formerly enslaved in the process (although novelist Gaëlle Bélem's recent account has Edmond choosing the surname Albius himself for a number of reasons having to do with prestige).[61] Edmond's 1848 freedom papers read, "Edmon [sic] son of Pamphile and Mélise, both deceased [. . .] presented himself and after having been recognized by us, he received the surname and name of Albius, Edmond."[62] In an 1862 letter, his former master notes curtly, "Edmond's freedom name is Albius."[63] The surname Albius has led to much speculation, because it derives from the Latin word for white. Some have associated the choice with the white flower of the vanilla plant he pollinated. Edmond's knowledge of technical Latin terms for plants made this explanation seem plausible and even empowering. However, others have interpreted the surname as a way of denying Edmond's Blackness or even as a kind of racial prank. After all, the phrasing of the 1848 freedom document suggests that Edmond may have been assigned his last name with no input in the matter, in keeping with what happened to thousands of other former slaves that year.[64] Various rules made it clear that slaves were to be given surnames different from those of the whites on the island. To further complicate matters, the 1848 naming campaign faced a time crunch. A rush was on for those emancipated to participate in upcoming elections, and all voters required a family name. An unprecedented scramble to concoct surnames ensued. Some newly freed people ended up with names that referenced their new status, with one Toussaint, from Edmond's hometown of Sainte-Suzanne, taking the surname of Affranchi, meaning "manumitted." One Parisian planning document even recommended "a system of [new] names with infinite variation, created by interchanging the letters of certain randomly selected words." And so, some ended up with neologisms, others with first names as family names, others place names, others still with names that former owners devised as deliberately odd, ridiculous, or insulting.[65] Given Bellier-Beaumont's spirited defense of Edmond's discovery, it seems unlikely he would have sought to humiliate him in such a manner. Nevertheless, the motives behind the name Albius remain open to interpretation. They call to mind previous ambiguous surnames, starting with the early sixteenth-century Black trumpeter in England named John Blancke. According to Imtiaz Habib, Blancke's "surname [was] most likely an affectionate pun on his skin color"—perhaps derived from the word *blanco*, meaning white in Spanish.[66]

The enduring ambiguity of Albius's surname is evoked in Marcel Proust's 1920–21 *The Guermantes Way*, the third installment of his legendary *Remembrance of Things Past*. One of the characters, Mr. de Bréauté, seizes the opportunity of being served vanilla ice cream to show off his knowledge. He pontificates at meal's end:

> The flavor of vanilla we tasted in the excellent ice cream you gave us this evening, Duchess, comes from the vanilla plant. This plant produces flowers which are both male and female, but a sort of solid wall set up between them prevents any communication. And so we could never get any fruit from them until a young negro, a native of Réunion, by the name of Albins [sic], which by the way is rather a funny name for a black man since it means "white," had the happy thought of using the point of a needle to bring the separate organs into contact.[67]

This passage is typical of Proust's famous roman à clef style, wherein a veneer of fiction is overlaid onto recent history. It also accurately summarizes Edmond's discovery. But to my point about naming, in Bréauté's impulse to impress and amuse, he cannot help but quip at Albius's name.[68] Regardless of whether Edmond chose his surname, Albius was being subjected to readings that focused more on a racial joke than on the accomplishment of cracking the white orchid's secret.

While some chuckled at his name, others contested Edmond's discovery. The earliest challenge was the most credible and came from neighboring Mauritius. There, in October 1842, Wenceslas Bojer, the Bohemian-born vice president of the local society of natural history, triumphantly declared that he had overcome the "overdevelopment of a membrane" in the vanilla flower, thereby enabling its artificial pollination. He achieved this on the property of Mr. Auguste Genève at Rivière Noire. Bojer mentioned that he utilized "a slight incision" to achieve the result. He added that three different estates in Mauritius, including Genève's, were producing vanilla.[69]

Had Bojer read of Morren's method, copied Albius's, or discovered his own? Scientists have identified a similar "tearing technique" as "a slight variation of the Albius method," distinct from Morren's.[70] In the absence of a detailed description of Bojer's "incisions," it is impossible to determine with certainty the Czech botanist's inspiration. Bojer's announcement came mere months after Albius's tour of plantations in Bourbon, in which he was asked to explain his technique to multiple audiences. News no doubt circulated through the enduring ties between elite planter families of the two previously connected islands. Mauritius had only been transferred from French to British sovereignty twenty-eight years earlier. Prior to that, Port-Louis, Mauritius's capital, had served as the prime port and hub for all the Mascarenes. Naturally, connections of all sorts endured. An 1850 article in the Réunion press shed light on the many Mauritian family and business ties of three families from Sainte-Suzanne. One was of these families was led by none other than Joseph Desbassayns, the same planter who had invited Edmond to present his discovery.[71]

Still on Mauritius, a document from 1831—in other words, prior to both Morren's and Edmond's discoveries—offers an intriguing alternative possibility. The minutes of the Mauritius Society of Natural History's September 1831 meeting reveal the following. The organization received and read out a letter from the same Auguste Genève from Rivière Noire, dated September 21, 1831. In it, the twenty-eight-year-old Mauritian planter asserted that he had successfully pollinated vanilla on his estate. He enclosed two flowers and two pods as proof.[72] Many questions arise from this rival claim, most of which cannot be answered. Had Genève beaten all others to the discovery? If so, why did he not trumpet it afterward, and why did vanilla production not spike on Mauritius? Was the method Bojer described in 1842 identical to Genève's from 1831? Could the knowhow have transferred in the other direction, from Mauritius to Bourbon? While such a reverse trajectory is conceivable, it would not explain why Bojer triumphantly claimed the discovery only eleven years later. Nor can one imagine how transmission from Mauritius to Bourbon would have been directed solely at the enslaved Edmond in 1841. By definition, a Mauritian planter had a greater platform than an enslaved Bourbon botanist. One hypothesis is that Genève, Morren, and Albius all achieved pollination in isolation from one another but Albius's needle or toothpick method endured because it was more straightforward than Bojer's incision procedure. Critically, Edmond and Bellier-Beaumont also shared Edmond's method; others may not have done the same with theirs. Timing, transmission, and technique all mattered.

Other would-be challengers to Albius came from the French Caribbean. In Martinique in 1842, a naval pharmacist named Pierre-Sébastien Dupuy announced a new pollination method involving cutting the vanilla orchid's membrane "with extremely slender scissors." The method proved far trickier than Edmond's. And yet, there is circumstantial evidence to support an independent pollination discovery on Martinique: records show the island suddenly exporting 305 kilos of vanilla in 1840, then 774 kilos in 1841, followed by a mysterious decline to 40 kilos in 1842 and a paltry 10 kilos in 1859. Furthermore, in the 1840s, the trading ship *Adèle* regularly purchased vanilla at Martinique's port of Saint-Pierre and brought it back to France. So Dupuy may indeed have invented a cutting technique at the end of the 1830s that provided modest short-term results between 1840 and 1842. He then made the method public in 1842, the date of disclosure precluding any external influence on Edmond's discovery.[73]

The next challenge to Edmond's claim, which was more far-fetched and ill-intentioned, originated closer to home. Ironically, the backlash against it produced the key body of printed evidence about Edmond's discovery. Without it, Edmond's story might have never been told. Indeed, had Ferréol Bellier-Beaumont not been provoked into expressing his slave owner's pride, sense of honor, or commitment to the truth in 1862, we would not have the correspondence that establishes in minute detail Edmond's remarkable achievement.

The spark occurred in 1862 when Claude Richard, director of Bourbon's main garden, the Jardin de l'Etat, brazenly denied Albius's discovery, dismissing it as fake news. As the main botanical authority on the island and the founder of the first French-created botanical garden in Africa, located in Saint-Louis, Senegal, Richard wielded influence beyond the measures he took in 1836, which included banning unaccompanied slaves from park grounds, along with restricting the possession of wine, liquor, guns, horses, dogs, smoking, and plant vandalism.[74] In reality, Richard and his colleague Joseph Bernier had put forward a vanilla pollination technique of their own that had proven to be "a complete failure."[75] Richard fits the consummate vengeful villain mold. Twenty-one years after the fact, to deprive Albius of his discovery and claim it as his own, he put forth two arguments. First, he had himself slipped word of the technique to Edmond when the enslaved boy was around eight or nine years old. Richard claimed, without proof, to have known about the artificial pollination of vanilla since 1811 or 1815. Second, "an ignorant child" could not have made such a discovery alone. Ferréol Bellier-Beaumont took immediate offense and felt his word was at stake. He also expressed sympathy and even admiration for Edmond.[76]

And so Bellier-Beaumont drew up a rebuttal, in the form of a detailed December 1862 letter to the legal clerk and local naturalist and historian Eugène Volsy-Focard. In it, Bellier-Beaumont described Edmond's expertise and indeed erudition in the field of botany. He rejected as preposterous the notion that Richard could have whispered a secret to the young man who would have failed to act on it for years. Also, if artificial pollination were common knowledge, why did the discovery elicit such widespread attention from local planters in 1841? Next, Bellier-Beaumont offered a theory as to how Richard might have otherwise known about artificial pollination. Charles Morren had discovered a method in Belgium in 1836. Perhaps Richard had learned of it the way Ferréol Bellier-Beaumont himself recently did, by reading a short description of Morren's method in the *Dictionnaire pittoresque d'histoire naturelle* at the museum in Saint-Denis. Still, Bellier-Beaumont rightly pointed out, that would not account for Richard's claim about knowing of a method since 1811 or 1815. What is more, Bellier-Beaumont hastened to add, Morren's method was different from Edmond's, for the *Dictionnaire pittoresque* described the Belgian cutting the vanilla flower's "veil."

In 1863, Volsy-Focard grew a second offshoot to this storyline. He recounted how in 1848 his vanilla planter friend David de Floris had contacted Paris, asking the government to support the budding sector of Réunion vanilla. Floris was generally pleased with Paris's response, including a pledge to reduce tariffs on the product. However, a strange jibe accompanied the good news. The minister of the navy and the colonies informed Floris of an "artificial fertilization procedure" used at Paris's Jardin des Plantes, from which Réunion could profit. This startled Floris. How could the ministry be so out of touch? Was this a classic example of the metropole's arrogance towards the colonial periphery? Was it simply incompetence? Did the ministry not know that Edmond Albius had discovered vanilla's artificial fertilization technique seven years earlier? And how could Paris's botanical gardens be using the technique in question without realizing it originated in Réunion?[77]

Volsy-Focard offered two interpretations (not knowing about Joseph Neumann's 1838 rediscovery): Either the Ministry of the Colonies was ignorant of the exchanges between Réunion and Paris's botanical gardens, or perhaps the Jardin des Plantes was using Charles Morren's earlier method. Volsy-Focard clearly leaned toward the former explanation. After all, he explained, based on the same dictionary entry, Morren's approach had involved "cutting the labellum."[78] What is more, Morren had poked holes in the vanilla vine. Neither of these actions bore any resemblance to Edmond Albius's technique.

The distance between Belgium and Réunion had led to a broken telephone. Morren had certainly carved holes into vanilla vines to encourage flowering. However, this was distinct from artificial pollination. As for the cutting of the "veil," we saw in the previous chapter that it was one of several possible options discussed by the Belgian.[79] In other words, on the one hand, Volsy-Focard's and Bellier-Beaumont's evidence is not as irrefutable as they might have imagined, because they did not draw it from the horse's mouth. On the other hand, the very fact that they could not access the original source (as evidenced by the fact that Bellier-Beaumont drew his sole reference to Morren from a dictionary of natural history) invalidates any notion that Edmond copied Morren's method.

The controversy over Richard's attempt to claim credit for Albius's discovery died down after Ferréol Bellier-Beaumont witnessed Richard's reaction to his rebuttal. Bellier-Beaumont regretted having brought shame to the man "in his old age" and decided that Richard had somehow convinced himself of his own lie. "Let's leave him his chimera," he resolved.[80] The matter had tested Ferréol Bellier-Beaumont's dual ties to his white planter-class fraternity and his former slave, whom he knew to be the inventor of a new method. Still, Bellier-Beaumont expressed satisfaction that local planter David de Floris, in his new notice on the cultivation of vanilla, had "recognized the truth" by naming Albius as the inventor of the method that had brought fresh prosperity to Réunion.[81] Twelve years after the abolition of slavery, Floris's description made no mention of Edmond's unfree status at the time of the revelation, but it did spell out other aspects of his identity: "We owe the discovery of the pollination of vanilla to Edmond, a Creole, the domestic and gardener of Mr. Bellier-Beaumont, residing in Sainte-Suzanne. It is thanks to his discovery that we owe the increased culture of this plant, which had been previously sterile in the colony."[82]

Given the power imbalance, it is remarkable that Albius's discovery was not stolen from him. He received tardy recognition, although no material compensation, for an advancement that transformed Réunion's economy. (Several individuals did plead in vain for Edmond to be monetarily rewarded, including Bellier-Beaumont.) His likeness is featured as an engraving in Antoine Roussin's pantheon of great local figures and places, which was published in the 1863 installment of the *Album de la Réunion*. He is depicted in a dignified pose, holding a vanilla flower in his left hand. The legend reads simply, "Edmond Albius, inventor of the artificial pollination of the vanilla plant."

Roussin's was either the first or the second known representation of Edmond Albius. In 1924, a local textbook presented what it purported to be a historical photograph of a much younger Albius, presumably dating from the 1850s, due to his more youthful appearance compared to Roussin's rendition.[83] However, this claim is implausible since photographic portraiture in Réunion only began in the 1860s and Albius was born in 1829. The age of the subject in the photo simply does not align with that chronological bracket. It also seems strange that Bellier-Beaumont would fail to reference a photo of the young Edmond in his correspondence. Perhaps the textbook

FIGURE 7. Edmond Albius depicted by Antoine
Louis Roussin in the *Album de la Réunion*, vol. 3, 1863.
Courtesy Archives nationales d'outre-mer.

included a representation of someone who played Albius during a historical reenactment in the early twentieth century?

In other words, the only reliable visual representation of Albius is Roussin's. We do know that Edmond Albius received copies of the Roussin engraving and was thankful for them. Ferréol Bellier-Beaumont penned the following addendum to a September 21, 1863, letter to Volsy-Focard: "Edmond asks me to have you kindly pass on to Mr. Roussin his thanks for the lithographs [. . .]. The ingenious inventor of the fecundation of vanilla was indeed able to distribute copies of it to his friends and family, avid consumers of drawings and engravings, like all Black people."[84] What are we to make of this sweeping generalization? While certainly betraying Bellier-Beaumont's prejudice, it may also reflect a social reality that visual portraits resonated strongly among recently emancipated, nonliterate populations.

However, despite the dual recognition of David de Floris's pamphlet and the 1863 Roussin volume, resistance to the idea of an enslaved twelve-year-old person of color making a major botanical discovery endured. The field was by then too crowded for others to lay claim to the invention. Instead, new critics took aim at the improbability of Albius's profile. Such allegations of fraud, copying, mimicry, or plagiarism took on special resonance in a colonial context. Their meaning was clear: A Black youngster simply could not have knowingly, let alone scientifically, cracked the case.

These challenges have come in varied forms and from different quarters. Some are especially jarring. In 1938, Georges Limbour, a philosophy teacher and close friend of painter André Masson, poet Robert Desnos, and other surrealists, dedicated a novel to vanilla production. His *Les Vanilliers* begins in Mexico; this section features the trope about vanilla resembling green beans. The scene then shifts to a fictionalized Bourbon, an island presented as ravaged by deforestation. Edmond is introduced as an enslaved teenager, fearing his master's temper. Bourbon's vanilla, in turn, is presented as "cursed" and "sterile" prior to 1841. However, in this novel, Edmond's discovery is associated with his puberty and specifically his interest in the young Jeannette. While the two are playing, he breaks a tooth of her comb and decides to "plunge it into the [vanilla] flower." "Oh, now she, too, is a woman," exclaims Jeannette. Edmond then begins "piercing each flower several times, in all directions, with the clumsiness of an ignorant insect." Here, Edmond is denied his achievement, which is instead attributed to chance, clumsiness, and even animalistic traits. Limbour goes on to describe the frenzied piercing motion as nothing short of "rape." Edmond somehow emerges with a reputation as a "great seducer" of white girls. In this novel teeming with surrealist-inspired dreams and allegories, the discovery of vanilla is rendered as a carnal awakening. Oddly, rather than ushering in artificial pollination, in Limbour's narrative Edmond's discovery prompts Bourbon's planters to introduce boatloads of hummingbirds to fertilize vanilla.[85] These birds occupy a special place in the surrealist bestiary and were one of the vectors of vanilla pollination wrongly suspected by Charles Morren. The net effect of this fictionalized version is to present Edmond's discovery as an accidental byproduct of teenage, stereotypically distorted Black sexuality. Surrealism's penchant for sexualized readings, impulsive action, and the irrational subverts Edmond's deliberate, careful, and skillful operation. Clearly, Limbour never took the time to try pollinating vanilla himself!

Another rumor about the 1841 discovery runs as follows. Edmond was allegedly rebellious and clumsy. After being "reprimanded" by his master, he trampled a vanilla flower in a vengeful rage, leading to its "involuntary" fecundation.[86] A 2012 young adult novel has Albius mashing vanilla in frustration after having seen a fellow slave being raped.[87] Each of these versions flouts botanical common sense, as the Albius maneuver, undertaken with a needle or a toothpick, is extremely delicate and cannot be achieved by stabbing or stomping.

Despite his method achieving global success, Albius faced many challenges in his adult life. In the wake of the 1848 abolition, many former slaves, including Albius, moved to the island's only city, Saint-Denis. There, in 1851, three short years after emancipation, he worked for a certain Captain Marchand as a cook and gardener. His employer soon accused him of thieving silver bracelets, a necklace, and a box of seashells. A court sentenced Albius to five years of forced labor.[88] After three years, he obtained early release for good behavior, partly on the basis of his discovery. He returned to Sainte-Suzanne to live on the plantation where he had been enslaved.[89] Edmond Albius died in relative poverty in the dwindling village of Sainte-Suzanne in 1880. The qualifier "relative" is based on a recent find in the Réunion archives. It would appear that Albius became a co-landowner through his marriage to Marie Pauline Bassana in 1871, and so did not perish in utter squalor as was previously assumed.[90]

The broad contours of Edmond's discovery were known in the early twentieth century, as Proust's passage reminds us. Yet Edmond's reputation was still limited. Even on Réunion, one was hard-pressed to find memorials to him prior to the 1980s. I have uncovered a few references to a portrait of Albius that hung at Réunion's Chamber of Agriculture, and its description matches that of the Roussin portrait. In 1923, it was sent to Madagascar to be displayed at that island's first commercial fair. There, the local press described Edmond as "a benefactor to humanity."[91] Two decades later, a

AN ENSLAVED TEEN CRACKS THE CASE

July 1945 article in a Réunion newspaper highlighted that no plaque or monument had been erected in Albius's honor, with only the same solitary depiction of him still present on the walls of Réunion's Chamber of Agriculture.[92] Since then, Edmond has achieved some local recognition in Réunion, but I would argue that his fame has not extended beyond the island's shores. On Réunion, a middle school has been named in his honor, and two monuments now commemorate him.

The first was a municipal effort, spearheaded by then-Mayor Lucet Langenier. Despite hailing from a working-class family, he managed to win the mayorship of Sainte-Suzanne, wresting power from a string of landholding incumbents. He was deeply involved in politics, advocating for local culture and autonomy from France, with a particular focus on promoting Réunionese identity. This led him to erect a stela in honor of Edmond Albius in 1981, which was the year France shifted to François Mitterrand's Socialist Party. The modest monument, comprising a pedestal in the shape of the island, on which stands a small bust of Albius, is located at Bellevue, precisely where Edmond grew up and made his discovery. It is rendered in a local folk-art style. Online sources suggest that the bust of Edmond had previously been painted white, but at the time of my visit in 2022 it was gray.[93]

A second monument honoring Edmond Albius stands outside coastal Sainte-Suzanne and was inaugurated in December 2004. The statue of Albius, wearing a jacket and bow tie, was clearly inspired by the Roussin print. A photo of the unveiling shows Paul Vergès, a key figure in Réunion politics, resting his hand on the shoulder of Edmond Albius's likeness. Vergès served as both the Communist president of the island's regional council and a senator in Paris. He never tired of invoking Albius, the "slave who made a great discovery for Réunion and was never rewarded by his masters." In 2021, the solitary statue was enhanced with a frame for it, designed by another artist, which was covered in depictions of vanilla vines. On the eve of the day commemorating the definitive end of slavery on Réunion, students from Edmond Albius Middle School were enlisted to inscribe local meaning, in Creole, to Edmond on individual stones, which they deposited at his feet. Edmond has been reinvented as a champion and vector of Creole identity.[94]

CHAPTER 4

Queen of Vanilla
Réunion Surpasses Mexico

CONTRARY TO EDMOND ALBIUS, WHO NEVER PROFITED FROM his discovery, Réunion achieved some prosperity from vanilla. A concerted campaign began a few years following Edmond's 1841 breakthrough. In 1848, the Ministry of the Navy and the Colonies responded to Réunion vanilla planter David de Floris's letter containing vanilla attachments and seeking Paris's aid for the new sector. Several samples of Bourbon vanilla had reached the ministry in that revolutionary year, suggesting a strong effort to capitalize on the Albius revolution. The minister promised to contact the French chargé d'affaires in Mexico to learn about Mexican vanilla preparation methods, which he pledged to share with Réunion's planters.[1] Here is proof of a coordinated effort to have French colonies vie with Mexico in the vanilla business, using Mexican expertise, no less. In other words, initial state promotion was key in enabling the French empire to top Central American production. Once again, nations and their empires engaged in concerted competition over vanilla pods.

The French Ministry of the Navy and the Colonies kept its vow, liaising with the Ministries of Commerce and Finance to "encourage, as much as possible, the development on the Island of Réunion, of this new branch of industry." One result of the discussions was a plan to reduce by one franc per kilo customs duties on vanilla coming from French colonies. The ministry also pressed the authorities in Réunion to promote vanilla cultivation by all means possible.[2] Meanwhile, officials in Réunion received valuable intelligence. Réunion's archives contain a June 1852 report from Bordeaux, detailing the quality and quantity of vanilla leaving Mexico: 356,950 pods had left Veracruz for New Orleans, 528,450 for New York, 19,000 for

Le Havre, 8,000 for Britain, and 436,000 for Bordeaux. The beans, which were considered splendid, traveled in tin boxes. Réunion's planters and exporters were learning from Bordeaux traders and government agencies in Paris the tricks of the trade and the markets to target.[3]

These coordinated efforts yielded remarkable results. In 1848, Réunion produced a mere fifty kilos of vanilla; this increased to 136 kilos in 1852. That year, only three planters appeared on a list of major vanilla producers: Mrs. Patu de Rosemont at Saint-Benoît, whose estate Edmond had visited in 1841; Mr. David de Floris at nearby Champ-Borne; and Mrs. Devillaine in Saint-Denis. The latter had written to the administration in 1849 to explain how she struggled to pay the "eight Black workers" on her estate, now that the emancipation of slaves had been proclaimed.[4] Clearly, enslaved agricultural workers on her grounds had practiced and perfected vanilla cultivation prior to emancipation; these same workers, now free, continued to undertake the same tasks afterward. The archives show that the estates of these three early vanilla magnates alone accounted for 125,000 vanilla pods, with all other producers on the island bringing in another 125,000.[5] Thanks to Edmond's method, and its application on a large scale by dexterous pollinators, often women known as the plant's "matchmakers" (*marieuses*), vanilla production boomed on Bourbon.

In 1855, Réunion produced 899 kilos of vanilla and dispatched 140 kilos of the previous year's harvest to mainland France, in exchange for an impressive total of 35,000 francs.[6] Two years on, Réunion produced 1.6 metric tons of vanilla. Its agricultural experts took stock of "vanilla's success which has surpassed even the boldest predictions." They boasted that competition from Mexico need no longer be feared.[7] Indeed, by 1862, the island exported just shy of twenty-eight metric tons of vanilla for a total of 593,582 francs. By then, vanilla had emerged as the second most lucrative crop for Réunion after sugar, and ahead of coffee.[8] In 1877, Réunion surpassed Mexico's production, 37.94 tons to 25.37, and seldom looked back. Admittedly, Mexico did achieve substantial output in the first years of the twentieth century, but by then Tahiti and Madagascar's vanilla ascendancy were well underway.[9] In 1879, Réunion produced 73 metric tons for just over 4 million francs.[10] As a moneymaking export crop—scarcely any of it was consumed on location—vanilla served as a "social motor," drawing an entire coast of the island into a sector of the world economy.[11]

This social engine is all the more powerful because the entire commodity chain prior to the point of retail, from propagation to pollination and preparation, is concentrated on-site. This is in stark contrast to chocolate's supply chain, for example. Today, the West African nation of Côte d'Ivoire leads the world in raw cacao output; yet very little of it is processed into chocolate in the country. And of course, it is the transformation of the raw cacao into chocolate that yields the greatest profits.[12] Vanilla bucks this raw extraction trend. Like sugar, whose processing on location in the Caribbean in some ways prefigured the Industrial Revolution, vanilla preparation has always taken place on-site, although it requires none of sugar's heavy industry.[13] Yet, precisely because most everything having to do with vanilla is by definition manual—no machine can pollinate flowers, determine the exact moment to pick the pods, or blanket and sun dry it for just the right length of time—it ranks as one of the most labor-intensive products per gram. As one visitor to Réunion in 1868 noted, although "vanilla yielded considerable benefits, [. . .] exorbitant care was required to achieve even a passable harvest, and the slightest storm can wipe out in just a few minutes a planter's dearest hopes."[14] In that sense, vanilla was a high-risk, high-reward cash crop. In January 1878, for instance, a hurricane killed some fifty Réunionese and inflicted significant losses on the island's vanilla groves, slicing production by one-third.[15]

Vanilla has always been remarkably labor-intensive, particularly during the pollination and preparation phases. Individually hand-pollinating each flower early on the very morning it blooms represents a daunting task. That said, vanilla requires far more than just pollination. The pod's subsequent preparation is also notoriously complex and to this day involves its share of trade secrets and regional variations. In the wake of Edmond's discovery, growers experimented widely with curing techniques. Some hung bundles of pods in the shade so that they would not dry up. Ultimately, that method proved counterproductive, leading to cracked vanilla beans, whose precious seeds spilled out and failed to keep.[16] In 1851, Ernest Loupy, a Saint-André planter, applied the boiling water treatment.[17] This short scalding phase kills the pod and halts maturation, thereby preventing cracking. It precedes a series of drying stages, aimed at reducing a pod's water content and intensifying flavors and aromas. Yet there was no rapid homogenizing of methods on Réunion. Even Loupy's boiling could be applied multiple times and for different amounts of time. For decades, several techniques continued to compete on the island.

One source provides insight into different methods used on Réunion in 1875. Eugène Chauvet was born there in 1818 but left for the United States in 1846, marrying an American and living for decades in New Orleans and New York. After many adventures, including gunrunning in Southeast Asia, he returned to his native isle in 1874. There, in May 1875, Chauvet outlined different techniques in his journal:

> Several pounds [of vanilla beans] are put into a basket and immerged three times in succession in boiling hot water, as quickly as it can be done, and withdrawn just as quickly. After the third withdrawal, when the last drop of water has fallen, the beans are wrapped up, still steaming, in woolen blankets, and placed in a cool place for 24 hours. The following day they are exposed to the hot sun for several hours [. . .], each bean separated from each other, and so on every day until they have assumed a dark brown appearance, when instead of remaining under blankets in the cool place, they are put on shelves, uncovered, to perfect themselves until they are fit for market. When so fitted, they are put up in tin boxes.[18]

However, Chauvet hastened to add that some of his relatives prepared the pods differently. They boiled them only once, "and just the time to count from one to twenty-one as quickly as one can do, and then put them into the blanket to steam the whole day under the sun." Next, the pods were "taken into a room at sunset and remain[ed] in the blanket the whole night." The following day, the pods were placed directly on the shelves. Finally, Chauvet mentioned a third, more "dangerous" method in which the beans were never boiled but instead placed in an oven. This involved the greatest risk of overheating, overdrying, and therefore of "losing" the beans.[19] In other words, notwithstanding the increased standardization of grade and size, considerable variation endured in preparation on Réunion Island itself and globally. Preparing vanilla was specialized work, involving trade secrets, oral transmission, as well as trial and error. To this day, countless variations remain in scalding and drying modes and times.

Vanilla made all these efforts worthwhile thanks to its high cost. By the 1870s, with the vanilla boom in full swing, pod theft became rampant on Réunion. The authorities made examples of the few ever caught redhanded. On January 28, 1875, a court in Réunion sentenced one Alexandre Fontaine to six months in prison and a 100 franc fine for vanilla larceny. In a report sent to Paris, the governor of the island explained that Fontaine lived in dire poverty and that theft of vanilla was "extremely frequent" due to its high value and ease of theft. Stealing vanilla was literally picking low-hanging fruit. It must have been especially tempting for the destitute. Fontaine pleaded for clemency on the grounds that he had lived "in utter indigence, in complete misery." The governor even recognized that Fontaine had shown contrition. Still, the governor insisted on upholding the sentence to dissuade others. Fontaine's appeal was therefore denied. The archival file containing his appeal bears the laconic response "rejected."[20] At least in the way it exposed inequalities, the rush on vanilla was comparable to those on precious metals that occurred during the same era in nearby South Africa and faraway North America.

Officials struggled to stem the intractable theft problem. Planters urged government officials to increase traceability by drawing up certificates for all individuals moving vanilla. One such document delivered by a police official in 1879 specifies that thirty-seven kilos of green (unprocessed) vanilla were transported for twenty minutes "atop a man's head" while "in town."[21] Given vanilla prices, this short walk was recorded as a company might register the comings and goings of a Brink's convoy today.

The second half of the nineteenth century witnessed Bourbon vanilla's meteoric ascent. Despite Bourbon being an outdated term for the isle, the connection between the two names persisted. In 1850, the New York–based *Merchants' Magazine* ran a piece titled "The Vanilla of the Island of Bourbon." On the strength of sampling two boxes freshly arrived from Réunion, the writer concluded, "We have ascertained that [Bourbon] vanilla is in no respect inferior to the best commercial vanilla" (read Mexican vanilla).[22] And so new doors opened.

Prices began to drop as the Mexican monopoly broke. Vanilla had once been so pricey as to remain unattainable for many middle-class Europeans. For instance, a financially strapped character in Honoré de Balzac's 1842 novel *Les deux frères* serves his guest *pots de crème* flavored with burned oats instead of vanilla, which the writer notes is like trying to replace coffee with chicory. A few decades on, owing to Albius, a large slice of the bourgeoisie no longer required such substitutions. By 1867, a Parisian newspaper reported that vanilla, which had sold for two francs or more a pod in 1860, now went for twenty-five centimes a pod, thanks to the influx of Réunion beans.[23]

As Bourbon vanilla became cheaper and surpassed its Mexican rival, a parallel can be seen with Indian tea closing the gap on its Chinese competitor. In both instances, European imperial powers, France and Britain respectively, entwined patriotic, imperial, and quality rationales to bolster their upstart colonial products against an established sector in the article's land of origin.[24] There was some isolated resistance to Bourbon vanilla, of course, as there was to Indian tea, and as there had been to Morren's more modest attempt to promote Belgian vanilla. Already in 1858, an ad in the *Boston Evening Transcript* advertised "extract of true Mexican vanilla," to distinguish it from other provenances.[25] In 1869, Chauvet remarked that although his family's Réunion vanilla was "good and handsome," it remained less sought-after than Mexico's. He added that Mexican vanilla fetched higher prices even on the French market.[26] Decades later, the US producer and distributor Joseph Burnett Company (a pioneer in creating vanilla extracts in the 1840s) pulled no punches in a 1900 booklet defending Central American vanilla:

> France, some years ago, inaugurated the culture of this most esteemed variety—namely, the Mexican vanilla—in the Bourbon islands [sic], where the soil and climate were thought to be in every way favorable, but Nature frowned upon this attempt, and after her favorite had been borne away from Papantla, to alien soil, it degenerated. The result of this effort on the part of French industry has been an inferior product, known as Bourbon vanilla.[27]

Using notions of terroir, uprooting, and degeneration, the American company presented its attachment to Mexican vanilla as a matter of quality and principle. Of course, Burnett was promoting its own product and discrediting new competition while prioritizing its own interests. But regardless of the company's motives, Burnett was fighting a losing battle. Over the next decades, many a US firm would proudly advertise its use of "Bourbon vanilla." For example, a 1921 Fort Wayne, Indiana, ad for Dreier's ice cream soda boasted of resorting to "no synthetic flavors and no artificial coloring" and using only "the best materials we can buy." Those included "pure Bourbon vanilla bean extract."[28] By then, Bourbon was becoming a shorthand for all Indian Ocean vanillas, including Madagascar's.

Burnett's campaign seems not to have had much effect. The Réunion vanilla curve continued its upwards trend, at least until the turn of the century. The island reached its production zenith in 1898 with a staggering two hundred metric tons exported, during a year when Mexico's exports totaled forty-four.[29] Vanilla's contributions to the island proved all the more important when sugar prices fell. In 1900, cane sugar cost more to produce on Réunion than it fetched at market.[30] As for vanilla, in the span of just forty years, it had gone from a Central American monopoly to a predominantly Indian Ocean–produced spice.

Exactly what kind of vanilla was Réunion producing? Subcategories abounded under the broad label "Bourbon vanilla," although they all belonged to a single varietal, the Mexican-originating *Vanilla planifolia*. On Réunion, the descendants of Philibert's Guianese *Vanilla pompona* ceased to matter economically by the middle of the nineteenth century. Even though some reports from the 1890s mention the export of *vanillons*, a term usually denoting *Vanilla pompona*, this was a regional misnomer. On Réunion, the term *vanillons* was used as a diminutive to designate any pod measuring under fourteen centimeters (about five and a half inches) in length.[31] Such specific subcategories mattered for quality and pricing gradations. For example, in January 1891, records show that Réunion shipped 10,263 kilos of longer pods to mainland France and a mere 859 kilos (about 1,893 pounds) of pods under fourteen centimeters. These two categories were subdivided into several more quality gradations: first, second, and third tiers for the long pods and first and second for the shorter ones.[32]

The rankings coincided with a new focus on bundling, packaging, and sizing vanilla in a manner that both shaped and reflected new consumer expectations. The idea of vanillas of similar sizes, sheens, and qualities bundled together became standard in the late nineteenth century, much as the finish and hue of indigo were homogenized in this era.[33] By the early twentieth century, this homogenization emerged as a key part of pod preparation, on Réunion and beyond. A 1930 photo shows two Réunionese women bundling vanilla pods of the same length and tying them with raffia strings, the latter undoubtedly coming from nearby Madagascar. André Albany, part of a family of Réunionese photographers, took the picture to illustrate one of Réunion's main economic sectors at the 1931 International Colonial Exhibit in Paris's Bois de Vincennes.[34]

FIGURE 8. "Vanilla preparer," Réunion Island, 1930. Photo © André Albany.

The dexterous manual task being performed by the worker in the photo's foreground presents several parallels with needlework. To start, of course, the earlier stage of vanilla pollinizing also involved the use of a needlelike instrument, needles having long been linked to female labor across many cultures. The worker shown here holds a strand of raffia between her lips, much as seamstresses did with string. She binds a bunch of identically sized pods. Unlike manual pollination, this task might well have been subject to mechanization. And yet, it was not, first because it took place in a colonial context of underpaid labor, and second because the entire vanilla supply chain was located on-site. Whereas the nineteenth-century sewing machine had made possible the easy relocation of garment manufacturing (redefining conceptions of female labor along the way), the enduringly artisanal nature of vanilla production precluded a similar transformation.[35] Most steps in the process did not lend themselves to industrialization, starting with pollination, picking, and curing. Spot mechanization simply did not make sense in such a context, if only because the necessarily manual nature of the rest of the chain would have been unable to keep up.

After being bundled and placed in tin boxes, Réunion's vanilla was shipped overseas. Whereas Mexican vanilla had reached land at Bordeaux, Réunion's vanilla steamed into the ports of Marseille and Le Havre in the second half of the nineteenth century.[36] Marseille's share of colonial commerce exploded at this time, with its import tonnage from the French empire nearly tripling between 1874 and 1898.[37] This was partly the result of the opening of the Suez Canal in 1869. Réunion often marked the final or penultimate stopover for long-haul shipping that connected the Pacific and Indian Oceans to Europe. Thus, in March 1889 the Messageries Maritime's *Sydney* reached Marseille with 112 cases of vanilla from Réunion. But the ship had previously stopped in Tahiti, New Caledonia, Australia, and Mauritius. The vanilla cases therefore shared the hold with 2,789 balls of Australian wool, nearly 3,000 bags of New Caledonian nickel, 10,518 Australian copper ingots, and 100 cases of Tahitian cultural objects bound for the same Paris Universal Exposition for which the Eiffel Tower had been erected that very month. Although officially an ocean liner, the *Sydney* carried only 103 passengers; its main treasures rested below deck.[38] One final revolution, the proliferation of steam and metal hull ships, also helped shorten the trip to market. The opening of Réunion's vastly improved port at the Pointe des Galets in 1886 coincided with the disappearance of its last wooden-hull ships. For decades, chambers of commerce and traders in French port cities had clamored for Réunion to build a new, deep-water port. (Neighboring Mauritius had one, but it was under British control.)[39]

Until the early twentieth century, Réunion's vanilla left port exclusively for mainland France, mostly Marseille, and from there was consumed domestically or reexported to the United States, Italy, and Russia, among others. The traders who called at Réunion's main port of Pointe aux Galets typically dealt in a host of goods and wares. In the 1890s, Marseille buyer and trader Alfred Dor, having inherited his import-export business from his father in 1887, dispatched three steamers through the Suez Canal. They ran multiple circuits to Zanzibar, the Seychelles Islands, Mauritius, Madagascar, and Réunion. At those destinations, his employees purchased cloves, vanilla, sugar, geranium, perfume essences, and turtle shells, keeping Dor abreast of commodity prices throughout. Vanilla, rum, and geranium (the latter for the perfumeries of Grasse) were the main goods to board in Réunion.[40] Here was a relatively modest firm with a limited but experienced team and fleet specializing in circular trade within the Indian Ocean out of Marseille.

A far larger company entered the fray to compete with these regional circuits at the turn of the twentieth century. In 1904, the US vanilla importers Dodge and Olcott arranged for the first direct pod shipments from Réunion to New York, circumventing mainland France altogether.[41] In fact, Dodge and Olcott soon opened a branch on the island. By the 1920s, this New York–based vanilla import company operated offices not just in Réunion but also in Madagascar (in Tamatave and Nosy Be), the Comoros, Guadeloupe, Mexico (in Veracruz, Papantla, and Gutierrez Zamora), Tahiti, and Java—in addition to its US venues in New York, Philadelphia, Chicago, Boston, St. Louis, and Los Angeles. In the 1920s, its leadership claimed vertical control over the vanilla business, advertising themselves as "planters, curers and merchants."[42]

Dodge and Olcott were no newcomers to the international spice business. The company was founded in 1798 by Robert Bach, who started out selling pharmaceuticals, soaps, essential oils, and perfumes in Manhattan, a stone's throw from Wall Street. By 1840, Bach had teamed up with a number of associates and expanded to London under the name Dodge, Cuming, and Company. A decade later, it opened a branch in Paris under the brand Dodge and Colvill. The firm increasingly specialized in essential oils, including sandalwood, cumin, cloves, and nutmeg. Vanilla came into its orbit in this manner, for its role in perfumery. In 1880, the company established a plant in Brooklyn, New York, and in 1904, another in Bayonne, New Jersey. By 1925, Dodge and Olcott hired a young chemist named Ernest Guenther, who was tasked with traveling to Provence to study the production of lavender essences and perfumes. (One source quipped that the Bayonne plant became "Grasse in New Jersey.") Dodge and Olcott emerged as a remarkably successful multinational firm by leveraging the centuries-old fascination that Westerners have had with spices. However, it brought these flavors to mass markets through distillation and industrial techniques, which were studied and perfected at multiple sites. Dodge and Olcott's presence on the ground in faraway Réunion, and its executives' desire to bypass Marseille to ship vanilla directly from the Indian Ocean to the East Coast of the United States, speak to the firm's reach and depth. Here was a company with a hand in production, conditioning, trading, shipping, and distribution of pods. As a titan in the field, it soon wielded enough influence to affect vanilla pricing.[43]

Pragmatic Réunionnais producers proved eager to deal with Dodge and Olcott, just as they sought opportunities elsewhere. Indeed, ever since they had put themselves in competition with Mexico in 1848 and had succeeded in that challenge thanks to government support, Bourbon vanilla producers demonstrated savvy awareness of their position in the global market. In 1906, for instance, they learned of a production drop in Mexico. This, combined with a typhoon that had just ravaged Tahiti, led to a considerable spike in prices. Réunionese planters seized the chance to extend their reach into Russia and some other central and eastern European markets that had until then retained their preference for Mexican vanilla.[44]

Clearly, Réunion's vanilla was booming and reaching distant markets. But who was involved in the minute and specialized labor required to produce the stuff? We saw that the formerly enslaved played an important role at such key early vanilla estates as Mrs. Devillaine's in Saint-Denis. Soon, other groups joined the sector. After the 1848 abolition of slavery, taking their lead from British colonists in the Caribbean and nearby Mauritius, French plantation owners brought scores of indentured workers from South Asia to replace bondage labor. In 1851, an agricultural assembly convened at Albius's hometown of Sainte-Suzanne. At the heart of discussions were the connected issues of "how much work are the newly affranchised undertaking" and "how much labor is being provided by the twenty-four thousand Indians who have been introduced into the colony since 1848."[45]

New South Asian immigrants came to play a major role in the vanilla sector, reminding us that this colonial "franchise venture" reflected the cultural mosaic that was Réunion. And like most franchises, vanilla offered a path toward social advancement. A nineteenth-century legal case allows us to reconstitute one such path. Two indentured workers, Ranguin Livambarom and Virapin Moutien, had arrived together in Réunion on August 24, 1856. They served several contracts as *engagés*—indentured laborers. Virapin Moutien's final indentured contract ran from 1869 to 1871.[46] That very year of 1871, Ranguin Livambarom purchased and started to cultivate a plot alongside the Rivière des Pluies, uphill from the capital, Saint-Denis. "There, he devoted much care to establish a vanilla grove," noted a legal brief. The question of where Ranguin Livambarom's property ended caused much ink to spill, with the authorities claiming that he had "usurped" public land adjacent to his own, along a bank of the Rivière des Pluies. Another source used the verb *invade*.[47] Yet another document made the point that Ranguin Livambarom was but one of many Indians and Creoles to settle an upland area at that time, precisely as the rugged and remote valleys of Cilaos and

Mafate were attracting pioneers.[48] Government officials concurred on one thing: Regardless of his legal claim to the entire plot, Livambarom's vanilla grove had become very lucrative.[49]

Ranguin Livambarom perished from unnamed causes in September 1874 and left no direct heirs, which led to this case being brought to court. The lack of legal descendants was common for former indentured workers, given the gender imbalance on most plantations. At his death, the estate of his fellow traveler Virapin Moutien claimed that he had been coproprietor of the vanilla plants. The government reached a settlement, paying Livambarom's estate and a Miss Mallarma, representing Moutien's estate, 400 francs each.[50] This March 1875 settlement meant that both the land and the vanilla on it were now in the administration's hands, although the property's exact lines remained blurry.

The government then jumped to action, assigning a forestry official to guard the vanilla from possible theft.[51] Time was of the essence. The forestry official determined that the vanilla grove of the deceased would produce at least 2,000 francs' worth of pods. A certain Jacquemand agreed to tend to the precious crop, pick it, and prepare it for market. He was paid thirty francs a month for this task. However, in November and December 1875, the department entrusted a specialist named Bec to undertake the arduous, delicate, and specialized work of artificially pollinating the vanilla flowers, for only eight francs.[52] Then, with little notice, Jacquemand changed his mind about the entire undertaking, citing inadequate drying and preparing facilities for the pods after they were picked. The government was forced to scramble to sell the vanilla green (i.e., unprepared) for the considerably lower price of 453.66 francs.[53]

With Ranguin Livambarom gone, his vanilla business slipped into chaos, especially after Jacquemand absconded. Indeed, an attentive visitor to a vanilla grove set in a natural setting will attest that without daily tending, the vanilla vines can become overrun with weeds, grow too far up trees to loop back, lose their delicate sun-shade balance, or even strangle one another!

After the authorities reached a settlement with the two estates, in March 1875 Livambarom's plot "reverted" to government land. Thereafter, the authorities rented the plot to Debuisson, a property owner in Saint-Denis, at the rate of fifty francs per year plus another 1,200 francs for the 1,200 vanilla vines already on location. However, the legal file reveals that "the vanilla grove on which the renter had pinned his hopes was completely ravaged by disease." Unfortunately, it remains silent about which affliction decimated the grove. It was in all likelihood the fusarium fungus, a scourge that attacks the roots and prevents them from absorbing water properly. Changes in environment can trigger an outbreak. The available evidence suggests that rapid shifts of ownership had resulted in the neglect and subsequent disease of the vines. Fusarium is one of countless fungal scourges, reminiscent of potato blight or the oidium that ravages vines. Burdened with vanilla debt, having paid 1,200 francs for nearly worthless vines, Debuisson decided to plant and harvest filao trees instead, in a bid to pay his rent and cut his losses.[54]

Several questions endure around this story. A key mystery involves how, where, and when Livambarom and Moutien acquired their vanilla know-how, which was extensive, inasmuch as things fell apart without them. Maybe one or both of them had served as indentured laborers at a vanilla plantation, or they might have crossed paths with vanilla workers who could have shared their trade secrets. Regardless of how they arrived at the Rivière des Pluies, their story is one of death coming just as economic success and rapid social ascension via vanilla seemed within reach. Their example also reminds us that every tessera of Réunion's rich cultural mosaic was involved in vanilla: from nineteenth-century South and East Asian migrants, to descendants of enslaved Africans and Malagasy, to the progeny of European planters, all were implicated in the Bourbon vanilla boom. Different ages and genders were also involved. An 1885 report on school attendance at Saint-Philippe noted that girls were skipping class to harvest vanilla.[55]

In addition to specialized pollinators, cultivators, and preparers, in Réunion (as in Mexico) vanilla gave rise to a class of middlemen. In July 1877, the police department in the district of Saint-Joseph put pen to paper. The requisite report contained few surprises, few events really, with no disturbances anywhere. And so, in that quiet month, the constable fleshed out the usually terse "agriculture" section. We thereby learn that the vanilla harvest in Saint-Joseph was proving "quite abundant" that year and that *accapareurs* (translatable as either monopolists or hoarders, terms reminiscent of the New Spanish context) from the next district over in Saint-Benoît had come to purchase as much as possible.[56] Vanilla speculation was thriving. To this day, producers are better off selling their vanilla black (prepared) than green (unprepared). However, some do not have the deep pockets, secured facilities, or time to undertake the process. When buyers purchased the pods green, they entrusted the vanilla to specialized preparers. Volume mattered, and modest producers were left selling their pods green, in contrast to the owners of larger estates.

Réunion's vanilla dominance did not last long. Already at the turn of the twentieth century, Tahiti surpassed its output. During World War I, Madagascar and the Comoros outpaced both Réunion and Tahiti. In 1912, Madagascar produced just over 113 tons of vanilla.[57] A chart preserved in Madagascar's national archives shows similar vanilla output for Madagascar and Réunion between 1901 and 1915, before Madagascar's production skyrocketed, reducing Réunion's to specks in the span of three years. Then, in the 1930s, Réunion's production tumbles to levels rarely seen before 1865.[58]

To add insult to injury, wealthy settlers in Madagascar and the Comoros were recruiting Réunion's best vanilla preparers. In 1901, a Réunion newspaper railed at the colonial authorities in Madagascar for unscrupulously enticing young Réunionese into working as pod preparers on their island. The article highlighted Madagascar's "murderous climate" and hinted that young Réunionese men would be corrupted there.[59] Another source emphasized the pull factors at play. Plantations on Madagascar offered higher wages, combined with a lower cost of living. This proved appealing to specialized young Réunionese Creoles. Planters in Madagascar and the Comoros pulled off this talent drain thanks to their deep pockets. (Although culturally and religiously distinct, the Comoros Islands were tied to Madagascar administratively between 1908 and 1960.) One plantation, that of Regoin et Bouin in Anjouan—part of the vast Société Comores Bambao—produced a staggering twenty thousand kilos of vanilla, while the output of Réunion's largest plantations hovered around three thousand kilos. A Réunion vanilla expert feared that this imbalance did not bode well for the island ever regaining its crown as "queen of vanilla."[60]

Of course, all this competition proved beneficial to the social category in question: skilled Réunionese vanilla preparers who were willing to travel overseas. Consider this 1928 correspondence within the ranks of the wealthy La Motte Saint-Pierre vanilla family, owners of sprawling vanilla estates on Nosy Be and in northeastern Madagascar.

> Because a Réunionese vanilla preparer showed up here (off to exercise his profession in the Comoros)—albeit a rather young one—I felt obliged to ask Vital if we could still count on him. He responded that he had never been

sure about leaving and that we could count on him for the upcoming preparation of the crop so long as we provide him with a three-month holiday to ward off his fatigue, including covering his trip home to Réunion. Monsieur de Lastelle believes he doesn't really expect us to pay for his holiday expenses, but we should at least figure out what his holiday salary would be. I therefore responded that I would ask you by mail. Could you kindly get back to me by telegram, as he is scheduled to set sail [soon]?[61]

In other words, sought-after Réunionese preparers profited from interisland competition and earned paid vacations before they became common (paid holidays were only introduced in France under the Popular Front government in 1936). These skilled workers were some of the most precious assets of vanilla franchises.

On the eve of World War II, despite its clear retreat, vanilla nevertheless remained a significant crop for Réunion, if only in terms of the number of small-scale growers. The island counted between four thousand and five thousand individual producers, out of a total population of roughly 210,000 inhabitants.[62] During the war, Réunion's authorities initially sided with the pro-Nazi Vichy regime, ushering in a period of partial autarky and restrictions. Foreign vanilla outlets were virtually shut, as the US War Production Board restricted vanilla entries from Vichy-controlled colonies. Even sending vanilla to mainland France became challenging due to a British naval blockade. Then, thanks to a Fighting French commando operation, Réunion swung back to the Allied side in November 1942. When the island finally rejoined the world economy, expectations for the vanilla sector ran high. American demand had been pent-up. Indeed, only a single shipment of vanilla from the Indian Ocean (from Madagascar, not Réunion) had reached the United States directly between 1940 and 1942, docking at New York in February 1942.[63]

However, just when prospects should have looked rosy in 1945, Réunion found itself at an unexpected vanilla disadvantage. To understand why, one must go back to an incident that transpired at the war's outset. On the very day of the Nazi onslaught against France, on May 9, 1940, the French-American Banking Company in New York had sent word that an unspecified number of vanilla shipments from Réunion had arrived moldy.[64] Within months, the new Vichy regime's minister of the colonies cabled that the incident risked driving the US back toward Mexican producers.[65] The French-

American Banking Company complaint unleashed fierce debate in Réunion. Vichy officials tried to get to the bottom of the matter. The Chamber of Commerce consulted preparers, producers, and exporters alike. Some wrote back, indicating that the molded pods could not possibly have been prepared by them.[66] One suggested that he had nothing to hide, inviting officials to keep his vanilla under observation in a hanger for a month.[67] In March 1941, one exporter, E. Sauger, dismissed the matter as straightforward: "Nearly all problems encountered by exporters come from poorly picked vanilla, which is to say vanilla that was picked unripe." His colleague, the planter Alexis de Villeneuve, concurred: "With properly ripe pods, one cannot go wrong with preparation."[68] However, a scientist at Réunion's agricultural laboratory drew a more nuanced picture. In February 1941, he confessed that he could find no scientific work on proper modern vanilla preservation techniques. However, he did provide informed advice that the exported pods should not contain more than 14 percent water and must be inspected for parasites and mold. He warned against seemingly simple solutions, including the use of formaldehyde, salicylic acid, and any other antiseptic agent, on the grounds that they would be counterproductive and violate French food regulations. Finally, he recommended that, prior to export, vanilla shipments be inspected by both a chemist and an agricultural specialist.[69]

The issue remained unresolved and took on new urgency when international shipping returned to normal levels. In 1946, the Réunionese vanilla preparer Joseph Suzony Boyer shared his practical thoughts on the matter. The water content on Réunion's vanilla needed to be reduced prior to export, he opined. This could readily be adjusted during the preparation process. Preparers should also be on the lookout for mold and mites before shipping their vanilla overseas. Boyer then came to the transportation conundrum, for which he offered no solution. Tin boxes had shown their limits during long-haul travel, sometimes arriving rusted because of the oil released by vanilla pods.[70] However, even these tin boxes were in short supply because of the war and the dislocations it caused. In 1941, despite rationing and recycling projects, the containers had become prohibitively expensive.[71] By 1944, people in Réunion's vanilla sector faced daunting challenges: exporting their product without wax paper, special string, or tin boxes, convincing US authorities that the fiasco of rancid vanillas would not recur, and, last but not least, coping with the devastating effects of an April 1944 cyclone.[72] The greatest challenge by far, however, remained competition from Madagascar and the Comoros due to their low labor costs. Long before our current globalization, internal competition and wage disparities were looming large within France's colonial empire.

Réunion produced some eighty tons in 1955. However, in the following decades, instability became the norm (thirty-three tons in 1962, sixty-one tons in 1963, forty-four tons in 1964), followed by collapse in the last decade of the twentieth century. In 1990, the island produced a mere twenty-five tons of vanilla, a figure not seen since 1875. Large Sainte-Suzanne and Saint-André vanilla producers who had been central to the sector since the nineteenth century abruptly abandoned it. The collapse continued, unabated: Edmond Albius's home district of Sainte-Suzanne went from having 151 vanilla producers in 1992 to only 39 in 1995.[73] In 1993, vanilla growers on Réunion faced multiple challenges, such as falling prices and the devastation wrought by Hurricane Colina. The underlying structural crisis in the 1990s, however, involved the undercutting of the Indian Ocean vanilla cartel, which had set base prices since the 1960s, which I will present in greater detail in chapter 8. It had come unraveled in the 1980s for two main reasons: Madagascar's move, under pressure from the International Monetary Fund, to raise output, and the ascendancy of another actor on the vanilla scene, Indonesia. The result was a catastrophic decline in prices, on the order of 70 percent.[74]

French authorities despaired that the European Union was not moving rapidly enough to stabilize vanilla prices. In concert with local tiers of government and a modest European contribution, they turned to support Réunion's vanilla cooperatives, including its largest, Provanille, to the tune of 28 million francs over five years.[75] Yet there was no stemming the bleeding. Le Bras Panon's famed vanilla plantation failed in 1995. Even the Floris family's legendary Grand Hazier estate closed in 2006, at a time when it still accounted for roughly one-third of the island's production. However, it soon came back to life thanks to its new owners, Betrand Côme and Elisabeth de Cambiaire. They have not only revived Grand Hazier but won a host of prestigious prizes, including the gold medal for top vanilla from France's *concours général agricole* in 2019.[76]

Grand Hazier and the Provanille cooperative, which still collects from tiny producers, are some of the rare recent success stories. Nowadays, Réunion's vanilla sector barely clings to life. In 2009, the island produced four metric tons of prepared vanilla. How could Réunion's pods compete when, in 2012, Madagascar's vanilla was ten times cheaper?[77] Some are now betting on upscale direct sourcing to elite restaurants on mainland France. Others look to distinguish their Bourbon vanilla from Madagascar's by obtaining formal EU organic certification.[78] Others still are turning to tourism, opening boutiques on their plantations. With nearby Madagascar's wages so low compared to Réunion's European Union salaries, creativity has become the name of the game. Some have taken this quite far. For instance, one producer couple in Saint-Philippe is selling "blue vanilla," which they claim can be eaten whole, casing included. It has achieved success, thanks to savvy marketing. Yet its detractors counter, off the record, that it contains less vanillin than standard *planifolia* beans, which may explain why its promoters vaunt its flavor as "milder and subtler" than most.[79] Without taking sides in the dispute, it seems to me that the main takeaway from "blue vanilla" is that distinguishing oneself has become key for vanilla producers on Réunion.

This is a far cry from the state of affairs in the late nineteenth and early twentieth centuries, when Réunion's vanilla dominated the planet. Restricting our analysis to Réunion proper, the tale may seem like one of loss and decline. However, viewed from another angle, the hub of production has not shifted far from where Edmond transformed the sector. The world's largest producer, Madagascar, which lies only 944 kilometers (586.5 miles) west of Réunion, overtook it for good in 1915. So, if we adjust our lens to consider Madagascar, Réunion, and the Comoros Islands as an interconnected southwestern Indian Ocean ensemble, the vast majority of the planet's vanilla has been produced in this area since the 1870s. Indeed, by 1967, those three alone combined to produce a staggering 80 percent of all vanilla: 666 tons from Madagascar, 145 from the Comoros, and 18 from Réunion.[80] The initial swing from Mesoamerican to Indian Ocean production, which took place in a remarkably short span, hinged on two interconnected factors: the site of Edmond's discovery and a determined effort by French authorities to parlay it into global vanilla dominance. Although in this chapter I showed how Réunionese interests came to resent Madagascar's vanilla ascendancy, the following one will make clear that the scheme to place Madagascar at the top of the vanilla pod-ium was, ironically, of Réunionese design.

CHAPTER 5

Madagascar's Mr. Vanilla

THE REASONS FOR RÉUNION PLANTERS RELOCATING VANILLA production offshore to Madagascar were no mystery. In 1848, Réunionese doctor Louis Lacaille published a book whose title said it all: *The Importance and Necessity of Colonizing the Island of Madagascar*. One of the many arguments he advanced was that Réunionese planters could bring vanilla to the great island and have it grown more cheaply by local peoples. With slavery abolished the very year he put pen to paper, Lacaille imagined that Madagascar would provide extremely low-wage labor on vast vanilla plantations—the next best thing to slave labor in his opinion. His solution served multiple purposes, answering the call of Réunion planters who complained of struggling to remunerate their vanilla workers. From the standpoint of demand, extending vanilla's cultivation zone to the world's fourth-largest island promised to make the pod more affordable for new categories of European and North American consumers. The net result, he predicted, would be to redefine vanilla, which would no longer be a "luxury plant."[1] In other words, vanilla's consumption could be democratized at home through colonial conquest overseas. Another reason Lacaille wished to transform Madagascar into an outlet for Réunion is worth exposing. He was one of many Réunionese clamoring for a colony for their colony, a dual imperial dynamic that reinforced their Frenchness.

A slew of early colonial schemes for Madagascar turned out to be pipe dreams, starting with the notion that the "Red Island"—so named because of its ferrous soil—might become a settlement colony like South Africa, Canada, New Zealand, or Australia.[2] Unlike so many of these designs, Lacaille's vanilla scheme did come to pass (in fact, the process had already begun), although not as he had imagined it. He had recommended immediate annexation of the vast island, followed by mass introduction. Instead, vanilla found its way to a still-independent island of Madagascar through trade and botanical circuits. France annexed two small islands off the eastern and northwestern coasts of Madagascar in 1820 and 1841. These outposts, known respectively as Sainte-Marie (Nosy Boraha) and Nosy Be, would become vanilla bridgeheads. The botanical transfers to these two satellites, and even to Madagascar's terra firma, would occur long before the French took control of the main island in 1895.

Prior to the French invasion, the main island of Madagascar had been ruled by kings and queens from its highland capital, Antananarivo. These ethnic Merina (highlander) monarchs conquered the isle over several centuries, culminating in the efforts of King Radama. Radama forged an alliance with Britain that opened the door to the London Missionary Society, which shared some of his centralizing impulses. In the wake of Radama's conquests, the island was, in the words of historians Solofo Randrianja and Stephen Ellis, "a sovereign state [. . .] a fledgling member of the international family of states."[3] The kingdom was ethnically diverse but institutionally and linguistically unified—Malagasy, a language belonging to the Malayo-Polynesian family, reflects ancient maritime migration from that part of the world. The island therefore presented a markedly different situation on the eve of colonial conquest in comparison to most of the nearby African continent.

Radama and his successors governed a powerful state, undertook a census, and developed a large standing army as well as a sizeable bureaucracy. Wanting to incorporate European knowledge, Radama dispatched select Malagasy youngsters to be trained in Britain and Mauritius. Other young people received an increasingly "Western" education on location in the heart of the great island. Indeed, due in part to missionary activity, literacy rates were high in nineteenth-century highland Madagascar. As Faranirina Rajaonah and Phares Mutibwa have noted, school enrollment in 1880s Madagascar was comparable to that of most European nations.[4] The Malagasy state's educated lead officials, many of them military figures, held significant positions and controlled a substantial portion of the island's trade. In the name of the monarchy, they organized sweeping *corvées*, forms of unpaid and mandatory work, encompassing both manual labor and military service. *Corvées* were especially resented in recently conquered coastal regions peopled by non-Merina populations.

Independent Madagascar's relations with the outside world were plural and complex. Its main exports in the second half of the nineteenth century included beef, rubber, gold, orchil, salt, sugar, rice, and fine woods.[5] The chief transport corridor for these goods ran between the port of Tamatave (Toamasina in Malagasy) on Madagascar's eastern coast, and the Mascarene islands, themselves warehouses and outposts for British and French interests. Connections with the United Kingdom were numerous. We saw that Radama's agreements with Great Britain opened the door to the Protestant London Missionary Society to proselytize, with considerable success, in the highlands especially. Yet King Radama spoke French as his first foreign language, rather than English. A number of French entrepreneurs and technical experts were also welcomed into the kingdom, in addition to American business interests. By the late nineteenth century, France and Britain vied for control over Madagascar. Although the Franco-Malagasy War of 1883–85 ended with no clear victor, it resulted in a large indemnity that the island kingdom was obliged to pay France. Loans were taken out to repay it, and the Malagasy kingdom enacted increasingly desperate measures to raise cash, including legalizing gold mining under the umbrella of a crown monopoly. After this proved insufficient, a Parisian bank foreclosed on the country's debt and took over the operation of Madagascar's main ports. Since the 1870s, these had started exporting vanilla as a cash crop. Finally, in 1890, Britain and France agreed that Madagascar would fall under a French zone of influence, giving Britain a free hand elsewhere. The path was paved for France to formally invade and then colonize the island in 1895–96. The colonial era did not mark a clear break with the past in every regard, of course. Vanilla and gold continued to be exported. Institutionally, forced labor and some facets of central authority were simply repackaged under a new guise.[6]

After the conquest of 1895, the French utilized a classic divide-and-rule strategy known as the *politique des races*. In coastal regions, the new colonial authorities played on existing resentment toward Merina domination. The Betsimisaraka people constitute the majority in the parts of Madagascar that came to specialize in vanilla (along what became the Sava coast, although not on Nosy Be, which was ethnically composed of Sakalava and Antakarana). In the eighteenth century, Ratsimilaho, son of a Malagasy noblewoman and an English pirate, had broken away from Sakalava rule to create a Betsimisaraka Confederation. (The ethnonym Betsimisaraka means "the many undivided.") According to David Graeber, the confederation borrowed in part from the principles of pirate egalitarianism to foster a Northern Malagasy Enlightenment. Ratsimilaho also built a formidable army, equipped with British firearms. However, by 1817 Radama's forces defeated the Betsimisaraka and imposed harsh subjugation on them. In the wake of the French conquest of 1895, Betsimisaraka people voiced grievances about their former overlords. At Vatomandry, some remembered "an extremely harsh authority." Others testified that royal representatives had demanded that they bow before their palanquins. The legacy of Merina domination was even etched in place names. Consider the case of the nearby village of Lañijadoña, which means "smacks of despotism." Little wonder that some Betsimisaraka welcomed the French conquest of 1895. But many ultimately saw their hopes dashed. Betsimisaraka lands would later erupt in revolt against French rule on several occasions. In fact, they would serve as the inception point for a vast insurrection in 1947. In this sense, the *politique des races* backfired.[7]

Vanilla fits into this long story of tensions between coastal and highlander peoples, insofar as it grows only on the isle's tropical coastlines, predominantly in Betsimisaraka regions. However, to this day, pod pricing and production targets are established in the highland Merina capital, Antananarivo. The Malagasy past has shaped the vanilla sector in other ways as well. On the Red Island, vanilla has been entangled in local histories of *corvée* labor, forged during both precolonial and colonial times. Paradoxically, in Madagascar, vanilla cultivation has had both dispossessing and coercive effects as well as empowering ones.

One last point of context should be established. To the outside world, Madagascar has long been associated with a pervasive sense of otherness, especially in the realm of natural history. Indeed, the island's fossil testimonials to gigantic prehistoric birds, along with its endemic species of lemurs and chameleons, led many colonial sources to view it as outright bizarre. Preserving that uniqueness emerged as a key imperative for outsiders. As an anthropologist has pointed out, that impetus has led to flattened visions of Malagasy people either as victims or "killers" and "burners" of their own environment, itself in need of rescue.[8] However, one interesting feature of vanilla is that it reflects the reverse dynamic. Although there are several varietals of indigenous vanilla orchids on the island, none of them is edible. *Vanilla planifolia* was first imported by outsiders in the early 1820s and was subsequently embraced by a wide range of Malagasy people who made the finicky orchid their own. Madagascar's becoming the world's top producer of edible vanilla in under a century tells a rather different story, one of universalism and resourcefulness.

Prior to 1822, edible vanilla did not grow anywhere in Madagascar. We saw that in 1820, France claimed one of Madagascar's subsidiary isles, the former pirate haven known as Sainte-Marie. It is there that edible vanilla was first introduced. This is revealed by a fleeting reference in the records of French naval captain Auguste Samuel Massieu de Clerval. In August 1822, he noted during his visit to the newly acquired territory that two intrepid planters on Sainte-Marie had "even" introduced vanilla, although they concentrated their efforts on cotton, coffee, cloves, and cinnamon.[9] One of the two men, Fortuné Albrand, had previously served on Île Bourbon, where he probably acquired the vanilla cutting. He would be named commandant of Sainte-Marie in 1823. At this point, however, vanilla was not yet bearing fruit. It subsequently became a minor cash crop on Sainte-Marie. The isle exported 8.2 kilos of vanilla in 1882, then 15 kilos in 1887.[10]

Vanilla reached another Madagascar's fringe areas a few decades later, to greater success. Between 1847 and 1852, French botanist Louis-Hyacinthe Boivin sailed to several points around the Indian Ocean. France had annexed the small isle of Nosy Be in 1841, trying to compensate for the loss of Mauritius. A botanist trained by Antoine Laurent de Jussieu, Boivin took copious notes and samples during his travels. On Nosy Be, at some point between 1847 and 1852, he drew up a column for "plants of which there are only a few specimens here" and then another for "plants of which there is but one specimen on the island."[11] Vanilla appeared on the second list. Boivin did not specify its provenance, but given the timing, the cutting almost certainly came from Réunion or Sainte-Marie.

According to the island's commandant, a second introduction of vanilla occurred on Nosy Be in 1872. The previous specimen may have died. The commandant relates that by the late 1870s, "some settlers were growing a few vanilla plants around their properties."[12] In the following decade, a sugar crisis, combined with a coffee disease, boosted vanilla's importance. By 1896, local planters on Nosy Be were turning away from sugar in favor of vanilla, producing some two metric tons of green vanilla that year.[13] Two years later, a local newspaper predicted that "because of the sugar sector's downturn, coffee and vanilla cultivation are destined to be the future of Nosy Be."[14] Colonial officials encouraged its spread and met little resistance, given the rates of return. Consequently, vanilla came to thrive on Nosy Be.

The Lastelle brothers, whose plantation lay northeast of the main town of Hell-Ville, added between twenty thousand and sixty thousand vanilla vines per year to their plantation between 1897 and 1900.[15]

Nosy Be may have been remote, but it was remarkably cosmopolitan, located at the crossroads of different worlds. Mainland Madagascar's coast was within sight, and Sakalava people moved between the French-held island and the Kingdom of Madagascar. Multiple Hamburg trading companies, including the Deutsche-Östafrikanische Gessellschaft (DOAG), had outlets on Nosy Be. Several Chinese merchants opened shops on the island, and many became involved in vanilla preparation and sales. So, too, did South Asian traders, who connected Nosy Be to broader Indian Ocean networks.[16] In other words, in addition to serving as a springboard for France to intervene in mainland Madagascar, Nosy Be featured a complex social mosaic of its own.

Nosy Be's vanilla left for Marseille as well as Hamburg. Records for 1888 show 337 kilos of vanilla departing Nosy Be, worth a total of 4,007.5 francs. Vanilla, unlike rice, sandalwood, or sugar, wasn't loaded onto the Arab, Indian, or German ships at Nosy Be but was instead shipped on seventeen French boats to Marseille.[17] After the opening of the Suez Canal in 1869 and the emergence of steamships and steel hulls, the southern French port had become much easier to reach.

Soon, the great island itself outpaced Nosy Be. The first vanilla cuttings to reach Madagascar's terra firma did so at Vatomandry in 1873, introduced by one Joseph Lucien Edouard Guénot, a customs official who moonlit as a vanilla planter.[18] That double life proved ideal for learning about and cultivating vanilla plants. His profile was not unique: planters in this part of eastern Madagascar around Tamatave often doubled as merchants, port agents, or traders. His vanilla groves, the first on the great isle, were located at Ambohimanarivo, along the Sakaleona River.[19] Guénot appears to have turned to vanilla for much the same reasons as Nosy Be planters did: His coffee trees had been decimated by disease in the 1870s.[20] By 1876, a New England journalist reported from Tamatave that "there are [. . .] one or two plantations here for growing vanilla, owned by foreigners, and I have seen some very nice, large, highly scented pods."[21] Other visitors took note. In 1890, explorer Louis Catat observed that near Mahanoro, vanilla was replacing coffee. He counted no fewer than twenty plantations along the Mangoro River that had shifted to vanilla cultivation, with each growing some six thousand vines.[22] Vanilla's appeal was obvious: It was remarkably lucrative. In 1881, the eastern coast of Madagascar already exported vanilla worth 4,000 piastres (roughly 20,000 francs). The document reporting this data added, "Sugar and vanilla production are increasing right now, coffee is dropping."[23]

Unsurprisingly, given that the plant was introduced from overseas, outsiders played a significant role in vanilla's early years on the Red Island, starting with several Mauritians and an American. This was the result of the Kingdom of Madagascar's recent decision to open up. Debts had forced the hands of the royal regime in Antananarivo, which had long preferred a policy of economic independence. Consequently, since the reign of King Radama II and then increasingly in the wake of the Franco-Malagasy War of 1883–85, there had been a "massive" influx of Europeans on the island.[24]

Among them was the Franco-American vanilla grower Eugène Chauvet, whom we met in the previous chapter. Born in Saint-Paul, Réunion, in 1818, he left for the United States in 1846, married a US national, and lived in both New York and New Orleans. He also traveled widely to Mexico, North Africa, Asia, and around the Indian Ocean. After a short return to his native island in 1874, the fifty-seven-year-old widower decided to seek fortune in Madagascar, which he reached in September 1875. After disembarking in Tamatave, Chauvet spent his first six days on the island at the Watkins plantation while seeking out a plot of his own "for planting coffee." He quickly found one, bordering a lake near Tamatave. His diary provides details about the previous landholder, Calvata. Chauvet explained that she was a "woman chief of a *tanambé* (village)." Because female Betsimisaraka chiefs were uncommon, it is possible that Chauvet was dealing with a high-status Creole woman. Dominique Bois has studied the reasons why nineteenth-century Betsimisaraka women entered into alliances with outsiders via marriage. Some appear to have taken on the title of chief when their union produced a child. If this were the case, perhaps Calvata's marriage had now come under strain, or she had some other urgent need for funds. As for Chauvet, he seemed pleased with his purchase. Before assembled local villagers, he handed Calvata the equivalent of ten dollars (roughly $240 today), as well as a piece of brown sheet metal, in exchange for over one hundred hectares of land. Further on, Chauvet specifies that a partner joined him in the land purchase. That man was none other than Colonel William Robinson, US consul in Tamatave from 1875 to 1886, and veteran of the US Civil War. His partnership with the diplomat no doubt enabled Chauvet to avoid some of the paperwork and obstacles involved in dealing with the local representatives of the Malagasy crown.[25]

In April 1876, Chauvet's diary noted the onsite death of Louis Lacaille, who had hatched the idea of making the island a vanilla colony in the first place back in 1848. Chauvet and Lacaille were both born the same year, 1818, in the same town on Réunion. They likely had been schoolmates.[26]

We saw that Chauvet had coffee in mind when he first reached Madagascar, but by April 1876, his priorities had changed. He now wrote of "a coffee and vanilla plantation." While the majority of his vanilla was of the "Bourbon" or *planifolia* varietal, he specifies in his diary that smaller amounts were "native."[27] (Madagascar possesses seven varietals of endemic vanilla.) Some of his vanilla climbed on fences, another patch was left in the forest, and a third section was planted at the foot of host trees.[28] It bears reminding that vanilla thrives in forest undergrowth, relying on trees for support and shade. Therefore, its cultivation usually causes less ecological damage than the more predatory extraction of rubber or timber, for example.[29]

In September 1877, after two years of growing vanilla, Chauvet was jubilant; he had tripled the surface of his lands devoted to the orchid. He basked in the moment: "[The vanilla] vines have grown faster than my most sanguine expectations." This didn't stop the Franco-American from complaining about local holidays. The following month, he grumbled that the *fandroana* or queen's bath celebration would "prevent work for a whole week" on his plantation.[30] The *fandroana*, a Merina festival closely resembling water rites in Cambodia, symbolized the sacred and magical powers associated with the royal body. An annual ritual of renewal, it crystallized popular adherence to the monarchy while reviving monarchical lineage. The queen's bath at the heart of the ceremony had agricultural meanings as well, as it augured the arrival of the rainy season.[31] For Chauvet, however, all this was little more than an irritant, depriving him of his workforce.

In addition to griping about local holidays, Chauvet acted as a man under siege from Madagascar's nature and environment. On his vanilla groves, he shot at least three snakes, one of them a six-footer locals called a menarana snake (*Leioheterodon madagascariensis*), as well as numerous crocodiles and caimans, one of them "sixteen feet," and another purportedly "the size of an ox." He dubbed one of the reptiles "Mr. Eatman" and recounted in October 1878 how a crocodile devoured one of his former vanilla plantation employees. Less seriously, he related how fossa broke into his pigeon pens. And interestingly, Chauvet's vanilla laborers regaled him with tales of two mythical beasts common in Malagasy lore: the *bakobako*, which resembles a dog, and the *songomby*, which resembles a donkey and is considered "very dangerous." Finally, despite taking quinine, Chauvet complained of fevers as debilitating as those he had suffered in Algeria and Mauritius. Madagascar's biological otherness was a recurring theme for Chauvet.[32]

In October 1878, Chauvet related undertaking the first artificial pollination of the vanilla orchids on his plantation, serving as a reminder of the significant amount of time required before being able to harvest vanilla—usually three years from planting. Chauvet became convinced that Madagascar offered better conditions for vanilla than did Réunion. In the same entry, he observed, "[One of the flowers] I fecundated [. . .] was already 24 hours old, but I think that owing to the dampness of this climate the operation will succeed. Not so at Réunion where after 3 o'clock PM it would have been too late." At this point, his journal no longer mentioned coffee at all.[33]

In November 1881, Chauvet's journal turned to exports. He diligently packed seven tin boxes with vanilla, each weighting roughly half a kilo (1.1 pounds). These, in turn, were protected in three wooden cases. He tapped into his American networks and dispatched the whole package to Boston through his contacts at the F. O. Whitney Company. In January of the following year, Chauvet provided further details on his highly personalized shipping arrangements: "I went to town [Tamatave] to see the shipment of my vanilla per Bark Glide, captain of the *Beadle*, of Salem, Massachusetts."[34] Chauvet's vanilla was heading straight to the insatiable US market, surely the first Malagasy pods to reach the American continent.

While American citizens were a rarity even in the cosmopolitan Tamatave area, Mauritians were not. Given that their home island had been French prior to the British takeover in 1810, Mauritians generally spoke French in addition to English, Creole, and Malagasy, in the case of Mauritians settled on the Red Island. In fact, Britain and its overseas holdings, rather than France, constituted the Kingdom of Madagascar's top commercial partner until the Franco-Malagasy War.[35] Mauritians therefore occupied a key space as French-speaking British nationals, on an island that was shifting between British and French spheres of influence.

The 1883 war, which France waged in hopes of establishing a protectorate over Madagascar, triggered a slew of vanilla-related grievances from this key intermediary community. One stands out in particular. A Mauritian national by the name of Antoine Joseph Talbot drew up the following claim to the local British consul in Tamatave in January 1884:

> Although without any proof at present, I am drawing to your attention that I own in the countryside, at the place known as the Voloïna River, one and a half hours outside of Tamatave, a vanilla property dubbed "Mon Espoir" [My Hope]. Vanilla was in full bloom then. Now last year's harvest is certainly lost for me, as well as that of the next two years, not to mention that my plantations are going without any tending and are abandoned. I am therefore requesting the sum of 5000 dollars.

Talbot added that his now presumably destroyed vanilla vines were "a very sought-after and esteemed" plant.[36]

Several points can be gleaned from Talbot's grievance. He submitted it before even being able to survey the damage done, as one might for a property left in haste during a hurricane. His lands might have been targeted as "French" by Malagasy forces knowing he was a French speaker; this hints at the delicate position of Madagascar's Mauritian community as France and Britain competed for influence over the Red Island. Mostly, Talbot highlighted how valuable vanilla had become. He felt the need to explain to the British consul that pods were a luxury crop. Finally, the very name that Talbot had lent to his vanilla estate—"My Hope"—evokes the upward social mobility that vanilla offered when it wasn't being destroyed by war. Chauvet and Talbot were two external actors embarking on vanilla ventures on Madagascar's eastern shores under the still independent Kingdom of Madagascar. Their cases show how vanilla was emerging as a significant cash crop in those coastal regions well before the French invasion of 1895.

The French conquest involved far larger objectives than just vanilla, of course. It had more to do with the scramble for the Indian Ocean and the colonial settlement schemes we briefly surveyed. Even so, in the heat of battle, at least one French invader had vanilla on his mind. Cavalry officer Emile Edmond de Cointet noted with wonder that "the island [...] seems to lend itself easily to so-called specialty crops, such as coffee and vanilla, which deliver large profits. Concessions have already been registered."[37] A few years later, in 1899, a French guidebook for incoming colonials tied cultivation to the logic that had underpinned slavery: "Tilling the earth is forbidden to Europeans in warm lands." However, according to this source, vanilla stood as an exception to this rule not because it grew on vines above the soil but due to its need for cerebral rather than manual labor.[38] By 1909, Madagascar was seen no longer as a kind of Eden but rather as an island rife with disease. A new governor flatly pronounced that "Europeans cannot be agriculturalists here [...] what Europeans can do instead is export."[39] This set the stage for colonial vanilla planters making extensive use of local labor, both paid and unpaid.

In 1896, French authorities deposed Madagascar's last monarch, Queen Ranavalona III; the following year, they banished her to Réunion. Madagascar became a full-fledged French colony. In 1898, the satellite islands of Nosy Be and Sainte-Marie were subsumed into Madagascar's administration, run from a capital that changed names from Antananarivo to the more Gallic-sounding Tananarive. Frenchification efforts were in full swing, even within the deeply transnational and cosmopolitan vanilla sector. And Malagasy royal symbols were not their only target. In 1903, Paul Legras presided over a new union of Nosy Be vanilla planters, whose stated goal was to emancipate French colonial planters from the clutches of German traders. His organization's manifesto reads:

> Most vanilla planters on Nosy Be lack the necessary capital to prepare their vanilla themselves, to send it to Europe and wait for the profits from their sales. They were previously at the mercy of the Hamburg-based DOAG, which signed contracts for advances on their harvests and then bought it but imposed conditions. Our planters have therefore created a union to have their vanilla prepared by someone of their choosing and sold to France by a broker of their choice.[40]

In other words, Nosy Be planters knew well that selling their vanilla green to the DOAG meant they made a tiny share of the profits. They also realized that a German firm was serving as a link within an otherwise French chain: the DOAG bought from French colonial planters and sold largely to French import houses. (A decade later, in 1913, Germany imported 6 metric tons of Madagascar vanilla compared to France's 51.5 metric tons.) The planters involved in this plan clearly resented the DOAG's activities on both capitalist and patriotic grounds. The lead local official on Nosy Be backed the project, highlighting how it would "take away, inasmuch as possible, from the obligation of submitting to the whims of a foreign company which is exploiting the current situation." However, the planters' union stumbled over major hurdles. First, some within the colonial administration referred to it as an association, rather than a union, doubting its legality. Second, and more seriously, the new central colonial authorities in Tananarive refused to pay the 50,000 francs the planters requested as a subsidy for their union. As a result, in 1906, the entire scheme failed.[41] The DOAG won this round. However, the Hamburg firm had little time to savor its victory. In 1914, it and all other German companies active in the vanilla sector across the French empire were expelled at the onset of the First World War.

Despite the union's collapse, Nosy Be growers continued to produce vanilla, undeterred. Plantations came in different shapes and sizes and were owned by people from various walks of life. At first blush, the lead missionary of the Congrégation du Saint-Esprit's Nosy Be outpost, Father Clément Raimbault, might seem a surprising producer. Admittedly, vanilla was not his only occupation. Correspondence with his parents reveals his many activities: running the mission, tending to the ill, managing Catholic schools, converting non-Christians, officiating at various events (e.g., communions, catechisms, weddings, funerals), and engaging in verbal jousts with officials he considered anticlerical. That said, shortly after arriving on Nosy Be, Raimbault decided that cash crops were the best way to fund his mission, now that church and state had been separated in France by a 1905 law. By 1906, the enterprising missionary stood at the helm of a lucrative side business, producing everything from vanilla to rubber, rice, coffee, grapes, and cacao. In the following years, new crops were added, including pepper, ylang-ylang, and other perfume plants, which the missionaries distilled and then sent in exchange for handsome profits to the perfumeries in Grasse.

Raimbault's letters to his relatives provide a rich vein of material about the local vanilla sector. In 1906, he explained that due to what he called the high cost of labor—roughly a franc per day—only forty of the mission's three hundred hectares of land, located on several points of the island and on the neighboring isle of Nosy Komba, were cultivated. In 1907, he accounted for the shortness of one of his letters home by invoking how busy he was "pollinating and planting vanilla." He added that he had dispatched one hundred kilos of prepared vanilla to France that year and hoped to send twice that amount the year following.[42]

FIGURE 9. Six vanilla pollinators, Madagascar. Photo by Guillame Grandidier, circa 1900. Courtesy Archives nationales d'outre-mer, reference 35 Fi39/132.

Although he mostly wrote in the first person, it is obvious from context that Raimbault performed little of the manual vanilla labor himself. His letters to his parents cast indirect light on the plight of workers on the mission's plantations. In May 1907, he complained of just how closely he needed to watch over his vanilla and coffee laborers: "From morning to evening one has to look over the shoulder of the workers and yell at the top of one's lungs to get even a bit of work out of them." Later that year, he admitted to resorting to an "ingenious"—read deceptive—method for "recruiting personnel." Labor on Nosy Be was far too expensive, he often griped. Manual vanilla pollination especially constituted "absorbing work that requires much labor." And so, "to get a few men, I had to become *fatidra* with them, which is to say blood brothers. As much as I felt repugnance for a ceremony that I can't even bring myself to describe to you, so vulgar was it, I had no choice but to do it." A French official on Nosy Be had described the Sakalava *fatidra* bond in the 1840s as follows: "The partners are considered to be so close that when one dies, the other will die soon after." A British missionary added in the 1890s, "This covenant gives an absolute guarantee for safety and assistance from the king or chief with whom it is made."[43] In other words, the vanilla workers who entered into this bond expected protection and benefits in return. Raimbault's use of the custom appears to have been more casual and cynical. After mentioning *fatidra* in his letter, he abruptly turned to figures: eight thousand to ten thousand vanilla flowers were now being pollinated each day.[44]

In 1909, Raimbault revealed something else about the profiles of some of his vanilla laborers. Pollination time had come, he wrote his parents: "This delicate work, with which children are usually tasked, needs to be closely overseen." Much the same logic was applied on coffee plantations in other parts of the world, where some tasks were considered especially suited to children. Raimbault's specific motives seem open to interpretation. Did he assign the task to children because they worked for lower wages than adults, or because he believed their little fingers to be nimbler at undertaking the Edmond technique? Either way, he showed no compunction about sharing this detail with his parents. By 1910, he wrote that "the work of pollinating vanilla on our different plots requires much care and personnel: some twenty men, and roughly ten children are running about the vanilla groves from morning to evening marrying the flowers as they open."[45]

To child labor, we should add adult forced labor. In 1927, Raimbault requested exactly 131 *engagés* to work on his many plantations.[46] *Engagé* in this context did not denote South Asian indentured workers, as it did on Réunion. Instead, the designation was hatched by Governor General Joseph Gallieni as a kind of euphemism for and reinvention of prestation labor—work conducted without remuneration at the arbitrary discretion of a French official or in lieu of taxes. It was commonplace in French colonies, but on Madagascar it also built on the precolonial royal Malagasy *fanompoana*, a distinct local form of forced labor from precolonial times. Prior to 1895, *fanompoana* could either serve as a way of paying taxes in kind or involve mandatory military service to the sovereign. Interestingly, the Malagasy monarchy had briefly considered applying it to eastern coast plantations, before opting for outright slavery instead.[47] In the words of Gallieni, this *fanompoana*, now repackaged as *engagisme*, was viewed as necessary on settler plantations so as not to "let the Malagasy fall back into their native laziness and indolence."[48] And Father Raimbault was not about to miss out on unpaid labor, whatever it might be called.

Raimbault's letters also provide insights into some of the weather events that dictated vanilla's boom and bust cycles. In 1910, as drought devastated the vanilla groves, Raimbault listed the many scourges his pods faced on Nosy Be: floods, hurricanes, droughts, and locusts. In 1911, he observed vanilla vines near the ocean being "burned" by the saline breezes. Just a few years later, in 1913, a cyclone "annihilated" the mission's vanilla plants. Different lessons were learned from these incidents: vanilla was moved upland away from the shore, vanilla rows were reoriented to better face the winds, and the mission even decided for a time to privilege "sturdier" coffee over vanilla. But ultimately, vanilla's profits were too good to pass up.[49]

Last but not least, Raimbault's correspondence reveals his business acumen. In October 1910, he wrote his parents, "Right now, I am very much absorbed by a shipment of vanilla—packaging and customs forms. I am sending it to Belgium where prices seem firmer to me, no doubt because of the [Brussels] World Fair. I was warned of a coming price drop for this product, but every year the same thing happens: a drop occurs after the first shipments, but then vanilla prices rise once more." Raimbault must have had a commodity index in his head, not to mention teams of informants. He certainly strategized about when, where, and to whom to ship his vanilla. Interestingly, the following year, he once again sent his vanilla to Belgium, this time to Liège, where unbeknownst to him, Charles Morren had first pollinated the orchid. The letters also show how clearly and swiftly Raimbault grasped shifting market conditions. In 1915, in the midst of World War I, he noted, "I won't make much from vanilla for it is a consumer good to be sure, but a luxury one and this is no time for luxury."[50]

The roaring twenties reversed his fortunes once more, and in July 1920 profits from the mission's plantations were such that Raimbault decided to expand operations to mainland Madagascar.[51] By 1924, Raimbault was no longer writing to his relatives on missionary letterhead but on new stationery that read, "The Missionary Fathers of Nosy-Be [. . .] Colonial products: vanilla, coffee, pepper, ylang-ylang essence."[52] That four-item list was somewhat deceptive, because vanilla remained the star of the show. In the 1920s, the company's vanilla profits stood four times higher than those of the next commodity on the list, coffee.[53] If final proof were needed, it was vanilla beans, rather than pepper or coffee, that Raimbault periodically sent home as a gift to his family and friends, as in November 1930, when he posted five containers of vanilla, preserved in tin cases.[54]

Despite the best efforts of the agricultural workers on Raimbault's plantations, Nosy Be was actually lagging behind new centers of production. By 1900, the hub of vanilla cultivation shifted from Nosy Be and the Tamatave districts to Sava in northeastern Madagascar. There, Betsimisaraka farmers had been embracing and mastering pod production for several years.

Significantly, in the early days of imperial domination, overseas settlers from the Mascarenes and beyond were not the only ones to take up vanilla cultivation. Malagasy people quickly embraced and mastered the exogenous plant. An 1898 table for Vohémar province draws up a list of "crops and farms owned by natives." Several points jump off the page. The first Betsimisaraka vanilla growers hailed largely from the town of Sambava and its vicinity. They practiced cash crop monoculture, rather than dabbling in rubber or coffee, as did the *vazaha* planters—a Malagasy term combining aspects of "outsider" and "white." However, subsistence farming is not shown on the table, so it is likely they also grew plants with which to feed themselves. Four Malagasy vanilla planters are identified by name, which is interesting, given that no Malagasy rice, manioc, or sugar farmers appear in that manner (instead, there is a summary of totals by ethnicity). The French colonial authorities who drew up these tables evidently considered vanilla to be a noble harvest. The document presents the Malagasy vanilla cultivators as follows: "Poly, Malagasy woman, Petifera, Totozafy, and Benasory [Malagasy men]." Of the four, Totozafy owned the largest plantation, spanning two hectares.[55] My conversations with experts in Antalaha's vanilla sector in 2022 suggest that 0.3 hectares is roughly the maximum amount of land on which a single family can cultivate vanilla without having to hire extra help.[56] So these four Malagasy planters must certainly have recruited workers.

Farther south, too, at the head of Antongil Bay, in 1909 an official observed the gradual inroads being made by Malagasy vanilla producers. "Some natives," he wrote with obvious contempt, "have thrown themselves into rich European crops, including vanilla. This crop requires much labor and care, and they have therefore only partially been able to succeed, with roughly twenty hectares in their hands."[57] Colonization was first and foremost an act of dispossession. That said, the percentage of Malagasy-owned vanilla-producing lands would continue to grow after 1910, culminating at 80 percent in 1956, on the eve of independence. That year, out of 3,100 hectares dedicated to vanilla, 2,500 were Malagasy-owned. The trend reveals not so much an effort at colonial reform but rather the increasing popularity of vanilla production among Malagasy people and the emergence of a rural elite around it.[58]

By 1928, the local administrator called vanilla Antalaha's "main crop, and sole preoccupation for European, Asian and Native planters." He added, "Its output seems to be breaking all previous records." The following year, he noted:

> Everyone has started planting vanilla: old and young, women and men, all set about growing vanilla; our colonial subjects would have chopped down the forest if they could have, to grow more vanilla. It is almost as if having a plot of land planted with vanilla confers a noble title; one who does not own one feels dishonored.[59]

As on Réunion, the vanilla fever he described transcended communities, age groups, and genders. The official also draped himself in an environmentalist mantle to condemn the rising vanilla monoculture. However, presenting himself as a champion against "chopping down the forest" was absurd, given that vanilla *needs* a forest.

In addition to Malagasy, Réunionese, mainland French, Mauritian, and American planters, sources point to several Chinese cultivators, preparers, and resellers involved in the vanilla sector early on. One of them, appearing in the records under the name Attave, was born in Hong Kong in 1866 and arrived in Madagascar in 1891. He became owner of a vanilla plantation in Antalaha. His compatriot, Wock-Su, hailing from Canton, landed in Madagascar via Mauritius. He, too, cultivated vanilla in Antalaha, although on a smaller scale. A third Chinese national, named Affocka, born in Hong Kong in 1864, was listed as both the owner of a major vanilla plantation and a representative of the Ah-Thu import-export firm.[60] Many East Asian and South Asian immigrants also served as exporters, operating out of the deeper water port of Tamatave. Sava's vanilla is still expedited there on flat-bottom boats capable of braving Antalaha's treacherous reefs, which continue to gore ships to this day.

Expertise did not come solely from the private sector. At the turn of the twentieth century, some key colonial officials also contributed to the rise of Sava's vanilla. René Jules Edouard Moriceau, an Alsatian-born naval officer who transferred to the Ministry of the Colonies and then spent time as an official in the South Pacific, served as head of the district encompassing

Sava between 1899 and 1901. No vanilla angle was too obscure for the former navy man. In Madagascar, he studied the orchid's host plants, drawing from knowledge of vanilla cultivation in Tahiti and New Caledonia. For instance, he wrote that Sava planters would do well to embrace the following South Pacific technique:

> The finest vanilla groves on Tahiti, where it has achieved considerable development, are always located in natural forests, with vanilla vines growing two meters above ground, on soft woods, such as the *burao* [hibiscus tileaceus], which happens to be very abundant in Madagascar. Vanilla runs along these soft woods, which form a sort of shaded trellis.[61]

Moriceau added that in Madagascar he had "observed numerous vines of wild vanilla in the forest near the ocean." He pondered how the flowers had been pollinated. He also anticipated later attempts to cross-fertilize *Vanilla planifolia* with local varietals, aiming to improve its genetic resistance to disease. Moriceau was a consummately transcolonial expert. As a well-travelled naval official, he alternated between Tahitian and Malagasy techniques, providing linkages and comparisons at an early date. The navy was an institution that, by its very nature, enabled these kinds of lateral vanilla connections.

Finally, Moriceau drew up schemes for vanilla to emerge as more than a "minor crop." He saw it as one day becoming one of Madagascar's chief exports. His enthusiasm was based on local data from Sava: "Prepared vanilla sells in Sambava for 40 francs a kilo. Settlers hope to sell five hundred kilos of it this year for a total of 2,000 francs. They believe they can quintuple that figure next year and then produce 200,000 francs of vanilla by 1901. I sincerely hope so, especially because serious efforts have been undertaken."[62] His broader vision certainly came to pass, although some of his concrete suggestions did not. For example, the *burao* never caught on locally, with everything from banana stalks to nut trees and the local *zatrofa* (also spelled jatropha) being used as hosts plants instead.

Madagascar's vanilla sector thus rested the shoulders of naval experts, Betsimisaraka and Sakalava cultivators, Reunionese preparers, and hyphenated or "bridge" communities, be they Chinese or Mauritian. These different groups within the vanilla franchise formed a complex mosaic and soon accumulated considerable capital. *Vazaha* settlers, some of whom owned massive conglomerated vanilla estates, were turning even more handsome profits. In 1924, at the height of Sava vanilla's golden age, a Tananarive newspaper depicted the French vanilla planter on the Red Island as an upstart:

> You may know Mr. Vanilla. Now that he is rich, he shows off his wealth in the four corners of France; you have probably spotted him at all of Paris's top sites. But you likely never saw him back in the time of his obscurity; he was a little person, tiny in fact. Don't imagine some illiterate worker or mediocre merchant, though. No doubt those make excellent nouveaux riches, but Mr. Vanilla, previously an impoverished cashier, had built up enough pent-up capitalist desires to make the perfect upstart. [...] He began by impressing his old acquaintances. He ended up impressing the whole world. He only regretted that his wife didn't keep the price tags on the dresses she was wearing so that all could see them.[63]

Tananarive's high society evidently enjoyed lampooning vanilla nouveaux riches. If one were to look beyond the stereotypes, it is obvious that there were genuine success stories happening not only in Sava but also beyond. The colonies were often perceived in Europe as a rare means of attaining upward social mobility. And this particular social elevator ran on a combination of vanilla and cheap labor, including coerced, colonized labor.

On balance, when prices permitted, vanilla could be an empowering crop, enabling some Betsimisaraka people on the Sava coast to top up their income or become full-fledged plantation owners. A Betsimisaraka middle class came to thrive thanks to vanilla.[64] However, as we have also seen, there is another side to this story. Dr. Lacaille's dream of exploiting cheap labor on Madagascar proved enduring, as did Father Raimbault's recruitment of children and *corvée* laborers. This was a fixture of many vanilla plantations on the Red Island.

A 1906 report from Nosy Be discusses the Giraud vanilla plantation, which spanned some hundred hectares. Giraud reached out to the administration after having tried in vain to recruit one hundred workers to pollinate vanilla. He persuaded only half that number, and now brought the quandary to a local official, who spelled out the problem as he saw it: "If the flowers are not fecundated on the very day they bloom, they are irremediably lost." Therefore, "not helping Giraud" would lead to "a very compromised vanilla harvest." The official added as a given that "it is public knowledge that the natives of Nosy Be have a repugnance for work in the fields." Instead of providing a decent salary to workers, his solution was to order local subaltern officials, all of them Malagasy, to "recruit all natives who are not working for themselves."[65] In other words, being a vanilla planter oneself was one of the few ways to avoid being rounded up to conduct unpaid vanilla work for settlers.

By 1938, the situation on Nosy Be had not fundamentally changed. If anything, forced labor had been codified. Some of the island's 580 prisoners were sent to work gratis on plantations whose owners "complained of not being able to find free workers." On the main island's Sambirano region, nonincarcerated Malagasy people worked without pay on vanilla plantations to cover the taxes they owed; in 1938, the daily rate of labor to repay tax arrears stood at six francs.[66]

In addition to child labor, tax-remediation labor, and prison labor, many planters relied heavily on female labor. Although local lore suggests that women were hired for vanilla pollination because of their smaller fingers and deft touch, the archives indicate that baser motives were at play. For instance, a report from Maroantsetra province from 1906 reads plainly that "during vanilla fertilization season, growers prefer to call upon female labor which is less expensive."[67]

Power relations on vanilla estates are not always fleshed out in colonial documents. However, a 1903 photo of Mauritian vanilla planter Henri Dupavillon directing a worker in Maroantsetra speaks a thousand words. Dupavillon stands, dressed entirely in white, giving orders with the aid of a stick. His commanding body language is that of an overseer and expert. Meanwhile, the worker, who may possess greater vanilla knowledge and experience, can be seen kneeling at the foot of the vanilla, receiving instructions. He wears a raffia smock, known as *akanjobe*. As for the vanilla, it winds around its host trees in the forest undergrowth. Other sources specify that in 1902, Dupavillon owned thirty hectares of vanilla and cacao plantations. Vanilla was spreading rapidly at Maroantsetra more generally, with two hundred thousand new vines added in under a year.[68] In the absence of information about whether this worker was even paid or data on how many of his colleagues fled or resorted to other "weapons of the weak" on the plantation, we are left with only the determination seen in the eyes of this *akanjobe*-clad man.

By the 1920s, some were giving voice to the grievances of the colonized toiling in vanilla groves. Jean Ralaimongo and Paul Dussac's *L'Opinion de*

FIGURE 10. "Maroantsetra, Dupavillon's vanilla estate, 1903."
Courtesy Muséum d'histoire naturelle, Paris. MS 3131.

Diego-Suarez was a notable newspaper for denouncing colonial abuses. For example, a 1928 article took aim at the *indigénat*, a loose legal ensemble that enabled local officials to arbitrarily detain and punish the colonized.[69] The piece reads as follows:

> Sambirano: We are informed that nearly all inhabitants here, men and women alike, undertake a few years of *indigénat* labor per year. The motives are usually trumped up, the most often natives want to tend to their own vanilla and subsistence cultures, instead of working for settlers who are the administration's favorites, and who promise forty-five francs to women and men working to pollinate vanilla, but actually pay them twenty-five francs.[70]

Thus, by 1928 in this part of northwestern Madagascar, even owning a vanilla grove of one's own provided no protection from being rounded up to conduct unpaid or meagerly paid labor for *vazaha* vanilla planters. Imagine for a moment a Malagasy vanilla producer having to neglect their vines, in their ephemeral flowering phase, to perform the same work on a neighboring *vazaha* estate.

In the face of injustices of this kind, some vanilla workers rebelled or committed acts of sabotage. Suspicious fires broke out in warehouses, where fortunes' worth of pods dried for months in wooden, flammable crates.[71] Others took even more radical action. In 1909, Comorian vanilla workers murdered their Réunionese vanilla overseer, the unfortunately named César (French for Caesar). On one of the Comoros Islands' massive Société Bambao estates, seven vanilla employees grabbed hold of axes used to cut back foliage and turned them on César and his family. The governor's office curtly described the workers' motives as "revenge." Upon closer scrutiny, it would seem that laborers on the Bambao vanilla plantations resented the company's surveillance practices, which César had intensified to satisfy his own superiors. It was probably no coincidence that the company's associate director had just been dispatched to step up discipline on the plantation. In other words, César himself had been under pressure to increase yields. Five of the accused vanilla laborers were sentenced to death.[72]

Other forms of opposition were more explicitly political. Jean Ralaimongo was a leading Malagasy dissident and close friend of Ho Chi Minh, whom he met in Paris. In 1924, Ralaimongo was pulled into local Antalaha conflicts. *Vazaha* planters claimed that Malagasy-produced pods were being poorly prepared. In response, Malagasy laborers threatened to stop working on *vazaha*-owned plantations. The ensuing strike was more specifically aimed at raising the salaries of pickers and pollinators. The island's new governor hatched an improbable way of breaking the labor action by bribing workers to concoct racketeering charges against Ralaimongo. During the trial that followed, many Betsimisaraka vanilla pickers and pollinators spoke up to defend him.

A few months after being exonerated in 1926, Ralaimongo planned to travel to France, with his ticket paid by one of his Antalaha vanilla allies. In exchange for the boat fare, Ralaimongo agreed to work on securing outlets in Europe for the planter's vanilla. The trip was ultimately canceled for unknown reasons. Ralaimongo then conceived a plan to build cooperatives of Malagasy vanilla planters. The idea was to ensure that smaller Malagasy growers would no longer be at the mercy of *vazaha*-owned networks and holding companies.[73] The vanilla cooperatives he championed were reminiscent of vineyard cooperatives in southern France during this same era, which were built on a more egalitarian economic model. The experiment proved short-lived, however, because the Second World War brought an abrupt slowdown to vanilla exports from the great isle.[74]

During World War II, Madagascar suffered much the same fate as Réunion. Following the choice of Madagascar's governor to side with the Vichy regime in 1940, vanilla exports plunged from 376 tons in 1938 to 107 tons in 1943. It took years to overcome the damage wrought by the war. Prior to it, Madagascar and Réunion had combined to export on average an astonishing thirty-five tons of vanilla to the United States per month, compared to Mexico's eight. That state of affairs ended abruptly in late 1940 and throughout 1941, with Madagascar being subjected to a partial British naval blockade. By 1948, the island was still struggling to recover its position as the top vanilla exporter to America.[75] Here, competition once again became a key driving force. After Madagascar was dethroned from its top rank, local authorities scrambled to find new ways to regain it.

At war's end, colonial authorities enlisted scientists to improve *planifolia* yields. Three main goals were spelled out in 1945, all focused on improvements to output and quality. They included "refining the pods' perfume, increasing yields, and fighting efficiently against diseases that attack this delicate orchid." A laboratory located at Ambohitsara, near Antalaha, was called on to achieve these objectives via hybridization. The team began by collecting wild indigenous vanillas. In December 1945, Madagascar's governor launched an even vaster collection campaign "across the French empire and around the world."[76] Such prospecting continued Moriceau's earlier attempts to link vanilla techniques and even graft local nonedible variants onto *planifolia*. In the wake of World War II, Vanilla *planifolia*'s notorious sameness was being stretched in new directions. Crossings with nonedible varietals were once again being undertaken to improve Malagasy *planifolia*'s resistance and reestablish its global dominance.

Soon, a web of laboratories, with Ambohitsara as its headquarters, emerged under the umbrella of the Office de la recherche scientifique coloniale, later renamed the Office de la recherche scientifique et technique outre-mer (ORSTOM). By 1950, the Madagascar laboratories were reporting at least one "satisfying" result with a hybrid vanilla. It came from a 1946 crossing in Anjouan on the Comoros Islands between *Vanilla planifolia* and a local Comorian vanilla known as *Vanilla humblotii*.[77] By 1955, a host of other hybrid varieties were being studied. In 1959, Antalaha's vanilla laboratory requested new specimens from Indonesia, South America, and the Caribbean. The key objective remained increasing the Red Island's output, as the average annual four hundred tons produced by Madagascar the previous few years were now deemed "insufficient."[78]

Madagascar's vanilla gene laboratory network grew out of previous suggestions, including Moriceau's from 1901, that hybridization with local varietals might enhance *Vanilla planifolia*'s resistance to disease, specifically fusarium. That quest continues to this day. In Réunion and Madagascar, I was fortunate enough to visit with CIRAD (Centre de coopération internationale en recherche agronimique pour le développement) scientist Michel Grisoni, who is leading these efforts, as well as working on sequencing vanilla's genome. His hybridizing work draws on an incredibly wide range of vanilla plants, varying from leafless or nearly leafless varietals from dry climes to the thick-stemmed tropical African *Vanilla imperialis*.

In 1960, Madagascar gained independence. Its first president, Philibert Tsiranana, has long been depicted as pro-French, even neocolonial. The archives do point to some carryovers between colonial and postcolonial practices in the vanilla sector. (And more broadly, France did retain influence over elected bodies, the nation's officer school, and other areas.) In one of many continuities, ORSTOM's vanilla laboratories remained active on the island. Moreover, vanilla was still being purchased by Hamburg firms. For instance, in 1969, Aust and Hachmann imported three tons of dried vanilla from Sava's 1967 harvest.[79] Yet, on balance, during his time in power between 1960 and 1972, Tsiranana did not just toe Paris's line. He forged lasting contacts with West Germany, and despite his ardent anticommunism, he even tried to export Madagascar's vanilla to the Soviet Union. On his clock, vanilla's production curve shot upward, making it by far the island's top cash crop.[80] Madagascar was synonymous with vanilla once again. Consider the figures. In 1966, Madagascar's vanilla exports totaled an astonishing 712 metric tons. The next closest competitors were the Comoros Islands—which remained under French control until they gained independence in 1975—with 134 tons, followed by French Polynesia's 110 tons, Indonesia's 90 tons, Réunion's 17 tons, and Mexico's 14 tons. All the world's other producers (Sri Lanka, Uganda, the Seychelles Islands, Mauritius, Tonga, and Costa Rica, most notably) combined for a paltry 20 tons.[81] By this point, Madagascar's overproduction had become a problem, as it pushed down prices. Some Malagasy vanilla reserves had to be destroyed for this reason in 1967. The issue resurfaced in 1972, when tons of excess production could not find a market. In the words of one report from that year, "The situation is preoccupying the government and some twenty exporters, most of them from the Chinese community, and a few Europeans, who have export quotas."[82]

In 1975, Madagascar engaged in a political U-turn. At the height of the Cold War, its new leader, Didier Ratsiraka, sometimes called the Red Admiral, took only a few months to sign an economic agreement with the Soviet Union that elicited anxiety in both Paris and Washington. The accord as presented in the Malagasy press spelled a rapprochement with Russia. Moscow expressed interest in building dams, producing cement, and enhancing Antananarivo's radio emitter. On the list of Madagascar's purchases were electrical generators, mining machines, cranes and port equipment, as well as food-processing and road-building machinery. Madagascar's export side of the ledger begins with "coffee, vanilla, cloves, pepper, rice, peanuts, pine nuts, lima beans, manioc, cotton, tropical fruit."[83] Madagascar's vanilla beans were poised to stream into the USSR to become ingredients in late Soviet ice-cream. However, the island's relationship with the Eastern Bloc did not last, as Ratsiraka shed his Marxist mantle and returned Madagascar to the Western Bloc in the 1980s.

In Sava today, one can identify several vanilla continuities from precolonial and colonial times. Pods still represent an empowering cash crop while also serving as complex markers of the island's relationship with the former imperial power and the West more generally. On good years, in the twenty-first century, vanilla rains cash down twice annually on parts of the otherwise extremely poor island nation. In 2016, Sava vanilla cultivator Cécile Zafy explained that over the previous two years, thanks to vanilla, she had been able to build two houses, buy a motorcycle as well as a sound system, and afford three varied meals a day.[84] However, sudden cash influxes sometimes bring unexpected consequences. Anthropologist Annah Zhu has studied *vola mafana*, or hot money sprees, resulting from vanilla's boom and bust cycles. She explains how abundance around the time the product goes to market has led to stories of vanilla madness. In one extreme example, a vanilla producer allegedly boiled their currency bills—just as one briefly boils vanilla—and ate them as soup, only to be found dead the next day. One of the most revealing and persistent rumors runs as follows: consumers in

Europe and North America use vanilla not as a foodstuff but instead as an explosive or as a component in tires. These ideas are reminiscent of others circulating in northern Madagascar about sapphires going into weapons systems rather than jewelry settings. Such readings are unsurprising given vanilla's cash crop status: Malagasy people sell it to eager intermediaries willing to pay a fortune for pods. The vanilla is then shipped overseas from the port of Antalaha or the airport at Sambava. The finished product in the form of desserts or snacks is seldom seen back in Sava. After all, Zhu's Malagasy interlocutors all pointed out that only *vazaha* consumed vanilla. Cécile Zafy reported the same. Such "fantastical responses" to global capitalism are instructive historically as well.[85] Precolonial and colonial planters did not explain vanilla's endpoint to the local populations they recruited, often forcibly, as pollinators, pickers, and preparers. This may seem hard to reconcile with the incredible breadth of local vanilla knowledge. It highlights how vanilla knowhow was and remains remarkably compartmentalized, with production "franchises" located a world away from consumers.

The story of Madagascar rising to the top of the pod-ium also bridges the eras into which historians have tended to divide the island. Vanilla emerged as a significant crop long before the French invasion of 1895 not only on Nosy Be but also on the eastern coast of the main isle. There, pods empowered local Betsimisaraka people, who made vanilla their own. Within the slim margin available under colonial rule, they became leading specialists of the crop within a single generation. Vanilla vines climbed the dense and diverse forests the Betsimisaraka tended across the Sava district. In fact, vanilla brought into contact the entire Malagasy mosaic: Sakalava and Betsimisaraka farmers, Merina officials, South and East Asian merchants, planters of Mauritian and Réunionese origin, as well as *vazaha* traders, be they American, French, or German. However, Madagascar was not the only Southern Hemisphere island to specialize in vanilla in the wake of Edmond's discovery. Intracolonial networks, both naval and missionary, also brought vanilla and vanilla knowledge from the southwestern Indian Ocean to the French South Pacific. In turn, the region emerged as a serious competitor to Madagascar in the first decades of the twentieth century.

CHAPTER 6

Tahiti's Black Gold

IN 1908, A THIRTY-EIGHT-YEAR-OLD SWISS VANILLA IMPORTER and retailer was found bound, gagged, and murdered in his Paris apartment on the boulevard Voltaire. The victim, Eugène Hänni, had set off to Tahiti in 1894 with the idea of establishing postal services and then profiting from stamp speculation. It was only the year following, on the nearby Leeward Islands, that he became interested in vanilla. There, shortly before departing the South Pacific for good, he noted enviously the fortunes others were making by exporting vanilla. Hänni was drawn to the import side in Europe in 1900, when a compatriot friend on the Polynesian Leeward isle of Huahine sent along some of his pods. A few years on, Hänni placed ads in the Swiss press, vaunting "vanilla imported directly from the colonies." He sold it in packs of ten beans, two hundred grams, or in sample glass tubes containing four pods.[1] By the time of his mysterious murder in 1908, Hänni was selling Polynesian vanilla at his door as well. In fact, that's how his body was discovered: suspicions were aroused when a customer came knocking for vanilla and heard no answer. The police then forced the door. In addition to the body, they found vanilla samples scattered atop the fireplace and on a desk. Many large boxes of vanilla also lay strewn across the floor. Two vanilla brokers, Alexandre Terrien of Nantes and Jean Bechat of Paris, were interviewed by police and cleared of any wrongdoing.[2] The sensationalist press soon seized the story: "Who strangled Father Vanilla?," asked *Le Matin*, using the nickname Hänni's friends had given him. The article mentioned that Hänni had just completed his will and testament; perhaps some of his "vanilla clients"—in quotes, as if vanilla were a front—wanted to settle scores, and he knew his life was in danger? A Belgian past felon named Isodore Vermeire was charged with the crime but later acquitted. The case, worthy of a film noir, remains unsolved.[3]

However, the crime scene itself tells us a great deal about the vanilla Hänni sold. First, he stockpiled pods in his Paris apartment, which doubled as a warehouse. This was no doubt an effort to cut costs, which is easier to do with compact vanilla than with coconuts or mineral ores. Second, his business was conducted at once through brokers in Europe and direct personal Swiss connections in Polynesia. These communities of middlemen were some of the countless cogs operating to promote this fractured, luxury commodity. They implicated Polynesian planters and pod preparers as well as Chinese intermediaries on location in Tahiti, French brokers in Marseille, Paris, and beyond, producers in Taha'a, Huahine, and Tahiti, teams of experts, and a web of smaller actors including Hänni himself, two of the initial suspects in his murder, along with his Swiss contacts. Third, and most important for us, the unfortunate victim had advertised Polynesian vanilla in the vaguest of terms as "coming from the colonies." Here was a sign that he did not wish to draw attention to its specific provenance. Polynesian vanilla was crucially of a third type, neither *planifolia* nor *pompona*. At the time, it faced constant accusations that it was somehow inferior in taste.

Whereas Madagascar and Réunion's vanilla belong to the Mexican *planifolia* varietal, French Polynesia's is unique. Its pods are on average thicker, its leaves far narrower, its aroma distinctive. Its flavor palate provides hints of anise, licorice, and caramel. Former three-star Michelin chef Olivier Roellinger describes Tahitian vanilla as "shorter and thicker, often oilier than the *planifolia* variety, but presenting perhaps a finer aroma."[4] *Vanilla tahitensis*, as it is known, may be a niche varietal, yet it has some avid supporters.

Before we can discuss the polarized views on Tahiti's unique vanilla or the constellation of communities and stakeholders involved in Polynesian pod franchises, we need to answer the question of where the highly distinctive *Vanilla tahitensis* came from. Apart from some basic elements, there is little consensus on the topic among geneticists. They agree that all edible vanilla originated in the Americas and that *Vanilla planifolia* was Tahitian vanilla's mother. Beyond that, it has yet to be determined where and how the hybridization occurred and with what father.[5] In 2008, a team of vanilla biologists found that *Vanilla tahitensis* might present the closest genetic profile to pre-Columbian Mayan vanilla. In their words:

The closest approximation of a pre-Columbian Maya vanilla cultivar may be *Vanilla tahitensis*. Although completely unknown in a wild form, this cultigen may have traded along the Pacific littoral of Mesoamerica after Contact, introduced over the Pacific to the Philippines as the "vanilla of Guatemala" via the Manila Galleon, and finally taken in the mid-nineteenth century from the Philippines to French Polynesia.[6]

The evidence I present here contradicts the historical interpretation of this team's conclusions though not its genetic core. My archival findings rule out the Philippines as a possible point of origin in all the vanilla introductions to Tahiti between 1846 and 1886.

The fact that vanilla arrived in French Polynesia in several waves does not simplify matters. Whereas in Madagascar vanilla schemes preceded colonization, in French Polynesia the reverse occurred, albeit a mere four years after conquest. Given that chronology, a brief discussion of the colonization of Tahiti and the other islands that eventually became French Polynesia seems in order.

Tahiti does present some analogies with Madagascar. The languages spoken on the two islands belong to the same family, for one thing. For another, shortly before conquest by French colonizers, both lands experienced a wave of internal colonization of their own. That process was undertaken by a ruling family that had transformed a series of chiefdoms into a monarchy in the case of Tahiti, and by the Merina kingdom in the case of Madagascar. Prior to first contact with Europeans in the 1760s, Tahitians had conducted regular trade with the Leeward Islands, some ninety miles to the northwest. (Together, the Leeward Islands and Tahiti plus Moorea comprise the Society Islands.) In the words of historian Colin Newberry, there is evidence that "commercial imperialism was [also] indigenous." Besides trading with the Leeward Islands, Tahiti's ruling elites sourced fish and coconut oil from various other local holdings, including Tetiaroa Atoll. Tahiti's ascendant monarchs subsequently grafted their own Pacific imperial ambitions onto those of France and Britain.[7]

Indeed, by the early nineteenth century, Tahiti became the subject of intense international competition between French, British, and American interests. In the 1830s, France alternated between pursuing grandiose Pacific designs and playing spoiler. Some of the key imperatives for the French navy involved countering British ambitions and exacting revenge for the loss

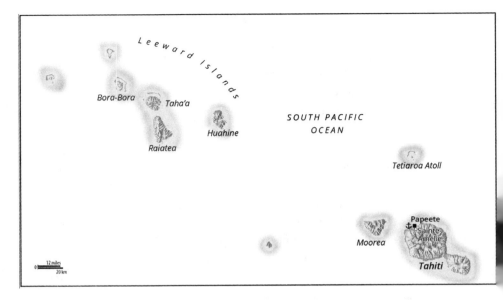

FIGURE 11. The Society Islands, part of French Polynesia.
Map by Isabelle Lewis.

of New Zealand, where French settlement plans had been foiled. But even in the halls of power in Paris, London, and Washington, differing agendas competed. Until 1839, for instance, some within the French naval ministry still favored "competitive coexistence" with other powers in the Pacific. In its minimalist version, external influence could have been limited to using Tahiti as a key rest and provisioning stopover on Asian trade routes. Just a few years later, though, Paris adopted a more aggressive stance, seeking out islands to annex outright. The maximalist option prevailed.

Rival navies were not the only ones with eyes on Tahiti. While Catholic and Protestant missionaries of various nationalities vied to convert Polynesians, and maritime powers descended on the island to replenish their supplies for their transpacific voyages, whale hunters competed for prey in the region's deep blue waters. In fact, finding a port of call for whalers was the reason invoked to justify Admiral Abel Aubert du Petit-Thouars's invasion of the Marquises archipelago and then Tahiti in 1842. Tahiti's Queen Pomare IV initially agreed under duress to a French protectorate, which in principle distinguished between Tahitian control of the land and French "external sovereignty." The next year ushered in formal French colonial rule. However, major insurrections broke out in 1844, led in part by members of Pomare's family and backed by large segments of Tahiti's population.[8] Heated Franco-British discussions ensued regarding control over the Leeward Islands, comprising Raiatea, Taha'a, Bora-Bora and Huahine. Each side buttressed its claims with colonial and missionary readings of Polynesian kingship and chieftaincy. Locally and internationally brokered treaties brought the fighting on Tahiti to an end in 1847, leaving the Leeward Islands independent for a time. However, Tahiti, by far the largest landmass in the area with its 1,042 square kilometers (about 402 square miles), now found itself under French control. In late 1846, the press reported that agriculture on Tahiti had ground to a halt, due to the devastation caused by war and repression. By 1850, the new colonizers were radically changing local landholding by mandating enclosures and implementing compulsory agricultural labor.[9]

As is often the case, the invaders showed little unity of purpose. Some leading officials were of two minds themselves. In 1847, the second governor of French Oceania, Charles Lavaud, explained that he had initially believed Tahiti best suited to becoming a French naval base rather than a colony. The compromise "military settlement" experiment he decided to conduct only "partly succeeded," by his own admission. He blamed French sailors for trying to make a quick fortune and then dashing. Given the lack of "love" these naval settlers showed for the land, in the governor's opinion, only one narrow path remained for Tahiti becoming a prosperous and viable French colony. It involved fostering "important commodities for export." Ending on a more optimistic note, Lavaud concluded that such a path remained open if sufficient resources were invested. Only then could Tahiti become "in these seas what the Isle of France had been in the Indian Ocean."[10] In this vision, vanilla, introduced by a French admiral only ten months earlier, cultivated using knowhow from Réunion, represented a uniquely French tool to compensate for the loss of Mauritius. The South Seas could become France's new Mascarenes.

Tahiti had attracted external interest in part because of its location as a stopover between the Americas and Asia. The story of vanilla's introduction has itself been caught up in that middle ground. Standard genealogies have vanilla first arriving in Tahiti from the Philippines in 1848.[11] However, a box in the French colonial archives contains several critical pieces of evidence to the contrary. Some concern the date of vanilla's arrival in Tahiti, others more crucially its point of origin. In November 1849, naval lieutenant François

Valentin Petit, at the helm of Tahiti's horticultural services, revealed that Admiral Ferdinand Hamelin had brought vanilla from Mexico to Tahiti in December 1846.[12] Another document in the same file gives an identical provenance, adding that the vanilla in question had flowered by 1850 and then thrived in Papeete's "government's garden." That source specifies that "subsequently, Rear-Admiral Bonnard sent more vanilla plants [to Tahiti] from Paris, but they did not surpass in quality those brought aboard the *Virginie*."[13] One more document, a table signed by naval pharmacist Georges Cuzent, dated January 1857, shows the two arrivals of vanilla on Tahiti. It records the dual introductions as follows: "*Vanilla aromatica*, from Mexico, 1846 by Admiral Hamelin; *Vanilla planifolia*, from Manila, 1850 by Admiral Bonnard." However, this Manila connection must have been an error. Indeed, in the very same carton, we are fortunate to have the detailed seed and cuttings manifest from the 1850 crossing to Tahiti organized by Admiral Bonnard. The vanilla on board the *Thisbé* is listed as having originated in Paris's National Museum of Natural History. And to reach Tahiti, the *Thisbé* sailed around Cape Horn, not through the Singapore Straits.[14] Clearly, vanilla first reached Tahiti from Mexico in 1846 on board the *Virginie*, and not from the Philippines in 1848 as has been commonly held. Naval and press records confirm this: In December 1846, Hamelin took the *Virginie* eastward to California (which still belonged to Mexico), not westward to the Philippines.[15] Seven years after the fact, Cuzent got it wrong. And Cuzent's version, taken up by one publication and website after another, became doxa.

Add to this the fact that the *Vanilla aromatica* varietal Cuzent listed is no longer accepted as a botanical category, having been conflated with *Vanilla planifolia*, and the plot thickens.[16] How and when did Polynesia's vanilla become *tahitensis*? For hybridization to have happened in situ, another varietal and a common pollinator to both would have had to be present on location, or a deliberate, complex hybridization project would have had to be carried out. The latter seems improbable, as there is no mention of one in the archives and botanists place the first human-created orchid hybrid in 1856. With those options highly unlikely, we must assume that *tahitensis* came to the island from outside. Ascertaining that the Americas are where Tahitian vanilla originated is one thing, understanding how, when, and where *Vanilla tahitensis* came into being is quite another. The most likely scenario would be that either Hamelin's or Bonnard's vanilla was *tahitensis*. The fact that scientists have recently uncovered a reverse parentage version of *Tahitensis*, with *planifolia* as the father rather than the mother, in the rainforests of Colombia, close to the Pacific coast, reinforces the Hamelin hypothesis. Indeed, Bonnard's specimen came from Paris and was almost certainly *planifolia* (Parisian botanists would have noticed the distinctive flower of *tahitensis*), while Hamelin's vessel was last seen sailing southward along the coast of Mexico in 1846. In the words of Alan Chambers, lead author of the scientific study in question, his team's findings "further support the hypothesis that *Vanilla tahitensis* is the result of a natural, although rare, hybridization event between species with overlapping native ranges."[17] The weight of evidence thus supports the idea that *tahitensis* did not emerge on location but was brought to the islands from the Americas.

Lieutenant Petit provided other key details in his reports. They show previous French techniques quickly reaching Polynesia and point to new experimentations on location. In 1849, Petit wrote, "The vanilla is growing well and looks like it will be productive. It has been planted in all different parts of the island so as to determine where it will thrive."[18] This mirrors the practice utilized on Bourbon a few decades prior: precious cuttings were scattered across the island's microclimates at various altitudes and shores to increase the chances of success. Therefore, in some respects, vanilla's military champions were applying earlier lessons. There is also substantial evidence of new experimentation being undertaken in Tahiti, which was shared across French colonial networks, within the ranks of the navy, and beyond. A November 1850 report lists all agricultural efforts conducted at Papeete since the French invasion. In the vanilla column, one reads, "Twenty meters of vanilla, led along ropes, a method that allows us to follow pollination, have been set up at the foot of trees of medium height. Four vanillas are flowering at present. This method of cultivation is probably unique."[19] To my knowledge, the rope method is no longer used along tree hosts. That said, having witnessed the stretching, tiptoeing, and crouching involved in pollinating vanilla, whether it's a few inches off the ground or halfway up a tree trunk, I certainly understand the appeal of leading vanilla along trellises of uniform height. All this further suggests how much vanilla mattered in key naval circles whose influence reached the very top of France's colonial project. Indeed, in France, the Ministry of the Navy was twinned with the Ministry of the Colonies until 1889.

Lieutenant Petit's split identity as a member of Paris's horticultural society as well as an officer of the first naval infantry regiment should therefore not come as a surprise. The French navy presented his horticultural mission to the South Pacific as "being useful to bringing prosperity to our holdings in this region."[20] Petit himself ascribed a more specific purpose to his undertakings: "To the natives as well [my horticulture] has had the effect I had hoped; for after having carefully examined the work I was undertaking, and the results I obtained every day, they were able to appreciate all the benefits they could gain from it. Several of them went to work and [. . .] began selling the product of their labor."[21] Tahiti in the 1850s thus witnessed multiple transfers of vanilla knowledge. Officials at the government's small garden in Papeete at once conducted their own experiments and set about "converting" Polynesians to vanilla planting.

The navy remained deeply implicated in the cultivation of Tahitian vanilla. In the 1850s, naval vice commissioner Honoré Trastour established a vanilla grove at Sainte-Amélie, just outside Papeete. His 1858–59 harvest yielded fifteen pounds of pods. Trastour boasted that its "delicious aromas are at the least the equal of the best vanillas from the Americas." He foretold bright prospects for vanilla: "After sugar, no culture is promised a more brilliant future than vanilla." He even offered to hand out vanilla cuttings to prospective planters, so long as they took him to the site of their future groves so that he might dispense the best advice.[22]

The clergy soon matched and even surpassed the French navy's role in promoting Tahitian vanilla. For although there was little unity of purpose to the process of colonizing Tahiti, naval, religious, and civilian authorities were able to coalesce around the seemingly fantastical scheme of making the island a major pod producer. Monsignor Florentin-Etienne Jaussen, Tahiti's apostolic vicar (and titular bishop of Axieri), was at the center of these schemes. Born in Ardèche in 1815, the year of the Battle of Waterloo, Jaussen entered the priesthood in 1840. After three years spent in Chile, he was posted to Tahiti in 1849. His interests there proved to be sweeping: he sought to build a cathedral in Papeete and proselytize among Polynesians, of course, but he also established an acclimatization garden that rivaled the government's and closely studied enigmatic tablets found on Easter Island. Now, in 1860, he formulated a surprising suggestion: he urged the naval ministry to introduce vanilla to Tahiti.[23] Given that vanilla had reached the isle in December 1846, I initially took this to mean that Jaussen was somehow out of touch, fourteen years behind the times. But another sentence from Jaussen's hand, preserved in Rome, proves otherwise. It is part of a seemingly incongruous to-do list of "good measures to adopt," which he drafted between 1860 and 1863. Fourth on this list of ten, long before "banning divorce" and "establishing strict morality," one finds "introduce true vanilla, the only luxury crop that poor settlers and lazy natives alike can undertake."[24] Beyond the aspersions directed at local people, this means that Jaussen thought little of vanilla on location, so much so that he did not consider it "true vanilla." And that strongly suggests that the vanilla on Tahiti, introduced in 1846, was the Mayan-descendant *Vanilla tahitensis*. This would explain Jaussen's dismissal of it as inferior, for *tahitensis* has been the object of constant criticism.

Jaussen followed up on his plan. One note in his archives describes eight different species of vanilla, most of which have since been incorporated into other taxonomies. Another undated note from his hand reads "correct type of vanilla = Micentella." Micentella probably refers to the Mexican town of Misantla.[25] Below that, the bishop listed three different methods of preparation, without any further detail: Misantla's, Tentilla's, and "Jicáltepec, French," referring to the French community's vanilla plantations in that coastal region of Mexico. In 1886, the bishop received a letter from a scientist whom he had previously contacted regarding vanilla. He, in turn, connected Jaussen with prizewinning gardener Désiré Fleureau, who was "tasked" with bringing the bishop a case containing multiple types of vanilla—including "samples from different packets"—raising the possibility that some might have been non-*planifolia*.[26] Just like the unfortunate Hänni decades later, Jaussen mobilized an entire vanilla team, including a gardener, a botanist, a range of informants, a squad dispatched on a mission to Mexico, and part of the Church hierarchy.

All of this points to the fact that Jaussen was orchestrating another introduction of vanilla to Tahiti from Central America, one based on deep research and extensive sampling. When it occurred and which varietal it involved are points on which the sources remain frustratingly silent. One intriguing but remote possibility is that the bishop's quest for "real" vanilla may have brought Tahiti a descendent of Mayan vanilla. After all, of the many missions we have followed, only Jaussen's explicitly referenced new bioprospecting in Central America. Then again, Jaussen's initial quip about "real vanilla" is itself compelling evidence that *tahitensis* came to Tahiti in 1846 with Hamelin.

The Roman Catholic Church did not limit itself to trying to improve the quality of Tahiti's vanilla. In lockstep with the colonial administration—a local alliance partly compelled by Protestantism's sway in the area—the Church also sought to step up production. In 1864, the governor of French Oceania wrote to Monsignor Jaussen. The islands under French control witnessed ferocious competition between Catholic and Protestant missionary orders. The governor now tried to put that tension to productive use, getting the rival orders to race to convert Polynesians to agriculture, so as to "steer them away from idleness." Although officially committed to "equal balance" between Catholics and Protestants, the governor saw no reason why he could not "grant certain favors to those who succeed at educating and professionally instructing the natives." The winning orders would take home both cash and honorific rewards.[27] Vanilla cultivation was being incentivized. But it wasn't cultivated only to satisfy colonial government demands. An 1885 letter from a Spiritan missionary shows one Father Nicolas Blanc turning profits from vanilla the previous year.[28]

There are also isolated signs that demand for Tahitian vanilla emerged spontaneously from British, American, and German firms. On the last day of 1854, the New Zealand–based Hort brothers put out an ad in the Tahitian press, announcing that they were keen to buy "any vanilla" that might be available.[29]

International corporations evidently had their eyes riveted on this new source of pods. This only reinforced the administration's idée fixe that vanilla could reap profits and perhaps even transform Tahiti into a new Mauritius. In 1862, the colonial authorities in Papeete decided to invest in vanilla, earmarking 5,000 francs to support the creation of new groves.[30] Just as the Ministry of the Colonies and local Réunionese authorities had championed the plan to dethrone Mexico, so did initial state investment matter deeply in the Polynesian case. The results were close to immediate, as much as vanilla's nine-month gestation allowed. By 1864, vanilla was appearing on Tahitian customs ledgers, albeit in modest quantities. The first quarter of that year saw a mere five kilos of vanilla exported for 400 francs, the second quarter another five kilos. By the third quarter of 1864, vanilla exports leapt to seventy-six kilos, for 5,350 francs. In the final quarter, Tahiti exported ninety-five kilos of vanilla, for a total of 9,350 francs. The island's main exports remained coconut oil, oranges, lemons, and mother-of-pearl, but vanilla had found its way to the list.[31]

The following year, a Tahitian newspaper announced that Réunionese planter David de Floris's 1860 article and pamphlet *Notice sur la culture du vanillier* was available at the periodical's headquarters, for the price of twenty-five centimes. A copy even shows up in the collections of Monsignor Jaussen. The pamphlet, which recognized Edmond Albius as the discoverer of vanilla's artificial pollination, also taught readers how to select host trees, tend to the vines, maintain the correct light-to-shade ratio, prepare the pods, and package them. In other words, this eight-page document was highly practical. The fact that it was sold in Papeete demonstrates how vanilla knowledge voyaged along French colonial circuits, from the Indian to the Pacific Oceans.[32]

Over the next two decades, Tahitian vanilla's production began rising, from 350 kilos in 1882 to 8,431 kilos in 1885. A US consular report from the vanilla-importing port of Bordeaux in 1888 showed Tahitian vanilla jockeying for second place in the French colonial world, well behind Réunion's 164 metric tons in 1886 but neck and neck with Sainte-Marie off the eastern coast of Madagascar and Guadeloupe in the Caribbean.[33] Two decades later, Tahiti would dethrone them all to become by far the world's largest vanilla producer for a time. Tahitian vanilla took off in the 1890s, precisely as two of French Polynesia's other exports, cotton and oranges, collapsed. In 1892, Tahiti exported 11.6 metric tons of vanilla, compared to 1.2 metric tons in 1883.[34]

To the Europeans who introduced vanilla to the South Pacific, it may have provided some grand pathway to Tahiti becoming a new Mauritius. However, for local Polynesians who quickly made the new crop their own, vanilla allowed entry into a global franchise venture. White settler domination over the Tahitian vanilla sector broke between roughly 1880 and 1900, when the crop started to take the form of "microproperty" Polynesian cultivation.[35] An 1894 British report described the "native mode" of vanilla cultivation in the following terms: "[It] is, as a rule, simply to plant the cuttings of the vine under the shade of trees, and then to leave them to grow and twine round supports as best they can. Occasionally attention is paid to keep the vines trained round the trees and to prevent them from attaining a greater height than 9 feet, so that during the inoculating season the flowers may be reached without difficulty."[36] Once again, the question of ease of reach came up. It is clear from these observations that the 1850 naval practice of stringing vanilla horizontally was no longer being used. Instead, according to this source, Polynesian planters tended to loop vanilla vines downward so that they did not climb all the way up tree trunks and make it difficult to reach flowers and pods alike.

Tahitian vanilla was by now generating wealth on-site. As in Madagascar, local peoples swiftly mastered vanilla production and preparation. Vanilla was certainly not the only exogenous crop to thrive in this way, although unlike breadfruit, which had been introduced by Polynesians themselves, vanilla was brought in on the invaders' ships.[37]

Vanilla gained favor across all segments of French Polynesian society. As grand chief of Papara, Tati Salmon was an important member of Tahiti's ruling class. In addition to producing pods, Salmon exported oranges to New Zealand and provided cotton to a German firm and sugar to an American one. Salmon was also an English speaker who learned the language while growing up with his paternal grandparents in Hastings. (This English connection had made him a British subject before he acquired French nationality in 1880.) He befriended several American and British tourists of note, including novelist Robert Louis Stevenson and historian Henry Adams, whom he regaled with local histories and tales. His letters to Adams have survived. Vanilla first appears in their correspondence in November 1892, in the form of a gift. (We saw Father Raimbault of Nosy Be doing the same.) That month, as he passed through San Francisco, Salmon left two packages of vanilla, one bound for Adams in Boston, the other for a mutual New Englander friend.[38] These modest parcels followed Polynesian vanilla's well-trodden path to market, via the port of San Francisco. That said, Tahiti to San Francisco was no marine highway. As late as 1899, Salmon bemoaned that a regular and reliable shipping line to California had yet to be established. He blamed Paris for blocking such plans, presumably over fears of French Polynesia growing too close to the United States.[39]

In 1893, Salmon turned from giving vanilla as a gift to exploring its production. He reported that the vanilla harvest lay ahead of him. He added that he knew his situation "would never allow him to become rich." The following year, he explained why: Revenue from his crops, be they oranges, sugar, or vanilla, paid off his mounting debt to a Hamburg firm, the Société Commerciale de l'Océanie (SCO).[40] A few months later, he railed against the German company, raising the prospect of personal bankruptcy and its accompanying "dishonor."[41] Indeed, SCO records confirm that Salmon, who had once ranked among Tahiti's largest landholders in the 1880s, grew increasingly indebted to the Hamburg firm between 1895 and 1900 (partly due to his poor investments, adds historian Claus Gossler). Several historians have analyzed the practices of the SCO, which was founded in Hamburg in

1876 and arrived in French Polynesia that same year. At its zenith, the firm controlled half of French Polynesia's exports and imports, not to mention Tati Salmon's mortgage. It was without question "the dominant trading organization in French Oceania."[42]

In 1895, Salmon returned to the topic of vanilla, this time expressing his hope of finding a way to reduce his debts to the SCO. He worried about falling sugar prices and noted that his "coffee and vanilla plantations will begin to earn a profit next year." As for the future of Tahitian vanilla, Salmon mused, "Only time will tell." But one thing was certain: There was suddenly "heavy demand" for the two commodities, not just in San Francisco but across Europe as well. In 1904, a disillusioned Salmon brought up vanilla's volatility. In January of that year, vanilla had sold for five francs a kilo. The following month, it went for half that. At that rate, it was "hardly worth planting," he griped. Two years later, Salmon blamed wages, not prices. With the current cost of labor, he wrote, vanilla simply cannot be grown: "Some natives continue to cultivate it [...] but they won't last long."[43] The larger problems that Salmon detailed had less to do with pods and more to do with cycles of indebtedness and the SCO's near monopoly in an insular setting.

As in Madagascar, one can identify two stages to vanilla's takeoff in Polynesia. After having been initially promoted by state officials, naval authorities, botanists, entrepreneurs, and especially missionaries, vanilla next brought into contact established elites, local farmers, and outsiders. Some of the latter were fleeting stakeholders. Polynesian vanilla captured the attention of short-term visitors, who were enraptured by Tahiti's emerging exotic, erotic, and idyllic mystique.[44] During his first stay in Tahiti (1891-93), famed fauvist artist Paul Gauguin sketched a vanilla vine in all its zigzagging splendor. The artist scrawled the word *vanille* alongside the plant, a possible sign that he was not previously familiar with it. The vine appears alone in Gauguin's sketchbook, yet it was necessarily climbing some host plant. In this charcoal rendition, only the vanilla remains, as a minimalist tribute to the edible orchid. It discernibly bears three or four pods. The drawing appears in the right sidebar of a sketch of a Polynesian performing agricultural work. The vanilla is boxed out from the portrait, as if to be stashed for further inspiration. It might have been a preliminary sketch for a background detail of his 1891 painting *Dans la vanillère, homme et cheval* (In the vanilla grove, man and horse). That title is deceptive, as vanilla plays a minor role in the setting.

FIGURE 12. Detail from Paul Gauguin's sketchbook.
WBC ART / Alamy Stock Photo.

Gauguin wasn't done with vanilla. After a two-year hiatus in France (1893–95), the painter returned to Tahiti. Over the course of that second stay, his vanilla ambitions appear far more revealing, albeit unrealistic. The artist had by then sunk into addictions to morphine and alcohol. Moreover, in the words of Devika Ponnambalam, he had "taken up with several Tahitian girls, who'd become his 'muses,' lovers and unofficial wives."[45] By May 1897, when he wrote to his fellow painter and collector Georges-Daniel de Monfreid, Gauguin was short on funds and had just taken out a loan. His planned way out of insolvency involved a vanilla plantation. He explained, "If my health allows it, and I still have a few funds left to spend, I plan on planting vanilla, which has a good cost-benefit ratio, without requiring too much labor." Gauguin was misinformed about vanilla being easy work. Of course, the project came to naught, and a year later the artist complained to the same friend that "he could not get even a centime's credit from the local Chinese [store] to buy bread." Although Gauguin's vanilla groves never materialized, the fact that he floated the plan sheds light on vanilla's reputation as a possible lifeline for colonials who were at risk of sinking into a "poor white" status that threatened the very existence of colonialism. Vanilla continued to be associated with quick money, rapid social ascension, and, for Gauguin, hopes for a second chance. By 1900, however, a disillusioned Gauguin took stock of vanilla's limitations, in particular its requirements for undergrowth.[46] Vanilla proved harder to produce than he had first assumed, and he soon realized it was neither a lifeline nor a line of credit. While vanilla remained a chimera for Gauguin, other outsiders in the same era used it as an allegory to paint a grim portrait of imperial conduct.

Also sailing the South Seas in this era was Scottish writer Robert Louis Stevenson. His relationship to vanilla tells a rather different story, insofar as he was largely interested in scandals tied to extraction and colonial mistreatment. His unfinished novel *Sophia Scarlet* features a vanilla magnate as one of its main characters. It is a story of labor abuses, land dispossession, and violence on a South Pacific vanilla plantation. Around the plantation's decadent table sit a Frenchman, a Briton, and a German, "all of more or less military cast."[47] Stevenson was more familiar with Samoa than Tahiti, but there is much evidence to suggest that the inspiration for his vanilla estate was indeed Tahitian. In an October 1894 letter to British literary critic Sidney Colvin, Stevenson wrote of *Sophia Scarlet*, "It is a *regular novel*, heroine and hero, and false accusation, and love and marriage, and all the rest of it—all planted in a big South Sea plantation run by ex-English officers—à la Stewart's plantation in Tahiti."[48] Here Stevenson referred to the notorious Terre Eugénie plantation at Atimaono, Tahiti, established by fellow Scot, William Stewart. Stewart introduced 1,018 laborers from China to work in the expansive fields of his Tahiti Cotton and Coffee Plantation Company. The Eugénie estate, named in honor of Napoleon III's wife, was founded in 1862, as entrepreneurs moved to satisfy demand from European cotton importers desperate for new providers as the US Civil War raged. However, after the Union prevailed in 1865, Stewart's plantation faced financial struggles and public relations problems. Articles regularly accused Stewart of slavery-like practices; he was even caught redhanded purchasing a boatload of Arorae people from the Gilbert Islands, who refused to be taken into slavery and resisted. The main point for our purposes, however, is that Stewart's lands grew cotton, coffee, and even sugarcane but not vanilla, which tended to be cultivated locally on smaller, privately owned plots.

So why did the author of *Treasure Island* use his literary license to change crops? At a basic level, it is revealing that Stevenson would have turned to a Tahitian vanilla estate as a canvass in the early 1890s, when vanilla had only been introduced to Polynesia some fifty years prior. As for the details, the mention of the German, British, and French military personnel suggests that Stevenson grasped at once vanilla's cosmopolitanism and the French navy's interest in it, not to mention the lure of vanilla wealth. Yet the fit remains imperfect, as vanilla did not lend itself to Eugénie's economies of scale. A more cynical reading runs as follows: Stevenson may have decided to substitute vanilla for cotton to lend a vaguely South Seas aftertaste to a novel the author himself described as having an "*Uncle Tom's Cabin* flavor."[49]

So far, I have discussed vanilla on the main isle of Tahiti. The island's status, as well as its relationship with the rest of what would become French Polynesia, evolved significantly in the second half of the nineteenth century. In 1880, after the death of King Pomare V, France formally annexed Tahiti. By 1886, liquid lines were being drawn between South Pacific isles that call to mind the carving up of Africa, except that this particular cast of colonizing nations included the United States, Germany, Britain, and France. At that juncture, the westernmost of the Society Islands—Huahine, Raiatea, Taha'a, and Bora-Bora—retained independence.[50] However, in 1895, France zeroed in on those four. In January 1897, Gauguin noted the arrival of an expeditionary force from New Caledonia along with the warship *L'Aube*, all dispatched, in his words, to "take the Leeward Islands by force, [they which] had refused to be part of the [1842] annexation of Tahiti."[51] Indeed, in March 1898, Paris seized the isles in question.

The diffusion of vanilla to those islands is a key point given that today vanilla has nearly disappeared from Tahiti proper (its point of first contact) and grows predominantly in the western Society Islands of Taha'a, Raiatea, and Huahine. In 1863, one finds signs of vanilla growing on Moorea, located some twenty-eight kilometers (17.4 miles) from Tahiti.[52] Then, in 1899, a source reported that vanilla was "progressing in Tahiti, Moorea, and the Leeward islands," the latter having just been annexed by France.[53] This squares with historian Pierre-Yves Toullelan's two-stage chronology: after 1900, the focus of cultivation of many crops in Polynesia, including vanilla and coconuts, shifted from Tahiti to the archipelagos. By 1918, the Leeward isles had become major pod producers. That year, Taha'a and Raiatea, which are twinned insomuch as they share a reef, combined for fifty-one tons of prepared vanilla, Huahine twenty-five tons, and Bora-Bora ten tons.[54]

Island-to-island diffusion continued, unabated, even across colossal distances. Although it is part of French Polynesia, the remote Gambier archipelago sits some 1,600 kilometers (994 miles) southwest from Tahiti, well on the way to Chile. In 1929, its lead administrator reported the following: "The cultivation of vanilla, begun back when this product fetched high prices, seemed to be giving positive results; but the day when prices tumbled, the natives neglected their plantations, so much so that some are now fallow."[55] Although he did not specify when vanilla cultivation had begun on the Gambiers, the official did raise the interesting point that vanilla ebbed and flowed. Indeed, vines can be left unattended for decades in forests and then be recultivated. Since 2011, a Polynesian couple on Akamaru Island on the Gambiers have taken up vanilla production once more. The fact that they had to turn to the internet to learn cultivation and preparation techniques on an island where most of the population now raises pearls suggests that Gambier vanilla dormancy must have lasted several generations. This long break shattered any chance for oral transmission of vanilla knowhow.[56]

The 1910–11 vanilla harvest rankings marked Polynesian vanilla's first apogee. That year, it outperformed all other vanilla producers with 250 metric tons. Next came Mexico, which rebounded with 135 tons, Madagascar (including the Comoros) with 110 tons, and Réunion with 46 tons. Emerging smaller players, rounded out the list, including the Seychelles Islands with 22 tons, Java and Ceylon with 10 tons apiece, Guadeloupe with 9 tons, Fiji with 5, and Mauritius with 2 tons.[57] For a short span, Tahiti achieved the top global vanilla ranking, bracketed between Réunion's past dominance and Madagascar's ascendancy.

Despite Tahiti's meteoric rise on the vanilla charts, insecurities abounded. For decades, some had claimed that Polynesia's vanilla was somehow inferior, its pods less flavorful or aromatic than Réunionese or Mexican *Vanilla planifolia*. In 1879, a commission tasked with inspecting Tahiti's agricultural products concluded that nearly all the vanillas it sampled "leave a great deal to be desired in their preparation."[58] In 1883, Parisian buyers charged that recently arrived Tahitian pods were "lacking in perfume."[59] That same year, a journalist traveled to San Francisco to investigate how Tahitian vanilla was regarded in that key port city. He interviewed vanilla importers and chocolatiers alike. Prominent among the latter would have been Domenico Ghirardelli and Etienne Guittard, European chocolate manufacturers who arrived in Northern California during the Gold Rush. All agreed: Mexican vanilla was far superior. Some invoked Tahitian vanilla's supposed flatness. The journalist himself noted that Mexican vanilla sold in "much smaller packs" of twenty-five to thirty beans. He added by way of praise that these Mexican pods were "cylindrical and dry as wood, pencil shaped."[60]

Tastes evolve, as do preservation techniques, but certainly "dry as wood" is no selling point for vanilla beans at present. This speaks to shifting conventions around vanilla consumption. These sets of "self-evident rules that everyone submits to without reflecting" concern all consumer goods.[61] In the case of vanilla in the late nineteenth century, conventions were beginning to govern luster, texture, container shapes, as well as flavor and aroma. Texture shifts are not altogether surprising, insofar as they are dictated by preparation techniques, particularly the water-shedding drying phase. At the time, a dryer pod probably served to extend the product's shelf life.

Some of these conventions lay at the heart of the challenge facing Tahitian vanilla. Negative press toward *tahitensis* endured and even intensified.[62] In 1895, local authorities sought to understand the "lack of appreciation" for Tahitian vanilla abroad. They concluded that "defective preparation" was the crux of the problem and published a bilingual French-Polynesian pamphlet outlining best practices. The detailed instructions appear to be based on knowhow learned on Réunion. The pamphlet chastised locals for the "rudimentary" methods they used in vanilla preparation. It squarely blamed producers in Tahiti for the fact that their pods were selling three to four times cheaper than the competition.[63] By 1903, Tahitian vanilla was going unsold, piling up in hangers in Hamburg and San Francisco. Word on the street was that it smelled of heliotrope, a flowering plant reputed to smell like ... vanilla.[64] In 1912, Singapore Botanic Gardens Director Henry Ridley summarized the claims against Tahitian vanilla as follows: "The vanilla of Tahiti resembles that of *Vanilla pompona*, *vanillons*, in having a flavor of heliotrope or piperonal, which makes it unsuitable for high-class confectionary, and it is therefore used chiefly for perfumery."[65]

Even when the French South Pacific experienced its vanilla boom, a cloud of negativity continued to hover over its pods. In 1912, two French vanilla experts noted snidely, "Tahiti is currently the first producer of vanilla at least in quantity, if not in quality." They then pronounced it "inferior" to the vanilla of both Réunion and Mexico. Interestingly, these authors, Désiré Bois and his colleague Julien Constantin, were also some of the first to posit Tahitian vanilla's uniqueness, although in their opinion it remained a subcategory of *planifolia*.[66] They were not alone in heaping scorn on Tahiti's orchid, for the markets did much the same. In July 1914, Tahitian vanilla sold for twenty-three or twenty-four francs a kilo, versus twenty-seven to thirty-five francs a kilo for Réunionese vanilla, and forty to seventy francs a kilo for Mexican vanilla.[67] By 1920, Tahitian vanilla's reputation had not recovered. In fact, that year, one source reported that "all inferior or spoiled vanillas are now sold under the denomination 'Tahitian.'"[68]

Who or what was to blame? In 1904, Charles Chalot, a leading botanist from Jardin Colonial in Nogent-sur-Marne (founded in 1899), and a former director of the experimental gardens in Libreville, Gabon, was sent to Tahiti by the French Ministry of the Colonies. His mission involved determining the reasons for the "inferiority" of the island's pods. Did it have to do with preparation or cultivation? In 1908, an agricultural inspector compiled a list of guilty parties: "The main causes for denigration of Tahiti's vanilla seems to reside in a very defective preparation process and a seemingly near total ignorance of the rules drawn up in Réunion, for instance." The head of the Jardin Colonial concurred, identifying three problems: "defective cultivation methods, hurried harvesting, and poor preparation."[69]

The obvious answer to improving the quality of Polynesian pods seemed to involve greater oversight over the picking, preparing, and packing processes. A series of new laws accomplished just that. The first, in 1910, cracked down on the selling of green, unprepared vanilla. The accompanying texts make clear that this measure targeted ethnic Chinese vanilla buyers, who were suspected of being at the root of Tahitian vanilla's shoddy reputation. The next law, drafted the following year, ensured that all vanilla exported from Polynesia underwent strict quality-control tests.[70]

However, some worried that these measures might prove counterproductive. One immediate and practical concern involved duration of transport. Already in May 1911, a lobby group known as the French Colonial Union noted that from January to April 1911, a mere one and a half metric tons of Tahitian vanilla had been shipped to France, compared to eighty metric tons to San Francisco. The reason for the imbalance was simple: the crossing to California took only twelve days, as opposed to the two months necessary to reach France. Over the course of sixty days, the pods could "ferment," and

French buyers mindful of the new quality regulations preferred to source their vanilla elsewhere.[71]

In January 1911, Governor of French Polynesia Adrien Bonhoure led the charge against the new legislation on other grounds. He wrote to the ministry in Paris that the new rules would "deal a blow to both the cultivation and export of vanilla," thereby killing the hen with the golden egg. He explained that in the past few years:

> The vanilla business had become one of the most flourishing branches of the colony's commerce. The preparation improved so much that 200 tons of vanilla were exported last year, while never before had we surpassed the figure of 125 tons. This represented a considerable resource for Tahiti. I should add that all the Indigenous planters took the habit of handing over the preparation of their [green] vanilla to the Chinese small merchants, who bought it from them on the spot. And it's precisely the Chinese vanilla preparers whom this measure seeks to target and see disappear. Only, who would replace them? [. . .] I cannot figure it out.[72]

That same month, an anonymous letter from Tahiti reached Paris, protesting the new measures. "The Chinese community's inveterate enemies have reached their objective, to the great detriment of the colony's overall interests," thundered the complainant. It went on to explain that local Chinese traders possessed immense vanilla knowhow and had recently introduced improvements in pod processing. Finally, this community enjoyed countless global connections; would Tahitian vanilla ever sell as well without them?[73]

In 1912, Tahiti's Chamber of Commerce took up the matter of vanilla quality once again. One speaker opined that he was tired of hearing of Tahitian vanilla's supposed inferiority. Tahiti's pods were every bit the equal of any others, he insisted. If consumers did not appreciate Tahitian vanilla, it was because of "the complete manipulation [our vanilla] undergoes in America and especially in Germany." The Germans, he claimed, "transform it by artificially inducing *givre*." (The manipulation of Tahitian vanilla in Germany was described more harshly by a British source in 1905: "Vanillin is now being used in Hamburg to improve the flavor of the cheap vanilla produced in Tahiti.") The Chamber of Commerce speaker theorized that German tampering explained why "our vanilla is universally underappreciated." However, two of the speaker's peers identified other culprits, closer to home. Polynesians, they contended in a blanket assertion, continued to pick vanilla before it was ripe. As for "Chinese vanilla preparers," they asserted that this group remained in business despite being indirectly targeted by the 1910 law. Their work allegedly continued to be shoddy. These two members of the Chamber of Commerce concluded by blaming the colonial administration for granting vanilla-preparing licenses to Chinese individuals in the first place and not enforcing new 1911 vanilla measures.[74]

In other words, matters of "poor preparation" and "picking unripe vanilla" were all code words used to attack a perceived Chinese stranglehold over the local vanilla business. In 1911, the US consul in Papeete reported the new rules to Washington in the plainest of terms:

> The Chinese are quite numerous here, and are rapidly becoming the sole shippers of vanilla, in this way: the native, who still prefers the indolent carefree life of past ages, but whose taste has been cultivated to demand canned meats and bread made from American flower [sic], was naturally allured to the Chinese shops where credit was given much more readily than by the French and German merchants at Papeete. When the time for paying the Chinese merchant arrives, the native says "you may have my vanilla if you will cut it," and the Chinamen go into the field with only the idea of quantity never quality.

Consul North Winship concluded, "This law is directed almost entirely against the Chinese, who are the bête noire of the French officials here, but it is doubtful if it will prove satisfactory, since, if the Chinese merchants cannot collect their debts in vanilla, they will collect them by taking the native's land."[75]

Winship wasn't the only American to both reflect and comment on prevailing colonial attitudes toward Chinese people in Tahiti's vanilla trade. In his best-selling travel narrative *Mystic Isles of the South Seas*, Frederick O'Brien cast a Chinese vanilla broker as the victim of a crime. O'Brien had lived in Tahiti in 1914, but this book was not published until 1921. In it, an unscrupulous American has a Chinese merchant consign eighteen tins of vanilla to him, each valued at roughly $100 each. He then denies any knowledge of the deal, sells the vanilla, and, adding insult to injury, concocts a story of having assaulted and humiliated the Chinese vanilla trader.[76] The crime seems predicated on racial deniability—in other words, on the premise that he, as a white American, could never have swindled an ethnic Chinese trader.

Why was this community targeted, and what was its own history in Tahiti? In the nineteenth century, responding to what they considered a labor shortage, French authorities opened the doors to two waves of Chinese migration, involving Hakka and Cantonese groups, respectively. While the first migrants had been almost exclusively men, Chinese women began reaching Tahitian shores in larger numbers in the early twentieth century. The immigrants created mutual aid societies and developed closed-circuit flexible credit practices that soon rendered them powerful players in the vanilla sector, alongside the Hamburg SCO. The first restrictive measures against the community came in the late nineteenth century; then, in 1903, a local decree mandated the registration of all Chinese people in Tahiti. By the 1920s, colonial authorities, taking their cue from Australia and the United States, began restricting further Chinese migration. At that juncture, some French officials had come to view Polynesia's Chinese population as internal colonial rivals. In this sense, the 1910–11 vanilla laws aimed squarely at the Chinese community were part of a broader backlash.[77]

With the outbreak of World War I, the German firm SCO was thrown out of the French South Pacific. This redirected remaining vanilla resentment back to the Chinese community, now the sole remaining scapegoat. For instance, in 1937, a rambling grievance reached the Ministry of the Colonies in Paris. It made pointed allegations regarding various regions of the French South Pacific. In the Leeward Islands, Chinese middlemen supposedly purchased vanilla from Polynesians at a rate of three cents per pod. The governor of French Polynesia acknowledged that "Indigenous producers are often victims of the practices of Asian merchants." However, on balance, he found the allegations to be baseless generalizations. He assured Paris that vanilla could never be sold so cheaply in the Leeward Islands because it is sold at auction twice a year, and these auctions are open and transparent. The accuser had taken aim at a scapegoat in French Polynesia, pillorying Chinese merchants as a parasitic and profiteering merchant class. At a very time when anti-Semitism was overtaking much of Europe, other supposed internal enemies were being "unmasked" in much the same spirit in the South Pacific.[78]

Setting aside the odious attacks on the Chinese community, was there anything to the allegations of Tahitian vanilla's inferiority? *Vanilla tahitensis* does contain less vanillin than *planifolia*, but its other chemical ingredients make it the preferred choice to many palates. That is what pharmacist M. Rivière concluded in a 1912 study based on the first detailed chemical analysis of Tahiti's black gold. He flatly ruled out the presence of any heliotrope in Tahiti's pods. He added that "the aromatic elements that accompany vanillin have a great importance in the fruit's aroma." In other words, Polynesia's vanilla could be marketed as superior, thanks to its subtler, more varied aromas. The only concrete suggestion Rivière formulated was to increase the drying time for Tahitian vanilla to decrease its water content prior to export. That would allow at once for greater concentration of flavors and better preservation.[79]

On the eve of World War I, the bulk of Tahiti's vanilla steamed towards the US market. Chocolatiers had by then either abandoned their anti-*tahitensis* prejudice or reached the conclusion that Tahitian vanilla was worth its discounted price. In 1913, over 101 metric tons of Tahitian vanilla were exported to the United States. Next on the list came France with 24.8 tons, then Britain with 4.85, Australia with 2.28, and finally Germany with 1.5 tons. These exports generated some 4 million francs.[80]

The Great War marked a rupture. Already in October 1913, a few months before prior to its outbreak, a Franco-German vanilla skirmish erupted. A German publication alleged that Tahitian vanilla reeked of heliotrope and needed to be coated in German synthetic vanillin to achieve a passable scent. Better to use German colonial vanilla from Africa, the article advised.[81] The French fired back several salvos, although they, too, flattened the issue by failing to mention that Tahitian vanilla was mostly shipped to Europe via a Hamburg firm. The smear campaign against Tahitian vanilla had clearly crossed the Rhine. Next came the threats from actual war at sea. In September 1914, German warships bombed Papeete. By 1917, with shipping routes jeopardized by submarines, Tahitian officials pinned their hopes on a plan to transport their stockpiled pods to Europe via Australia. There was urgency, given that vanilla shipped from Madagascar and even Guadeloupe was making it to market in 1915 and 1916, but remote Tahiti's vanilla was not. Colonial officials attributed this partly to poor cooperation from France's British ally, which controlled the seas. Finally, a restrictive French export decree issued in October 1916 banned vanilla exports to not only Germany and its allies but also the neutral Netherlands and Sweden. As a varietal already considered inferior by some, Tahitian vanilla suffered greatly from these combined effects of the First World War.[82]

Tahitian vanilla production continued to slide in the wake of the Great War. For one thing, quality remained uneven. In July 1933, a complaint reached the Ministry of the Colonies in Paris. Two full cases of Tahitian vanilla had just arrived "completely rotten" aboard the steamer *La Boussole*. The complainant was certain that the vanilla had been sent spoiled from Tahiti and that lax oversight was to blame. They ended on an ominous note: Traders had previously turned away from Tahitian vanilla precisely because of such problems, only returning to it after the 1910–11 measures had taken effect. Nothing prevented them from turning their back on it again.[83]

Tahitian vanilla rebounded in a second golden age that began during World War II. At a time when Réunion and Madagascar could no longer export because they had fallen under Vichy French control, vanilla from Polynesia, which rallied to General de Gaulle's Free French in 1940, streamed into the United States to help make up the difference. This momentum carried into the postwar period. French Polynesia exported a record three hundred metric tons of pods in 1949. However, production began to decline in the 1950s, dropping to 137 tons in 1953, a nadir not seen since the Depression. The gradual downturn begun in the 1950s accelerated thereafter, as it became increasingly difficult for local producers to compete with Malagasy and Comorian prices. By 1973, Polynesia exported a mere nineteen metric tons of vanilla.[84]

In 1982, a hopeful report charted a way to pull French Polynesia out of vanilla decline. Thanks to its uniqueness, *Vanilla tahitensis* would prove less vulnerable than *planifolia* to price fluctuations, the document predicted. In other words, Tahitian vanilla's singularity ought to be celebrated; the days of hiding its provenance, the way Eugène Hänni once had, were over. Here was an optimistic reading that played on two registers. First, it rested on the distinctive flavor palate of *tahitensis*, which is the furthest removed from synthetic vanillin. Second, it relied on shifts in tastes, much as coffee connoisseurs have historically proven fickle, switching loyalties from one varietal, origin, and preparation method to another.[85]

The 1982 report also offered a snapshot of Polynesian vanilla production at the time. Most was grown on Taha'a and Raiatea, but a few producers remained on Moorea and Tahiti itself. Most importantly, the report highlighted a new vanilla cultivation method, introduced in 1979, which involved growing the plant more intensively under shade houses (*ombrières*) used to regulate sunlight. These settings allow air to circulate through the webbing, solving multiple problems such as the maintaining of host plants, which can be conveniently replaced with cement pillars. They also render moot the risks posed by birds and other animals, as well as the delicate balancing of sunlight. Moreover, they minimize the risk of introducing parasites through the host. And they eliminate the competition between host plant and vanilla for nutrients. Mostly, they do away with the long, steep hikes often required to harvest forest vanilla. In a broader perspective, they have unwittingly rekindled the French navy's experimental nineteenth-century technique, for *ombrière* vanilla vines grow along both vertical concrete rows and horizontal rails, enabling coordinated arm movement for pollination and cultivation. In short, this technology has brought about the level of resource optimization that Charles Morren had once dreamed of.[86]

As a visitor to Taha'a can observe, densely cultivated shade houses are located right in people's backyards. I learned that nowadays roughly half of Polynesia's vanilla is cultivated under *ombrières*, which are simpler to manage than forest vanilla. However, shade houses also present risks: Bands of thieves can and have swiftly combed through them, making off with a fortune in pods. In 2022, one Taha'a planter woke up to discover he had lost 90 percent of his "black gold."[87] Plant diseases also spread faster in confined spaces. I witnessed vanilla cultivators attempt to ward off these two banes in various ways, including the use of intimidating guard dogs and imposing strict restrictions on who can access the *ombrières*.

Taha'a has been dubbed Vanilla Island. Its contours roughly resemble a four-leaf clover, and its luxurious slopes offer breathtaking sunset views of Bora-Bora. Its four hundred vanilla producers span every one of its peninsulas as well as the interior. Unlike tourists, who flock instead to Bora-Bora, vanilla is ubiquitous on Taha'a. (The tourism economy took over in Bora-Bora after the collapse of phosphates and copra in the 1950s.)[88] On Taha'a, vanilla is sold at improvised stalls and in convenience stores.

Two of my informants on Taha'a, Cristiano and Naomi, are proud to produce some of the vanilla still grown upland, in the woods.[89] Cristiano had a previous career as a fisherman, and for a time he even kept up the fishing and vanilla work simultaneously, tending to the vanilla before dawn with a headlamp. Vanilla cultivation *sous bois* (in forest), they insist, involves daily work, which is especially intensive during the pollination and harvest times for their five thousand vanilla plants. That said, shade house and forest vanilla are not mutually exclusive: Another of my contacts, Rodrigo, who had previously worked for a hotel located on Taha'a's outer reef, now cultivates vanilla in both manners, on the hills behind his property. These three Polynesian cultivators operate differently. The couple rents the land and cedes a percentage of their vanilla earnings to the landlord, while Rodrigo is the landowner of a much smaller parcel. One interesting feature they share, along with seemingly all of Taha'a's roughly four hundred producers, is that they form family or even solo businesses, hiring neither pickers nor pollinators from outside their kinship group. Another point of commonality is that they typically sell their vanilla "green" at auction to buyers and preparers.

The distinctiveness of *Vanilla tahitensis* pods is thus mirrored in some unique and pioneering practices in Polynesia. The shade house revolution, which began in the Leeward Islands, has now spanned the world. More broadly, French Polynesia has maintained and even enhanced its reputation for vanilla experimentation. Today, on Raiatea, thousands of solar panels have been placed over two hectares of vanilla greenhouses in a bid to link "agricultural development with the energy transition," in partnership with a Chinese company.[90] Charles Morren's 1830s dream is materializing, although in the tropics rather than in northern Europe.

CHAPTER 7

Vanillamania

TAHITIAN VANILLA WAS FIRST EXPORTED IN MEASURABLE quantities around 1860; incredibly, French Polynesia was able to top the charts of global vanilla exporters a mere fifty years later. Other markers capture the astonishing rate and scope of change in vanilla production and consumption over the course of the nineteenth century. In 1805, a grocer's widow died in the Loire Valley city of Angers. The ninety-five-page inventory of the wares owned by Félicité Anne Hardye, daughter and granddaughter of local jewelers and spouse of the late Loire Valley grocer Jacob-Denis Abraham, constitutes a treasure trove of material for social and economic historians. For our purposes, it reveals five kilos of vanilla-flavored chocolate along with cloves and cinnamon. Here was a carryover from vanilla's Aztec function as a flavoring for chocolate. Yet it is unlikely that the entire stock contained more than a single vanilla bean as flavoring.[1] In other words, contrary to sugar, cacao, coffee, tobacco or cotton, vanilla usually flies below the radar in most archives, especially outside of production sites.

Some nine thousand kilometers (5,500 miles) away, and sixty-four years later, in 1869, US Consul to Veracruz E. H. Saulnier passed away from yellow fever.[2] His second-in-command dispatched all the deceased's earthly belongings to his widow in Brooklyn. They included a looking glass, white pantaloons, a kerosene lamp, and a "tin box with 200 vanilla beans." One can only imagine her reaction upon receiving the jumbled shipment. Why so much vanilla? As the US representative to the world's vanilla export hub, Saulnier likely kept a stock of pods either as a form of currency or as a side business. Occupation, geography, but mostly chronology explain the disparity between the two inventories. Unlike Hardye, Saulnier died in one of the planet's vanilla nerve centers, several decades after manual pollination had massively increased output.[3] A tide of vanillamania had begun sweeping the planet between the two deaths, only to intensify thereafter.

The wave of vanillamania led to a gradual democratization of pods, following the Albius revolution. This chapter begins by examining pod competition and the ramping up of production in Mexico, across Dutch and British colonies, as well as among new minor producers such as Japanese colonial Micronesia as well as French Indochina and Puerto Rico. Next, it turns to other facets of the vanilla rage that spilled over into the twentieth century: pod theft, smuggling, and surging global consumption.

Mexico stormed back as a significant vanilla power at several points in the second half of the nineteenth century. (In 1879–80, the country exported close to 41 metric tons, and after many lulls, it reached an all-time export zenith of 224.7 tons in 1906–7.)[4] The first rebound began in earnest in the 1850s with the Mexican adoption of the Edmond Albius pollination method, which traveled via a French connection. In the absence of direct testimony about the introducer or a precise date, we are left with varying secondhand accounts. In 1892, traveler Ludovic Chambon related the following after visiting the French settlement in Jicáltepec:

> [Prior to the 1840s] some years the number of pods was inconsequential. [French] settlers were beginning to tire of this unreliable and insufficiently profitable crop, when they learned from the head of the Jardin des Plantes in Paris a method for artificially pollinating vanilla, which had been used for a few years on Île Bourbon. This clinched their fortune: the simple process increased harvests tenfold.[5]

In this version, Paris relayed the method to the French community in Mexico. However, no sign of any such correspondence can be found in the archives of either the Jardin des Plantes or the French consulates in Mexico.

Long after the fact, Henry Bruman, a geography professor at UCLA, transcribed the following oral history of how the Albius method reached Mexico. He claimed to have heard it directly from members of the French colony of Jicáltepec:

> One of their number was sent home to France about 1840 to study tropical agriculture and brought back with him the technique of pollinating vanilla

flowers by hand. According to the story still current in the area the colonists soon harvested so many vanilla pods from their limited plantings that the Totonacs in the vicinity accused them of theft. This, of course, was a traditional justification for homicide, and so, in self-defense, the colonists had to teach the Indians the new technique. Vanilla production per hectare increased five-fold as a consequence.[6]

In this rendition, an unnamed individual from within the community introduced the method in the 1840s. Again, no archival source corroborates it. Bruman's version also describes conflicts with Indigenous people over the new technique. Yet it completely elides the fact that vanilla contacts and exchanges mostly worked in the other direction: Franco-Mexicans had learned where to find and how to gather forest vanilla from the Totonacs in the first place, and had acquired most of their curing and preparation knowledge from them as well.[7] By the 1860s, incidentally, a mere 5 percent of Mexican vanilla was collected in the wild; the vast majority was cultivated, predominantly by Totonac people who grew it as a cash crop and sold it to local middlemen. The French of Jicáltepec, conversely, both grew and prepared their pods, in some instances exporting them themselves as well.[8]

Although it remains unclear who brought the Albius method to Mexico and when, it was most likely introduced by and to the French community in Jicáltepec and nearby San Rafael. The Jicáltepec "colony," as the French consulate in Veracruz liked to refer to it, was founded in 1833 by some hundred immigrants hailing mainly from the village of Champlitte, at the crossroads of Burgundy and Franche-Comté. Inspired by utopian Fourierist ideals, the project's brainchild, Stéphane Guénot, brought the villagers squarely onto Indigenous Totonac lands. Although Guénot abandoned the agricultural colony, and many families returned before the vanilla breakthrough, some persevered, and others joined them from other parts of France. In the 1850s, Jicáltepec's French population became intensive vanilla cultivators.[9] By 1906, the colony counted eight hundred souls, of whom only eighty at that point had been born in France. A report from that year confirms that all remained deeply involved in the vanilla sector, and that the French community alone produced two million pods annually.[10] By 1899, the French settlements in and around Jicáltepec / San Rafael were by far Mexico's leading vanilla producers.[11] Intense vanilla specialization lasted from the 1850s until the outbreak of World War I, when exports declined. This community from remote, rural, inland France had become significant actors in the global vanilla trade by parlaying its linguistic skills and impeccable timing (arriving in Mexico less than a decade before the Albius breakthrough) into networks with Bordeaux and beyond.[12] The settlers also benefited from a perfect setting: their villages lay in the heart of vanilla country, and most estates were situated along the Nautla River or its tributaries, which greatly facilitated exports.

The late Abbot Jean-Christophe Demard, an expert on these French settlements, gained access to the private papers of several of their members, which show French planters forging networks in the 1850s. For example, in 1857, Pierre Belin crossed back from Mexico to Europe, dutifully accompanying his prepared pods, which he then sold to the Bayonne firm of Delvaille and Attias. (Three years later, the pods won a prize at the Briançon international fair.) At its core, the Belin-Delvaille-Attias transaction was transdiasporic. Delvaille and Attias were of Spanish Jewish background. Their families had settled in Bayonne, at Spain's doorstep, after the Spanish crown expelled all Jews from Spain in 1492. By 1857, they had established connections with the Americas, including with the French colony in Mexico.[13] Other Jicáltepec / San Rafael producers stayed in Mexico and prayed that their vanilla would safely reach European ports unaccompanied. For example, in 1859, Claude-François Pauffret dispatched his vanilla from Veracruz to the Wittenet family firm. Less successfully, Claude Groissaint, formerly a winemaker back in France, sent his vanilla to the Guibert Company in Bordeaux, which promptly complained that it had arrived spoiled.[14]

Jicáltepec / San Rafael, in turn, was transformed into a springboard for vanilla knowledge. By the twilight of the nineteenth century, French authorities in Jicáltepec were receiving queries about "their" way of pollinating and preparing vanilla. In 1894, French diplomats in Venezuela reached out for information on how to start a vanilla plantation, in hopes that French adventurers in South America could found vanilla groves there. In other words, vanilla had become one manifestation of paracolonial soft power, part of a web of French influence cast across Latin America.[15]

In 1902, Pierre/Pedro Naudé, a fifty-seven-year-old French resident and honorary consul of Jicáltepec, answered a request from the main consulate in Veracruz to distill his vanilla knowledge, specifically the process of manual pollination. Naudé responded that he possessed a longhand document dating back to 1875, which he sent along. (It drew from the notes of vanilla planters François Lavoignet and Eugène Mahé.) The piece, titled "Cultiva-

FIGURE 13. Detail from the 1875 document transmitted by Pablo Naudé. The text reads, "Manner of holding the flower while it is being pollinated." Courtesy Archives du Ministère des Affaires étrangères, France, 725PO/1/8.

tion of *Vanilla planifolia*," included multiple hand-drawn diagrams, one of which depicted "the manner in which to hold the flower while pollinating it." Angles mattered as much as dexterity. The text explained when and how to plant, pollinate, tend to, and cure vanilla. It advised against letting vines grow more than four meters (13.1 feet) up a tree, lest the pods and flowers escape easy reach. It further recommended that girls undertake the "minute labor" of manual pollination with their "agile hands." Interestingly, the detailed document provided no genealogy whatsoever and did not mention Albius.[16] Pollination knowledge had been appropriated and internalized as part and parcel of the community's Frenchness, to which it stubbornly clung and still does to this day (sometimes at its own peril, as during the Franco-Mexican War of 1861–67). However, this Frenchness never extended to tariffs. Try as these planters might to claim their vanilla as French, customs officials back in Europe continued to define it as Mexican.[17]

The proliferation and readership of such vanilla instruction manuals, both handwritten and printed, are instructive in their own right. One manual's diffusion speaks to what Emilio Kourí terms the Americanization of Mexico's vanilla sector.[18] In 1893, an American newspaper in Mexico City translated Agapito Fontecilla's 1861 vanilla grower's manual. The translator, O. W. M. Hillier, explained the need for an English version as follows: "There is no other treatise on the subject, and [...] very many English and Americans are investing in Mexican lands suitable for the cultivation of vanilla." The manual covered in painstaking detail everything from the choice of land

and soil to cultivation and preparation of vanilla, including the sweating and blanketing phases. It outlined the different types of plantations in Papantla: Some people positioned vanilla cuttings at the feet of existing trees, others planted rows of trees with vanilla in mind. It also divulged trade secrets: When sufficient days of "good sunshine" were lacking, as in December, an oven or *poscoyon* was utilized to dry the pods. *Poscoyon* signifies "half roasted" or "lightly baked" in Totonac—a sure sign of the practice's Indigenous roots. And yet, Fontecilla insists, "Don Juan Perez [. . .] was, it is said, the first to use the '*poscoyon*' and to give it the name, and he kept the secret to himself till a servant of his gave it away." Such alleged indiscretions presented a catch-22, for large vanilla estates could not function without an army of personnel. Fontecila's detailed description of the laborers required merely for the drying and sorting phases serves as a reminder of the specialization and sheer numbers involved in pod preparation. He recommended hiring two "*maestros* or experts to work on nothing else but the separations, revisions, etc., until the vanilla is tied up." Additionally, one should hire some twenty presumably less skilled "guys (*mozos*) for spreading vanilla in the sun."[19]

Armed with such manuals, American entrepreneurs quickly set their sights on Mexican vanilla. In 1903, Cleveland-born William Vernon Backus made an offer to the Mexican authorities. He would introduce the first-ever vanilla extract facility to Mexico. Backus had acquired vast tracts of land around Veracruz, growing rubber, tobacco, and vanilla. He also stood at the helm of a "maze of companies."[20] His operations were part of a broader US run on Mexican natural resources. But Backus was careful to couch his proposed extract factories in terms that might appeal to the local authorities. His factory, the first of its kind in Central America, would use cutting-edge equipment, and he planned to make significant investments over the next decade. Mexican students would be retained to learn the process of extracting vanilla.[21]

The vanilla craze, coupled with regional ebbs and flows, led transnational businesses to either dabble in vanilla or outright specialize in it. At first blush, Alfred/Alfredo Lefebvre and his son André/Andres fit the first category, although their knowledge appears remarkably deep for mere "dabblers." The Lefebvres were French importers-exporters, at the helm of a lucrative wholesale and retail business that mainly imported and sold French wares in Mexico. Occasionally, however, thanks to their dual headquarters in Mexico City and Paris, they seized the opportunity to trade Mexican commodities.

On May 25, 1890, André Lefebvre wrote in Spanish to Alberto Schaar in Misantla, in the heart of vanilla country, asking him to warehouse as much vanilla as he could. Two days later, André wrote in French to his New York trading partners Struller, Meyer, and Schumacher, requesting that they keep him abreast of vanilla prices. How much vanilla could they consign for an "easy sale," Lefebvre asked? On June 13, André turned his attention back to Schaar in Misantla, who had just written him. He regretted that the purchase of vanilla had caused Schaar "annoyances and difficulties," but expressed confidence that the "game would be successful" thanks to the vanilla's "fine preparation." On June 24, Lefebvre contacted his New York interlocutors once more, requesting updates on the "fluctuations of the vanilla market." A few days after that, he reconnected with Schaar, inquiring as to how the preparation of vanilla was progressing on location. Then, on July 1, 1890, André Lefebvre asked Charles Boucher, the company's contact at Jicáltepec, to oversee the transfer of the vanilla originating from Jicáltepec to Veracruz and provide detailed descriptions of each case. That same day, André wrote to Loustau and Company in Veracruz. He indicated that he intended to send the vanilla shipment to Paris but found the first transport quote he received too high. Might Loustau try obtaining another estimate from the American Veracruz Shipping Company in New York? As for insurance, he would take care of it through other channels. On July 5, from Mexico City, André wrote to his father in Paris. He was finally shipping him fourteen cases of vanilla via a French steamer set to leave Veracruz on July 12. He boasted of having "negotiated the price very well," thereby ensuring a hefty profit margin. On July 11, Alfred wrote his father once more. He explained that at each stop (Jicáltepec, Misantla, Veracruz), the pods had undergone quality control. They were shipped in tin containers within cedar cases. Each case was in turn branded with the company's initials. The vanilla pods themselves were divided into three class categories based on length, sheen, and weight.[22]

What can this microhistory of a Mexican vanilla shipment tell us? The entire operation required a set of complex familial but also multilingual, multicontinental, multicultural, and probably multifaith exchanges. The interactions themselves were rapid, prolific, and intense, a point we tend to forget when we associate frequent back and forth with the information age. Furthermore, every actor involved took a cut, from Jicáltepec and Misantla in the production zone to the port city of Veracruz, the New York firm, and the shipping and insurance companies, in addition to intermediaries like Loustau, who compared shipping rates. Specialized vanilla knowledge was required at every stage, as expressed by Schaar's frustrations over preparation, and André Lefebvre's detailed description of packaging. Last but not least, the "vanilla game" the younger Lefebvre played involved constant attention paid to both market reception on the one hand, and production and warehousing on the other. Even more than reaching markets, André Lefebvre was deeply involved in reading them.

While closely connected through the Lefebvres and Jicáltepec settlers, Mexico and imperial France jockeyed for supremacy in vanilla production. Indeed, throughout the nineteenth century, Paris sought to extract Mexico's riches, especially vanilla, as it did when it studied Mexican export strategies to share them with Réunion planters in the 1840s. Some of these efforts were half-baked. Consider an episode from Napoleon III's disastrous 1861–67 Mexican military campaign. Like his more illustrious uncle Bonaparte, Napoleon III ordered legions of experts to follow in the wake of his advancing troops. An ambitious scientist working for one his commissions recommended transferring vanilla cuttings from Mexico to Paris greenhouses. The same source noted that caution should be exercised to identify the right kind of vanilla. Recently, he added, entrepreneurs from Martinique and Guadeloupe had purchased Mexican cuttings and planted them in the Caribbean, only to realize after exporting their first pods to France that they had grown lesser-valued *Vanilla pompona*, not *planifolia*.[23] The whole story reeked of amateurism.

From a broader perspective, neither Mexico nor France ever held complete vanilla monopolies, although both exceeded 85 percent of global production at their respective apogees. Ensuring that a monopoly was averted, Dutch, British, German, and US planters took up vanilla cultivation on a small scale in the nineteenth and early twentieth centuries, everywhere from Java to the Seychelles, Uganda, and Puerto Rico. Let's now turn to some of these vanilla second fiddles. Their forays into vanilla betray the unprecedented demand that swept the world in the second half of the nineteenth century.

Leiden tropical botanist M. H. de Vries's early history of vanilla suggests that a Dutch expedition brought *Vanilla planifolia* to Java from the Netherlands in 1841. (This was an offshoot of Charles Morren's cutting.) Others contended that vanilla already existed on location in Java, which prompts the question of whether it was of the same type. Still according to de Vries, only in 1850 did the recently introduced *Vanilla planifolia* begin to flower and bear fruit on Java.[24] The near simultaneity with Tahiti and Jicáltepec is striking. Had local officials studied Edmond Albius's method? If not, why had nine years elapsed between the introduction of *planifolia* and its cultivation? In 1905, one source hinted, based on the notes of Dutch colonial horticulturalist S. Binnendijk, that the Dutch team had rediscovered vanilla's manual pollination method on their own. If this were the case, and the Dutch team somehow remained ignorant of Albius, then perhaps they were aided by the writings of Charles Morren, whose work had been translated into Dutch?[25]

Given how much research, even espionage, the Dutch devoted to pod preparation, one can reasonably doubt whether they could have been unaware of the Albius method that had been practiced on Réunion for nearly a decade. A set of documents preserved at the Dutch National Archives reveal that like the French on Réunion, the Dutch in Java initially acquired their curing and preparation knowhow from Mexico. A diplomatic dispatch from the Dutch consular authorities in Mexico in 1852 relayed locally sourced "information about the treatment of the vanilla pod." Presented in both the original Spanish and a Dutch translation, the short piece of horticultural intelligence outlined the best curing and preparation processes. It recommended carefully drying the pods in the sun for six weeks until they lost "all moisture."[26] This fact-finding mission shows how Dutch horticulturalists and diplomats went directly to vanilla's birthplace to better understand how to commercialize their pods.

Meanwhile, vanilla was thriving back on Java. By 1851, botanist Johannes Teijsmann was sending de Vries whole vines bearing multiple pods.[27] We are fortunate to have a detailed portrait of this early phase of Javanese pod production from the writings of Karl Sherzer, a member of a scientific expedition that circumnavigated the globe between 1857 and 1859, under the patronage of Austrian Archduke Ferdinand Maximilian (who would soon become the ill-fated emperor of Mexico). In Java, Sherzer marveled at the Buitenzorg botanical gardens, known today as Bogor Gardens. He wrote of the head gardener:

> Mr. [Johannes] Teijsmann has the great merit of having been the first to introduce into Java the cultivation of the valuable and costly vanilla plant (*Vanilla*

planifolia), by using artificial means of fructification, after all the many expensive experiments previously made had failed, because the insect which effects the fructification of the plant in its original climate [...] is not found in Java. At present the yield is so great, that not alone does Mr. Teijsmann annually secure and send to market seral hundredweights of this aromatic pod, but several other landowners have applied themselves to the laying out of vanilla plantations.[28]

Teijsmann was evidently falsely claiming credit for both introducing vanilla to Java and discovering the method of vanilla's manual pollination. For our purposes, however, the passage reveals the rapid spread of vanilla on Java and concerted Dutch colonial efforts to monetize the crop.

Precisely as Javanese vanilla was beginning to thrive under Dutch colonial auspices, British production in the Indian Ocean increased. Thanks in part to family ties with neighboring Réunion, vanilla developed rapidly in British colonial Mauritius. In 1858, the island exported just over 316 pounds (143.33 kilos) of vanilla, a figure that increased to 3,182 pounds (1.44 metric tons) in 1870, and 4.5 metric tons in 1900. In 1865, a local newspaper reported that all other attempts at achieving diversification and abandoning sugar monoculture had failed. Only "vanilla has succeeded," the paper noted, but it hastened to add that prices fluctuated too much for vanilla to become an outright replacement for sugar. Many evidently persevered in growing vanilla: by 1888, the island's forty-two arpents (35.48 acres) of land cultivated with vanilla dwarfed the total acreage devoted to cacao, indigo, tobacco and coffee but lagged far behind sugar and aloes.[29] Just as in Réunion, vanilla on Mauritius grew on a vast number of estates but in small quantities. A local vanilla commission estimated that Mauritius counted three thousand vanilla planters in 1903 but that only one hundred of them produced more than fifty kilos (110 pounds) of pods a year.[30]

In 1865 and 1866, Mauritius presented its vanilla at the Dublin world's fair. The pods representing the island came from the Brousse and Levieux estates. James Morris, the secretary for the Mauritius committee at the fair, expressed hope the island's vanilla would win a prize; however, in the absence of any competitor, it received an honorary mention instead. Morris added, "I am informed that vanilla is, comparatively speaking, little used in Ireland." He later elucidated, "In Dublin, the real vanilla was hardly known [...]. The manufacture of *chocolat à la vanille* does not exist in Ireland; so that the demand for real vanilla was almost nominal."[31] Indeed, statistics confirm that Mauritian vanilla essentially went to satisfy the English market but was also exported to continental Europe to meet unrelenting French demand. In 1888, 1.34 metric tons of Mauritian vanilla was exported to the United Kingdom, and 2.3 metric tons to France.[32] Small amounts also made it to the United States, although we know from Cincinnati pharmacist John Uri Lloyd that in the 1890s Mauritian and Seychellois vanillas were "often sold as low-grade Bourbon vanilla in our market."[33]

In 1887, a new French duty, doubling existing ones on vanilla from outside the French empire, ushered in a phase of vanilla protectionism. As retaliatory tariffs were being proposed, it became all the more important for consuming nations to produce their own vanilla.[34] This led British vanilla efforts to extend beyond Mauritius. Vanilla cultivation spread from there to the Seychelles Islands, another multilingual and multiethnic former French colony in the Indian Ocean. On this archipelago, vanilla's ascendancy occurred later, with production commencing in the 1870s (sixty kilos in 1877).[35] A report from 1898 provides useful details about outside inspirations and local methods: "The Mexican system of allowing the vines to grow under trees nearly wild is almost universally adopted at present, and is a decided improvement on the old system of training the vine on artificial supports." Seychellois authorities lobbied hard for their British colonial vanilla. In 1897, the administrator of Seychelles boasted, "Some of the Seychelles vanilla sent home last year was pronounced by the experts to be the finest ever seen on the London market." They also sought the advice of one M. C. Meyjes, a chemist and druggist, who urged local producers to "tie the vanilla together in bundles containing pods all of the same length, or at least not varying more than one inch because the pods are paid by length as well as by appearance." On a negative note, Meyjes observed that the cost of vanilla was bound to decline, as it had been steadily increasing for years. In fact, its moment in the Seychellois sun proved remarkably brief.[36]

The Seychelles Islands reached a production peak in 1901 with 71.89 metric tons of vanilla exported. However, that same year one source remarked ominously, "There is a capriciousness about the yield of vanilla, and even a greater capriciousness about its price."[37] Indeed, the following year, production dropped to 60.8 metric tons, and in 1904 it tumbled to 41 tons. Terrible droughts hit Mahé and its surrounding areas in 1904 and 1905, wiping out the vines completely. In addition, fungal disease, likely fusarium, ravaged the crop, despite the advice of one expert in 1898 to space out vines to reduce contagion.[38] In 1908, the governor tried one last-ditch effort to save the sector, arranging for the distilling of local vanilla into a concentrated extract on location. (This mirrored the Comorian practice of distilling on the spot the fragile but intense ylang-ylang flower for the perfume industry.) Ever the entrepreneur, the Seychelles governor then sent samples to the three main British chocolate giants: Rowntree and Company, Cadbury Brothers, and A. J. Caley and Son Ltd. The latter ran experiments, before reporting back flatly in May 1909, "We regret to state that chocolates flavored with this extract do not give anything like so pleasant a result as those flavored with the actual vanilla pod. The extract seemed to impart a peculiar flavor, quite foreign to ordinary vanilla."[39] The Seychellois extract scheme had fallen flat.

In 1912, the press reported that with five to six tons expected, "these islands that recently generated seventy tons will disappear altogether from the market as notable producers."[40] By 1919, the Seychelles exported a mere four metric tons of vanilla. Disease was squarely blamed for the sector's collapse, probably fusarium. One wonders whether the local practice of applying manure to vanilla roots might have compounded the crisis; coconut shells and other composts are often used today, but manure is not recommended.[41] Because of these factors, the Seychelles Islands receded into vanilla obscurity, although small-scale production endured in the twentieth century. The isles represent a curious case of vanilla achieving a brief flash that faded rapidly.

British botanists also endeavored to introduce vanilla to India. A first clipping was sent from Kew Gardens to the Raj in 1835; it soon "died out." A subsequent introduction to Bengal took place from Mauritius. By 1855, Indian pods were sent to London for testing. However, the undertaking largely failed on the subcontinent. In 1873, George Henderson, head of Calcutta's botanical gardens, reached the following verdict: "The attempt to introduce vanilla culture into Bengal is a most disappointing and discouraging one. Here is a plant as readily propagated as a willow, which thrives everywhere it has been tried, and the fruit of which is almost worth its weight in silver, yet not a single native or European, as far as I am aware, has had the enterprise to continue the cultivation." Henderson added, "Some years ago a European gentleman [. . .] had many acres of vanilla, but he had soon to leave the country, and the estate being sold, the vanilla culture was given up." In 1881, one expert claimed that haphazard pollination was to blame. Other reasons surfaced to explain mixed results in vanilla cultivation near Bangalore in the 1870s. There, the pods split during preparation, spilling their beans.[42] Pollination and preparation made pod production far trickier than Henderson had suggested. Vanilla was no willow. By the late nineteenth century, production had shifted to Ceylon (today's Sri Lanka), which emerged as a minor exporter.

However, at the dawn of the twenty-first century, Indian vanilla finally experienced a revival in the Western Ghats. In under a decade, the nation went from no commercial vanilla output in 1997 to some three hundred metric tons in 2008. But just as quickly as the rebound occurred, in 2008 a global vanilla downturn nearly knocked out the entire sector. The man at the center of Indian vanilla's revival, Dr. R. Mahendran, was also one of the few entrepreneurs left standing in the wake of the crisis. Today, his company Expovan not only exports beans but also produces extract for the domestic market. Under the brand Goodness Vanilla, it helps meet the growing Indian middle-class appetite for natural vanilla ice cream; and in partnership with a large dairy cooperative, his vanilla flavors local milk.[43]

In addition to the British and Dutch, in the twentieth century the United States also entered the vanilla production fray, albeit on a limited scale. In 1919, D. W. May, the agronomist at the helm of Puerto Rico's Agricultural Experiment Station concluded, on the basis of several years of trials, that "vanilla is a very promising introduction into Puerto Rico, as it may be employed by the coffee growers of the island to diversify without in any way injuring their main crop and it will furnish employment for the women and children of the rural population." May's colleague, horticulturalist T. B. McClelland, based his arguments on mainland US demand. Vanilla's price never fell below $2.28 a pound, and sometimes reached over $7.00 a pound (in 1879). American imports had climbed uninterruptedly since 1865, hitting 1.1 million pounds (close to five hundred metric tons) in 1911. And thanks to Puerto Rico's lower duties, Puerto Rican vanilla held a competitive advantage in the United States. McClelland provided additional details about Puerto Rican vanilla. It had originated from the Subtropical Garden at Miami, which in turn had received its *Vanilla planifolia* samples from Papantla, Mexico but also, interestingly, from the Fiji Islands via Hawaii. McClelland specified that "no varietal difference whatever has been seen between the two."[44]

Some fancied they could open the continental United States to vanilla cultivation. In 1873, Mr. Nanès, a Réunionese living in mainland France, inquired about the possibility of starting a vanilla plantation in Texas. Nanès added confidently that as a Réunionese, he knew vanilla and understood that it required little capital for high profit margins. However, the French consulate in New Orleans killed the project. Vanilla could not grow on lands that experienced even occasional frost, and Tampico, Mexico, was therefore the northernmost point of cultivation in the Americas, consular officials insisted.[45] American businesses also explored the idea. In August 1894, the Land of Sunshine Company based in Merced, California (but headquartered in Chicago), wrote to the secretary of state after one of its directors read an article about French vanilla producers in Mexico. He asked that Washington solicit the opinion of the US consul in Mexico "as to whether the bean could be cultivated in the frostless, irrigated lands of California, Arizona, New Mexico, etc."[46] These might seem like pipe dreams, but today vanilla cultivation has begun in earnest in the continental United States, this time in southern Florida. A University of Florida project initially had vanilla growing on avocado trees.[47]

The US, British, Dutch, and French overseas empires were certainly not the only ones engaging in vanilla research, circulation, and production. In the 1920s, prolific Japanese agronomist Hoshino Shūtarō introduced vanilla from Java to a newly created research station on the Micronesian island of Ponape. (The Japanese had seized these isles from Germany in 1914.) Neither Japan nor its colonies ever emerged as major vanilla producers, although Shūtarō's introduction speaks to Japanese specialists engaging in global pod experimentation and competition via expansion into tropical zones.[48]

In the nineteenth century, vanilla fever ran so high that even as Réunion was rising into a vanilla titan, other parts of the French empire began to dabble in pods. In 1847, the head of Pépinière centrale d'Alger (Algiers's plant nursery), Auguste Hardy, introduced vanilla from Martinique to Algeria. This was tricky business; most cuttings perished en route. However, one was miraculously rescued, and by 1852, vanilla was growing on the garden's trellises. Nonetheless, Hardy never persuaded Algerian settlers to turn to pods.[49]

Algeria's climate is probably too dry for vanilla to have thrived. But in the second half of the nineteenth century, France had also widely colonized in western and central Africa. Botanist Charles Eugène Aubry-Lecomte introduced vanilla to Gabon in 1852. In 1892, missionaries took vanilla cuttings from the experimental gardens in Libreville to their coastal mission in Mayumba. However, Gabon never produced more than a few kilos of vanilla. Conversely, neighboring French Congo, where vanilla was introduced in the early twentieth century, exported four hundred kilos (882 pounds) of pods in 1911. In 1930, French Congo and Gabon combined for some three hundred kilos (661 pounds) of prepared vanilla, exported solely to France.[50]

In 1899, the botanical gardens in Pondicherry, French India, were experimenting with vanilla cultivation; the following year, its directors dispatched samples to Marseille.[51] Ultimately, though, these vanilla experiments amounted to little more than local consumption or decorative use, with the net result being a repeat of earlier British failures in Bengal.

Vanilla did achieve a minor breakthrough farther east, in what is now Vietnam. The first introduction occurred in 1865 at the Saigon botanical gardens, but vanilla seems not to have spread beyond its gates.[52] In 1887, a Hanoi baker asked the authorities whether vanilla might be planted widely in French Indochina, no doubt to provide ingredients for his pastries. Nearly simultaneously, the lead official in Dinh Binh province in South-Central Vietnam expressed interest in cultivating vanilla, alongside other experimental crops including litchi and cacao.[53] After his first attempt to introduce Réunionese vanilla cuttings to Indochina failed in 1913, planter Henri Le Guidec tried again in 1918. He then started a single hectare vanilla plantation at Honquan, near Thudaumot. By 1921, it was yielding twenty-two thousand pods. Le Guidec opted to grow the vines on what he called Japanese lilacs (*Melia azedarach*) for its ability to provide partial shading. This appears to be the only Asian concession or twist to French Indochinese vanilla production.[54] In 1924, Le Guidec's vanilla drew mixed reviews from the Institute for Colonial Agronomy of Nogent-sur-Marne. On the one hand, its length and quality secured its place in the top vanilla category. On the other hand, the vanilla's "new provenance" rendered it less attractive to customers (force of habit mattered). So, too, did the more worrisome fact that the pods arrived excessively dried. The authorities at Nogent suggested that the second issue was easy to rectify.[55]

A less savory character swiftly tried to emulate Le Guidec's relative success. Jean Giorgi launched a rival plantation near Bien Hoa circa 1926. However, Giorgi gained notoriety not for his vanilla but for his abusive, murderous bent. In 1929, he pulled out a firearm after refusing to concede his clear election loss for a local council seat. A year later, he stabbed and wounded a Muslim resident of Saigon; then, in a separate incident, he stabbed and murdered a Vietnamese witness to the domestic violence he had just committed. He avoided prison by pleading insanity, a case that undoubtedly would have yielded a different outcome had the tables been turned, with a colonized assassin and a colonizer victim. Given Giorgi's pattern of cruelty, one can only imagine what the employees on his vanilla estate must have endured.[56]

Seemingly spontaneously, around the world, missionaries, bakers, and murderous adventurers all turned to vanilla. This was another sign of vanilla's appeal. In the larger scheme of things, however, Giorgi and Le Guidec remained outliers. Neither the Asian nor for that matter the African continent proper ever became major vanilla producers. Outside of Mexico, vanilla remained an insular crop, tied primarily to the Indian and Pacific Oceans. Indeed, to this day, vanilla is mostly associated with islands, be they Java, Taha'a, Tonga, or of course Madagascar.

Islands, nations, and empires weren't the only ones fiercely competing over vanilla. On a smaller scale, we already saw vanilla larceny and piracy at work in the eighteenth-century Atlantic, nineteenth-century Réunion, and twenty-first-century Taha'a. Such thefts persisted and in fact intensified as vanilla went global. They became the bane of producers the world over. In late nineteenth-century Jicáltepec / San Rafael, for instance, French cultivators hired armed guards to watch over the pods near harvest time, day and night. Totonacs, too, experienced vanilla theft within their ranks. More often than not, prevention efforts were in vain.[57] To this day, vanilla growers deploy a range of strategies to ward off thieves, including one that anthropologist Genese Sodikoff recorded just south of the Sava region in 2000: steadfast denial that they grow or own any vanilla at all.[58]

Similar issues surfaced on the French Caribbean island of Guadeloupe, which remained a significant vanilla producer. (Although harvests proved uneven from year to year, the isle exported close to five tons in 1885 and thirty-one tons in 1908.) However, the island's vanilla sector was devastated by a 1928 hurricane that badly damaged 80 percent of the crop. The very next year, as planters scrambled to recover, authorities reported that vanilla theft had become so widespread that growers were picking their pods prematurely to avoid losing them altogether. Vanilla theft and natural disasters came to be perceived as twin decimators of the island's crop.[59]

VANILLAMANIA

Indeed, larcenies occurred at every point of the production-to-consumption chain, including on the high seas. In August 1938, the Messageries Maritimes navigation company contacted the Dzoumogné vanilla plantation in Mayotte. Because of a recent rash of thefts and accompanying concerns from insurance companies, the shippers explained that henceforth they would only accept specially sealed boxes of vanilla. The company emphasized that the sender was solely responsible for proper sealing and provided a how-to diagram.[60]

Sometimes vanilla robbing, and reactions to it, took on epic proportions. This happened in British colonial Mauritius, where vanilla theft allegations quickly devolved into finger-pointing and judicial overreactions. Pod pilfering has a long, documented history on Mauritius. In May 1873, the Mauritian press reported vanilla larceny in the district of Flacq on the isle's eastern coast.[61] In 1874, more vanilla was declared stolen at Rivière Noire. In a separate incident, a pod thief was caught red-handed at Plaines Wilhems. In several robberies that year, thieves not only stole green pods but also cuttings, which suggests they were starting groves of their own. The authorities responded with a draft ordinance mandating that anyone found traveling with vanilla should produce a permit for it.[62] The measure failed. That same November, more pods were stolen in Pamplemousses. The press clamored for the establishment of a powerful secret pod police force to handle the problem.

Inspired by steps taken on Réunion, an enterprising goldsmith by the name of J. Jaume devised a special stamp for marking green pods permanently. An announcement in a Mauritian newspaper offered to show readers the pods stamped by Jaume's device. The following month, when another vanilla theft occurred at Pamplemousses, the same source posited that the stamp might have averted it. Predictably, others copied the idea, and by 1875, E. Groéme, a Port-Louis clockmaker, was advertising his "moderately priced" vanilla stamper in the press. Another paper hailed Groéme's invention as "almost an objet d'art"; more to the point, although it obviously could not eliminate vanilla thefts, it was bound to reduce their frequency.[63]

In 1884, with vanilla thefts still a regular occurrence, some small planters became increasingly incensed by the way authorities handled cases. One claimed that the local police responded to a vanilla larceny in Creole by saying, "Don't plant vanilla, plant manioc instead. Nobody will steal that." As with truffles or opium poppies, vanilla's lure seemed too powerful to resist.[64]

All this was child's play next to the furor that erupted around the turn of the century. In April 1902, a member of Mauritius's Franco-Mauritian elite, vanilla planter Paul Léonce Le Juge de Segrais took the floor at a public hearing. In addition to overseeing his own vanilla plantations, the sixty-two-year-old Segrais worked as a stockbroker. His family typified patrician Creole society: His ancestors hailed from Mauritius, Bourbon, and the Loire Valley, and his spouse was from Paris. Before a newly formed public inquiry, he solemnly described an epidemic of vanilla thefts:

> There are many larcenies now. I [have been] a vanilla grower for the last fifteen years. I was personally robbed lately, during the night, for the amount of about 2,000 rupees of vanilla pods, besides the depredations caused on the plantations, the pods and creepers having been stripped off. That was in May last year. My vanilla pods were marked *S*. The mark was deposited at the police station of Pamplemousses in March 1900. My overseer reported the matter to me. I made my declaration at the Pamplemousses station. The police inspector came to my place, visited it, and made report. The police never succeeded in finding out the thieves. I went to the police station and found out in the books there, a mark similar to mine, deposited by one Soomaror, an Indian of the same district, residing at about two miles from my place. The Indian's mark was deposited after mine [. . .]. In October, Mr. Contanceau called me to come and see a lot of vanilla he intended to purchase from Mr. Offman, preparer of vanilla, in d'Artois Street, Port-Louis. I inspected the vanilla, and found it was very inferior in quality owing to the immaturity of the pods when prepared, and inside one of the bundles, I found my mark *S* on a few pods. I opened only one bundle. I recognized the mark to be mine by the number of points composing the letter *S*. I made a remark to Mr. Offman, who replied that he had bought the vanilla from different Indians and Creoles who had taken it to his place at Long Mountain for sale. When I went to the police to make my declaration in May last, the officer in charge of the station told me that there was a slight difference between my mark and that deposited by Soomaroo [sic]. They differ in the number of points, my marks having one or two points more. I am almost positive that the vanilla I had seen with Mr. Offman was mine and which had been stolen from my property.[65]

The complaint is notable for many reasons. It shows that Jaume and Groéme's devices were still in use, although they turned out to be ineffectual at proving uncontested ownership. (To compound matters, some have suggested that marked vanilla is, on average, less valuable when sold.)[66] Segrais's grievance also highlights vanilla networks, with planters, preparers, and police all displaying vanilla knowledge. And of course, it exposes an accusation made by a leading French planter—that is, a member of a community still wielding much power in Mauritius—against an individual from the South Asian community, likely a descendant of an indentured worker brought to Mauritius from India. In other words, the establishment acted as vanilla gatekeepers.

The authorities took to heart Segrais's point about the inadequacies of both the police and the law. They proved especially sensitive to his point that "anyone can bring stolen vanilla pods to a preparer without being obliged to give the proof that the pods came from his place." To this, Segrais added other arguments: that the thefts led to poor quality vanilla (any vanilla that was ripe would have been harvested by the planter, so the vanilla picked by thieves was by definition unripe) and existing penalties for those caught were insufficient. Segrais concluded on a note of helplessness: "My plantation is about three or four acres in extent, and is very difficult to watch, unless there are three or four watchmen with loader-guns on the spot." To this planter, at least, it seemed that vanilla thieves always held the advantage.

Other planters piled on. Nemours Langlois relayed the following story. He co-owned a vanilla plantation with Mr. Rosnay. Despite deploying watchmen, dogs and guns, as well as "small boards with nails on them scattered across the plantation," pod thefts continued in large numbers. Then, Langlois's sleuthing revealed that some vanilla stolen from him had been taken to a preparer by "a relative of my watchman."[67] Another planter, Léon de Saint Pern, likewise concluded that the theft of his vanilla was an inside job, involving collusion between his "guardians [sic] and some accomplices."[68] Booby traps, dogs, and guards proved ineffective, as they were respectively avoided, mollified, or corrupted.

And so, the Mauritian authorities reacted with new laws, targeting specific nerve points in the preparation process: the production, sale, and transport of pods to preparers. The new measures included the creation of vanilla carrying permits that allow the transportation of vanilla explicitly for a single day, between daybreak and sunset. They made markings mandatory, despite the Segrais case casting doubt on the effectiveness of this practice. They obliged planters to declare by July 10 of every year the amount of their lands dedicated to vanilla. Every vanilla sale now required a special form signed by both seller and buyer—the law stipulated that the nonliterate could turn to the police for help. Some within the "vanilla committee," which represented planters, asked for more. "Full powers should be given to police to arrest delinquents with or without a warrant," they implored. They also pleaded for the creation of a powerful "vanilla Inspector" to oversee the crackdown on thefts. Additionally, all sellers and preparers of vanilla would need to be licensed.[69] These extraordinary lengths illustrate at once the value of vanilla and the power dynamics at work in Mauritius.

Nevertheless, the repressive arsenal failed to satisfy some of those concerned. The island's two largest vanilla producers at the time, Jean Péguilhan and Nemours Langlois, spoke out against the proposed red tape. Interestingly, the two vanilla magnates argued that the many declaration forms were bound to prove a burden for small vanilla producers, including those having "just a few vanilla plants in their courtyards."[70] The heavy-handed crackdown on vanilla theft had set off a backlash. There are hints that a similar 1888 measure aimed at preventing vanilla theft in the Seychelles Islands elicited nearly the same reaction.[71]

Still, Mauritian colonial authorities pressed on. In 1915 and again in 1918, they introduced ever more draconian ordinances. Buyers now had to file as many reports as sellers. A listing of the number, and later weight, of pods to be harvested had to be submitted at least fifteen days prior to harvesting. Vanilla sellers, preparers, and their agents were required to keep detailed registers, which the police could consult on demand.[72]

Closely related to theft was the question of vanilla smuggling. An 1863 article in the French press suggested that vanilla corruption was rampant in Mexico and "contraband" had taken on "colossal proportions."[73] Smuggling occurred at both the point of departure and arrival. At the French port of Saint-Nazaire in the spring of 1884, disembarking passengers entered medical quarantine. This left time for customs officials to search their ship. They uncovered a hidden cabinet containing 1,675 cigars, 19 kilos of coffee, and 1.5 kilos of vanilla. A member of the shipping line swiftly confessed to customs fraud.[74] Unsurprisingly, this smuggler dabbled in items with high value-to-size ratios and capitalized on wares transited through the Veracruz-Havana-Europe lines. Unfortunately, by definition, smuggling mostly went unreported, and the few incidents like these that dot the historical record are only the tip of the iceberg.

What drove this spate of vanilla competition, theft, and smuggling? The American appetite for all things vanilla proved voracious. In 1890, the United States still lagged well behind France in terms of vanilla consumption.[75] That changed rapidly. The two nations were nearly tied by 1902 (237 metric tons imported to the United States versus 259 metric tons to France), and America surpassed French vanilla imports for good in 1906 (nearly 400 tons imported by the United States versus 312.7 tons imported by France).[76] However, as the twentieth-century progressed, the ratio of synthetic vanillin to real vanilla purchased by US households kept climbing, a topic I return to in the next chapter. Even so, vanilla producers could find some solace in the enduring popularity of their flavor: out of every one hundred ice cream servings sold in the United States in 1958, fifty-three were vanilla flavored.[77] The United States remained the biggest market for vanilla, even as synthetic vanillin grew in popularity. In 1921, the United States imported 232.1 metric tons of vanilla from French colonies alone. By 1933, that figure had climbed to 552.2 metric tons, even as the Great Depression raged.[78] However, by 1938, the authorities in Paris, concerned about the sustainability of US demand and wanting to avoid putting all of their eggs in one basket, sought entries into the Australian market.[79] On balance, though, most vanilla was heading to the United States and France, with much smaller amounts going to Germany, Britain, Denmark, Italy, and the Netherlands. In 1929, Weimar Germany imported 66 metric tons of French colonial vanilla, Britain 39.4 tons, Denmark 21 tons, Italy 10 tons, and the Netherlands 8.5 tons.[80]

So, how was vanilla being used? Recipe books can provide an answer, although we should be mindful that they tended to target specific bourgeois audiences and that cooks did not always follow recipes to a tee.[81] Yet an unmistakable pattern emerges from them: with a handful of exceptions that we encountered in chapter 1, vanilla rarely appeared in pre-1841 cookbooks; thereafter, it permeated them.

More than just a recipe book, Baron Léon Brisse's menu-a-day for the year 1867 is an example of extreme regimentation. It also captures the moment when elite cuisine reached a broader market. The baron was certainly noble himself, but he was above all a food journalist, perhaps the world's first. He was also an unabashed gourmand, a pioneer in making elite cuisine more widely available to a bourgeois constituency, which craved this type of normative instructions from the nobility. Vanilla makes no fewer than thirty-five appearances in his legendary 1867 book of menus (compared to twenty-four for pork, for example). It takes the form of vanilla soufflé, vanilla tartlets, vanilla darioles, vanilla bavarois, vanilla blanc-manger, vanilla Chantilly or whipped cream, and vanilla ice cream, and serves as an ingredient in everything from apple desserts to oeufs à la neige. Some of the recipes called for vanilla powder, others for actual vanilla pods. The book proved enduringly influential enough for Julia Child to own a copy.[82]

Partly, then, Brisse's menu-a-day manual reflected the bourgeois emulation of noble tastes, which was nothing new—bearing in mind that neither the nobility nor the bourgeoisie were homogenous blocks. Where vanilla was concerned, however, a reversal was at work. The new cookery of the seventeenth century reflected a sea change; in Jeffrey Pilcher's words, spices no longer "convey[ed] aristocratic status when bourgeois families could also afford them." Here, a sumptuous and status-conferring new "spice" was once more being diffused from aristocratic to middle-class palates.[83] However, its reaching the bourgeoisie did not make vanilla any less appealing to the aristocracy. Quite the contrary. By the last third of the nineteenth century, the chefs of Sultan Abdulhamid II in Constantinople were ordering vanilla for "European" style desserts, such as apple bavarois flavored with vanilla. The court in Saint Petersburg was equally enthralled. At a lunch on October 6, 1898, French chef Pierre Cubat served the Russian Czar Nicholas II and his family a cauliflower potage, followed by veal cutlets, hare, and, for dessert, a vanilla soufflé.[84]

Pellegrino Artusi's 1891 *Science in the Kitchen and the Art of Eating Well* is often considered the foundational handbook of Italian cooking. Again, vanilla dots the book. It appears in a staggering thirty-eight nonfrozen desserts, including hazelnut cake, baba au rhum, dolce di chiare d'uovo (meringue cake), plum cake (in English), zuppa Inglese, uova di neve (floating islands), soufflè di castagne, and pasticcio a sorpresa. Numerous iced dishes and creams also included vanilla: pezzo in gelo, gelato di crema, gelato di amaretti, gelato di terroni, gelato di castagne, and ponce alla romana. Among these sweets, often a mere "dash" of vanilla was recommended; sometimes it appeared as an option, with lemon zest or even coriander listed as an alternative. (Artusi was not alone in this regard: a few years later, the German Dr. August Oetker's chocolate cake recipe called for either vanilla sugar or grated lemon zest.) Certainly, fewer of Artusi's dishes centered on vanilla compared to Brisse's text. Nevertheless, vanilla's ubiquity as a flavoring is startling. Artusi's savarin called for vanilla sugar, but the chef took no shortcuts; he recommended flavoring the sugar with a whole vanilla pod through slow infusion, presumably not just for this dish but for all recipes in his book.[85]

Vanilla also served as a key ingredient in the quintessential Italian panettoni. In the 1930s, the Motta company installed a hundred-foot conveyor belt at its headquarters on Milan's Viale Corsica to begin industrial-scale production of the Christmas specialty. In addition to the candied citrus and raisins that characterize the traditional Milanese recipe, vanilla evidently held a central place in this first mass-produced panettone. In 1938, the company contacted the French vanilla planters' association. The Milan firm wrote of being "large consumers of Bourbon vanilla" and sought to secure as much supply as possible. Perhaps its executives had read the writing on the wall that war was about to disrupt trade routes and isolate the Italian boot?[86]

Back in France, in the late nineteenth and early twentieth centuries, vanilla's popularity merged with a vogue for local specialties, precisely as regional identities came under threat or were being recast. Vanilla was grafted onto quintessentially local dishes at two sites that had historically served as pod import hubs: the port city of Bordeaux and the Basque Pyrenean border with Spain, which had long been a site of vanilla smuggling. In the Basque borderlands, the recipe for biskotxak, a kind of shortbread, was first recorded circa 1830 in the spa town of Cambo-les-Bains. But it was only after biskotxak was reinvented into gâteau basque in the late nineteenth century that vanilla cream was added to the recipe. Similarly, Bordeaux's famous cannelés, a local delicacy that is at once irresistibly chewy and crunchy, hark back several centuries. However, their defining vanilla and rum flavors date only to the first quarter of the twentieth century.[87] In some ways, the phenomenon is not unique: many an ingredient in southwestern French cuisine, from Espelette peppers to Barbary ducks, is of distant origin; kiwi fruit became the latest addition to Adour Valley production in the 1980s.[88] However, it is the lag that makes vanilla-flavored gâteau basque and cannelés stand out. In each case, ports of entry continued to matter centuries after trade began. In a potent yet invented nostalgic twist, vanilla was whisked into existing regional delicacies between 1890 and 1930 at the very points of contact where it had first reached France in the sixteenth and seventeenth centuries.

Not all consumption trends were backward-looking. Once used primarily to flavor cacao drinks, vanilla became a global mainstay of ice creams and, in the late nineteenth century, syrups. In 1886, the pod provided flavoring for just such a syrup that was gaining favor at that quintessentially American invention, the soda fountain. The recipe for Coca-Cola was kept secret, but we now know that vanilla was included in Frank Robinson's earliest formula. It called for nineteen ounces of vanilla extract to be added to eighteen gallons of water. (Thereafter, recipes identified vanilla in code as "merchandise 7.")[89]

Between 1898 and 1902, Coca-Cola went to court over how its product was taxed as medication. The company's cause was not helped by the fact that it had previously advertised its beverage as a remedy to treat headaches and "nervous exhaustion." This legal case produced an ingredient list at last. The company's lawyers contended that the "mere trace" levels of cocaine in the drink precluded its being labeled as medicine. They also sought to play down its alcohol content, asserting that Coca-Cola could best be compared to coffee and tea as a stimulant. Sugar and water were by far the "syrup's" main components, followed by coca leaves and kola nuts. However, "lemon, vanilla and calcium" appeared as the three flavoring agents.[90] Vanilla was no doubt enlisted at least in part to help counteract kola's natural bitterness.[91]

Due to the rise in demand for the beverage, even modest amounts of flavoring translated into significant vanilla imports. By the 1980s, when "New Coke" briefly emerged, which was made without pods, vanilla indexes tumbled amid rumors that 30 percent of the world's vanilla had previously been funneled into "Coke Classic." A company spokesperson responded that the 30 percent figure was exaggerated but declined to specify how much of the world's vanilla supply had gone into Coca-Cola.[92]

However, despite these major inroads by Coca-Cola, in the United States most vanilla still found its way into ice cream. In 1915, trailblazing dietary and domestic scientist and food writer Sarah Tyson Rorer published her influential *Dainty Dishes for All the Year Round*. It provided an abundance of advice on how to hand-crank ice creams from scratch. Vanilla extract or vanilla sugar make appearances in her burned almond, filbert, hazelnut, walnut, coconut, chocolate, chocolate Delmonico, bisque, caramel, caramel Neapolitan, hokeypokey, condensed milk, gelatin, and arrowroot ice creams, not to mention her iced chocolate, frozen Montrose pudding, frozen plum pudding, frozen custard, iced rice pudding, stuffed mousse, and French custard with golden sauce. As for vanilla ice cream proper, Rorer offered several variations, no doubt based on budget. They can be divided into two families: one for vanilla ice cream per se, which included "one vanilla bean," and another for "vanilla ice cream with extract," which required "two tablespoons of vanilla."[93] When iceboxes and hand-crank ice made way for steam-powered and later brine ones equipped with compressors, America's vanilla ice cream infatuation turned into an obsession.[94] Interestingly, vanilla was spared the US backlash against perceived European and especially French "fancy foods" that marked the 1910s through the 1930s.[95]

Post-1900 recipes in the Americas increasingly relied on convenient vanilla extract, a liquid derived from pods but diluted in large quantities of alcohol or water. The trend was not restricted to the United States. In 1902, in Mexico, the very birthplace of vanilla, a newspaper's recipe section revealed the widespread use of vanilla extract. It appeared in several ice creams, as well as a pudding and a vanilla cake.[96]

Other cuisines followed suit. The father of modern Greek cooking, Nicholas Tselementes, was inspired in part by French culinary traditions but also by his time as chef at the Hotel St. Moritz in New York. His foundational *Greek Cookery* appeared first in Greek in the 1930s, then in English in 1950. Six of the 1950 edition's desserts called for vanilla, but all, including vanilla koulouria, listed it in teaspoons—in other words in extract or powder form. Although genealogies are hard to establish, it seems likely that his widespread use of vanilla extract or powder can be linked to his time in New York and the expectations of his US readership.[97]

Industrial biscuit makers also turned to vanilla extract for flavoring. Back in France, Nantes-based Lefèvre-Utile, more commonly known as LU, already sold six types of vanilla biscuits in 1875. LU then entered the vanilla wafer business in 1896 after the firm sent a team to Britain, the pioneer in mass wafer production. The French delegation visited the Huntley and Palmers factory in Reading to study the firm's techniques.[98] While it lagged behind on the wafer front, LU seems to have surpassed its English competitors in the vanilla realm, as suggested by the tins and wrappers of each company. On Huntley and Palmers wafer tins, the eye is drawn to the words *sugar wafer*, which appear in a large contrasting font while *vanilla flavored* is relegated to an afterthought, rendered in a nearly monochromatic smaller typeface. Conversely, LU highlighted the vanilla in its wafers, according *vanilla* the same proportions as the word *wafers* itself. That said, vanilla's connotations remained vague: one LU floral décor resembled a daisy more than a vanilla orchid. By the turn of the century, LU hired renowned Czech art nouveau illustrator Alphonse Mucha to design the iconic feminized vanilla wafer image shown in chapter 9.

The British chocolate company Rowntree and Company—which later created Kit Kat—went a step further by vertically integrating vanilla production. In 1899, Wilhelm Rowntree purchased lands on Dominica in the British Caribbean. His idea was to "bring English energy and scientific knowledge to bear upon tropical culture and to combine our knowledge of English markets and requirements with the cultivation of a West Indian estate." The two main crops were to be cacao and vanilla, with bananas, pineapples, and coconuts grown on the side. Rowntree sought confirmation from the Colonial Office in London that *Vanilla planifolia* was the optimal varietal to plant.[99]

Beyond Europe and North America, in the late nineteenth century vanilla also achieved modest inroads in Asia. Japan opened to foreign trade in 1858, and vanilla wasted little time making its appearance. In 1865, the French community in Yokohama advertised the arrival from France of many cordials, including a vanilla liqueur cream. Clearly, at that juncture, vanilla remained a flavor enjoyed primarily by expatriates. External influences took other forms as well. In 1904, Satō Chūgi, who served on the Japanese army's reception committee for foreign military officers, requested that the General Staff Office in Tokyo send various foodstuffs, such as German sausages, drinks, as well as spices, including "a half dozen vanillas." By 1906, French officials in Madagascar checked with Japan's postal services to confirm that vanilla could be sent there in modest quantities by mail.[100]

By the following decade, signs emerged of Japanese people enjoying this foreign delicacy themselves. In 1919, several newspapers ran ads for Morinaga's "vanilla chocolate" bars that featured a quote by German medical chemist Julius von Liebig affirming the restorative virtues of chocolate. The ads specified that chocolate bars were "greatly enjoyed by businessmen all over the world." Despite the words *vanilla chocolate* figuring prominently on the wrapper in English, the text made no mention of vanilla.[101]

In 1925, the British embassy in Tokyo took on the case of a Kobe-produced "vanilla essence." The embassy's agents were not concerned by my key question—still unresolved—of whether the substance contained any actual vanilla. Rather, they worried that the producer's tag presented a "resemblance to the labels and names of well-known British manufacturers." They ultimately discovered that Yujiro Yoshida of Kobe produced this liquid bearing the misleading brand name "Great Henry Co. of London."[102] Whether the vanillin was real or synthetic, the flask's very existence, when combined with the spread of vanilla chocolate bars, betrays a budding consumer interest in vanilla flavor in Taishō-era Japan.

Demand continued to grow thereafter. In 1936, Japan imported half a metric ton of Tahitian vanilla.[103] In 1956, it purchased close to 305 kilos (672 pounds) of Réunionese vanilla, then 7.24 metric tons of Malagasy vanilla in 1971. Japanese consumption reached its zenith in 1979. That year, it imported 52.45 metric tons of vanilla pods. However, two years on, that figure was more than halved (twenty-one tons in 1981) as Japanese food manufacturers turned to synthetic vanillin.[104]

The large-scale embrace of vanilla in China followed a similar pattern. Foreigners consumed it in Shanghai as early as 1882, in the form of ice cream served at a charity ball. By 1917, the *China Press*, read by expatriate communities across the foreign concessions in China, included a tip in its segment "New Things Every Woman Ought to Know." It advised, "You might try vanilla in your cocoa," and specified, "The flavor will be wonderfully improved if a drop of vanilla is added in each cup just before serving." And in 1920, the Shanghai General Store advertised its "reasonably" priced "fresh vanilla beans."[105] As for broader Chinese consumption, surely the Chinese overseas communities involved in vanilla preparation and exports from Polynesia to Madagascar must have played a role in propagating vanilla in mainland China. Unfortunately, I have not been able to connect them back to Chinese consumption through existing sources.

One thing is certain: Already by the late nineteenth century, vanilla's entrancing flavor had bewitched palates the world over. However, despite its price drop resulting from the manual pollination revolution and the ensuing multiplication of cultivation zones from Java to Seychelles, some consumers still could not afford it. Synthetic vanillin would remedy this, making vanilla a mass flavoring, but at a tremendous cost to the vanilla sector. By mid-century, real vanilla began fighting back.

CHAPTER 8

Revenge of the Orchid

VANILLAMANIA REACHED A FEVER PITCH DURING THE SECOND World War. As the USS *Lexington* sank after a Japanese submarine attack in 1942, sailors scrambled to get their hands on the ice cream in the ship's freezers. They filled their helmets with it before descending into their life vessels. Vanilla ice cream must have obsessed these fighters for it to be *the* item to grab from a sinking battleship. Two years later, in August 1944, as American soldiers were being freed from the westernmost prisoner of war camps in Europe, the National Dairy Products Company placed a patriotic ad in *Life* magazine. Titled "558 Americans took vanilla!" it reads, "They boarded a Swedish ship in a Portuguese port after being released from German internment camps. And every one brought a long pent-up appetite for ice cream. [. . .] We must have eaten at least a quarter of a ton of it the first day out, one of the [. . .] passengers reported." The ad concludes by vaunting the merits of vanilla ice cream as a wholesome American food. This was at once a piece of a much larger marketing operation and the expression of a national obsession. By 1945, the US navy even created a floating ice cream–production barge to bring 135 million pounds of the treat to its servicemen in the Pacific.[1] Vanilla ice cream had become an American need.

In addition to bringing about a surprising spike in US ice cream consumption—by way of comparison, wartime Britons were urged to eat frozen carrots on sticks—World War II also marked a turning point for the vanilla flavor in that ice cream.[2] Ever since the 1930s, the amount of actual vanilla in US ice cream dropped, even as consumption of the frozen dessert skyrocketed. The Second World War greatly accelerated the trend because Madagascar, Réunion, and the Comoros Islands remained outside the Allied orbit until 1943 while Mexico and Tahiti strained to keep up with demand. It didn't help that a German U-boat sank one of the few wartime shipments of Bourbon vanilla—140 metric tons of Malagasy pods aboard the *Robin Goodfellow*—off the coast of South Africa in 1944.[3] Due to this supply crisis, and the mounting risks tied to maritime transport, synthetics were taking vanilla's place, mirroring a trend with other commodities during World War II, including rubber and diamonds.[4] Yet it seems unlikely many GIs, marines, or sailors noticed any difference from the ice cream of their childhoods that contained actual pods, because few taste buds can. And so, it follows, if synthetic vanillin provides nearly the same smell and taste as real vanilla, does it matter that it's a chemical replacement?

The rise of synthetic vanillin is the perfect encapsulation of what Goodman, Sorj, and Wilkinson call substitutionism, the effort to replace an agricultural crop with an industrially produced chemical proxy (or a substitute crop, as in the case of margarine in lieu of butter).[5] Battles over what constitutes vanilla—and more specifically about vanillin, the molecule present in both real vanilla and in its many synthetic substitutes—lie at the heart of this chapter. They extend back to the nineteenth century.

We should remember from the outset that vanillin levels vary even within natural vanillas. *Vanilla tahitensis* is a case in point; it contains less vanillin than *Vanilla planifolia*, and many of its complex aromas derive from its non-vanillin components, which are absent from synthetics. Indeed, there is no straightforward correlation between vanillin content and excellence in natural pods.[6] Therefore, claims of ideal substitutes, just like claims of absolute purity, need to be treated with some caution.

As Nadia Berenstein has shown, debates over synthetic vanillin stretch back the late nineteenth century. Vanillin was identified in 1858 by French chemist Théodore-Nicolas Gobley.[7] In 1874, German researchers Ferdinand Tiemann and Wilhelm Haarmann unlocked vanillin's molecular structure, synthesizing it from coniferin. Initially, the discovery had little impact: The factory at Holzmindin that first produced synthetic vanillin in 1876 yielded a substance that fetched a prohibitive $1,500 per kilo. However, proponents of chemical vanillin were soon arguing that their product could achieve greater purity, potency, and even aroma than what was possible with vanilla beans. Indeed, the two Germans contended that they had discovered the actual source of vanilla beans' flavor and perfume. Germany became a site where chemical vanillin was "naturalized." As Paulina Gennermann explains, the process involved a linguistic and conceptual slippage that occurred in that country in the late nineteenth and early twentieth century: Vanilla and vanillin became one and the same in popular discourse and in cookery, despite being demonstrably different insofar as additional flavors and molecules are present in real vanilla. By the 1890s, two laboratories, one French, the other German, established more affordable processes by which to produce vanillin from clove oil. In the 1920s came ethylvanillin, derived from a new chemical product featuring a more intense aroma. These different chemicals elicited considerable commercial interest.[8]

Cheap synthetics averted nearly all the challenges of natural vanilla, an unstable luxury good that—if it weren't stolen, lost to piracy, sunk by a U-boat, or destroyed by a hurricane—could crack, spoil, dry up, or mold. Real vanilla also presented countless variations in grade, quality, nose, texture, and size, whereas synthetics could achieve complete uniformity. Uniformity's appeal was no doubt increased by the amount of trickery present in the natural vanilla business. Already in 1859, a book described a widespread method for mimicking *givre* on vanilla. In 1895, a Belgian vanilla importer and trader stood trial for having faked *givre* on his pods to enhance their appeal and value. Finally, in 1927, J. Moroy, a female scientist working for France's central fraud prevention department, drew up a detailed case against so-called vanilla powders that incorporated minuscule quantities of actual vanilla, which they drowned in much cheaper sugar.[9]

Skulduggery of this kind might seem relatively harmless were it not for suspected cases of poisoning that had marked the previous century. Vanilla panic set in at the height of obsessions over food purity and tampering. Alleged vanilla poisonings occurred internationally, mostly in the summer months. The isolated events dotted the entire century and presented no particular sequence beyond seasonality. Such a series of unresolved cases over so many decades might have piqued Sherlock Holmes's interest. A first lineup of suspects included adulteration, tampering, rogue pods, and even the characteristics of real vanilla itself—before chemical vanillin joined the list. In July 1826, a doctor and his wife fell violently sick after eating vanilla ice cream on the terrace of the Café de la Rotonde in Paris's Palais-Royal. In July 1863, at a Viennese soirée hosted by Austria's minister of police, scores of high society guests doubled over in digestive distress they dared not describe, all attributed to vanilla ice cream. In New England in 1873, a scientist investigating vanilla poisoning mysteriously fell victim to the affliction himself. Five of his relatives who had eaten the same vanilla custard likewise suffered from "much gastric disturbance," while two others who had opted for alternate desserts reported no problems. The following year, the press reported a string of vanilla ice cream poisonings in Paris, France; Altona, Canada; Munich, Germany; and Vienna, Austria. Then, in Lawton, Michigan, in June 1886, eighteen customers fell sick after eating vanilla ice cream. Others who had enjoyed lemon sherbet at the same establishment were unharmed. Debates raged, accusations flew. One scientist pointed to "vanillism" as the culprit. An article about the incident in the *Detroit Free Press* claimed that "the [vanilla] bean often poisons the skins of workmen employed in picking and assorting it." However, Victor Vaughan, a bacteriologist at the University of Michigan, settled the matter by drinking large quantities of the wrongly incriminated vanilla extract and showing no ill effects. It turned out that the problem with nineteenth-century vanilla custards and ice creams had to do with dairy and refrigeration, not vanilla.[10]

The call for greater transparency, regulation, and standardization of vanilla can be traced to one so-called vanilla poisoning in particular. Fin-de-siècle Vienna was characterized by breathtaking art nouveau, Johann Strauss's waltzes, and Sigmund Freud's breakthroughs, of course, but also by a string of purported vanilla poisonings, several of them fatal. While some pointed to another outbreak of "vanilla disease," an 1898 article in *Scientific American* cast doubt as to whether actual vanilla was to blame. The piece explained that synthetic vanillin had begun to replace natural vanilla. Some was extracted from wood while some came from cardol. Although the latter could be an irritant, the author ruled it out as a cause of death. Still, the article suggested, rather than fault vanilla, "more knowledge regarding artificial vanillin is desirable."[11] Suspicions seemed to be switching to chemical vanillin. However, by 1907, a French toxicologist became rightly convinced that nearly all the previous century's so-called vanilla poisonings had nothing to do with either vanilla or vanillin.[12]

Still, standardizing vanilla, along with drawing a distinction between real and synthetic vanillin, remained powerful twin imperatives for regulators. In France, a 1905 law forced industrialists to indicate when their products contained synthetic vanillin. A cycle of transatlantic emulation ensued, and the following year, the United States followed suit with the 1906 Pure Food and Drug Act. In a country where most vanilla was consumed in extract form, standardization was meant to regulate the "purity and strength" of natural vanilla extracts. The legislation further required those using synthetic vanillin to include the words *imitation* or *compound* on their labels.[13] The law represented the culmination of decades of concerns over consumer fraud and adulterations. As Nadia Berenstein has highlighted, synthetic vanillin was not the intended target of the 1906 Act because it was not the product of adulteration so much as an exact chemical match for vanilla's key component. It still ended up falling under the Act's purview. Lines were drawn with a new vanilla standard relying on tests for botanical components rather than vanillin.[14]

The new 1906 labeling rules, in particular the uninviting term "imitation vanilla," had immediate effects. In the ensuing months, pod consumption surged in the United States, with the country suddenly surpassing France's consumption for the first time. American pod importers rejoiced. On the other side of the Atlantic, their French counterparts were quick to learn the lesson and demand a revision of that nation's 1905 law. In 1907, Bordeaux's Chamber of Commerce, representing real vanilla importers, launched a frontal attack on synthetics. They charged that chemical vanillin was nothing short of "consumer deception." France's 1905 law needed to be more rigorously enforced, they insisted. They further questioned synthetic vanillin's healthfulness. Finally, they asked their government to mandate that the words *chemical vanillin* be included on the label of any product containing the ersatz. The timing of their petition was no coincidence: Its authors noted that the US Pure Food and Drug Act had helped pod prices in that country rebound between 60 and 80 percent over the course of the previous year.[15]

But could these measures force the hand of the food industry? Certainly not in countries outside the new legislation's reach. Near the turn of the twentieth century, London's Imperial Institute worried that Seychellois vanilla was losing out to competition from Swiss and French synthetic vanillin and considered its options for defending British colonial pods. One strategy involved threatening English chocolate manufacturers into revealing their use of chemical vanillin while another aimed to shame them into turning away from vanillin. A third approach was to pass legislation "prohibiting the use of vanilla substitutes." Verification was bound to prove tricky, noted the Institute: "It may be difficult to discover the presence of vanillin by analysis." Consequently, the Institute floated the idea of informal inspections. It could send "a qualified official [. . .] to visit some manufacturers' premises and ask questions." Chemical vanillin detection was presenting a headache precisely because the same molecule was also present in real vanilla. In 1906, the Imperial Institute contacted Rowntree and Company, J. S. Fry and Sons, and Cadbury directly. Was there any truth, the Institute asked hopefully, to rumors that "chocolate manufacturers have of late to some extent given up using artificial vanillin for flavoring chocolate, and have reverted to the use of natural vanilla?" The rumor proved too good to be true. All answered negatively. The chocolate manufacturers J. S. Fry and Sons explained that chemical vanillin offered a far "greater flexibility in handling than [vanilla]."[16] It seemed there was no putting the chemical genie back in its bottle.

Despite the new battle lines, sometimes the boundary between vanillin and vanilla became blurred. In 1934, Jean Wade Rindlaub, a leading advertising executive and food consultant who worked most notably for the General Mills food and recipe brand Betty Crocker, pitched a proposed for a "vanilla capsule." Her invention was designed for convenience. Its casing was dissolvable and tasteless, so that the capsule, containing a single tablespoon of vanilla, could be deposited into any recipe (she cited puddings or fudge). It was not evident what the capsule would contain; however, based on the context and Rindlaub's use of the words *fresh vanilla*, in lieu of vanillin, it can be inferred that the contents were natural vanilla extract. But Rindlaub's container made even natural vanilla a perfect single-dose, ready-to-use product.[17]

Although her capsule never caught on, by the middle of the twentieth century American bakers and cooks were seldom buying actual vanilla pods. Betty Crocker's iconic 1950 *Picture Cook Book* called for vanilla extract exclusively, even in ice cream.[18] Real vanilla itself had become disembodied, which could only help the cause of synthetics. Why pay more for one liquid over another? And who was checking what went into the liquid in the first place?

The definition of real vanilla remained hotly contested. Even at the height of the reign of synthetics, food inspectors continued to worry about other natural products posing as vanilla. Substituting similar natural ingredients for vanilla has a long history, just as for centuries pricey peppercorns have been replaced by lookalikes.[19] Instances of burned oats, heliotrope, pandan (*Pandanus amaryllifolius*), or other substances passing for vanilla dot the historical record. By the twentieth century, new, more sophisticated ersatzes of natural origin made their appearance. Taking stock of his long career, the Food and Drug Administration's Gilbert Goldhammer, who rose through the ranks during and after the Second World War, remembered one case in particular.

Over the course of the war, a brand calling itself Plantation manufactured what it labeled as vanilla extract. It turned out that the product contained very little real vanilla and was predominantly composed of oleo resin derived from much cheaper Saint-John's-wort, sweetened to deceive consumers. The case initially stumped the FDA, but the organization ultimately prevailed, demonstrating fraud and sending several of those involved to jail.[20]

Natural replacements thus constituted one problem. However, synthetic vanillin posed a much greater set of challenges still. Artificial vanillin may have first been derived from cloves and beaver secretions (castoreum), but its primary source soon shifted to wood derivatives (lignin).[21] The US chemical giant Monsanto began producing artificial vanillin from lignin in 1906, soon followed by several rivals in wood-rich areas, including Scandinavian nations and Canada. In the Niagara region of Canada, the Ontario Paper Company took advantage of the abundance of local forests, cheap electricity from nearby Niagara Falls, and plentiful water to produce newsprint, which it started churning out in 1913. However, the toxic pulp paper sulfite waste the process generated was so abundant that by 1935 the company sought ways to process it. At that very time, with the support of the Canadian pulp and paper sector, McGill University chemistry professor Harold Hibbert was developing a new method of producing vanillin from waste sulfite liquor, itself derived from paper pulp. In 1937, he reported to the vice president of the US Flavoring Extract Manufacturers Association that Howard Smith Chemicals Ltd. in Montreal was putting his method into practice. The professor pronounced it a commercial success that generated a hundred pounds of synthetic vanillin "of the highest purity" per day. By 1941, Hibbert was reporting higher yields at a lower cost. On the strength of those innovations, in 1943 Ontario Paper Company transformed pulp waste into industrial alcohol, and in 1952 it began converting it into vanillin for the food and pharmaceutical industries (a transformation the *Chicago Tribune*'s mills had already undertaken in 1947). In 1964, the Ontario Paper Company announced that its new manufacturing process could generate three thousand pounds (1.36 metric tons) of chemical vanillin a year. (Note that synthetic vanillin is more potent per ounce, so three thousand pounds went a long way.) By the 1970s, it and Monsanto were vying for global chemical vanillin supremacy. Monsanto boasted of its vanillin's "exceptional flavor, purity and uniformity," while the Ontario Paper Company claimed that a "fresh breeze" of vanilla was "whispering through our towering forests." This came in jarring contrast to the

1959 complaints of local residents who told of "yellow stuff" billowing out of the vanillin plant that "ma[de] them sick," covered them and their gardens in sticky gunk, and stripped cars of their paint. This did not stop the firm from coining the advertising slogan "Vanillin by Ontario," linking the Canadian province to a flavor previously associated with a tropical orchid.[22]

Of course, Canada and the United States were only some of the many producers of synthetic vanillin. Others included Iran, Vietnam, Spain, Germany, the Netherlands and Japan. In other words, chemical vanillin manufacture and consumption were not limited to the so-called West. Already in 1926 Shanghai, Kraft was creating an increasingly popular "vanilla cake" that was actually made with chemical vanillin.[23] By 1972, the Ontario Paper Company had partnered with the Japanese Takasago Perfumery Company, resulting in the creation of a new vanillin plant at Iwakuni by Sanyo Pulp Company.[24]

The Iron Curtain proved no barrier to chemical vanillin, either. In 1965, at the height of the Cold War, both Communist Poland and Romania produced the stuff. Nevertheless, they also consumed some actual pods. The Soviet Union imported five metric tons of natural vanilla from Madagascar that same year, and Hungary also expressed interest in Sava vanilla.[25] However, the Eastern Bloc never emerged as a major pod consumer. Apart from a half decade of Didier Ratsiraka control over Madagascar between 1975 and 1980, when the Red Admiral prioritized trade with the USSR, most of the Soviet Union's iconic ice creams were produced with chemical vanillin, not vanilla.

With all these East-West continuities, the real divide between synthetic vanillin and real vanilla fell along North-South lines. The pod-producing Global South, articulated in the case of vanilla around Mexico, Polynesia, Indonesia, Madagascar, and the Comoros Islands, stood to lose most from synthetics while pulp-producing northern nations could gain the most. Little wonder, then, that Indian Ocean voices were at the origin of real vanilla's counterattack.

As chemical vanillin grew cheaper, diverging profit margins were such that synthetics could trounce their natural competitor. However, synthetics and natural vanilla managed to coexist between 1895 and roughly 1930. That balance broke for good during World War II.[26] In June 1968, a Parisian firm drew the following picture:

> While the production of ice cream in the United States increased by 500 percent between 1920 and 1961, [...] the percentage of natural vanilla

used for those ice creams has diminished, not just in relative terms, but even in absolute values, at the expense of chemical replacement products derived from cloves, petroleum, cellulose or wood, as well as ethylvanillin.

The same report showed that in the United States and Canada, the output of chemical and ethylvanillin rose by an astounding 700 percent between 1933 and 1963.[27]

Facing all these threats, the real vanilla sector needed to fight back, lest it vanish altogether. The origins of a concerted plan can be traced to the immediate post–World War II era. In 1945–46, Indian Ocean planters began to complain of their utter dependence on importer-exporters. Marseille trader Marcel Guyénot implied that the only winners in this situation were "American trusts." Then, in 1948, Madagascar overproduced, at the very time when consumption dipped and Mexican competition remained robust. This led to the unprecedented deliberate destruction of some six hundred tons of Malagasy vanilla.[28] Real vanilla beans were being destroyed while vanillin derived from pulp waste poured into ice creams.

The orchid's revenge involved the gradual formation of a production cartel, as well as deliberately stoking concerns in Europe and America about authenticity, purity, and lack of oversight. Profiteering from chemical firms and vanilla "trusts" alike also elicited public unease. As Kolleen Guy has noted, "Middlemen were not always seen as the guarantors of quality and the specter of excess profits, artificial shortages and dubious quality produced consumer anxieties and demands for market regulation."[29]

In 1955, Madagascar's Union Intersyndicale de la Vanille retained an American advertising firm to promote "natural vanilla" across the United States. It turned to Bernard L. Lewis Inc. to launch this nationwide operation across television, magazine, and radio. Bernard Lewis even created a dedicated subsidiary to handle the vanilla file. The Pure Vanilla Publicity Company established its headquarters in New York's Empire State Building, no less. It pushed vanilla in refrigerator pies, soda fountains, Victorian Christmas pudding, and molded vanilla plum pudding. It paid for articles across the press, including such evocatively titled pieces as "There Is an Orchid in the Kitchen" and "Make Mine Vanilla!" The company soon boasted of having reached 21,353,205 in circulation with its pod messaging.[30]

Not everyone approved of the campaign, however. In May 1955, the French embassy in Washington relayed the Bernard Lewis company's request for photos of vanilla groves to the authorities in Réunion. A local official scrawled across the page: "Absolutely not! [. . .] This is unfair competition from Madagascar vanilla which calls itself Bourbon Vanilla."[31] Lessons were learned: Future lobby groups of this kind would need to bring together all producers from the southern Indian Ocean.

Over the course of the 1960s, vanilla growers found reasons to be hopeful. In 1965, the FDA introduced new labeling that accentuated distinctions between real vanilla and chemical vanillin. That year, the United States imported 977 metric tons of vanilla beans, breaking previous records.[32] However, hopes pinned on the United States proved short-lived. New York importers began blaming producing countries for setting too high a base price for vanilla. The backlash led to vanilla piling up in hangers in American port cities in 1967. The United States even halted imports altogether for a while. This could not have come at a worse time, as Madagascar had just reached a new production peak of 1,600 metric tons.

In other words, the FDA-induced bump did not last. Before 1965, the United States had imported 70 percent of the world's real vanilla; that figure dropped to 60 percent a few short years later. Booming western European economies began picking up the slack. In 1967, the European Community (later the European Union) consumed 35 percent of the world's natural vanilla, with France bringing in 170 tons, West Germany 60, Italy 15, Belgium, and the Netherlands and Luxemburg a combined 20. Other major global consumers included Australia with nine tons, Argentina with six, and Britain and Canada with four tons apiece.[33]

For the nascent natural vanilla lobby, synthetics represented the prime enemy. Producing nations and regions responded with an international, Indian Ocean–centered cartel. I use this term not in a pejorative sense but in its classic definition of "a coalition or cooperative arrangement between political parties intended to promote a mutual interest."[34]

Real vanilla's counterattack began in earnest in 1966. In January, a preliminary agreement was reached between the authorities of the Republic of Madagascar (independent since 1960), the autonomous archipelago of the Comoros Islands, and the French overseas department of Réunion Island. Building on initiatives undertaken after 1943 in the late colonial era to apportion vanilla reserves, the three partners decided that pod exports to the United States should be allotted as follows: 405 metric tons from Madagascar, 20 metric tons from the Comoros, and another 20 tons for

Réunion.[35] Reflecting its output, Madagascar received the lion's share of the allotments.

Next, in October 1966, the Comoros Islands invited delegates from both Madagascar and Réunion to the Comorian capital, Moroni. On paper, at least, the structure of the governing troika was relatively fair, even favorable to developing countries. The project's initiator, who also presided over the 1966 session, was Abdourahim Mikidache, the Comoros Islands' minister of economy and finance.[36]

The group achieved some immediate success in the French market. A May 1966 French decree mandated that any product containing chemical vanillin bear a marker on the label reading "artificial" or "synthetic." Four years later, Malilé, a Paris-based vanilla company running a small workshop in the Loire Valley, faced charges for having breached that rule. Although most of their products contained actual Tahitian or Guadeloupean vanilla— under a label featuring a bare-chested racialized woman—food inspectors found that Malilé's "vanilla sugar with natural vanilla" was in fact composed of artificial vanillin instead of the real thing. Their so-called vanilla extracts also presented "irregularities." Accordingly, in August 1970 a prosecutor in Blois drew up charges against the company. In addition to invoking the recent 1966 decree, the prosecutor cited the 1905 law on doctored foodstuffs, noting that the label's words "containing natural vanilla flavor" were misleading.[37]

The Indian Ocean trio was emboldened by the 1965 and 1966 regulatory successes. A December 1966 follow-up meeting took place at Madagascar's embassy in Paris. There, representatives from Madagascar, Comoros, and Réunion mingled with vanilla traders and importers. They focused on "actions to take to defend pure vanilla in Europe." Purity was on their side. Long debates ensued under the dual leadership of Abdourahim Mikidache and Madagascar's ambassador to France, the biologist Albert Rakoto Ratsimamanga. After having discussed matters of price, reserves, and quality, the group agreed to foster "propaganda [. . .] to defend pure vanilla."[38] (The word propaganda did not yet have the negative connotations it does today.) This gave rise to a public relations firm initially dubbed Provanille (which turned out to be a name already taken on Réunion), then later Univanille. The title set the tone for the campaign: there was only one true vanilla, which was to say natural vanilla.

That very same month of December 1966, another team of vanilla specialists from Madagascar, Réunion, and the Comoros Islands met in Antananarivo to determine precise quotas for US and Canadian consumption and for each major American importer. The New York–based Vanilla Beans Association protested what it considered to be heavy-handed tactics, but the Indian Ocean producers stood firm.[39] Admittedly, some cracks were starting to appear in the united vanilla front. A Malagasy secret report concerning the December 1966 Paris talks suggested that the Comorians needed to be convinced not to cave to pressure from US companies. Still, the troika held. It put forward a two-pronged argument. First, the revenues of Indian Ocean, and especially Malagasy, vanilla farmers absolutely needed a boost for their quality of life to improve. Second, were the price of a gallon of American ice cream to rise 2 or 3 percent, it would not translate into an "upheaval in the cost price" to US consumers, whereas it certainly would boost vanilla rates. When the US firms protested that ice cream consumption was flattening, Madagascar's delegate countered with the idea that the US companies contribute at the very least to the new "vanilla propaganda" bureau (Provanille/Univanille). The 2–3 percent increase the trio was proposing could be earmarked for the new agency. The representatives from the American Flavor and Extract Manufacturers Association and McCormick Spices seemed taken aback.[40]

The forceful negotiating stance, along with the powerful role played by Malagasy and Comorian representatives who presided over these talks reflected the new weight held by the Global South following the 1955 Bandung Conference. The organization's genesis and formative years more or less mirrored those of more lucrative energy cartels, including OPEC (founded in Baghdad in 1960–61 and also articulated around the Global South).[41] A more cynical interpretation might have Réunion Island's position in the troika as a kind of French Trojan horse. In that light, via Réunion, France could have asserted postimperial vanilla influence through the nebulous network that was *Françafrique*. But it seems to me that the defense of real vanilla points to a different power dynamic. Réunion had little say in the deliberations because the island's production was dwarfed by Madagascar's. Moreover, the pod cartel was founded in the Comoros, run out of Madagascar's embassies, and showcased heavy Indian Ocean representation. None of this reflected a spirit of neocolonialism.

In 1968, the Comoros Islands, Madagascar, and Réunion once more dispatched delegates to Paris, where they met with Madagascar's interprofessional national vanilla board. At the headquarters of France's vanilla union, the delegates ratified a decision taken the year prior, to establish and fund the "propaganda center" devoted entirely to "defending natural vanilla" (note that the "natural" had replaced "pure"). Conceived at Madagascar's embassy in Paris a few years earlier, Univanille, the vanilla cartel's advertising service, was born. The national press in Madagascar relayed the exciting news. It reported that Europe would be Univanille's top priority, which was unsurprising given the reticence of US firms. Additionally, the fledgling agency had already coined an initial slogan: "Buy Indian Ocean vanilla."[42]

The first question was how to fund the ad agency. Producers balked at opening their wallets while warehouses overflowed with unsold pods. Ultimately, importers agreed in January 1968 on a tax to help support the firm.[43] Buyers, producers, and brokers now worked hand in hand to help rebrand vanilla and improve its image. A British source highlighted two unique features of Univanille: it united both decolonized (Madagascar) and nondecolonized regions (Comoros and Réunion), and its subsidies were tied to recent performance, meaning a North American decline would reduce attention to that market the following year.[44]

Univanille's initial findings were at once alarming and clear: "Natural vanilla seems to have almost entirely lost the industrial consumption sector." Supermarket biscuits, cookies, yogurts, ice creams, cake mixes, and custards all contained the synthetic stuff. The last remaining battlegrounds were in the realms of home cooking and haute cuisine.[45]

As Univanille was just beginning to take shape, the delegates sought to jump-start advertising on their own. One of their first measures involved making the case for authentic or real vanilla across western Europe, via Madagascar's embassies. However, they quickly ran into technical hurdles. The main challenge involved detecting synthetic vanillin in food, as it was nearly impossible without the use of highly advanced equipment. To make matters worse, the United States, which was moving full tilt ahead toward synthetics, held a monopoly over that machinery.[46] In some ways, the problem was not new. Ever since the nineteenth century, scientists, traders, and industrialists had quarreled over how to interpret laboratory testing of foodstuffs. However, this was no longer a matter of determining whether wine was watered down or butter contained lard but rather whether a product passing as vanilla was instead a chemical surrogate.[47]

Univanille was thus created to wage war on synthetic vanillin and simultaneously represent its different constituencies. The organization's charter ran as follows:

(a) Encourage in France and in all other countries, the consumption and use of vanilla, by means of propaganda, advertising, market studies, and all appropriate means.
(b) Develop [. . .] knowledge of vanilla and its uses, as well as its proper preparation.
(c) Bring together and use all documentary information, studies, and research on vanilla in view of the following:
　—Favoring the improvement of commercial methods of distribution, warehousing, and presentation of vanilla. [. . .]
　—Urging public authorities in France and abroad to enact measures defending natural vanilla.

Despite a broad global mandate, Univanille was mostly supposed to exert influence within Europe "so that in the future the countries of the Common Market should adopt common rules protecting natural vanilla against its chemical competitor, vanillin."[48] However, by 1971, it became clear that Italy, which by then had emerged as both a major producer and consumer of synthetic vanillin, opposed "natural vanilla" as a pan-European appellation.[49]

Challenges abounded, beyond European roadblocks. In 1968, Univanille readily admitted that its main obstacle was that "for most consumers, it has become hard to distinguish between the taste of real vanilla and that of its artificial substitutes."[50] Still, the firm's leadership held out hope of increased regulation. New US rules introduced by the FDA made food labels with lists of ingredients mandatory. If France's European partners followed the example of the FDA or the 1949 law in France that obliges ice cream and dairy producers to use real vanilla, it would result in a 300-ton increase in pod consumption. Univanille suggested creating a commercial designation for real vanilla. Again, this simply extended a precedent already established in France. Since 1966, any French product containing chemical vanillin was legally required to bear the words *artificial* or *synthetic* on its label. It was hoped that an intensive advertising campaign, coupled with regulatory reform, could stem the tide of chemical vanillin.

Whom should Univanille target with its ad campaign? The firm retained two advertising companies, Dupuy-Compton and ESSOR, to undertake separate studies. The first involved surveying a hundred or so retailers in Paris, Tours, and Strasbourg, the second a thousand French women across the country. The student-led upheavals of May 1968 delayed the first survey.[51] At the same time, Univanille deluged the media with materials and reached out to consumers as well as intermediaries. Ice cream makers, confectioners, and other retailers were explicitly targeted, as were food conventions and shows.[52]

An even broader category, women consumers, constituted Univanille's chief target. On the surface, this seems to conform to the notion of double-edged gendered consumerism, which elevated the middle-class "housewife" as a symbol of her class, family, or nation while confining her to a subordinate position. However, historians in recent decades have cautioned against reducing the "housewives" of the 1950s and 1960s to mere victims of advertising and instead have stressed their agency. This is readily applicable to the case of vanilla, where one can see a two-way dialogue in Univanille's surveys, in which female consumers often turn the tables on advertisers and psychologists alike.[53]

Dupuy-Compton dispatched its inquiries to Paris, Tours, and Strasbourg, focusing on vanilla retailers. One of its conclusions spoke to the gap between the capital city and the rest of the country: "It would seem that the demand for vanilla is weaker in Paris than in the provinces. This probably has to do with the fact that in the provinces, housewives devote more time to prepare traditional, homemade dishes."[54]

In August 1968, the second firm, ESSOR, conducted a more detailed survey that ran in two stages. First, psychologists were hired to conduct interviews with "housewives." Subsequently, a vast survey targeted a thousand French women. The analysis of these two surveys betrayed consumer trends that ran shivers down the spines of vanilla lobbyists. ESSOR explained that selling vanilla to younger women, with no family nostalgia for pods, would be an uphill battle: "Innovators, modern women, and active women more generally are refusing 'domestic slavery' by seeking the material convenience afforded by instant foods." In other words, ESSOR believed that modern women's busy lives led to the rise of synthetics, at the expense of natural products that required longer preparation times. The sociological details provided by the teams of psychologists are revealing. The anonymous woman who used the phrase *domestic slavery* was one of the few women surveyed to be gainfully employed outside the household, and certainly the only one in a management position, to be approached by ESSOR. The forty-four-year-old Parisian mother of a small child considered that "homemade desserts are a spent concept, a culinary habit on the way out based on the enslavement of women, and their relegation to the domestic realm, while active women lack time, and therefore seek out convenience, and in particular instant desserts."[55]

What can we make of these binary schemes of "liberated women" versus traditional cooks, and Parisians versus provincials? At an October 1968 meeting, Univanille's leadership put forth the following plan: "Housewives must use vanilla for very repetitive culinary preparations, and they should own some [pods], if only to perfume their sugar. We must distribute recipes in flyer format." This was a variation on the expression "If you can't beat them, join them." Rather than plead for the lost cause of traditional cuisine, Univanille believed it should move with the times. Roland Barthes's framework is useful here: instead of old-fashioned "dream cooking" or baroque "ornamental cuisine," Univanille was promoting "economical cooking" comprising "real dishes."[56]

In addition to producing recipe flyers, Univanille did not hesitate to mobilize all existing media. Its 1972 television commercial directly addressed French mothers. It features a middle-class couple and their lone teenage son, settled in the living room in front of their television. The husband is seen munching on a biscuit while his wife and son are enjoying yogurt (which underwent an industrial turn and accompanying mass consumption in France over the course of the previous decade). An expert on the TV addresses her directly: "Madame, you are thinking of vanilla, and you're right to do so. Because vanilla is a refined aroma. But be careful, in order to be certain that a product contains natural vanilla, check the packaging to ensure that the word *vanilla* is written on it." The teenage son then inspects the yogurt's label and proudly shows his contented mother that it does indeed bear the word *vanilla*. Meanwhile, the husband squints in vain for the designation on his cookie box while the television expert concludes, "If it were natural vanilla, it would have the word *vanilla* on it."[57] The "housewife" is triply solicited and vindicated in the clip, as she is directly addressed by the expert, then her son, and finally her husband, who looks sheepish as he fails to identify any sign of real vanilla in his snack.

However, such heavily gendered ads ran the risk of a backlash identified by ESSOR: that vanilla, already considered by many to be "bland" or a "diet food," might ultimately come to be seen as lacking "virility." According to an August 1968 report from the agency, "The dietary qualities of this essentially healthy and natural aroma, mean that it is usually recommended for children and the elderly [. . .]. That contains a real danger: if it were deemed too 'healthy,' vanilla might become demasculinized and trivialized."[58] Insisting on this orchid-derived product's so-called feminine virtues (elegance, subtlety, balance, healthfulness) in a society that still favored purportedly masculine values (strength, determination, meat consumption) ran the risk of backfiring. In a nutshell, making the husband wrong on the 1972 television commercial posed some challenges.

As part of its highly gendered campaign, Univanille also considered the importance of youth and transmission. It decided to target "household science" teachers—itself a field dedicated to training future homemakers. The organization placed an article in the October 1968 issue of *Enseignement ménager* (Household teaching), as well as in *Education rurale* (Rural education). It distributed seventy thousand copies of a brochure on vanilla to seven thousand household science schools across France. Indeed, *enseignement ménager* programs for young women received kits complete with brochures and slides titled "The Vanilla Lesson." They covered a range of natural vanilla products and explained the pollination, boiling, curing, and preparation processes.[59]

As this suggests, Univanille spared no expense or effort to spread its message in France. It retained the CEDAL (Centre de documentation de l'alimentation) food documentation center) to draft a public relations program. This was one of many such campaigns. The ambitious five-year plan included supporting "experimental cooking" to elaborate new recipes. In addition to the gastronomic side, CEDAL planned to reach some twenty thousand doctors with specifically tailored articles in the journal *Equilibre* (Balance). Meanwhile, in 1967 Dupuy-Compton drew up a list of professions its campaign should target. Doctors and dieticians came in fifth place, after "opinion leaders," "celebrity chefs like Raymond Oliver" (the sworn enemy of nouvelle cuisine), household science teachers, and food journalists.[60]

Univanille reached journalists in another creative manner by establishing a prize for the newspaper that published the "best documented and most accurate articles on vanilla." In 1970, the award went to Madeleine Beaumord and her Tours-based newspaper *La Nouvelle République du Centre-Ouest*. As part of her prize, she was accompanied by vanilla experts on a trip to Madagascar.[61]

Promoting natural vanilla also involved forging pragmatic alliances with the powerful sugar lobby. In July 1968, the French sugar documentation center (CEDUS: Le Centre d'études et de documentation du sucre) coordinated communication strategies with Univanille. One joint event was called the "beach round." Designed to coincide with the 1969 Tour de France, it promoted sugar consumption on French beaches, in concert with the French volleyball and yachting associations. Univanille added that CEDUS could provide expertise and experience in the realms of "public relations and psychological action." Indeed, Univanille emulated the achievements of CEDUS in the household science domain, in particular.[62]

Concretely, the two organizations copublished a brochure titled *Vanilla* and a book of "easy and fast recipes that can be made from prepared dishes." The former emphasized vanilla's nobility. It highlighted the hours of labor involved in vanilla preparation and conditioning and also underscored the wealth of knowledge in the vanilla sector. It mentioned that women and children with "dexterous fingers" undertook the pollination method invented by Edmond, a process romantically known as "marrying vanilla." Next, the brochure set its sights on vanilla's rival, "which is simply a chemical product." It praised French legislation that mandated clear labeling and curtailed the use of synthetics in yogurt. As for the cookbook, it included recipes for a date cake with vanilla sugar, as well as an almond cream made with a vanilla pod that was sliced down the middle and boiled in milk in the recipe's very first step.[63]

In concert with the two advertising firms it retained, Univanille sought to play up vanilla's nostalgic, Proustian connotations. Once again, the psychological campaign was aimed mainly at women. The results of ESSOR's August 1968 national poll were clear: "The attraction or rejection of the adult housewife for vanilla, and her likelihood to use it, can be specially explained by the way in which she experienced and accepted her own childhood." Moreover, based on ESSOR's investigations, female cooks who regularly used vanilla "first developed the habit by seeing their mother or their grandmother crafting deserts using pods or a packet of vanilla."[64] The psychologists ESSOR hired were persuaded that vanilla's appeal could best be understood in Freudian terms. It followed that the same framework could be used to manipulate demand and desire for natural vanilla.

However, ESSOR warned that recollections of childhood could also trigger rejections. Some of the women interviewed spoke of "horrid vanilla creams from their childhood." One of them remembered having snatched a whole vanilla bean in her kitchen as a child, mistaking it for licorice. She then snuck it in her mouth, averting her mother's vigilance: "Oh what despair, the taste was so foul," she recalled.[65]

At an October 1968 meeting with CEDAL and other food consortiums, ESSOR's turn to nostalgia met with serious criticism: "We should break with the past and orient our advertising to the future. Vanilla must not be a product that recalls childhood and traditional desserts, but instead a noble product that can 'perfume' or 'support' different culinary preparations. We should be capitalizing on the foodstuffs that accompany vanilla's perfume."[66] Vanilla nostalgia was a double-edged sword, but in the end it proved too powerful to be abandoned.

Univanille also tapped into other themes to sell real Indian Ocean vanilla. It tried to associate vanilla with a Malagasy exotic. Thus, for the October 1968 international food fair, Univanille asked Antananarivo to send "some objects typical of Madagascar which we could display [alongside vanilla] in our showcases." This was a well-established advertising technique: coffee, for instance, had long been marketed by geographical region, with Costa Rican, Java, and Ethiopian roasts all presented differently.[67]

But did exact provenance matter, so long as the vanilla was "pure" and "natural"? Most European consumers had no idea that the vanilla they consumed came almost entirely from Indian Ocean islands (followed in distant second place by the Pacific region). ESSOR seemed convinced that provenance mattered less than establishing an exotic-colonial mystique around pods. Among vanilla's strengths, ESSOR listed "its more or less precise exoticism, nonetheless palpable, which in the spirit of housewives constitutes an undeniable quality." Yet it disagreed with Dupuy-Compton's suggestion of an expansive "natural vanilla" label, preferring instead to develop elaborate niche colonial clichés: "Antillean vanilla would be a weaker expression, for example, than vanilla ripened in the Antillean sun, as this last formula completes notions of exoticism with the image of a healthy, natural product brimming with vitamins."[68] Of course, at this stage a negligible percentage of the European Union's vanilla came from the French Antilles (Martinique and Guadeloupe). Guadeloupean vanilla had experienced success between roughly 1893 and 1946, but it had slid down the rankings for the two decades since the island became a full-fledged French department in 1946.[69] That seemed not to matter; the whole project was a fiction, playing on the nostalgic thread ESSOR discovered in its surveys.

In that sense, the exoticism around real vanilla was hazy, sometimes completely eliding Mexico, Réunion, and even Madagascar. This "exotic aura," to borrow David Ciarlo's phrase, was deliberately blurred, which allowed advertisers to play on an imagined connection to the Caribbean, at a time when most vanilla came from islands in the Indian and Pacific Oceans. Among the respondents to ESSOR's nationwide inquiry in June 1968, one woman's linkage hinged on a rhyme in French: "Vanille, Antilles, for me the connection is automatic." ESSOR's analysis ran as follows: "Among the older women we interviewed, many remember having seen, while they were little girls, Creole women wearing madras textiles who sold vanilla on the markets. These indelible memories lend vanilla a rare emotional and folkloric value." A sixty-three-year-old Parisian woman cited "picturesque markets [...] where Creole women dressed in madras cloth sold pods individually that allowed one to prepare delicious desserts." ESSOR added, "The important role of childhood memories in the use that adult women make of vanilla lead one to fear that future generations will use it less and less, unless we restore its value in a modern context."[70] Vanilla nostalgia was back, and ESSOR ultimately embraced it. What also jumps out from this discussion is the recurring memory of an Antillean woman selling pods in the marketplace. Such women do indeed appear in early twentieth-century postcards as market vanilla vendors, carrying their precious merchandise in special wicker purses.

However, not all colonial clichés about vanilla were like this. For instance, a twenty-one-year-old Parisian interviewed in 1968 recycled a number of stereotypes about tropical lands, mediated and relayed by vanilla: "Vanilla appears as a naive, innocent product tied to regions whose climate, vegetation, and folklore evoke insouciance, a childlike serenity and joie de vivre."[71] No need for an elaborate postcolonial critique to see in this viewpoint a paternalist perception of the colonized as immature and primitive, presenting an insouciance at odds with modern European society.

According to another respondent, a thirty-four-year-old Parisian concierge, vanilla was a culinary interloper. ESSOR summarized her views as

FIGURE 14. Postcard stamped in southern France in 1909 depicting a Martinican "vanilla saleswoman" in a madras dress. Collection Collectivité Territoriale de Martinique, Archives, 2Fi 1223.

follows: "The dominant idea she has of vanilla is of a foreign product from warm lands—a product from the spice family, consumed in special cuisines from those lands, but bearing little relation to French culinary traditions (rather the sort of thing her Tunisian neighbor would use)."[72] In this way, vanilla's positive exoticism could easily morph into negative foreignness in a country that had just waged a prolonged war in North Africa.

ESSOR added another challenge to its list, this one related to taste. Nearly every woman the company interviewed failed to distinguish between vanillin-infused sugar and vanilla-infused sugar. Only 3 percent were able to tell the difference, with no margin of error provided. This "virtually nil perception of sensory differences" applied to aroma, taste, consistency, and hue. Furthermore, despite the word *vanillin* appearing on a label (*vanilline* in French), many hurried customers simply saw "vanilla" (*vanille*). According to the advertising firm, only the words *chemical* or *artificial* could serve as effective deterrents.[73]

Worse still, some consumers found vanilla bland in all its forms, reproaching it for "lacking personality." One of the June 1968 respondents, a twenty-eight-year-old Parisian woman, pulled no punches: Vanilla was little more than "a family myth, a bland product, devoid of color, shape, and flavor, which really adds nothing to a cake." According to another respondent, a twenty-nine-year-old psychologist from the Parisian suburb of Vanves, vanilla represented a "poor product, neutral and drab, without allure, sweet but soppy [. . .]. It's a sad food for elderly ill people. It's water, a cream with no flavor at all."[74]

Univanille would have its work cut out for it to convert ardent antivanillists. Perhaps the firm's only consolation was that these women weren't drawn to synthetic vanillin either. Still, the growing rejection of vanilla as not just "old" but also insipid and boring aligned with a trend that had already begun in English: the use of the term *vanilla* to describe something as plain, uninspiring, and unoriginal.[75]

Univanille did not easily admit defeat. The group turned to how vanilla was presented, seeking to improve displays in shops and supermarkets. Dupuy-Comton's research had revealed vanilla's lack of visibility in retail settings. The reason was simple: Because vanilla was not a big seller, it was relegated to the corners of shops and markets. Dupuy-Compton therefore insisted on the creation of "attractive displays." Moreover, vanilla should not be placed near the pepper and cloves, which were deemed insufficiently patrician neighbors.[76]

In its July 1968 inquiry into vanilla distribution, Dupuy-Compton carefully studied the presentation of vanilla in both grocery stores and supermarkets. Yet, it was not the difference in retail scales that drew the ad firm's attention. Instead, it was the gap between Paris and the provinces. According to the agency, "The integrated circuits are more modern in the provinces, and so pods in blister packs are more widespread there. The price of this modern package is slightly higher than that of glass tubes, which in Paris one finds in fourteen out of every sixteen stores." Naturally, cost depended on more than just packaging. The agency noted that an identical glass tube containing vanilla sold for sixty centimes in the working-class suburb of Montrouge, and one and a half francs in the upscale grocer boutiques of Paris's sixteenth arrondissement. However, in all the regions studied by the agency, pods came in second place in sales, far behind vanilla sugar. In the less affluent parts of Paris, the "twentieth arrondissement and suburbs," the gap between pod and vanilla sugar sales was even greater.[77]

In the least bourgeois quarters, vanilla sachets were clearly the most popular. ESSOR was especially appalled by their packaging. One female consumer stated in June 1968, "One doesn't feel like buying vanilla. It comes in little packs of powder. There are some products one wants to buy: because of their presentation, their appearance, one gets the impression that one will make extraordinary cakes with them. Not so with vanilla. The sachets are badly presented, poorly showcased, they don't elicit desire." Univanille proposed enhancing sachet opacity: Female consumers must absolutely be able to distinguish orchid pod powder from its chemical rival.[78] But it wasn't entirely clear how since vanilla sugar was and remains mostly white.

As for pods, their presentation was also the subject of much discussion. Some mostly young and urban female consumers hated the classic glass tube containing two vanilla beans. One respondent drew two troubling portraits of it: "Two dead fetuses locked in their shell, or hardened worms, it's really ugly!" Another, slightly gentler critic regretted the object's lack of modernity: "It's so granny-like, it's unbelievable." According to another, "it's designed for bored fifty-year-old women who have twelve kids and spend their Sunday morning making cakes, after having washed the kids." These reactions speak not only to consumer models but also to shifting social practices. A few weeks after the social revolution of May 1968, the younger generation didn't mince words. Interestingly, the respondent didn't even consider the possibility that the hypothetical fifty-year-old mother of twelve might spend Sunday morning in church, rather than tinkering with vanilla tubes. Finally, technology played a part in making glass vials seem out of date: refrigerators, not closet corners, had become the paragons of modern preservation, but vanilla specialists insist that refrigeration is counterproductive for preserving vanilla beans.[79]

However, just like the French May 1968 movement itself, the rejection of glass tubes proved to be a largely Parisian and ephemeral trend. The glass tube was certainly old hat at this point. Already in 1932, P. Lemerle vanilla importers in Paris were preparing tailored glass tubes for thirteen- to fourteen-centimeter-long vanilla pods (5 to 5.5 inches), with an eye to selling even larger pods in a separate format.[80] The container retained its fan base thirty-six years on and is still used today. According to ESSOR data, 68 percent of all female consumers in France still preferred this traditional container to plastic. One respondent noted that "plastic isn't pleasant, it's rubbery." Another added, "The glass helps preserve the flavors and is more natural." One more opined, "Glass is ideal for storage and conservation, because the tube comes with a hermetic blocker, and so prevents contact with the outside and with dust." Finally, 31 percent of female consumers put forward an environmental argument: Glass was reusable, plastic was not.[81]

Univanille's campaigns sent ripples across the Atlantic. In 1969, Stephen Manheimer, vice president of the Vanilla Bean Association of America (VBA), informed Univanille of his intention to launch a US sister company to promote Malagasy vanilla. Manheimer drew the following picture of American household budgets: Inflation had been driving up the price of milk, sugar, and labor. And because synthetic vanillin was twenty-six times cheaper than the real stuff, "natural vanilla [. . .] has become too expensive," especially given how little the public knew about it. Consequently, extract manufacturers were turning to synthetics. Manheimer therefore recommended educating US consumers. But the VBA would promote only Madagascar vanilla, not that of Réunion and the Comoros Islands.[82]

Manheimer believed that Madagascar vanilla could draw inspiration from Colombian coffee. Its iconic symbol, the Juan Valdez coffee farmer character, had conquered the American market. So, Manheimer recommended "a [similar] symbol for pure vanilla which can be easily recognized by housewives. It would then be advertised nationally in widely circulated women's magazines." The logo had to be eye-catching, "recognizable by the housewife at first glance." It would influence her as she made her way down the supermarket aisle, turning her away from synthetics. Better still, it would make her demand real vanilla from manufacturers. The Malagasy Juan Valdez never seems to have materialized. Yet there were precedents. During World War II, artist Alfred Bendiner had designed an ad campaign for ice cream containing Mexican vanilla that featured a stereotypical Mexican, Don Miguel, and his horse Plato.[83]

The key to Manheimer's argument ran as follows: "People in the vanilla industry are aware of their dishonest labeling (vanilla biscuits containing no vanilla) but the average female consumer is not." Lastly, Manheimer suggested highlighting a Malagasy connection, much as Univanille had. The goal was to link vanilla with "the Republic of Madagascar and all of its folklore as well as its enduringly attractive ambiance for readers and tourists."[84] Just as paternalist exoticism lay at the heart the Colombian coffee strategy, so was Malagasy Orientalism at the core of this ill-fated campaign.

Notwithstanding the failure of that US initiative, the Indian Ocean vanilla cartel held firm. In 1969, Madagascar sent 740 tons of pods to the United States and 378 tons to Europe; Réunion dispatched six tons to the States and thirty-five tons to Europe while the Comoros Islands sent ninety tons to the United States and seventy-five tons to Europe. Note that the percentages destined for Europe were increasing; Univanille seemed to be doing its work. The cartel next convened in Madagascar in 1970 and then in the Comoros Islands the following year. In 1970, it decided to raise the price for a kilo of third- and fourth-quality vanilla—the so-called base rate—to $11.70 by 1972. In 1971, it instructed Univanille to rekindle its activities in the United States, given the successes it had achieved in Europe.[85]

Later that decade, in 1979, Indian Ocean producing nations agreed that Madagascar would ship the United States 650 metric tons, the Comoros Islands 100 tons, and Réunion 5 tons. They continued to set quotas per importer. For example, the 650 tons were subdivided as follows: 380 tons for McCormick, 2,220 for Zink and Triest, and 50 tons for Charabot and Company. As for Europe's 410 metric tons, it would come from Madagascar to the tune of 350 tons, the Comoros (50 tons), and Réunion (10 tons). The group decided for the first time to separate Canada from the US market and grant it a maximum quota of fifty metric tons.[86] Meanwhile, Europe's consumption of natural vanilla continued to climb at the expense of the United States.

Despite this shift from the United States to Europe, on balance the Indian Ocean vanilla cartel succeeded at maintaining high prices and living wages for producing regions. At its apogee, the cartel generated 75 percent of the world's vanilla, but it gradually declined due to many long-term factors, notably the emergence of Indonesia as a new vanilla giant. Zink and Triest's imports from cartel members began dropping after 1965. This coincided with a jump in the company's imports from Indonesia, which bounded from 56 metric tons in 1963 to 129 tons in 1967.[87] The three big US importers were beginning to purchase outside the cartel while cartel members failed to bring Indonesia and Mexico into the fold. This demonstrated that in the end, the cartel remained regional, never succeeding in encompassing the entire Global South. The trend continued until the 1980s, when the cartel finally unraveled. Admittedly, the group did convene again in 1984 and 1985, apportioning Indian Ocean vanilla worldwide and expressing hope that Japan represented an emerging market for natural vanilla.[88] But at that point, the cartel had been undercut. Vanilla has been subject to wild price swings ever since, left at the mercy of speculation and hurricanes. This puts farmers in countries like Madagascar in a challenging situation. Large buyers and intermediaries can engage in speculation and stockpiling while producers cannot hedge their bets on markets the way their peers can with commodity futures—the scale of the vanilla economy simply will not allow it.[89]

As for vanilla's broader counterattack against its synthetic would-be replacement, it at least prevented outright annihilation. The collapse of the vanilla cartel certainly marked a setback, making it harder for farmers and others in the vanilla sector to earn a living. However, heightened consumer awareness of food provenance—the farm to table ethos—not to mention the aggressive advertising campaigns we just explored have borne some fruit. All that said, take a close look at labels in your kitchen. Outside of premium ice creams or yogurts, or foodstuffs containing vanilla purchased in health food or organic stores, synthetic vanillin has retained a near monopoly over processed foods. A small number of high-end brands take pride in listing "real vanilla" or actual "vanilla beans" in their list of ingredients. But they remain a minority the world over. Even the logos devised in the 1960s to identify real vanilla seem a thing of the past: for better or for worse, vanilla has no Juan Valdez.

CHAPTER 9

Toward Bland and White?

AS SHE STROLLED THE GROUNDS OF THE 1889 PARIS EXPOSItion Universelle, Polish novelist, playwright, and actor Gabriela Zapolska was struck not by the brand-new Eiffel Tower but instead by an entrancing smell. She let her nose be her guide:

> The vanilla already floats above in whole masses over the Esplanade des Invalides. Countless quantities of it are sold in all stalls, and its delicate, faint smell hangs constantly in the air. Even the main pavilion of the Ministry of War is shrouded in a subtle scent of vanilla, even the [gun]powder and saltpeter deposited nearby lose their bellicose scent and drown in the invisible mist of this delightful substance. In a Dutch bakery, flat cakes turn white from sugar mixed with dark vanilla flakes.[1]

Here, Zapolska celebrates vanilla's subtlety. The "delightful substance" seems to take the form of a magical fog that envelops the visitors to the exhibition. But the passage contains a key contradiction: Although described as "faint" and "delicate," vanilla still holds the power to drown out the smells of war. This is not an unusual duality: Some visitors to Papantla in Mexico and Sava in Madagascar report a wafting scent of vanilla in the air at preparation time that is at once subtle and overwhelming.

We saw that synthetics posed a serious challenge to real vanilla. A related problem reared its head around the same time. It had to do with the pod's transition from a refined fragrance and flavor, to a subtle one, and ultimately to being outright boring. As is often the case in cultural history, there was no straight line, running in this case from deluxe to dull. Indeed, the above passage reminds us that vanilla can represent several things at once. These different meanings are further complicated by ebbs and flows in vanilla's perceived olfactory intensity that Zapolska noted. Still, a trend is manifest in the direction of vanilla becoming increasingly bland in the nineteenth and twentieth centuries. The key question is why.

I would argue that the substitution process enabled this transformation. First of all, economically, the prodigious growth of vanilla ice cream between 1880 and 1960 was tied to the expanded use of synthetic vanillin. Put plainly, now that vanilla flavor was commonplace, it could no longer be luxurious. How could it remain a positional good when it was everywhere, from milkshakes to syrups and ice creams? Vanilla's shift to ordinary occurred over a remarkably short span. In 1832, prior to the dual manual pollination and synthetics revolutions, the fictional Mrs. Marsden in Eliza Leslie's short story had ridiculed her grocer for not knowing about vanilla; half a century on, it was ubiquitous.

Second, in terms of taste, the utter uniformity and homogenized muteness of early synthetic vanillin derived from cloves became readily associated with a kind of nothingness. This point is more tenuous because most consumers cannot tell the difference between real and synthetic vanillin's flavor or smell. Nevertheless, I contend that the sheer evenness, the complete flatness of the synthetic, which never deviates from batch to batch, produces a numbing effect. Synthetics also cannot reproduce natural vanilla's full range or many nuances. They copy only one of natural vanilla's molecules, vanillin, thereby missing out on the rest of the pod's olfactory and flavor complexities.

The evidence to back up the connection between the synthetic turn and the descent into dull is admittedly circumstantial. Yet it is at once geographical and chronological. Spatially, the tumble into bland was predominantly a US phenomenon, occurring precisely in the land where synthetics achieved the greatest inroads against real pods. Sequentially, the change in language coincided with the widespread commercialization of first clove and then lignin synthetics around the turn of the twentieth century, prior to the advent of more intense ethylvanillin in the 1920s. Seen in this light, vanilla became a victim of its own success as an immensely popular flavor. To further explain and analyze the phenomenon requires diving into sensory history.

A new generation of historians have begun grappling with the intersensorial.[2] My focus here is largely confined to the realms of smell, sight, and taste. That is because recovering the perception of vanilla in other senses presents practically insurmountable challenges. One does catch the occasional glancing reference. In Malagasy novelist Marie Ranjanoro's brilliant 2023 debut book about the 1947 insurrection in the Sava region, *Feux, fièvres, forêts*, vanilla marks all the senses. Ranjanoro describes the experience of a vanilla buyer as follows:

> Selling day had come. The previous weeks, growers had picked their vanilla under the trees and waited for the collector to come. They brought him large *gony* [sacks] that were fragrant and oily. He plunged his fingers in with delight and fished out a handful of pods, still pleasingly green and pleasingly plump. He broke one open to inspect the seeds. Then he whistled or grunted. He knew few words. His words were numbers.[3]

Such opulent references to touch are uncommon, given that few consumers have the luxury of diving their hands into entire sacks of vanilla beans. In fact, most people are completely disconnected from pods and end up engaging with vanilla only in the form of disembodied specks. To some extent, the same holds true with sight because so few vanilla consumers set their eyes on actual vanilla beans. Most only interact with a dark, alcohol-based liquid or a white powder that may or may not contain real vanilla. This chapter nevertheless tackles representations because visual cultures accompanied and reflected vanilla's descent into bland and white. Vanilla soundscapes pose an even greater challenge to re-create, notwithstanding occasional noises registered at the points of production and consumption. These include the rustling of undergrowth at the time of pollination and the distinctive calls of vanilla being sold at town markets.[4] But again, these sounds leave faint traces, if any. Consequently, this chapter concentrates on the senses on which vanilla leaves the clearest mark. In the dominions of taste, representation, and smell, vanilla experienced an interconnected, century-long downward spiral into bland.

In the olfactory realm, Jonathan Reinarz has pondered the gradual shift, in the twentieth and early twenty-first centuries, toward the "deodorization of society." He suggests that smell's frequent absence, in an increasingly antiseptic world, has led to a Proustian nostalgia for an era when smells were present and even powerful. Admittedly, Reinarz and others nuance the point, noting that many scents have endured. He adds that changes in "pungency" are also being registered.[5] The question of intensity proves critical in the case of vanilla, which has gone from sophisticated to boring, in ways that are connected to vanillin's becoming muted on its road from synthetic to ubiquitous.

Vanilla's cultural meanings shifted dramatically over the course of the nineteenth century. In some instances, we can see them being negotiated in real time. A mid-nineteenth-century Parisian vaudeville play bore the intriguing title *Une passion à la vanille* (A vanilla passion). Even reviewers at the time presumed that this implied some kind of adjectival judgement. And yet, to their disappointment, it turned out to be merely descriptive: one of the protagonists' families had made a fortune on colonial commodities. Then why not call their next plays "a pepper passion," "a tea passion," or even "a prune passion," joked the reviewers?[6] Clearly, at this point, vanilla did not mean insipid; if anything, it remained synonymous with wealth and luxury. Yet, tellingly, the play's reviewers seemed to will its title into some kind of value judgement. They were inviting vanilla to become an adjective.

Increasingly in the second half of the nineteenth century, the adjective chosen to describe vanilla was *subtle*. This shift happened at the same time that vanilla became tied to certain segments of society. We saw noble food critic Baron Léon Brisse vaunting the pod's merits to the bourgeoisie in 1867. I take Sarah Maza's point that the French bourgeoisie can constitute a slippery, even hollow social category. Nevertheless, vanilla was being increasingly *perceived* as bourgeois. Novelist Emile Zola referenced vanilla on more than one occasion as a quintessentially bourgeois flavor. In his 1880 novel *Nana*, familiar "vanilla perfumes" ascend from a chocolatier's workshop in the Passage des Panoramas, teasing bourgeois nostrils and inducing a flow of memories.[7] Like many of his contemporaries, Zola reveled in exposing what he saw as bourgeois hypocrisy. Others teased the dominant bourgeoisie for its overly regimented habits. The point is that vanilla's middle-class popularity wound up being a disadvantage, as the flavor became associated with the bourgeois and the bland.

In *La Curée* (1871), Zola stages smells dueling in a greenhouse. In that consummately confined space, the odors of a couple making love drown out a refined exchange of notes—rendered as a staccato—that vanilla and several other flowers are producing. Here, the carnal overpowered the floral.[8] Zola's metaphor, as well as his elaborate multisensorial assemblages, anticipated a broader use of sex as a way of rendering vanilla bland by association.

Over the course of the nineteenth and twentieth centuries, vanilla's subtlety morphed into blandness. In this last example, it constituted an odor that could be overwhelmed. It was but a small step from there to "neutral" and on to "plain." One manifestation of the trend was linguistic and occurred in US English. Already in 1846, as vanilla availability spiked thanks to the manual pollination revolution and increased use of extracts, a New York State newspaper was advertising, without punctuation, Clark's "plain vanilla and fancy chocolates." Here, the adjectives *plain* and *fancy* appear as antitheses.[9] An online sleuth seeking the genesis of vanilla-as-bland has uncovered an 1887 American reference in the *Fort Worth (TX) Daily Gazette* to some customers preferring "just plain vanilla" ice cream soda. However, this does not constitute a metaphorical use, so much as a literal flavor choice. The expression did provide a pathway to the metaphor, though. By 1942, figurative uses along these lines emerged, with *Life* magazine referencing a "plain vanilla foreign policy."[10]

This linguistic drift accompanied a change in tastes. Consider the respondents to the 1968 French survey we saw in the previous chapter, showing anonymous French women describing vanilla as "water, a cream with no flavor at all." There are other signals of vanilla becoming boring over time. One of the more surprising comes from within a family of vanilla experts. Offspring rejecting their parents' line of work is certainly not uncommon, and that filial reaction may partly (yet surely not wholly) explain the following example. Yvonne Kapp grew up to become the biographer of Karl Marx's daughter, Eleanor Marx. But Kapp's own grandfather and father, the German Jewish émigrés Hermann Mayer and Max Alfred Mayer, both worked in the vanilla business in London. Indeed, they each published on vanilla and its fluctuating prices. In 2003, Kapp drew the following portrait of her father:

> He took up all manner of pursuits outside the home: he played the violin in the Civil Service orchestra; was a chess player of tournament standard; won innumerable hideous trophies at golf and for fencing, all of which meant that he was out many evenings and always at the weekend. In old age, he confessed to me that he had for many years entertained a longing to retreat to one of the vanilla-growing islands in the Indian Ocean. (Vanilla, it should be said, was not only his merchandise but among his greatest interests: he knew of every region ringing the globe, all equidistant from the equator, where it grew and could talk about its provenance, cultivation and habits by the hour,

from which I learnt that the sex-life of the vanilla pod—whose name derives from "little vagina"—is decidedly rum).[11]

Rum in this sense means old-fashioned. The daughter was teasing her stodgy father for his vanilla fixation, which, coupled with his golfing, fencing, and other hobbies, made him the quintessential bourgeois conformist. If there was anything exotic about vanilla here, it could be reduced to a somewhat pathetic form of armchair travel.

Still, if one were to chart vanilla's turn to bland, one would register some ups and downs. Just as vanilla producers fought back against synthetics, so did vanilla's smell periodically shed the new label of boring. Like Jonathan Reinarz's fragrant city, which bucks the widespread "sterilizing" of odors, vanilla on occasion resists the marker of bland. I see three sets of instances when this occurs: one has to do with nostalgia, another with perfumes, and a third with intensity.

Despite the turn to bland, one can identify several cases of vanilla still being considered overpowering, even as mainstream cultures were tagging it as overly fine. Marie Morren's vanilla pods had triggered nausea and headaches at the 1848 Brussels fair, so they had to be kept under a bell jar like a potent substance. Decades later, an 1874 cartoon by Cham in *Le Monde illustré* made a similar point with humor. A school principal is seen clenching his face, wincing. He has been handing out awards to students. He groans, "What a headache! All my prizewinners are covered in vanilla ointment."[12] This cartoon, titled "Poor Principal!" provided a gentle critique of an overperfumed, overlotioned bourgeoisie. Alain Corbin has identified some of the dominant olfactory trends of nineteenth-century France. Ventilation and compulsive cleaning marked the era but so did what he terms the "proliferation of lotions" evident in Cham's cartoon. (In fact, complaints about overlotioning extend back to the eighteenth century.)[13] For our purposes, the drawing points specifically to vanilla's ongoing ability to overwhelm the senses—notwithstanding Zola's claim to the contrary—at a time when olfactory balances were being worked out. In this cartoon, vanilla's intensity is certainly a negative feature, yet the fragrance is anything but dull.

More broadly, then, perfumes offer another counterexample. They demonstrate vanilla's enduring appeal as a sophisticated fragrance. Some even bucked the trend toward synthetics. From the late nineteenth century on, as much of the world turned to chemical vanillin, the Chiris family increased

FIGURE 15. Cham's "Poor Principal!" cartoon, *Le Monde illustré*, September 5, 1874, p. 157. Author's collection.

the natural vanilla content in their flasks. After 1900, Georges Chiris built up the massive Société coloniale de Bambao on the Comoros Islands.[14] Although one critic accused the Chirises of never visiting their own vanilla groves, it is clear that they were able to manage them remotely, at board meetings, for instance.[15] There they set the price of vanilla sales and even followed when vanilla orchids flowered.[16] The company's vanilla perfumes proved popular and were emulated in France and beyond. For instance, the Russian perfume company Krasnaya Moskva introduced a vanilla-based scent in the 1920s.[17]

In fact, Chiris was one of many firms to incorporate vanilla into its most popular perfumes. In 1889, Guerlain launched Jicky, its first vanilla-dominant fragrance, which remains in circulation today. Rivals soon followed suit, either making vanilla the core of their fragrance or using it to soften other notes. By the 1920s, the term *Guerlinade* had come to refer to the vanillization of perfume. 1934 marked another turning point in Europe, with vanilla appearing for the first time in a men's fragrance, Caron's Pour un homme. Vanilla's widespread use in perfume between the 1880s and the 1930s certainly suggests the fragrance was retaining or even widening its appeal. However, by that point, substitution was affecting the fragrance sector as much as the food industry. By the interwar era, most perfume manufacturers had replaced vanilla proper with synthetic vanillin.[18]

The third and final case of vanilla resisting the tide of bland involves its powerful nostalgia-triggering effects, especially at sites of production. On Réunion in 1931, long after the island's vanilla production peak, local Creole authors Marius and Ary Leblond wrote, "The very words vanilla, vanilla grove, send us back, no plunge us back to Saint-Joseph, Vincendo, Langevin, those old neighborhoods of blessed names that maintain alive, like some naive incense, the perfume of vanilla with which they bade you the most aromatic welcome."[19] Here, vanilla enables time travel to the age when the island reigned as "queen of vanilla." Note the aroma's "naive," welcoming, and wholesome attributes. At the very least, the nostalgic qualities of vanilla have endured in the literature of the Indian Ocean. In Nobel Prize–winning Franco-Mauritian novelist Jean-Marie Le Clézio's 2003 *Révolutions*, vanilla-flavored tea conjures up remembrances of things past. As with Proust's madeleine (presumably vanilla-flavored itself), the vanilla tea opens a torrent of memories: songs and riddles from childhood, Creole expressions, and the sounds and rhythms of the Creole language itself. Such readings call to mind other powerful olfactory cues across global gastronomy, including matsutake mushrooms, which to Japanese aficionados similarly evoke "times past" and fond childhood memories in particular.[20]

And yet, those three registers of intensity, perfume, and nostalgia notwithstanding, the march toward boring proved inexorable in the Global North. Nowhere was this truer than in the United States in the twentieth century, where the term *vanilla sex* was coined. That expression, itself an offshoot of "plain vanilla," marked the zenith of vanilla as mundane. Vanilla's conventionality as it became bourgeois, more affordable, and even commonplace in extract and then in synthetic form certainly contributed to this development. It was surely no coincidence that "plain vanilla" and "vanilla sex" were coined in the country that was the world's largest global consumer of synthetic vanillin. By 1962, the United States absorbed a startling 53 percent of the world's chemical vanillin, followed by the Netherlands, Italy, and West Germany.[21]

Etymologist Pascal Tréguier has uncovered an early example of the term *vanilla sex* that links it squarely with the "plain vanilla" trope. It comes from the 1960 issue of a Hawaiian newspaper that reads:

> There are different flavors of sex just as there are of ice cream. Vanilla is the old stand-by, the most common, the average, the one everyone is sure to like. Thus, most sex is "vanilla" sex—good, sturdy, dependable. But the real connoisseur tries various flavors—chocolate, strawberry, and so on.[22]

Here the ice cream parlor origins of the expression are exposed. Vanilla's everydayness, its rank as by far the most popular ice cream flavor, has rendered it "dependable" but unoriginal—the very opposite of the lavishness the pod once connoted.

By the 1980s and 1990s, "vanilla sex" had become a negative buzzword. One source has highlighted the role queer people in North America played in popularizing the term as a way of denormalizing heterosexuality by making it boring. As a reaction, they elaborated the concept of "antivanilla sex." That said, an anthropologist has underlined that "vanilla sex" was never a stable category or an identity to begin with so much as a foil, used by many communities, including LGBTQ and BDSM ones, to describe what they "don't do." One informant summarized it as "heterosexual missionary-position sex within marriage." Yet another mooted that it was "sex without toys, costumes, or role playing."[23]

Has vanilla gone from boring to outright uninspired and unsexy? I would begin by cautioning that the term *vanilla sex* is not universal. The usage is largely restricted to English. Spanish, German, and French have not used vanilla as an adjective in this way. That may be changing but with an interesting caveat in the form of a backlash. In 2023, the French magazine *Elle* ran a piece explaining the meaning of the American expression yet celebrating "vanilla sex" as the opposite of pornography. It concluded that "if you prefer vanilla ice cream to an apple kiwi sorbet, then that's all to your credit!"[24] Here, vanilla admittedly stands for "ordinary," but it also denotes comfort and familiarity. Apple-kiwi, conversely, conveys needless and jarring convolution. In other words, while the expression "vanilla sex" may be crossing the Atlantic, its valence appears to be transforming along the way.

So how did "vanilla sex" and "plain vanilla" come into being in the first place? I posit that the two expressions first appeared in the land of soda fountains and ice cream parlors, where vanilla, often paired with chocolate or strawberry, came to represent blandness, partly due to the rise of uninspiring synthetics. Vanilla became a kind of vessel, like a cone, on which other flavors were heaped. This begins to explain how vanilla descended into blandness or even nothingness.

Racialized meanings were added to that bland foundation. As the poet Harryette Mullen has observed, "Whiteness is associated with cleanliness, purity but also blankness, the lack of color." Hence, she contends, the term *plain vanilla* took on the meaning of "normal," an "attribute," as it were, that is "desired but also boring."[25] In other words, vanilla became a shorthand for a quintessentially suburban, white, middle-class commodity, a bit like sliced white bread. Of course, as with vanilla, the construction of white bread is itself riddled with ironies and shifts of its own.

In this way, vanilla becoming white was often connected to its turning boring, especially in the United States. The myth of vanilla-as-white is at once transnational and elaborate. Fin-de-siècle European advertisers, starting with the Czech art nouveau artist Alphonse Mucha, created iconic representations of vanilla as female, pale, voluptuous, and blonde. The Nantes biscuit giant LU recruited Mucha to complete several designs for the company between 1896 and 1903, including four posters and thirteen tin covers. Along the way, Louis Lefèvre-Utile provided some mood and market feedback to the Czech. The "sensual and disrobed" models on the resulting visuals quickly lent LU a "unique graphic identity."

As one expert has observed, Mucha's first drawings for the Nantes biscuit company featured formally clad bourgeois women while his later ones, including the ad for vanilla wafers shown here, presented instead "lightly clothed sensual nymphs."[26] Sexuality and youth were both commodified. The crimson elements that stand out in the image include the poppies, the brand LU, the words *vanilla wafers*, and the model's lip and cheek color. The viewer's eye is ultimately drawn to the plate of inviting vanilla wafers she delicately balances on the right. Her ethereal cotton nightdress and long golden locks, contrasting with the image's reds and browns, all lend an impression of pristine whiteness.

FIGURE 16. Mucha's ad for LU's vanilla wafers, 1900.
Alphonse Mucha / Alamy Stock Photo.

The so-called West held no monopoly over these tropes. A 1905 advertisement appeared in the Japanese press for vanilla Oshiroi, the powder used by geishas on their faces and necks. Oshiroi, which literally means "white powder," can contain vanilla and was used to provide a white facial foundation. The ad further pronounced that its Oshiroi would not induce lead poisoning. Be that as it may, if the powder contained any actual vanilla, it would have had to be bleached or undergone some similar process, given that prepared vanilla is of course black—and raw vanilla is no whiter.[27]

Paradoxically, this pod with black seeds, whose pollination method was discovered by a Black teenager, became synonymous with whiteness throughout the twentieth century. Nowhere was this more evident than in the United States. We already heard Maya Angelou describe the racist banning of vanilla ice cream for African Americans. This was no isolated example. Leading African American feminist Audre Lorde told a similar story, recalling a scarring childhood memory: Her family taking her for vanilla ice cream in Washington, DC, one Fourth of July, only to be denied service. She wrote of the experience:

> The waitress was white, the counter was white, and the ice cream I never ate in Washington DC that summer I left childhood was white, and the white heat and white pavement and white stone monuments of my first Washington summer made me sick to my stomach for the rest of the trip.[28]

Clearly, in the Jim Crow era, the association between vanilla and whiteness was inextricably connected to racist extremism. African Americans were forcibly ousted from the world of vanilla. On top of that, in this passage, vanilla white serves not just as the ubiquitous and boring norm, it also takes on an oppressive, even sickening effect. It is reflected in the Lincoln Memorial Reflecting Pool at the foot of the Washington Monument, offering a picture of stark whiteness.

Vanilla's turn to white was reflected far beyond visual culture. By the 1990s, several popular music performers adopted names referencing vanilla. One was the Dallas, Texas, rapper Vanilla Ice, the second the Franco-German R & B group Milli Vanilli. The former was rapidly accused of faking his credentials, claiming to have grown up on the tough streets of Miami when he had not, while the latter became embroiled in a lip-syncing scandal. Their vanillaness remained vague, although for Vanilla Ice, it was his way of distinguishing himself as a white artist in a Black genre. Both were ultimately labeled hoaxes, and Vanilla Ice was accused of performing "faux rap."[29] Vanilla so embodied whiteness as to become part of the hoax. Of course, never was vanilla's original Blackness mobilized as an argument in either controversy.

Again, some counterexamples can be uncovered. Vanilla was not white in all places and contexts. A hazy racialized exoticism has also enshrouded some vanilla branding, especially when referencing points of production. The centerpiece of the 1931 International Colonial Exhibit at Paris's Bois de Vincennes was the permanent palace, whose surviving iconic art deco bas-relief shows commodities leaving the colonies for French ports. Vanilla appears among them, alongside pepper, sugarcane, cacao, cotton, and so on. However, vanilla shows up in the French Caribbean part of the frieze, linked to Martinique. The vanilla beans find themselves sandwiched between cacao fruit to their left and sugarcane to their right, as if inspired by Aztec *chocolatl*. The vanilla picker appears to be a Martinican woman. The scene, with its quasifictional provenance, calls to mind Univanille's 1960s advertising campaign. In reality, scarcely any vanilla was being produced in Martinique by 1931 (unlike its sister island of Guadeloupe). This imperial shrine rested on intricate fictions.[30]

One can uncover other examples of this sort. To this day, the Danish company Tørsleffs enlists the perplexing image of a man wearing a turban on its vanilla-flavored products. The visual apparently dates to the early twentieth century. One source identifies it as representing a "Sri Lankan man."[31]

Overall, though, vanilla remains enduringly associated with the color white, especially in North America. Next time you visit a supermarket, examine the labels on vanilla ice cream and yogurt. Many feature a white flower instead of the black pod from which the actual flavoring agent would emanate, if it were real vanilla. To make matters worse, the flower depicted is sometimes not even a vanilla orchid, or an orchid at all.[32] The shortcut has much to do with vanilla's association with cream, frozen or otherwise, as well as the perceived greater visual appeal of the flower over the bean.

Is vanilla headed toward complete irrelevance as a boring, white, and bland flavor and scent? Not necessarily, and to tip my hand, hopefully not. First of all, the turn to bland and white is predominantly a US phenomenon and may be running its course. Second, regardless of whether vanilla is

TOWARD BLAND AND WHITE?

FIGURE 17. Bas-relief on the permanent pavilion of the 1931 International Colonial Exhibition in Paris depicting vanilla harvesting. Author's photo.

considered potent, subtle, or dull, it has retained its appeal. In other words, vanilla can be simultaneously muted and appreciated. During the recent COVID-19 pandemic, vanilla's enduring global popularity and capacity to elicit nostalgia rendered it useful in unexpected ways.

In March 2020, the very month the WHO declared the new virus a pandemic, a French colleague emailed with news. She had contracted the virus, and her lone symptom was a complete loss of smell. Knowing about my project, she kindly sent along the surprising prescription she received from a Parisian hospital: nasal "exercises" to help the body's "sensory system" reboot. The patient was instructed to smell eleven products in sequence after having examined their labels. Repeat daily. Vanilla topped the list of easy-to-find items, followed by coffee, dill, thyme, cinnamon, cloves, lavender, coriander, vinegar, mint, and cumin. Vanilla had emerged as a key to olfactory recovery, in part thanks to its availability as a supermarket staple.

Vanilla represents a solution for sensory recovery for another reason as well. For all the negative press it has received for being boring, it remains a uniquely appreciated and recognized fragrance around the world. A recent study revealed that the scent preference for vanilla is universal.

However, the authors attribute this finding more to molecular structures than human agency or sociocultural constructions of smell.[33] The team of scientists behind the study tested ten scents across ten cultures. Vanillin outperformed all others in a striking example of "global consistency." (The Maniq people of Thailand were the only group that did not rank vanillin at or near the top of their preferences.)[34] Boring as it may have become to some, vanilla remains a global favorite. Today, its fragrance is used to scent baby toys and to stage homes.

Conclusion

VANILLA WAS ONE OF THE STARS OF THE SHOW AT THE hugely popular 1931 International Colonial Exhibition at Vincennes in the outskirts of Paris. In March 1930, the vanilla lobby persuaded the event's organizers to dedicate an entire pavilion to their product.[1] The resulting kiosk depicted vanilla's production, circulation, and consumption—with details that contradicted the message conveyed by the bas-relief at the nearby permanent pavilion. Within the kiosk, visitors' eyes were immediately drawn to the large slogan "Vanilla: France produces 85 percent of what the world consumes." A map displayed red lines representing imports streaming into Paris from Réunion, French Polynesia, Madagascar, and the Comoros Islands while blue lines depicted exports, radiating from Paris to all corners of the world. The reality that some Madagascar vanilla sailed directly to New York and nearly all Tahitian vanilla streamed into San Francisco was completely obscured. So, too, was Mexico's output, which was absorbed almost entirely by the United States. As was the challenge posed by synthetics. To the left of the idyllic image, which has been sanitized to eliminate any hint of child labor or other forms of coercion, one can make out representations of vanilla pickers and pollinators plying their trade. In the foreground, samples were presented at the art deco tasting counter, reminiscent of a trendy wine bar. There was no shortage of such venues at the 1931 exhibition, and a visitor could jump from one kiosk to another to test rum, coffee, and a range of fruit.[2]

The vanilla pavilion lends itself to both macro- and microanalyses. In the broadest sense, the entire commodity chain was laid bare behind this counter, albeit through a bowdlerized French colonial narrative. New Spain's

CONCLUSION

FIGURE 18. 1930 design for the pavilion at the 1931 International Colonial Exhibition in Paris. Author's collection.

near monopoly had given way to a modern French colonial one. Vanilla poured into Europe from mostly insular corners of the French empire. It came in all three edible varietals: *planifolia*, *pompona*, and *tahitensis*, from the isles of the Indian Ocean, from Guiana, and from French Polynesia, respectively. As the large map made clear, the pods had streamed from the Global South to the Global North. Finally, the pavilion itself was the doing of a French colonial empire that had bet on vanilla since the era of Louis XIV and had renewed its efforts in the 1840s. Now, vanilla warranted its own building.

From a microhistorical perspective, one can trace an individual vanilla bean's path from its genesis to this sleek countertop, exposing the full complexities of a luxury product.[3] The process and the journey both reveal the lead time and the artisanal meticulousness that vanilla requires. Some of the pods enjoyed at the counter had traveled from northeastern Réunion to

CONCLUSION

the International Colonial Exhibition. They had been deftly hand-pollinated early one morning in 1929. We know from vanilla carrier passes that a porter carried on his head two kilos of Raoul Ozoux's green pods in the late afternoon of May 31, 1930, in order to have them prepared. By December of that year, the beans had shed most of their weight, and Ozoux picked out six bundles that had been perfectly cured and developed a highly desirable *givre*. Ozoux took no chances. He entrusted his son with delivering them to the governor's office the day after Christmas, 1930. The prize parcel, appropriately insured, was then sent via the Suez Canal and the port of Marseille to the Bois de Vincennes. Ozoux pampered his star pods, even as the world began to slide into the Great Depression. Once in Vincennes, the beans were not only available for purchase and sampling but also entered to win a much sought-after award.[4]

Réunion's pods generated extensive discussion about precisely how to achieve excellence, which speaks to the fractured and luxury status of the vanilla industry. The exhibit organizers sent producers detailed questionnaires. Growers and preparers were asked about the particularities of their plantation and drying facilities. Given the breadth of queries, responses varied considerably. One producer boasted of his vanilla's top-notch "conservation and nose." Another planter in Sainte-Anne answered that his firm employed "ten women employees." Writing from the same town, Raoul Ozoux indicated that he, too, had ten people on his payroll. But then, in the next box available to him, he decided to share his mantra: "Good vanilla should be well-preserved, well-*givred*, and should release a pleasant perfume." He added that his vanilla was picked "at the perfect ripeness."[5] These seemingly divergent answers do share several points: an emphasis on artisanal and small-scale production, specific knowhow resulting in quality, and recognition of vanilla's diverse franchises and communities, encompassing pollinators, pickers, and preparers.

Superimposing this countertop view of Ozoux's pods atop the world map on display at Vincennes reveals vanilla's many features. Using Edmond's fecundation method, the pods sampled there had been hand-pollinated on Réunion Island, half a world away from vanilla's point of origin in Central America. Bypassing Mexican bees was a revolution in its own right. However, because vanilla never took an industrial turn and still required both manual pollination and intensive preparation, the pod remained expensive enough for a special carrier to be arranged. Preparation required specialized work that was reminiscent of the intricate labor performed in an haute couture workshop, marked by punctilious attention to detail. In contrast to rubber, cacao, coffee, or other raw materials that were transformed in the Global North, vanilla workshops were located on location in the colony. Some ten women worked in one of them. The final product was sorted and ranked by quality, with nose, *givre*, preservation, and presentation all dictated by a set of evolving, though largely unwritten, conventions. If my experience visiting vanilla groves in the twenty-first century is any indication, many pods ended up on the cutting room floor; not all were destined to become Ozoux's masterpieces. Nowadays, some of those outcasts wind up as makeshift home or car fresheners at sites of production; others find their way into sugar containers, which they slowly infuse with their aroma; others still are made into extract.

Although the exhibit organizers downplayed it, Réunion's vanilla was in fact competing with rivals within the French colonial empire and without (Java and Mexico most notably) but also with cheap synthetics. By 1931, synthetic alternatives were churned out from cloves and pulp paper waste. Today, they can be generated from cow dung. And in another serious blow to real vanilla, in recent decades the category-blurring label of "nature identical vanilla" has appeared. Designating a product entirely derived from wood, rice, or cloves, for example, and devoid of artificial or chemical ingredients, the practice leads customers to think of liquid vanilla substitutes as natural.

The tasting counter can also take us in another, more speculative direction that leaves the realm of history for the fields of oenology and vanilla science. Vanilla experts can be broadly divided into two schools of thought. The first includes those who believe that terroir shapes a bean just as it does a grape. According to that logic, a Malbec wine from the Andes bears little resemblance to one from Cahors, just as a pod grown on a bed of coconut shavings atop a volcanic base under a coastal *ombrière* presents little in common with another raised on a vine climbing an inland, old-growth forest on humid topsoil. Aromatic profiles do indeed tend to differ subtly from one producing region to another, although everyday consumers may not be able to distinguish them. This first school of thought is often championed by producing regions and nations themselves, which routinely tout their own vanillas as superior.

CONCLUSION

Others, however, assert that *planifolia* will always be *planifolia*—notwithstanding some of the hybridization efforts I have traced. While it is true that *pompona* still held a considerable share of the vanilla market in the mid-eighteenth century and *tahitensis* consumption surged in both 1910 and 1949, these are exceptions to the rule; *planifolia* is the main type of vanilla bean and overwhelmingly dominates the market. Another analogy can help us better understand the second school's argument. A bit like today's banana, although not to the same degree, *Vanilla planifolia* presents broad genetic similitude because of its mode of propagation. Consequently, there is no especially good or bad *Vanilla planifolia*, only variations in size and especially in preparation and preservation. To be sure, distinct markets have come to prefer vanillas derived from different preparation methods. Some companies based in Madagascar prepare pods differently for the American, French, and Japanese markets, for example. Furthermore, if it is picked too early or too late, if it is boiled for too long, if it receives too much or not enough sun, or if it mildews or dries up, one pod can clearly lag behind another. According to the second camp, careful cultivation, contingency, and curing still matter; terroir and provenance much less so.[6] Any pod that receives top-notch preparation and attention can develop a beautiful *givre*. Hence the kind of "unity of the diverse," or level playing field, that vanilla exemplifies. This also explains why specialists guard their preparation secrets, and why some are branching out to recover lost methods or discover new ones. Fostering and enhancing differences of this type are key strategies for vanilla producers.

Thus, in the wake of the manual pollination revolution, pod innovation and distinctiveness have historically hinged mostly on preparation. However, ever since the laboratory turn in post-1945 Madagascar, such developments have increasingly been linked with genetics. In recent years, an Israeli firm has claimed to be producing flavored vanillas thanks to both preparation and presumably genetic manipulation. The company offers an inventory that includes caramel-flavored pods as well as chocolate and smoky, woody ones. Representatives explain that the company uses an unspecified curing technique in addition to even vaguer "new technologies" and "other methods." This could change the grounds of the debate regarding the respective importance of terroir and preparation. Infusing outside flavors in this manner certainly marks a significant departure.[7]

CONCLUSION

That said, the two divergent schools can at least agree on two matters. First, major flavor differences do exist between *Vanilla planifolia, tahitensis,* and *pompona.* Second, real vanilla must not be allowed to dwindle, or even disappear, in the face of competition from its chemical competitors. That is a bona fide threat, given the challenge posed both by natural vanilla's price fluctuations and mostly by ever-cheaper synthetics. Does it matter that there is no real vanilla in most ice creams and yogurts, if most taste buds cannot tell the difference? Have provenance and authenticity become luxuries in their own right? Perhaps, but these pages do suggest some of the ways that real vanilla counts, especially to pollinators, harvesters, experts, preparers, and intermediaries, most of them from the Global South. Considering both the environmental and dietary impacts, it stands to reason that a natural product, derived from a plant that thrives in richly diverse forests across the Indian Ocean and in Central America, leaves a sounder ecological trail and presents greater benefits than a synthetic byproduct of pulp paper—even if natural vanilla comes from farther away.

Over the course of five centuries, the meanings of vanilla have proven to be particularly mutable, as it has been both an opulent spice and a source of balance, chocolate's constant companion, an aphrodisiac and a totem of blandness, a treatment for both depression and the plague. However, these endless contortions are in a sense the superstructure. They should not obscure the fundamentals of vanilla's phases: a precolonial era when it was used to flavor cacao beverages; the stage when Spain controlled nearly all distribution and the stuff was consumed largely by European elites, at first maintaining Central American uses as a flavoring for cacao; its globalization and shift to the French colonial world beginning in the 1840s, made possible by Edmond Albius's discovery of a teachable manual pollination method; the rise of synthetics in the twentieth century; and finally, real vanilla's attempted counteroffensive starting in the 1950s. These shifts have triggered vast geographical displacements from Central America to the Indian and Pacific Ocean worlds. Then, in a classic case of substitutionism, nations in the Global North began cornering the synthetic vanillin market. These ruptures mask some startling continuities, including vanilla's allure, its vulnerability to piracy and theft, and its nearly universal appeal as a fragrance.

The latest trends at the time of writing are not rosy for the real vanilla sector. Although new pod-producing nations, including Australia, Thailand, Cambodia, China, and Israel have emerged, the fact remains that a startling

99 percent of vanilla-flavored foods in the world contain artificial vanillin.[8] To be certain of eating real vanilla in a dessert, one either must pay a hefty premium or make it oneself, from scratch. Moreover, natural vanilla's boom and bust cycles endure. One might have expected the outbreak of COVID-19 and the accompanying home-baking fad to have boosted vanilla futures. On the contrary, pods reached a price peak of $600 a kilo (2.2 pounds) in 2019, just before the pandemic, only to see prices tumble since then, with some industrial food holdouts that still used real vanilla finally turning to cheaper synthetics. In the absence of a cartel, Madagascar's attempt to set a new bottom price on its own has also failed. All of this has had immediate and dire consequences on Sava, the world's leading vanilla-producing region, where some pod growers have had to sell their land and homes just to make ends meet.[9]

I have no crystal ball with which to predict vanilla's future. The ongoing battle against the fusarium fungus is one trend to watch; scientists seem to be closing in on fusarium-resistant hybrid vanillas. On a more concerning note, over the course of my research, many producers and cultivators expressed concern about shifts they have observed as a result of global warming. Vanilla requires heat to thrive but also several consecutive cool nights to flower. With that last condition at risk from Polynesia all the way to Madagascar, some growers are relocating their groves upland. This largely insular crop now stands at risk, much like some of the tropical islands on which it grows.

Notes

ABBREVIATIONS FOR ARCHIVES CONSULTED

AAT	Archives de l'Archevêché de Tahiti, Papeete, French Polynesia.
ACCM	Archives de la Chambre de Commerce et d'Industrie de Marseille, France.
ACFDT	Archives de la CFDT, Paris, France.
ACRBK	Archives Collection, Royal Botanical Gardens, Kew, UK.
ADE	Archives départementales de l'Essonnne, Chamarande, France.
ADG	Archives départementales de la Guadeloupe, Gourbeyre, France (Caribbean).
ADGIR	Archives départementales de la Gironde, Bordeaux, France.
ADIL	Archives départementales d'Indre-et-Loire, Tours, France.
ADIV	Archives départementales d'Ille-et-Vilaine, Rennes, France.
ADLA	Archives départementales de Loire-Atlantique, Nantes, France.
ADM	Archives départementales du Morbihan, Vannes, France.
ADML	Archives départementales de Maine-et-Loire, Angers, France.
ADN	Archives départementales du Nord, Lille, France.
ADPA	Archives départementales des Pyrénées Atlantiques, Bayonne, France.
ADR	Archives départementales de la Réunion, Saint-Denis, France (Indian Ocean).
AGCSE	Archives générales de la Congrégation du Saint-Esprit, Chevilly-Larue, France.
AGI	Archivo General de Indias, Seville, Spain.
AGN	Archivo General de la Nación, Mexico City, Mexico.
AGSSCC	Archivio Generale SSCC Picpus, Rome, Italy.
AMBAC	Archives du Musée des Beaux-Arts, Chartres, France.
ANF	Archives nationales de France, Paris and Pierrefitte, France.
ANM	Archives nationales de la République de Madagascar, Antananarivo, Madagascar.
ANMT	Archives nationales du Monde du Travail, Roubaix, France.
ANOM	Archives nationales d'outre-mer, Aix-en-Provence, France.
APPP	Archives de la Préfecture de Police de Paris, Le Pré–Saint-Gervais, France.
ARB	Archives de l'Académie royale de Belgique, Brussels, Belgium.
AUL	Archives de l'Université de Liège, Liège, Belgium.
BANC	Bancroft Library and Archives, University of California, Berkeley, CA, USA.
BSG	Bibliothèque Sainte-Geneviève, Paris, France.
BUA	Brock University Archives, St. Catharines, ON, Canada.
CADN	Centre des Archives diplomatiques de Nantes, France.

CHETOM	Centre d'histoire et d'études des troupes d'outre-mer, Fréjus, France.
KSLA	Kenneth Spencer Research Library and Archives, University of Kansas, Lawrence, KS, USA.
MCG	McGill University Archives, Montreal, QC, Canada.
MNHN	Muséum national d'Histoire naturelle (archive and library), Paris, France.
NADGM	National Archives Department, Government of Mauritius, Coromandel, Mauritius.
NAN	Nationaal Archief, The Hague, The Netherlands.
NARA	National Archives and Records Administration, College Park, MD, USA.
OSA	Österreichisches Staatsarchiv, Vienna, Austria.
SAH	Staatarchiv Hamburg, Germany.
SAPF	Service d'archives de Polynésie française, Papeete, French Polynesia.
SHDL	Service historique de la Défense (Marine), Lorient, France.
SHDM	Service historique de la Défense (Marine), Vincennes, France.
SLRIHU	Schlesinger Library, Radcliffe Institute, Harvard University, Cambridge, MA, USA.
TFLUT	Thomas Fisher Rare Books Library, University of Toronto, Canada.
TNA	The National Archives of the United Kingdom, Kew, UK.
UCDC	University of Cambridge Darwin Correspondence Project, Cambridge, UK.
VNA2	Vietnamese National Archives II, Ho Chi Minh City, Vietnam (Sách chỉ dẫn các phông, sưu tập lưu trữ bảo quản tại Trung tâm Lưu trữ Quốc gia II).

INTRODUCTION

1. In 2015, Malagasy vanilla producer Marcellin Zama explained that his pollinators only had until 10:30 a.m. to get to their flowers. However, others mention that they have until late morning or early afternoon. Cerveau Kotoson, "Ces gens-là... Zama Marcellin et sa femme, planteurs de vanille," *La Tribune de Diego-Suarez*, November 24, 2015.

2. Corey Ross, *Ecology and Power in the Age of Empire* (Oxford: Oxford University Press, 2017), 416.

3. David Goodman, Bernardo Sorj, and John Wilkinson, *From Farming to Biotechnology: A Theory of Agro-Industrial Development* (New York: Basil Blackwell, 1987), 2, 57, 69; Prakash Kumar, *Indigo Plantations in Colonial India* (Cambridge: Cambridge University Press, 2012), 159.

4. Sven Beckert, *Empire of Cotton: A Global History* (New York: Vintage Books, 2015), xix.

5. Paul Freedman, *Out of the East: Spices and the Medieval Imagination* (New Haven, CT: Yale University Press, 2008), 8.

6. Beckert, *Empire of Cotton*, xi, xii, xviii; Kumar, *Indigo Plantations*, 2–3.

7. Stephen Harp, *A World History of Rubber: Empire, Industry and the Everyday* (London: Wiley Blackwell, 2016), 4.

8. Sarah Abrevaya Stein, *Plumes: Ostrich Feathers, Jews, and a Lost World of Global Commerce* (New Haven, CT: Yale University Press, 2008), 79, 86; Kenneth Pomeranz and Steven Topik, *The World That Trade Created* (Armonk, NY: M. E. Sharpe, 2013), 91–93; Martin Lynn, *Commerce and Economic Change in West Africa: The Palm Oil Trade in the Nineteenth Century* (Cambridge: Cambridge University Press, 1997), 3; André Delcourt, *La France et les étab-*

lissements français au Sénégal entre 1713 et 1763 (Paris: Institut français d'Afrique noire, 1952), 184; Erika Rappaport, *A Thirst for Empire: How Tea Shaped the Modern World* (Princeton, NJ: Princeton University Press, 2017), 7; Judith Coffin, *The Politics of Women's Work: The Paris Garment Trades, 1750–1915* (Princeton, NJ: Princeton University Press, 1996), 53.

9. Sarah Osterhoudt, "'Good' Forests and Ambiguous Fields: Cultural Dimensions of Agroforestry Landscapes," in Frank Muttenzer, Gwyn Campbell and Jacques Pollini, eds., *Perceptions and Representations of the Malagasy Environment Across Cultures* (London: Palgrave, 2023), 34n, 39; Judith Klein, "La vanille Bourbon à La Réunion" *Géographie et Cultures* 50 (2004): 91–108.

10. Dan Koeppel, *Banana: The Fate of the Fruit That Changed the World* (New York: Plume Books, 2008), 101.

11. Tama Giles-Vernick, *Cutting the Vines of the Past: Environmental Histories of the Central African Rain Forest* (Charlottesville: University of Virginia Press, 2002), 163.

12. Emilio Kourí, *Pueblo Divided, Business, Property and Community in Papantla, Mexico* (Stanford, CA: Stanford University Press, 2004), 83, 100, 107–56.

13. Adam P. Karremans et al., "First Evidence for Multimodal Animal Seed Dispersal in Orchids," *Current Biology* 33, no. 2 (2023): 364, https://doi.org/10.1016/j.cub.2022.11.041; Adam Karremans, Charlotte Watteyn, Daniela Scaccabarozzi, Oscar A. Pérez-Escobar, and Diego Bogarín, "Evolution of Seed Dispersal Modes in the Orchidaceae: Has the Vanilla Mystery Been Solved?," *Horitculturae* 9, no. 12 (2023): 1270, https://doi.org/10.3390/horticulturae9121270.

14. Michael Pollan refers to plants as "willing partners in an intimate and reciprocal relationship." See Pollan, *The Botany of Desire: A Plant's-Eye View of the World* (New York: Random House, 2001), xiv, xxv.

15. Bruno Latour, "Pragmatogonies: A Mythical Account of How Humans and Nonhumans Swap Properties," *American Behavioral Scientist* 37, no. 6 (May 1994): 801.

16. On entanglements between people and mushrooms, see Anna Lowenhaupt Tsing, *The Mushroom at the End of the World: On the Possibility of Life in Capitalist Ruins* (Princeton, NJ: Princeton University Press, 2015), vii–viii.

17. Kourí provides a deeply researched study of vanilla in the Papantla region of Mexico. Patricia Rain's survey offers recipes, advice, and context but is not based on original research. Tim Ecott's lively vanilla voyages belong more to the travel-book genre, although they engage with Edmond Albius, Mexico, and Tahiti. Rosa Abreu-Runkel's short overview encompasses biology and uses but is not built on archival foundations. See Kourí, *Pueblo Divided*; Patricia Rain, *Vanilla: The Cultural History of the World's Most Popular Flavor and Fragrance* (New York: Jeremy Tarcher / Penguin, 2004); Tim Ecott, *Vanilla: Travels in Search of the Ice Cream Orchid* (New York: Grove Press, 2005); and Rosa Abreu-Runkel, *Vanilla: A Global History* (London: Reaktion Books, 2020).

18. Pesach Lubinsky, Gustavo A. Romero-González, Sylvia M. Heredia, and Stephanie Zabel, "Origins and Patterns of Vanilla Cultivation in Tropical America (1500–1900): No Support for an Independent Domestication of Vanilla in South America," in Daphna Havkin-Frenkel and Faith C. Belanger, eds., *Handbook of Vanilla Science and Technology* (London: Wiley Blackwell, 2019), 121–44; Pesach Lubinsky, "Historical and Evolutionary Origins of Cultivated Vanilla" (PhD diss., University of California, Riverside, 2007), 112–27.

19. Kourí, *Pueblo Divided*, 10–15, 88–99.

20. On Dampier, see Ecott, *Vanilla*, 25. On the act of piracy in 1704, see TNA, HCA 32/58/19. For Cádiz, see ANF, AE-B-I-216-fol. 34–26 and AE-B-I-216-fol. 58–59. The purse quote is from Adolphe Thiers, *Les Pyrénées et le Midi de la France pendant les mois de novembre et décembre 1822* (Paris: Ponthieu, 1823), 166. On smuggling more broadly and its habitual underestimation by historians, see Beverly Lemire, *Global Trade and the Transformation of Consumer Cultures* (Cambridge: Cambridge University Press, 2018), 139–89; and Michael Kwass, *Contraband: Louis Mandrin and the Making of a Global Underground* (Cambridge, MA: Harvard University Press, 2014).

21. On vanilla as aphrodisiac in eighteenth-century Europe, see Jim Endersby, *Orchid: A Cultural History* (Chicago: University of Chicago Press, 2016), 58–59. For Madame de Pompadour, see Madame du Hausset, *Memoirs of the Courts of Louis XV and XVI* (1899; Project Gutenberg, 2004), 40–41, https://www.gutenberg.org/ebooks/3883. On retaining the king's favor, see Colin Jones, *Madame de Pompadour: Images of a Mistress* (New Haven, CT: Yale University Press, 2002), 40. For the American example, see William Grimes, *Appetite City: A Culinary History of New York* (New York: North Point Press, 2009), 69; and Solon Robinson, *Hot Corn: Life Scenes in New York* (New York: De Witt and Davenport, 1854), 221. For the 1885 example, see Alexis Clerc, *Hygiène et médecine des deux sexes* (Paris: Jules Rouff et compagnie, 1885), 1:344.

22. The original recipe is held in the Thomas Jefferson Papers at the Library of Congress, Series 1: General Correspondence, 1651–1827, microfilm reel 56. Jefferson's July 28, 1791, request for fifty pods from William Short in France in 1791 is recorded in *The Works of Thomas Jefferson*, ed. Paul Leicester Ford (New York: G. P. Putnam's Sons, 1904–5), vol. 6.

23. Eliza Ripley, *Social Life in Old New Orleans Being Recollections of My Girlhood* (New York: D. Appleton, 1922).

24. Claire Bunschoten, "A Present and Absent Thing: How Nineteenth Century Vanilla Can Help Us Think About Edible Things," *Arcade* (Stanford Humanities Center), accessed November 4, 2024, https://shc.stanford.edu/arcade/interventions/present-and-absent-thing-how-nineteenth-century-vanilla-can-help-us-think; Eliza Leslie, *Mrs. Washington Potts, and Mr. Smith, Tales* (1832; repr., Philadelphia: Lee and Blanchard, 1843), 11.

25. On spice cravings in medieval Europe, see Freedman, *Out of the East*, 1–2. On luxuries versus needs in a modern context, see Immanuel Wallerstein, *The Modern World System*, vol. 3 (Berkeley: University of California Press, 2011), xvi, 131. On the 1792 food riots, see Colin Jones and Rebecca Spang, "Sans-culottes, *sans café, sans tabac*: Shifting Realms of Necessity and Luxury in Eighteenth-Century France," in Maxine Berg and Helen Clifford, eds., *Consumers and Luxury: Consumer Culture in Europe, 1650–1850* (Manchester: Manchester University Press, 1999), 37–62; and Rebecca Spang, *The Invention of the Restaurant* (Cambridge, MA: Harvard University Press, 2000), 106–7. Note that water was still a luxury, not a prime necessity. See Constance de Font-Réaulx, "Commercializing Water in Early Modern Paris," paper presented at the University of Toronto, March 24, 2022. On the luxury debate, see Michael Kwass, *The Consumer Revolution, 1650–1800* (Cambridge: Cambridge University Press, 2022), chap. 6.

26. Suzanne Marchand, *Porcelain: A History at the Heart of Europe* (Princeton, NJ: Princeton University Press, 2020), 18–19.

27. Kwass, *Consumer Revolution*, 102, 177.

28. Inga Saffron, *Caviar: The Strange History and Uncertain Future of the World's Most Coveted Delicacy* (New York: Broadway Books, 2002), 156; Kolleen Guy, *When Champagne Became French: Wine and the Making of National Identity* (Baltimore: Johns Hopkins University Press, 2003), 11–12. The quote is from Sidney Mintz, *Sweetness and Power: The Place of Sugar in Modern History* (Harmondsworth: Penguin Books, 1985), 95.

29. ACCM, MP 3.0.1.3.1./07, undated postwar document, "Séance de la commission du commerce extérieur." On Champagne capitalism, see David Todd, *A Velvet Empire: French Informal Imperialism in the Nineteenth Century* (Princeton, NJ: Princeton University Press, 2021), 123.

30. On vanilla as an example of "colonial globalization," see Genese Sodikoff, *Forest and Labor in Madagascar* (Bloomington: Indiana University Press, 2012), 117. On French luxury trades being on the defensive in the 1880s and 1890s, see Coffin, *Politics of Women's Work*, 202.

31. Maguelonne Toussaint-Samat, *A History of Food*, rev. ed. (Hoboken, NJ: Wiley-Blackwell, 2009), 393–400.

32. Todd, *Velvet Empire*, 123–174; ACCM, MP 3.1.9.

33. *Parte official de la Vigía de Cádiz*, no. 1, 1815. The 1802 glut was not limited to vanilla, of course. The same occurred with indigo. See John Fisher, *Trade, War and Revolution: Exports from Spain to Spanish America, 1797–1820* (Liverpool: Institute of Latin American Studies, 1992), 63. For the coffee figure, see Kwass, *Contraband*.

34. Henri Vermond, "La vanille aux colonies françaises," *La dépêche coloniale illustrée*, December 15, 1909, 290. The Mexican figures have been slightly adjusted on the basis of Kourí's table in *Pueblo Divided*, 299.

35. ANOM, 100 APOM 400.

36. Antoine François Prévost, *Manuel Lexique ou Dictionnaire portatif des mots français dont la signification n'est pas familière à tout le monde* (Paris: Didot, 1750), 2:758.

37. Vermond, "La vanille," 289–300.

38. Donatien Alphonse François de Sade, *La Vanille et la Manille* (Paris: Droressa, 1950), 7; Neil Schaeffer, *The Marquis de Sade: A Life* (Cambridge, MA: Harvard University Press, 1999), 131–132; Amanda Fortini, "The White Stuff: How Vanilla Became Shorthand for Bland," *Slate*, August 10, 2005, https://slate.com/human-interest/2005/08/how-vanilla-became-shorthand-for-bland.html.

39. Nadia Berenstein, "Making a Global Sensation: Vanilla Flavor, Synthetic Chemistry, and the Meanings of Purity," *History of Science* 54, no. 4 (2016): 401–2.

40. BUA, Ontario Paper Company Ltd., RG 75-12; Martin Hocking, "Vanillin: Synthetic Flavouring from Spent Sulfite Liquor," *Journal of Chemical Education* 74, no. 9 (1997): 1057. On cow dung, see "Ig Nobel Prizes Stranger Than Fiction," *Science*, October 5, 2007, https://www.science.org/content/article/ig-nobel-prizes-stranger-fiction.

41. Tracy Schuhmacher, "Wegmans Is the Latest Target in a Series of Lawsuits Pertaining to Vanilla," *Rochester (NY) Democrat and Chronicle*, October 9, 2019.

42. Maya Angelou, *I Know Why the Caged Bird Sings* (New York: Random House, 1969), 47; Michael W. Twitty, "Black People Were Denied Vanilla Ice Cream in the Jim Crow South," *Guardian*, July 4, 2014.

43. NASA, *Space Food and Nutrition: An Educator's Guide with Activities in Science and Mathematics*, July 2009, https://www.nasa.gov/wp-content/uploads/2009/07/143163main_space.food_.and_.nutrition.pdf; Christoph Pelzl, "Ecological Power Storage Battery Made of Vanillin," *Tu Graz*, January 10, 2020, https://www.tugraz.at/en/tu-graz/university/climate-neutral-tu-graz/singleview/article/oekologischer-stromspeicher-aus-vanillin.

44. Vínarterta incorporated few ingredients from Iceland itself, and its genesis by way of Vienna and Copenhagen coincided with an era of increased Icelandic trade in the late nineteenth century. See L. K. Bertram, *The Viking Immigrants: Icelandic North Americans* (Toronto: University of Toronto Press, 2019), 137–38.

ONE. NEW SPAIN'S NEAR MONOPOLY

1. Sophie D. Coe, *America's First Cuisines* (Austin: University of Texas Press, 1994), 58; Kourí, *Pueblo Divided*, 5, 9, 10.

2. Andrew Lawler, "In Biblical City of Armageddon, Signs of Early Vanilla and Elaborate Medical Care" *Science*, November 28, 2018, https://www.science.org/content/article/biblical-city-armageddon-signs-early-vanilla-and-elaborate-medical-care; Jonathan E. Robins, *Oil Palm: A Global History* (Chapel Hill: University of North Carolina Press, 2021), 3.

3. Pierre Chaunu, *Séville et l'Amérique, XVIe–XVIIe siècle* (Paris: Flammarion, 1977), 127.

4. Marcy Norton, *Sacred Gifts, Profane Pleasures: A History of Tobacco and Chocolate in the Atlantic World* (Ithaca, NY: Cornell University Press, 2008), 30–33.

5. Gilbert Bouriquet, *Le vanillier et la vanille dans le monde* (Paris: Paul Lechevalier, 1954), 11; Tim Ecott, *Vanilla: Travels in Search of the Ice Cream Orchid* (New York: Grove Press, 2005), 10, 23.

6. Miguel León Portilla, *Bernardino de Sahagún: First Anthropologist* (Norman: University of Oklahoma Press, 2002), 3.

7. AGI, Patronato 237, no. 1, Doce cartas con anexos, de Martín de Ursúa y Arizmendi, sobre la apertura del camino desde Yucatán a Guatemala y progresión del mismo, y sobre la conquista de varios indios que había en el distrito, 1695–96; Henry Bruman, "The Culture History of Mexican Vanilla," *Hispanic American Historical Review* 28, no. 3 (August 1948): 362. On cacao's religious function, see Norton, *Sacred Gifts*.

8. AGI, Quito 68, Testimonio de autos sobre la visita y ordenanzas hechas por el oidor don Diego Inclán Valdés, visitador de la gobernación de Popayán, para las ciudades de dicha gobernación, 1638–72.

9. AGI, México 37, no. 18, Carta del virrey duque de Alburquerque al rey sobre los crímenes y opresión que causa Andrés de Aramburu, alcalde mayor de Villa Alta [de los Zapotecas], 1653-11-18, México. "Usually a demand" appears in fol. 29v.

10. Laura Caso Barrera and Mario Aliphant Fernández, "Cacao, Vanilla and Annatto: Three Production and Exchange Systems in the Southern Maya Lowlands, 16th–17th Centuries," *Journal of Latin American Geography* 5, no. 2 (2006): 45; Brian Hamnett, *Politics and Trade in Southern Mexico, 1750–1821* (Cambridge: Cambridge University Press, 1971), 6, 21.

11. Alexander von Humboldt, *Political Essay on the Kingdom of New Spain*, trans. John Black (London: Longman, 1814), 3:31, 35.

12. BSG, MS 3877, fols. 68–69.

13. Ana Crespo Solana, "Legal Strategies and Smuggling Mechanisms in the Trade with the Hispanic Caribbean by Foreign Merchants in Cadiz: The Dutch and Flemish Case, 1680–1750," *Jahrbuch für Geschichte Lateinamerikas* 47 (2010): 182.

14. Solana, "Legal Strategies," 183.

15. ANF, AE-B-1-212-fol. 254.

16. ANF, AE-B-1-213-fol. 269. Vanilla constituted an important source of royal revenue for Madrid. In 1671, the treasury seized incoming vanilla beans on which duties had not been paid. AGI, Indiferente 31, Madrid, October 3, 1672.

17. AGI, Filipinas 205, no. 1, Expediente sobre el comercio entre Filipinas y Nueva España, 1708.

18. *Daily Journal* (London), June 6, 1728, 1.

19. Chaunu, *Séville et l'Amérique*, 229.

20. AGI, Contratación 2550, no. 3, Registros de venida: De las naos sueltas que vinieron de Veracruz y San Juan de Ulúa, Año de 1756.

21. ANF, MAR B7 369. Vanilla amounts appear in "Etat du chargement"; the definition of "fruit" comes up in the letter dated July 21, 1749; the crackdown on smuggling is mentioned in the letter dated June 24, 1749, responding to the court dispatch of May 31, 1749. See also "Mémoire concernant le commerce" January 18, 1698, in *Economie et négoce des Français dans l'Espagne de l'époque moderne*, ed. Didier Ozanam (Paris: Archives nationales, 2011), 41.

22. For the term *biopirate*, see Londa Schiebinger, *Plants and Empire: Colonial Bioprospecting in the Atlantic World* (Cambridge, MA: Harvard University Press, 2004), 39–44.

23. Albert Girard, *Le commerce français à Séville et Cadiz au temps des Habsbourg* (Paris: Bocard, 1932), 394; Chaunu, *Séville et l'Amérique*, 326–29. For the average of ninety-one days from Cádiz to Veracruz, see Geoffrey Scammell, *The First Imperial Age* (London: Unwin Hyman, 1989), 141.

24. TNA, HCA 32/111D/16, esp. CRA 152.

25. Colonel Hooke, *Secret History of Colonel Hooke's Negotiations in Scotland, in Favor of the Pretender in 1707* (London: T. Becket, 1760), 73; "Rome, October 7," *Independent Chronicle* (London), October 27–30, 1769.

26. Mario Trujillo Bolio, *El Péndulo Marítimo-Mercantil en el Atlántico Novohispano (1798–1825)* (Cádiz: Servico de Publicationes de la Universidad de Cádiz, 2009), 200.

27. ACCM, Roux L9, liasse 1137, Cádiz, October 2, 1729. On their global reach, see Jean-François Brière, "Le commerce triangulaire entre les ports terre-neuviers français, les pêcheries d'Amérique du Nord et Marseille au 18e siècle: Nouvelles perspectives," *Revue d'histoire de l'Amérique française* 40, no. 2 (1986): 193–214. Regarding Marseille's increased global trade after 1669, see Junko Takeda, *Between Crown and Commerce: Marseille and the Early Modern Mediterranean* (Baltimore: Johns Hopkins University Press, 2011), 31. In addition to Marseille, Bordeaux was already a pod importer in the eighteenth century. *Négociant* Jean Pellet dabbled in vanilla in 1724. ADGIR, 7B 1828, letter to Pellet from Martinique, April 4, 1724.

28. ACCM, Roux L9, liasse 830, Cádiz, August 9, 1729; September 20, 1729; March 7, 1730; July 2, 1731; November 27, 1731. See also Brière, "Le commerce triangulaire," 197–98.

29. Abbé Raynal, *Histoire philosophique*, cited in Michel Morineau, *Incroyables gazettes et fabuleux métaux: Les retours des trésors américains d'après les gazettes hollandaises* (Cambridge: Cambridge University Press, 1985), 494–95.

30. Kwass, *Consumer Revolution*, 102; Colin Jones and Rebecca Spang, "Sans-culottes, *sans café, sans tabac*: Shifting Realms of Necessity and Luxury in Eighteenth-Century France," in Maxine Berg and Helen Clifford, eds., *Consumers and Luxury: Consumer Culture in Europe, 1650–1850* (Manchester: Manchester University Press, 1999), 48.

31. On another gradual democratization, that of clothing and the accompanying "fashion revolution," whose precise dates and contours historians continue to debate, see Nancy Green, *Ready-to-Wear and Ready-to-Work: A Century of Industry and Immigration in Paris and New York* (Durham, NC: Duke University Press, 1997), 24.

32. Cillart de Kérampoul, Clément Vincent, *Dictionnaire François-breton ou François-celtique du dialecte de Vannes* (Leiden: La Compagnie, 1744), 395.

33. Rachel Laudan, *Cuisine and Empire: Cooking in World History* (Berkeley: University of California Press, 2013), 202.

34. Norton, *Sacred Gifts*, 9

35. AGN, Indiferente Virreinal, caja 5025, exp. 14, August 11, 1647.

36. Sor Juana Inés de la Cruz, *Libro de cocina del Convento de San Jerónimo* (Mexico City: Imprenta de la Enciclopedia de Mexico, 1979) (the author died in 1695); Dominga de Guzmán, *Recetario Mexiquense Siglo XVIII* (Mexico City: Consejo Nacional para la Cultura y las Artes, 2015); Gerónimo de San Pelayo, *Libro de cocina del hermano fray Gerónimo de San Pelayo* (Mexico City: Consejo Nacional para la Cultura y las Artes, 2015).

37. TFLUT, MSS 01287, anonymous Italian-language cookery manuscript, circa 1650–1750.

38. Marie-Pierre Rey, *Le premier des chefs: L'exceptionnel destin d'Antonin Carême* (Paris: Flammarion, 2021), 6, 65, 87; Marion Godfroy-Tayart de Borms, "Du maître queux au cuisinier du XIXe siècle: La construction de la figure du chef à travers la carrière de Marie-Antoine Carême," *Bulletin de l'Institut Pierre Renouvin* 50 (2019): 101–10; Marie-Antoine Carême, *Le pâtissier national parisien, ou traité élémentaire et pratique de la pâtisserie ancienne et moderne* (Paris: Garnier frères, 1879), 2:121, 184, 205, 211, 231 (quote), 388; *L'art culinaire au XIXe siècle, Antonin Carême* (Paris: Mairie de Paris, 1984).

39. Ad for Debauve et Gallais, *La semaine: Journal hebdomadaire*, December 28, 1828, 4; Jean-Paul Aron, *Essai sur la sensibilité alimentaire à Paris au XIXe siècle* (Paris: Armand Colin, 1967), 36–37.

40. Emma Spary, *Feeding France: New Sciences of Food, 1760–1815* (Cambridge: Cambridge University Press, 2017), 142–151 (quote on 151); Emma Spary, *Eating the Enlightenment: Food and the Sciences in Paris, 1670–1760* (Chicago: University of Chicago Press, 2012), 105. Regarding New Orleans, see the announcement in *The Courier* (New Orleans), December 4, 1830, 1. The observation on ancient Greece is from Jack Goody, *Cooking, Cuisine and Class: A Study in Comparative Sociology* (Cambridge: Cambridge University Press, 1981), 171.

41. David Courtwright, *Forces of Habit: Drugs and the Making of the Modern World* (Cambridge, MA: Harvard University Press, 2001); Kwass, *Consumer Revolution*, 30.

42. OSA, FHKA SUS Patente 211.15.

43. Jacques Donis, *Préservatifs contre la peste pour un chacun* (Grenoble: André Faure, 1721), 3.

44. Philippe Fermin, *Description générale, historique, géographique et physique de la Colonie de Surinam* (Amsterdam: E. Van Harrevelt, 1769), 191–92.

45. NAN, Tweede West-Indische Compagnie (WIC), 1.05.01.02, inventarisnummer 1025. This translation is drawn from Samuel Oppenheim, "An Early Jewish Colony in Western Guiana, 1658–1666," *American Jewish Historical Society* 16 (1907): 158. It is also quoted by Patricia Rain in *Vanilla: The Cultural History of the World's Most Popular Flavor and Fragrance* (New York: Jeremy Tarcher / Penguin, 2004), 59.

46. Natalie Zemon Davis, "Braided Histories: Jews, Africans and Philosophies in Eighteenth-Century Suriname," paper presented at Old Dominion University, 2002; Mordechai Arbell, "The Jewish Settlement in Pomeroon/Pauroma (Guyana), 1657–1666," *Revue d'études juives* 154, no. 3-4 (July–December 1995): 343.

47. Arbell, "Jewish Settlement," 360.

48. Andreas Motsch, "Le ginseng d'Amérique: Un lien entre les deux Indes, entre curiosité et science," *Etudes Epistémè* 26 (2014): https://journals.openedition.org/episteme/331.

49. "Les voyages de Mr. Goupy faits aux Isles d'Amérique et aux côtes d'Afrique en 1681," cited in Martijn Van Den Bel, "Les Amérindiens de Guyane par Jean Goupy, c. 1690," *Bulletin de la Société d'Histoire de la Guadeloupe*, no. 184-85 (2019-20): 32.

50. See Jacques François Artur, *Histoire des colonies françoises de la Guianne* (Cayenne: Ibis Rouge, 2002), 213n70, for the biographical information, 269 for the mill and etymology, and 311 for the engagement to his niece.

51. Artur, *Histoire des colonies françoises*, 268. See also ANOM, COL B 11, 145, instructions from Versailles, April 30, 1685.

52. ANOM, COL B 13, 37-38, instructions from Versailles, August 8, 1687.

53. ANOM, COL B 14, 295, instructions from Versailles, September 24, 1691. Another source registered the arrival of an entire bundle of vanilla from Cayenne that month in the port of Rochefort. See Pascal Even, "Les collections 'américaines' de l'intendant Michel Bégon," in *Le rôle des voyages dans la constitution des collections ethnographiques, historiques et scientifiques: Actes du Congrès national des sociétés historiques et scientifiques Voyages et voyageurs* (Paris: Editions du CTHS, 2008), 62.

54. ANOM, COL B 14, 436, instructions from Versailles, September 6, 1692.

55. Schiebinger, *Plants and Empire*, 36; Philippe Minard, *La fortune du Colbertisme: Etat et industrie dans la France des Lumières* (Paris: Fayard, 1998), 224–34.

56. ANOM, COL C 14/3, 5, Cayenne, May 5, 1693.

57. ANOM, COL B 14, 547, instructions from Versailles, July 29, 1693.

58. ANOM, COL C 14/3, 34, Cayenne, February 23, 1694.

59. ANOM, COL C 14/3, 47, 68, Cayenne, September 14, 1694, May 18, 1695. Only in 1790 would Cayenne formally obtain a botanical garden. See Hélène Blais, *L'Empire de la nature* (Paris: Champ Vallon, 2023), 27.

60. ANOM, COL B 18, 51, instructions from Versailles, September 15, 1694.

61. Victor de Nouvion, ed., *Extraits des auteurs et voyageurs qui ont écrit sur la Guyane* (Paris: Plon, 1844), 56, 121. Not all this Guianese vanilla was necessarily *pompona*. In the early

eighteenth century, Pierre Barrère, who served as the king's botanist in Cayenne between 1722 and 1725, indicated that two types of vanilla coexisted in French Guiana: "one large with a pleasant smell, the other small with hardly any odor, improperly locally called *vanille musquée* or small vanilla." The former thrived natively along the Oyapok River. The small vanilla remains a mystery. Its "fruit" were tiny: only two inches long. Their fragrance resembled violets more than standard vanilla. Another, later source corroborated this version of two Guianese vanillas. *Ordonnateur* César-Jacques de Lacroix, who arrived in Cayenne in 1774, insisted that "there are two types of vanillas in Guiana." The one with pods "smaller than pinky fingers" was "totally lacking in that essential oil that makes it so appropriate as a medication and a spice." The other featured seven- to eight-inch-long pods" and produced a "most pleasant smell." He pronounced the second to be the equal of "Spanish vanillas." This may point to the tiny ones being a type of vanilla now considered nonedible, perhaps *Vanilla hartii*. The large vanilla, however, was certainly *Vanilla pompona*. See MNHN, MS 683, "Description de deux espèces de vanille à Cayenne"; and Pesach Lubinsky, Gustavo A. Romero-González, Sylvia M. Heredia, and Stephanie Zabel, "Origins and Patterns of Vanilla Cultivation in Tropical America (1500–1900): No Support for an Independent Domestication of Vanilla in South America," in Daphna Havkin-Frenkel and Faith C. Belanger, eds., *Handbook of Vanilla Science and Technology* (London: Wiley Blackwell, 2019), 133. Thanks to Michel Grisoni for the *Vanilla hartii* hypothesis.

62. Charlotte Watteyn et al., "Trick or Treat? Pollinator Attraction in *Vanilla pompona*" *Biotropica* 54, no. 1 (2022): 268–74.

63. Jean-Baptiste Labat, *Nouveau voyage aux isles de l'Amérique* (The Hague: P. Husson, 1724), 2:380–86. The 1701 Robert report can be found in ANOM, C8 A13, fol. 206. On Versailles ordering the botanical mission, see Erick Noël, *Le goût des îles sur les tables des Lumières* (La Crèche: La Geste, 2020), 89–90.

64. Jacques Savary des Bruslons, *Dictionnaire universel de commerce, contenant tout ce qui concerne le commerce qui se fait dans les quatre parties du monde* (Amsterdam: Jansons and Waesberge, 1732), 1:853; Etienne François Geoffroy, *Traité de la matière médicale ou De l'histoire, des vertus, du choix et de l'usage des remèdes simples* (Paris: Jean Desaint, 1743), 3:182; "Vanille inodore d'Haïti," in Michel Étienne Descourtilz, *Flore pittoresque et médicale des Antilles ou traité des plantes usuelles* (Paris: Crosnier, 1829), 7:119–22; Marie Armande Jeanne Gacon-Dufour, *Manuel du Parfumeur* (Paris: Boret, 1825), 256.

65. Amy Butler Greenfield, *A Perfect Red: Empire, Espionage and the Quest for the Color of Desire* (New York: HarperCollins, 2006), 169–82 (quotes on 169 and 171); Shiebinger, *Plants and Empire*, 40–43; Danielle Trichaud-Buti and Gilbert Buti, *Rouge cochenille: Histoire d'un insecte qui colora le monde* (Paris: CNRS Editions, 2021), 251–70.

66. Thiéry de Menonville, *Traité de la culture du nopal, et de l'éducation de la cochenille dans les colonies françaises d'Amérique* (Cap-Français: Veuve Herbault, 1787), pt. 1, p. lv, and in the second section of this same first part, titled "Voyage à Guaxaca, capitale de la province du Mexique du même nom" (which uses Arabic numbers for pagination), 143–45, 198, 224, 231; Butler Greenfield, *Perfect Red*, 173, 181; Shiebinger, *Plants and Empire*, 35–43 (esp. 35 for the term *biopirate*).

67. There are signs of additional introductions of *pompona*. In 1820, an author seeking to "compensate" French settlers who fled during the Haitian Revolution explained that in the second half of the eighteenth century, vanilla had been introduced to Saint-Domingue from French Guiana, supposedly on instructions from botanist Pierre Poivre. See Georges-Christophe Würtz, *Mémoire sur le moyen de réparer les torts faits au commerce de la France par l'insurrection de l'isle de Saint-Domingue* (Paris: Treuttel et Würtz, 1820), 11.

68. Denis Diderot and Jean Le Rond d'Alembert, eds., *L'Encyclopédie*, vol. 40, *Recueil de planches sur les sciences* (Paris, 1780), 2.

69. "Importations," *Morning Courier and New-York Enquirer*, May 29, 1837, 2; *New-Orleans Price-Current and Commercial Intelligencer*, May 23, 1829, 2.

TWO. A BELGIAN WINS THE RACE

1. "Intérieur," *L'Emancipation politique, commerciale, religieuse et littéraire* (Brussels), November 11, 1831, 3.

2. Jan de Vries, *The Industrious Revolution: Consumer Behavior and the Household Economy, 1650 to the Present* (Cambridge: Cambridge University Press, 2008), 23, 52.

3. Kourí, *Pueblo Divided*, 87, 288 (table A.2).

4. Paul Arblaster, *A History of the Low Countries* (London: Palgrave, 2006), 170–77; Patrick Weber, *La grande histoire de la Belgique* (Paris: Perrin, 2013), 168–69, 191; Octave Servais, *Liège révolutionnaire* (Liège: Gillet-Jacques, 1930), 16.

5. Erik Buyst, "The Causes of Growth During Belgium's Industrial Revolution," *Journal of Interdisciplinary History* 49, no. 1 (2018): 71–92.

6. ARB, 19345-1367, Morren to Stassart, August 28, 1835; Edouard Morren, *Notice sur Charles Morren* (Brussels: Hayez, 1860), 9–21.

7. ARB, 19345-1367, Morren to Stassart, August 28, 1835.

8. Morren, *Notice sur Charles Morren*, 9–21.

9. Bestor, "Verrassel (Morren), Marie (1812–1865)," last modified January 28, 2021, 09:18 (UTC), https://www.bestor.be/wiki/index.php/Verrassel_(Morren),_Marie_(1812-1865).

10. Morren, *Notice sur Charles Morren*; François Crépin, "Charles Morren," *Biographie nationale* (Belgium) 15 (1899): 280.

11. Crépin, "Charles Morren," 276.

12. Morren, *Notice sur Charles Morren*, 8, 16–17; "Réponse [au] professeur extraordinaire van Breda," *Le Belge, Ami du Roi et de la Patrie* (Brussels), January 15, 1828, 3–4. On the meanings of beached whales in the Dutch golden age, see Simon Schama, *The Embarrassment of Riches: An Interpretation of Dutch Culture in the Golden Age* (London: Collins, 1987), 130–38. Duels were banned in Belgium in 1841, thanks in part to pressure from Morren. See ARB, 19345-1367, Morren to Stassart, October 11, 1836; and Thierry Evens, "Supprimons Les Duels Du Code Penal," *Le Soir* (Brussels), August 10, 1996, https://www.lesoir.be/art/supprimons-les-duels-du-code-penal_t-19960810-Z0CGAY.html.

13. Goswin de Stassart was elected director of the Royal Academy in January 1835. See Marie-Rose Thielemans, *Goswin, baron de Stassart, 1780–1854: Politique et Franc-maçonnerie* (Louvain: Académie Royale, 2008), 485, 590, 601, 748–52.

14. ARB, 19345-1367, Morren to Stassart, August 28, 1835.

15. Morren, *Notice sur Charles Morren*, 25–26; Eugène M. O. Dognée et al., *Liège, histoire, arts, lettres, sciences, industrie, travaux publics* (Liège: Daxhelet, 1881), 463. Gaëde's cause of death is listed in *Courrier de la Meuse* (Liège), January 9, 1834, 3. Courtois's appears in *Courrier de la Meuse* (Liège), April 17, 1835, 2.

16. ARB, 19345-1367, Morren to Stassart, May 3, 1836.

17. Samuel Clark, "Nobility, Bourgeoisie and the Industrial Revolution in Belgium," *Past and Present* 105 (November 1984): 150.

18. Victor Hugo, *Le Rhin: Lettres à un ami* (1842; repr., Paris: Imprimerie nationale, 1906), 58–59.

19. Servais, *Liège révolutionnaire*, 34–37; Paul Servais, "L'évolution du niveau de vie dans la périphérie liégeoiose au XIXe siècle d'après les inventaires et ventes de meubles après décès" *Social History / Histoire sociale* 21, no. 41 (May 1988): 113–28.

20. Charles Morren, "Sur la fructification de la vanille obtenue à moyen de la fécondation artificielle," *Comptes-rendus hebdomadaires des séances de l'Académie des Sciences de Paris* 6 (January–June 1838): 490; Charles Morren, "Fructification de la vanille au moyen de la fécondation artificielle," *Journal d'agriculture pratique, de jardinage et d'économie domestique* 1 (July 1838): 115.

21. AUL, MS 2647-58, letter dated May 5, 1829.

22. Charles Morren, "Note sur la première fructification du vanillier en Europe," in *Prémices d'anatomie et de physiologie végétales* (Brussels: Muquardt, 1841), first published in *Annales de la Société Royale d'Horticulture de Paris* 20 (May 1837): 1; Morren, "Sur la fructification de la vanille," 491.

23. Jim Endersby, "Deceived by Orchids: Sex, Fiction and Darwin," *British Society for the History of Science* 49, no. 2 (2016): 205.

24. Charles Morren, "Sur la fécondation, la fructification, le semis et la germination des orchidées," *Horticulteur Belge* 3 (January 1835): 9.

25. Nicolas Bouvier, *Une orchidée qu'on appela vanille* (Geneva: Metropolis, 1998), 50.

26. It is possible to pinpoint some of his influences, including German botanist Christian Sprengel, whose 1793 *Structure and Fertilization of Flowers* demonstrated that plants attracted insects to reproduce. Morren also acknowledged British botanist Robert Brown's 1831 article "On the Organs and Mode of Fecundation in Orchideae and Asclepiadaceae." To the Parisian Academy of Science in 1838, he pointed to a different inspiration: the work by French botanists Charles-François Brisseau de Mirbel and Adolphe Brongniart. In 1840, Morren confirmed each of these genealogies. See Tim Ecott, *Vanilla: Travels in Search of the Ice Cream Orchid* (New York: Grove Press, 2005), 115; Joseph Beaujean, "Petite histoire de l'introduction de la fructification du vanillier au jardin botanique de l'Université de Liège et à l'île de la Réunion," *Natura Mosana* 54, no. 4 (October–December 2002): 76; Morren, "Sur la fructification de la vanille," 489; Charles Morren, "Fructification de la vanille obtenue au moyen de la fécondation artificielle," *Journal de chimie médicale, de pharmacie et de toxicologie* 1, no. 4 (1838): 293; and Charles Morren, "Notice sur la vanille indigène," *Bulletin de l'académie royale de Bruxelles* 4, no. 5 (1837–38): 225–38.

27. Charles Morren, "On the Production of Vanilla in Europe," *Annals of Natural History* 3, no. 14 (March 1839): 6.

28. AUL, MS 4622, "La vanille est actuellement en fleur," *Journal de Liège*, February 17, 1836.

29. On botanical science as consumption, see James Livesey, *Provincializing Global History: Money, Ideas, and Things in the Languedoc, 1680–1830* (New Haven, CT: Yale University Press, 2020), 87. On reality as spectacle, see Vanessa Schwartz, *Spectacular Realities: Early Mass Culture in Fin-de-Siècle Paris* (Berkeley: University of California Press, 1998), 150.

30. "Botanique, Culture de la vanille à Liège" *L'Emancipation* (Belgium), February 19, 1837, 3.

31. Morren, "Note sur la première fructification du vanillier en Europe," 3.

32. Charles Morren, "Correspondance," *Comptes-rendus hebdomadaires des séances de l'Académie des Sciences de Paris* 8 (January–June 1839): 842.

33. Morren, "On the Production of Vanilla in Europe," 5–6; Charles Morren, "Botanique," *Bulletin de l'Académie royale des sciences et belles-lettres de Bruxelles* 4 (1837): 226.

34. Morren, "Notice sur la vanille indigène," 11.

35. Morren, "Fructification de la vanille" (*Journal de chimie médicale*), 293.

36. Morren, "Note sur la première fructification du vanillier en Europe," 2.

37. Clifton Crais and Pamela Scully, *Sara Baartman and the Hottentot Venus* (Princeton, NJ: Princeton University Press, 2009), 125–41 (quote on 134). The "oddity" quote is from Robin Mitchell, *Vénus Noire: Black Women and Colonial Fantasies in Nineteenth-Century France* (Athens: University of Georgia Press, 2020), 30; see also 41–42 on Baartman's firm no to Cuvier. On Cuvier having taught and encouraged Morren in Paris, see Edouard Morren, *Notice sur Charles Morren*, 18.

38. Morren, "Note sur la première fructification du vanillier en Europe," 2.

39. Morren, "Sur la fructification de la vanille," 491.

40. Kourí, *Pueblo Divided*, 18.

41. Morren, "Note sur la première fructification du vanillier," 2; Ecott, *Vanilla*, 115.

42. Gilbert Bouriquet, *Le vanillier et la vanille dans le monde* (Paris: Paul Lechevalier, 1954), 20. On Joseph Neumann, see Philippe Jaussaud and Edouard-Raoul Brygoo, *Du Jardin au Museum en 516 biographies* (Paris: Muséum national d'Histoire naturelle, 2004). As late as the 1980s, some still attributed the discovery to Neumann. See Maguelonne Toussaint-Samat, *A History of Food*, rev. ed. (Hoboken, NJ: Wiley-Blackwell, 2009), 525.

43. Alire Raffeneau-Delile, "Notice d'un voyage horticole et botanique en Belgique" *Bulletin de la société d'agriculture du département de l'Hérault* 25 (1838): 68–71 (quote on 71); Morren, "Sur la fructification de la vanille," 490; Conrad de Gourcy, *Second voyage agricole en Belgique, en Hollande et dans plusieurs départements de la France* (Paris: Librairie d'agriculture, 1850): 292.

44. ARB, 19345-1367, Morren to Stassart, May 5, 1837.

45. ARB, 19345-1367, Morren to Stassart, May 8, 1837.

46. Thielemans, *Goswin, baron de Stassart*, 357.

47. "Nouvelles diverses," *L'Indépendance Belge* (Brussels), May 12, 1837, 3.

48. As Kristy Leissle writes, "the place of *manufacture* became more important to appreciating chocolate than the place of origin of the beans. 'Belgian chocolate' has more

purchase than 'Ghanaian cocoa.'" Cacao was only starting to be produced in Africa at the time of Morren's discovery. See Leissle, "Invisible West Africa: The Politics of Single Origin Chocolate," *Gastronomica: The Journal of Food and Culture*, 13, no. 3 (2013): 2, 22.

49. ARB, 19345-1367, Morren to Stassart, May 4, 1838.

50. ARB, 19345-1367, Morren to Stassart, May 12, 1838.

51. *Bulletin de la Société de Médecine de Gand*, 1837, 42.

52. Morren, *Notice sur Charles Morren*, 21; Marie Morren, *De l'importance des premières impressions: Histoire d'Emma Nesbit* (Brussels: Deprez et parent, 1833); "Publication d'un *Manuel Héraldique*," *Le Belge* (Brussels), December 10, 1939, 2.

53. ACRBK, letters to Lindley, fol. 647, April 29, 1837; Morren, *Notice sur Charles Morren*, 25-26.

54. ACRBK, letters to Lindley, fol. 654, May 2, 1840.

55. Greenhouses/glasshouses were undergoing major structural evolutions in this era. See Kate Colquhoun, *The Busiest Man in England: A Life of Joseph Paxton, Gardener, Architect and Victorian Visionary* (Boston: David Godine, 2006), 13.

56. Anne-Marie Bogaert-Damin, "L'Illustration des revues d'horticulture en Belgique au 19e siècle," *In Monte Artium* 7 (2014): 155-76.

57. Natalie Zemon Davis, *Women on the Margins: Three Seventeenth-Century Lives* (Cambridge, MA: Harvard University Press, 1997), 152; Gabriella Berti Logan, "Women and Botany in Risorgimento Italy," *Journal of the History of Science* 19, no. 2 (2004): 601-28.

58. Ann B. Shteir, "Gender and 'Modern' Botany in Victorian England," *Osiris* 12 (1997): 33-36. On Lindley's part in this backlash, see also Ann B. Shteir, *Cultivating Women, Cultivating Science: Flora's Daughters and Botany in England, 1760-1860* (Baltimore: Johns Hopkins University Press, 1996), 165-66.

59. Joy Harvey, "'Darwin's Angels': The Women Correspondents of Charles Darwin," *Intellectual History Review* 19, no. 2 (2009): 207.

60. H. Haquin, "Camellia Japonica var. Maria Morren," *Annales de la société royale d'agriculture et de botanique de Gand* 3 (1847): 337-38; Hyacinthe Haquin, "Choix des meilleurs dahlias mis dans le commerce pour la première fois en 1851," *La Belgique horticole* 2 (1852): 108.

61. Charles Morren, "Fruits de serre," *Annales de la société royale d'agriculture et de botanique de Gand* 5 (1849): 13-15.

62. Charles Morren, *Palmes et Couronnes de l'horticulture de Belgique depuis 1845 à 1851* (Liège: Belgique horticole, 1851), 145-46.

63. Charles Morren, *Memorandum sur la vanille, son histoire et sa culture* (Brussels: Hayez, 1851), 32; Morren, "Fruits de serre," 13.

64. Morren, "Fruits de serre," plate.

65. "On écrit de Liège," *Le Belge* (Brussels), March 24, 1837, 2.

66. AUL, MS 4720, letters from the Prussian embassy and from King Leopold's assistant, May 3, 1837, and July 6, 1840, and a letter from the Austrian legation, October 24, 1837.

67. Baron d'Hombres-Firmas, "Horticulture. Souvenirs d'un voyage en Belgique et en Hollande, 1840," *Le Cultivateur: Journal des progrès agricoles* 15 (1843): 397.

68. *Rapports sur l'exposition nationale des produits de l'agriculture et de l'horticulture de 1848* (Brussels: Imp. Parent, 1849), 330-31.

69. Morren, *Memorandum sur la vanille*, 30.

70. "Rapport de M. Germain de St. Pierre sur la visite au jardin botanique de Liège," *Bulletin de la Société botanique de France* 20 (July 1873): 118n1.

71. Steven Topik, Carlos Marichal, and Zephyr Frank, "Introduction: Commodity Chains in Theory and in Latin American History," in Topik, Marichal, and Frank, eds., *Commodity Chains in Theory and in Latin American History* (Durham, NC: Duke University Press, 2006), 3.

72. Sarah Easterby-Smith, *Cultivating Commerce: Cultures of Botany in Britain and France, 1760–1815* (Cambridge: Cambridge University Press, 2018), 189.

73. Morren, *Memorandum sur la vanille*, 31.

74. Morren, "On the Production of Vanilla in Europe," 1.

75. On some of these questions, see Mark Smith, "Producing Sense, Consuming Sense, Making Sense: Perils and Prospects for Sensory History," *Journal of Social History* 40, no. 4 (2007): 847.

76. Morren, "Sur la fructification de la vanille," 489.

77. Morren, "Notice sur la vanille indigène," 7.

78. Pesach Lubinsky, Gustavo A. Romero-González, Sylvia M. Heredia, and Stephanie Zabel, "Origins and Patterns of Vanilla Cultivation in Tropical America (1500–1900): No Support for an Independent Domestication of Vanilla in South America," in Daphna Havkin-Frenkel and Faith C. Belanger, eds., *Handbook of Vanilla Science and Technology* (London: Wiley Blackwell, 2019), 133.

79. Jean-Baptiste Christophe Fusée-Aublet, *Histoire des plantes de la Guiane française* (Paris: Pierre-François Didot, 1775), supp. to vol. 2, 79–84.

80. Morren, "Fruits de serre," 13.

81. Morren, *Memorandum sur la vanille*, 32.

82. On period and place-specific "noses," see Smith, "Producing Sense," 847.

83. Filip van Noort, "Vanilla in Dutch Greenhouses: A Discovery: From Research to Production," in Daphna Havkin-Frenkel and Faith C. Belanger, eds., *Handbook of Vanilla Science and Technology* (London: Wiley Blackwell, 2019), 163; Maude Brulard, "Vanilla and Spice, Next to Bloom in Dutch Greenhouses," Phys.org, November 12, 2016, https://phys.org/news/2016-11-vanilla-spice-bloom-dutch-greenhouses.html; "Dutch Efforts to Grown Vanilla Commercially Flop," *Dutch News*, February 14, 2019, https://www.dutchnews.nl/news/2019/02/dutch-efforts-to-grow-vanilla-commercially-flop.

84. Michael Osborne, "Acclimatizing the World: A History of the Paradigmatic Colonial Science" *Osiris* 15 (2000): 137.

85. Jean-Alexandre Cazaud, quoted in Emma Rothschild, *An Infinite History. The Story of a Family in France over Three Centuries* (Princeton, NJ: Princeton University Press, 2021), 102.

86. Sidney Mintz, *Sweetness and Power: The Place of Sugar in Modern History* (Harmondsworth: Penguin Books, 1985), 148.

87. Steven Topik and William Gervase Clarence-Smith, "Introduction," in William Gervase Clarence-Smith and Steven Topik, eds., *The Global Coffee Economy in Africa, Asia and Latin America, 1500–1989* (Cambridge: Cambridge University Press, 2003), 2.

88. "Botanique, Culture de la vanille à Liège" *L'Emancipation* (Belgium), February 19, 1837, 3.

89. Morren, "Notice sur la vanille indigène," 1–2.

90. Morren, "Sur la fructification de la vanille," 492.

91. That said, attempts to introduce tropical rice varietals to Spain and France occurred in the eighteenth century, and the blockade's impact should therefore not be overstated, given the much longer tradition of acclimatization. See Livesey, *Provincializing Global History*, 97.

92. Londa Schiebinger, "The European Colonial Science Complex," *Isis* 96, no. 1 (2005): 52–55. For the argument that there was no "unity of purpose" and hence no "system" or "complex," see Loïc Charles and Paul Cheney, "The Colonial Machine Dismantled: Knowledge and Empire in the French Atlantic," *Past and Present*, no. 219 (May 2013): 128.

93. On empires as impediments to free trade and globalization in the second half of the nineteenth century, see Elizabeth Heath, *Wine, Sugar and the Making of Modern France* (Cambridge: Cambridge University Press, 2014), 269.

94. Morren, "Botanique," 236.

95. Henri Vermond was unsure whether Albius had been influenced by Morren, leaving open the possibility that the two had independently achieved similar results a few years apart. See Vermond, "La vanille aux colonies françaises," *La dépêche coloniale illustrée*, December 15, 1909, 290.

96. ARB, 19345-1367, Morren to Stassart, February 22, 1841.

97. UCDC, Charles Darwin to J. O. Westwood, July 9, 1860, letter DCP LETT 2862.

98. UCDC, letter DCP LETT 3252, Charles Darwin to the *Gardeners' Chronicle and Agricultural Gazette*, September 14, 1861, 831.

99. Harvey, "'Darwin's Angels,'" 199.

100. Charles Darwin, *On the Various Contrivances by Which British and Foreign Orchids Are Fertilised by Insects* (London: John Murray, 1862), 270.

101. Michael Pollan, *The Botany of Desire: A Plant's-Eye View of the World* (New York: Random House, 2001), 134.

THREE. AN ENSLAVED TEEN CRACKS THE CASE

1. MNHN, MS 308, notes indicatives sur l'emballage des végétaux, July 23, 1810, and projet d'établissement de correspondance entre les colonies françaises et le Jardin du Roi.

2. Hélène Blais, *L'Empire de la nature* (Paris: Champ Vallon, 2023), 41–44; Hélène Blais, "La caisse Ward," in Sylvain Venayre and Pierre Singaravélou, eds., *Le magasin du monde: La monodialisation par les objets du XVIIIe siècle à nos jours* (Paris: Fayard, 2020), 90–94. Earlier French cases are described in Yannick Romieux, "Le transport maritime des plantes au XVIIIe siècle," in *Botanique et horticulture d'outre-mer à la Loire-Atlantique* (Nantes: Archives départementales, 2004), 97–103.

3. That said, Poivre held a grudge. He falsely accused his colleague Fusée-Aublet of having destroyed his nutmeg. See Emma Spary, "Of Nutmegs and Botanists: The Colonial Cultivation of Botanical Identity," in Londa Schiebinger and Claudia Swan, eds., *Colonial Botany: Science, Commerce and Politics in the Early Modern World* (Philadelphia: University of Pennsylvania Press, 2005), 192–93.

4. Richard Grove, *Green Imperialism: Colonial Expansion, Tropical Island Edens and the Origins of Environmentalism, 1600–1860* (Cambridge: Cambridge University Press, 1995), 5, 11, 14, 146, 188, 196, 209.

5. MNHN, MS 308, Bourbon plant catalog, 1783.

6. We know that some vanilla had already reached Bourbon's sister island, the Isle of France. Well after the fact, Fusée-Aublet claimed that he had succeeded in making it flower and fructify in the Réduit Garden near Moka in the 1750s. By 1786, Jean-Nicolas de Céré on the Isle of France and his Bourbon colleague Joseph Hubert exchanged notes. Céré remarked in frustration that his vanilla was not bearing fruit. So, either Fusée-Aublet embellished his accomplishment, or it proved ephemeral. See MNHN, MS 454 (3), Fusée-Aublet, "Observations sur la nature de la vanille," 2; and Emile Trouette, ed., *Papiers de Joseph Hubert* (Saint-Denis: G and GL, 1881), 32.

7. MNHN, MS 1980, Mezières Lépervanche to Thouin, November 28, 1815, and August 1, 1816. Mauritius would play a pivotal role as a launchpad for other economic crops, including oil palm. See Jonathan E. Robins, *Oil Palm: A Global History* (Chapel Hill: University of North Carolina Press, 2021), 152.

8. Denis Lamaison, "De la vanille et des hommes: L'expédition du botaniste-voyageur Perrotet, 1819–1821," *Une saison en Guyane*, January 9, 2013, 96–101.

9. On April 2, 1819, Saint-Cyr wrote to Geoffroy Saint-Hilaire, a leading proponent of environmentally driven evolution. The governor bemoaned that local planters in Guiana had neglected vanilla. He asked the naturalist to send him whatever information he could on how better to prepare the pods, because the method currently used in Cayenne "fails adequately to set the fruit's aroma." ANOM, GUY 62, Saint-Cyr to Saint-Hilaire, April 2, 1819.

10. SHDM, BBP⁴ 409 (microfilm DE 2015 SA 57), Philibert to the Governor of Bourbon, July 3, 1819, 140; ANOM, GUY 54, Saint-Cyr report dated February 26, 1819.

11. ANOM, GUY 54, Saint-Cyr to Saint-Hilaire, February 26, 1819., Ministry of the Navy and Colonies to the Conseil des Ministres, August 14, 1820

12. ADR, 7M 27, Philibert to Milius, June 26, 1819.

13. ANOM, GUY 54, Philibert in Bourbon to the Minister of the Navy and Colonies, September 20, 1820.

14. ADR, 7M27, Philibert to Milius, July 3, 1819.

15. Perrottet, "Introduction de la vanille à la Réunion," *Annales de l'agriculture des colonies et des regions tropicales*, 1860, 374–75.

16. ANOM, GUY 54, Philibert in Manila, February 17, 1820, and Philibert in Manila, March 8, 1820; Eugène Volsy-Focard, "Introduction et fécondation du vanillier à l'Ile Bourbon," *Société des sciences et des arts de la Réunion*, 1862, 226.

17. Pesach Lubinsky, "Historical and Evolutionary Origins of Cultivated Vanilla" (PhD diss., University of California, Riverside, 2007), 113.

18. Arthur Delteil, *Etude sur la vanille* (Paris: Challamel aîné, 1874), 10.

19. ANOM, GUY 62, Governor Saint-Cyr to Paris, August 20, 1820; Lawrence Jennings, "Dreams vs. Reality: Plans to Colonize French Guiana, 1817–1822," in Serge Mam Lam Fouk, Juan Gonzalez Mendoza, Jacques Adélaïde-Merlande, Jacqueline Zonzon, and Rodolphe

Alexandre, eds., *Regards sur l'histoire de la Caraïbe, des Guyanes aux Grandes Antilles* (Cayenne: Ibis Rouge, 2001), 91–92.

20. ADR, 4J71, Hubert papers.

21. "Végétaux dont s'est enrichie récemment la colonie de l'île de Bourbon," *Annales de l'Agriculture française*, September–October 1823, 387; Corine Babeix, "La collecte des végétaux" in *Le voyage des plantes: Le jardin botanique de la marine* (La Seyne-sur-Mer: Musée Balaguier, 2008), 35.

22. Trouette, *Papiers de Joseph Hubert*, 32–33. On the Jardin du Roi, see Emma Spary, *Utopia's Garden: French Natural History from Old Régime to Revolution* (Chicago: University of Chicago Press, 2000), 67–78.

23. Frédéric Régent, Gilda Gonfier, and Bruno Maillard, *Libres et sans fers: Paroles d'esclaves français* (Paris: Fayard, 2015), 8–14; Prosper Eve, *Le Bruit du Silence: Paroles des esclaves de Bourbon* (Saint-André: Océans éditions, 2010), 30–35, 66.

24. Max Guérout and Thomas Romon, *Tromelin l'île aux esclaves oubliés* (Paris: CNRS Editions, 2010), 53, 67, 81, 91, 107–8.

25. On Bourbon, the enslaved came from many different parts of Africa and Madagascar. See Richard B. Allen, "The Constant Demand of the French: The Mascarene Slave Trade and the Worlds of the Indian Ocean and Atlantic During the Eighteenth and Nineteenth Centuries," *Journal of African History* 49 (2008): 43–72; Pier Larson, "La diaspora malgache aux Mascareignes: Notes sur la démographie et la langue," *Revue historique de l'océan Indien* 1 (2005): 143–55; Jean-François Géraud, Albert Jauze, and Eric Turpin, "Un schéma d'intelligibilité du monde servile à Bourbon: Les variations du prix des esclaves, 1789–1848," *Outre-mers* 98 (2010): 333, 351, 368–69, 376; Prosper Eve, "Les esclaves de Bourbon à l'œuvre," *Revue d'histoire des Mascareignes* 2 (2000): 47; Jean-François Géraud, "Esclaves et machines à Bourbon," in *Île de la Réunion: Regards croisés sur l'esclavage, 1794–1848* (Paris: Somogy, 1998), 119–27; Sudel Fuma, *L'esclavagisme à la Réunion, 1794–1848* (Paris: L'Harmattan, 1992), 36, 106–8; and Prosper Eve, *Un quartier du "bon pays": Sainte-Suzanne de 1649 à nos jours* (Saint-André: Océan éditions, 1996), 33, 71.

26. Géraud, Jauze, and Turpin, "Un schéma d'intelligibilité," 369; Fuma, *L'esclavagisme à la Réunion*, 76.

27. Fuma, *L'esclavagisme à la Réunion*, 68; Audrey Carotenuto, *Esclaves et résistances à l'île Bourbon (1750–1848)* (Paris: Les Indes savantes, 2021), 83, 349–79, 389–96. On the Middle Passage, see Terri L. Snyder, *The Power to Die: Slavery and Suicide in British North America* (Chicago: University of Chicago Press, 2015), 17, 29, 34.

28. Sue Peabody, *Madeleine's Children: Family, Freedom, Secrets and Lies in France's Indian Ocean Colonies* (Oxford: Oxford University Press, 2017), 67–69.

29. Bruno Maillard, "L'impossible bagne: Les 'envoyés' de l'île Bourbon à Sainte-Marie de Madagascar," *Annales historiques de la Révolution française* 375 (2014): 115–38.

30. Benoît Julien, "Quelques aspects de l'île Bourbon dans la première moitié du XIXe siècle," in *Île de la Réunion*, 25.

31. Julien, "Quelques aspects," 23; Géraud, Jauze, and Turpin, "Un schema d'intelligibilité," 351; Fuma, *L'esclavagisme à la Réunion*, 28.

32. Prosper Eve, *Naître et mourir à l'île Bourbon à l'époque de l'esclavage* (Paris: L'Harmattan, 1999), 149-51, 158; Prosper Eve, *Histoire d'une renommée: L'aveneture du caféier à Bourbon / La Réunion des années 1710 à nos jours* (Saint-Denis: CRESOI, 2006), 125, 156; Peabody, *Madeleine's Children*, 90-91, 110; Albert Jauze, "Coups de vent, avalasses, café, girofle et habitants de l'île Bonaparte au début du XIXe siècle," *Outre-mers, revue d'histoire* 382-83 (2014): 261-75.

33. See Lawrence Jennings, *French Anti-Slavery: The Movement for the Abolition of Slavery in France, 1802-1848* (Cambridge: Cambridge University Press, 2000), p. 25, for the metropole's new sugar demand, and p. 27 for lending rates.

34. Peabody, *Madeleine's Children*, 90-91, 110; Jauze, "Coups de vent"; Eve, *Histoire d'une renommée*, 239-40; Julien, "Quelques aspects," 26; Jean-François Géraud, "Esclaves et machines à Bourbon," in *Île de la Réunion*, 121. On the perils of monoculture in a French Caribbean context, see Elizabeth Heath, *Wine, Sugar and the Making of Modern France* (Cambridge: Cambridge University Press, 2014), 19-30, 83-91.

35. *L'Indicateur colonial: Feuille politique, littéraire, et d'annonces de l'Ile Bourbon*, October 30, 1841, 3.

36. William Gervase Clarence-Smith, *Cocoa and Chocolate, 1765-1914* (London: Routledge, 2000), 16, 117.

37. Eugène Volsy-Focard, *Dix-huit mois de République à l'Ile Bourbon, 1848-1849* (Saint-Denis: Gabriel Lahuppe, 1863), 247-48. On Peruvian guano reaching Réunion, see Gregory Cushman, *Guano and the Opening of the Pacific World* (Cambridge: Cambridge University Press, 2013), 47.

38. Pernille Røge, *Economistes and the Reinvention of Empire: France in the Americas and Africa, 1750-1802* (Cambridge: Cambridge University Press, 2019), 248.

39. On the history of that term, see Marie Hardy-Seguette, *Couleurs café: Le monde du café à la Martinique du début du XVIIIe siècle aux années 1860* (Rennes: Presses universitaires de Rennes, 2022), 272n39.

40. Eve, *Histoire d'une renommée*, 180, 243.

41. Fuma, *L'esclavagisme à la Réunion*, 39; Paul Cheney, *Cul-de-Sac: Patrimony, Capitalism, and Slavery in French Saint-Domingue* (Chicago University of Chicago Press, 2017), 77.

42. Eve, "Les esclaves de Bourbon à l'œuvre," 47, 58; Eve, *Le Bruit du Silence*, 48; Régent, Gonfier, and Maillard, *Libres et sans fers*, 64-65; Carotenuto, *Esclaves et résistances*, 83.

43. Pier Larson, *Ocean of Letters: Language and Creolization in an Indian Ocean Diaspora* (Cambridge: Cambridge University Press, 2009), 117-18.

44. Peabody, *Madeleine's Children*, 141-43; Christiane Connan-Pintado and Sylvie Lalagüe-Dulae, "A la recherche d'Edmond Albius, esclave réunionnais, 'fantôme' de l'histoire," *Modernités* 45 (2020): 88. Another source confirms Edmond's nonliteracy: Volsy-Focard, "Introduction et fécondation du vanillier à l'Ile Bourbon," 233.

45. Régent, Gonfier, and Maillard, *Libres et sans fers*, 27-28.

46. ADR, 6M 452, recensement Bellier. Edmond does not appear on the 1841 survey, which lists only three enslaved people. See ADR, 6M443.

47. ADR, 7M 27, Mézières Lépervanche to the Governor, December 8, 1853, reproduced in *Recueil de documents et travaux inédits pour servir à l'histoire des îles françaises de l'océan Indien*

et Bulletin d'information de la direction départementale des services d'archives de la Réunion (hereafter *RDT*) 10 (May 1981): 467.

48. ADR, 7M 27 Ferréol Bellier-Beaumont to Mr. Ganne, February 17, 1861, reproduced in *RDT* 10 (May 1981): 471; ADR, 7M 27 Ferréol Bellier-Beaumont to Volsy-Focard, December 9, 1862, reproduced in *RDT* 10 (May 1981): 475. Also see Edward Alpers, "Agency and Acquired Plant Knowledge among Enslaved Laborers: The Acclimatization of Vanilla and Cloves in the Indian Ocean World," *Monsoon, Journal of the Indian Ocean Rim*, 2:2 (November 2024): 92.

49. ADR, 7M 27, Ferréol Bellier-Beaumont to Mr. Ganne, February 17, 1861, reproduced in *RDT* 10 (May 1981): 471.

50. ADR, 7M 27, notice by Ferréol Bellier-Beaumont, reproduced in *RDT* 10 (May 1981): 472.

51. Eve, *Un quartier du "bon pays,"* 74–75; Jim Damour, dir., *Edmond Albius, l'esclave prodige* (Arte documentary, 1998); Megan Vaughan, *Creating the Creole Island: Slavery in Eighteenth-Century Mauritius* (Durham, NC: Duke University Press, 2005), 255.

52. ADR, 7M 27, Ferréol Bellier-Beaumont to Volsy-Focard, December 12, 1862, reproduced in *RDT* 10 (May 1981): 479.

53. This mode of locomotion was widespread on Bourbon, including for trips to the island's two spas. See Eve, "Les esclaves de Bourbon à l'œuvre," 49; and Eric Jennings, *Curing the Colonizers* (Durham, NC: Duke University Press, 2006), 110–13.

54. ADR, 7M 27, Mézières Lépervanche to the Governor, December 8, 1853, reproduced in *RDT* 10 (May 1981): 468.

55. Prosper Eve, *Les esclaves de Bourbon: La mer et la montagne* (Paris: Karthala, 2003), 325–28.

56. Judith Carney and Richard Rosomoff, *In the Shadow of Slavery: Africa's Botanical Legacy in the Atlantic World* (Berkeley: University of California Press, 2009), 89–90, 124–35; Londa Schiebinger, *Secret Cures of Slaves: People, Plants and Medicine in the Eighteenth-Century Atlantic World* (Stanford, CA: Stanford University Press, 2017), 46–48, 155; Londa Schiebinger, *Plants and Empire: Colonial Bioprospecting in the Atlantic World* (Cambridge, MA: Harvard University Press, 2004), 80–81.

57. Natalie Zemon Davis, "Physicians, Healers and their Remedies in Colonial Suriname," *Canadian Bulletin of the History of Medicine* 33, no. 1 (2016): 15–16; Londa Schiebinger, *Plants and Empire*, 211–14.

58. Dorit Brixius, "A Hard Nut to Crack: Nutmeg Cultivation and the Application of Natural History Between the Maluku Islands and Isle de France," *British Society for the History of Science* 51, no. 4 (2018): 590–95.

59. Eve, *Les esclaves de Bourbon*, 59.

60. Fuma, *L'esclavagisme à la Réunion*, 47.

61. "Affranchissements," *L'Indicateur colonial: Feuille politique, littéraire, et d'annonces de l'Ile Bourbon*, January 30, 1841, 1; Gaëlle Bélem, *Le fruit le plus rare ou la vie d'Edmond Albius* (Paris: Gallimard, 2024), 154.

62. ADR, E Dépôt 3/163, reproduced in *Les noms de la liberté, 1664–1848: De l'esclave au Citoyen, dossier pédagogique pour les enseignants*, 44.

63. ADR, 7M 27, Ferréol Bellier-Beaumont to Eugène Volsy-Focard, April 23, 1862, reproduced in *RDT* 10 (May 1981): 473.

64. This is also the interpretation of a recent graphic novel about Edmond, although I differ with the authors about the notion that the surname Albius was attributed solely based on alphabetical order. See Appolo and Telem, *Vingt décembre, chroniques de l'abolition* (Paris: Dargaud, 2023), 75.

65. Michaël Ferrier, *Sympathie pour le fantôme* (Paris: Gallimard, 2010), 248-49; Emmanuel Gordien, "Les patronymes attribués aux anciens esclaves des colonies françaises," *In Situ, Revue des patrimoines* 20 (2013): 1-8; Philippe Chanson, "Du nom à la scription, la trace indélibile du nom," *Sens-Dessous* 10 (2012): 4-14; Geneviève Payet, "Nom et filiation à la Réunion: De l'histoire à la clinique," *Cliniques méditerranéennes* 63 (2001): 179-92. On Toussaint Affranchi, see ADR, Pierrette and Bernard Nourigat, *Affranchissement d'esclaves*, Sainte-Suzanne registry, 69.

66. Imtiaz Habib, *Black Lives in the English Archives, 1500-1677* (New York: Routledge, 2016), 39 (quote), n. 62.

67. Marcel Proust, *The Guermantes Way*, trans. C. K. Scott-Moncrieff (New York: Random House, 1934), 285. I have used most of this translation but have changed the adjective *odd* to *funny* to reflect the original French *comique*. I have also removed "vanilla tree," which I consider to be a poor rendition of *vanillier*. For the original, see Marcel Proust, *Le côté de Guermantes* (1920-21; repr., Paris: Gallimard, 1954), 516.

68. Unusually for the punctilious Proust, Edmond's surname is misspelled Albins, which is another rendering of the Latin word for white. The error did not begin with Proust. Rather, multiple publications had misspelled Edmond's surname as Albins. See, for example, Jean Rambosson, *Histoire et légendes des plantes utiles et curieuses* (Paris: Firmin Didot, 1869), 325; and Alistair Mackenzie Ferguson, *All About Vanilla* (Chicago: University of Chicago, 1905), 12.

69. *Travaux de la société d'histoire naturelle de l'île Maurice du 6 octobre 1842 au 24 août 1846*, October 6, 1842, 4.

70. Jean Gabriel Fouché and Laurent Jouve, "*Vanilla Planifolia*: History, Botany and Culture in Réunion Island," *Agronomie* 19, no. 8 (1999): 699.

71. "Nécessité d'une société agricole à la Réunion," *L'Union coloniale* (Saint-Paul), August 30, 1850, 1.

72. ACRBK, DC 53/50, Société d'histoire naturelle de l'île Maurice, procès-verbal de la séance du jeudi 22 septembre 1831. Genève's age is drawn from NADGM, KK 17, recensement, Rivière Noire.

73. A later source claimed that Guadeloupean doctor Louis-Daniel Beauperthuy had been behind Dupuy's breakthrough. (Beauperthuy gained fame in 1854 for discovering the mosquito vector of yellow fever.) However, Beauperthuy left for Venezuela in 1839 and could hardly have overseen vanilla experimentation in the French Caribbean at the same time. Beauperthuy's putative discovery is raised in "La production de la vanille," *Bulletin de l'Office colonial*, 1914, 211-14. Dupuy is discussed in Delteil, *Etude sur la vanille*, 9, 13. For Beauperthuy's biography, see Rosario Beauperthuy de Benedetti, "Répercussion en Argentine en 1871 de la découverte du vecteur de la fièvre jaune réalisée par Beauperthuy au Vénézuela," *Histoire des sciences médicales* 12, no. 3 (1878): 283-89. Proof of Martinican vanilla aboard the *Adèle* in the 1840s can be found in ADIV, 4F G 38. Dupuy's full name appears in the *Bulletin officiel de la Guadeloupe*, January 1, 1841, 110; and in the *Gazette des Tribunaux*, March 5, 1848, 2.

74. Michel Chabin, "Le jardin d'Etat et le Museum," *RDT* 8 (August 1980): 357, 369. On Richard and his garden regulations, also see Blais, *L'Empire de la nature*, 37, 132; as well as Marc Tomas, "Propager l'acclimatation à La Réunion: Un enseignement impossible?," *Tsingy* 25 (2022): 136.

75. ADR, 7M 27, Mézières Lépervanche to the Governor, December 8, 1853, reproduced in *RDT* 10 (May 1981): 468.

76. ADR, 7M 27, Ferréol Bellier-Beaumont to Eugène Volsy-Focard, December 9, 1862, reproduced in *RDT* 10 (May 1981): 475.

77. Volsy-Focard, *Dix-huit mois*, 248–49. This question of Paris not realizing what was happening on Réunion as late as 1848 brings me to yet another alternative theory. Adam Karremans moots the idea that Perrottet introduced Neuman's pollination technique to Réunion in 1839 and shared it with Bellier-Beaumont at the time. He bases this on a Perrottet letter dated 1860, published in Pondicherry. I see several issues with the theory. Why would Bellier-Beaumont emphatically recognize Edmond as the inventor of a method if Perrottet had told him about Neumann at the time? Moreover, why would Réunion's planter and botanical elite (minus Richard) side with Bellier-Beaumont's interpretation in 1862 if they had evidence to the contrary? It is also worth noting that while claiming to have introduced Neumann's technique, Perrottet himself acknowledged Edmond's contribution to "putting" pollination "into practice." The question hinges in part on local versus metropolitan knowledge and in part on the issue of "invention" itself. See Adam P. Karremans, "A Historical Review of the Artificial Pollination of *Vanilla planifolia*: The Importance of Collaborative Research in a Changing World," Plants 13, no. 22 (2024): 3203, https://doi.org/10.3390/plants13223203; and Perrottet, "Introduction de la vanille à la Réunion," 378.

78. Volsy-Focard, *Dix-huit mois*, 249–53.

79. "Vanille," in M. F. E. Guérin, *Dictionnaire pittoresque d'histoire naturelle et des phénomènes de la nature* (Paris: Au bureau de souscription, 1839), 9:526.

80. ADR, 7M 27, Ferréol Bellier-Beaumont to Eugène Volsy-Focard, December 12, 1862, reproduced in *RDT* 10 (May 1981): 477. On the indirect nature of Bellier-Beaumont's accusations, see Blais, *L'Empire de la nature*, 203.

81. ADR, 7M 27, Ferréol Bellier-Beaumont to Eugène Volsy-Focard, December 12, 1862, reproduced in *RDT* 10 (May 1981): 477.

82. David de Floris, "Notice sur la culture du vanillier," *Annales de l'Agriculture des Colonies et des régions tropicales* 1 (January 1860): 20–27. The article was then turned into a pamphlet (Bibliothèque nationale de France, Paris [SP-10937]).

83. The textbook was Paul Hermann's *La Réunion au Cours élémentaire* (La Chapelle-Monligeon: Imprimerie de Montligeon, 1924), 51.

84. ADR, 7M 27, Ferréol Bellier-Beaumont to Eugène Volsy-Focard, September 21, 1863, reproduced in *RDT* 10 (May 1981): 482.

85. Georges Limbour, *Les Vanillliers* (Paris: Gallimard, 1938), 14, 32, 40, 44, 47, 64–67, 112–14, 118, 163.

86. The rumor is described in Joseph Beaujean, "Petite histoire de l'introduction de la fructification du vanillier au jardin botanique de l'Université de Liège et à l'île de la

Réunion," *Natura Mosana* 54, no. 4 (October–December 2002): 78; Tim Ecott heard this same rumor about Albius in Tahiti. See Ecott, *Vanilla: Travels in Search of the Ice Cream Orchid* (New York: Grove Press, 2005), 131.

87. Sophie Chérer, *La vraie couleur de la vanille* (Paris: L'Ecole des loisirs, 2012).

88. ADR, 2U 110; the story was recounted at an exhibit at the Réunion archives in 2022.

89. Ecott, *Vanilla*, 101.

90. Information shared by then-Director of the Departmental Archives of Reunion Island Damien Vaïsse in a 2022 email.

91. "La Réunion à notre foire," *Le Madécasse*, October 25, 1923, 1.

92. "Edmond Albius," *Le Cri du peuple* (Saint-Denis), July 20, 1945: 1.

93. Miguel Cally, dir., *Kunta Kinté: Le maire, Lucet Langenier* (Kapali Studios and France Télévision documentary, 2020). See also the photo available on Wikimedia Commons at https://commons.wikimedia.org/wiki/File:EdmondAlbius_Stele.JPG.

94. ADR, 48J866; "D'Edmond Albius à l'Alliance des Réunionnais," *Témoignages*, March 3, 2010.

FOUR. RÉUNION, QUEEN OF VANILLA

1. Eugène Volsy-Focard, *Dix-huit mois de République à l'Ile Bourbon, 1848–1849* (Saint-Denis: Gabriel Lahuppe, 1863), 249.

2. ADLA, 1ET F110, Ministry of the Navy and the Colonies, August 9, 1848.

3. ADR, 7M 27, Evaluation de la récolte de vanille du Mexique, 1852.

4. ADR, 7M 27, letter from Madame Devillaine, June 19, 1849.

5. ADR, 7M 27, liste des principaux cultivateurs, récolte de 1852.

6. Raoul Lucas, *La Réunion île de vanille* (Saint-André: Océan Editions, 1990), 75; Direction générale des douanes, *Tableau général du commerce de la France avec ses colonies* (Paris, 1855), 12, 62–63, 188.

7. "Ile de la Réunion: Exposition dans la colonie des produits de l'agriculture et de l'industrie locales," *Revue coloniale*, April 1857, 305; Lucas, *La Réunion île de vanille*, 75.

8. ADR, 6M 1332, provides a total of 27,701 kilos exported from Réunion in 1862. For the comparison with other products, see Sudel Fuma, *Une colonie île à sucre: L'économie de la Réunion au XIXe siècle* (Saint-André: Océan Editions, 1989), 300.

9. Kourí, *Pueblo Divided*, 294, 298.

10. "La production de la vanille," *Bulletin de l'Office colonial*, 1914, 232.

11. Steven Topik and William Gervase Clarence-Smith, "Introduction," in Clarence-Smith and Topik, eds., *The Global Coffee Economy in Africa, Asia and Latin America, 1500–1989* (Cambridge: Cambridge University Press, 2003), 4.

12. Elian Peltier, "Ivory Coast Supplies the World with Cacao: Now It Wants Some for Itself," *New York Times*, August 13, 2022.

13. Sidney Mintz, *Sweetness and Power: The Place of Sugar in Modern History* (Harmondsworth: Penguin Books, 1985), 48, 64.

14. Charles Buet, *Madagascar, la Reine des Iles africaines* (Brussels: J. Albanel, 1883), 332.

15. ADR, M65, report for Saint Paul, February 1878.

16. Yves Pérotin, André Scherer, Urbain Lartin, and Suzy Bachaud, *Notes historiques sur des sujets divers* (Saint-Denis: Archives départementales de La Réunion, 1957), 53n27.

17. Arthur Delteil, *Etude sur la vanille* (Paris: Challamel aîné, 1874), 13–14.

18. KSLA, Chauvet papers, MS E59, 4:56–57.

19. KSLA, Chauvet papers, MS E59, 4:57.

20. ANOM, REU SG 422, vols de vanille.

21. ADR, 7M 27, Expédition délivrée à M. Gustave Lecomte, May 1879.

22. "The Vanilla of the Island of Bourbon," *Merchants' Magazine* 23, no. 2 (August 1850): 249.

23. Honoré de Balzac, *Les deux frères* (Paris: H. Souverain, 1842), 78; "Revue scientifique," *La Gazette de France*, July 31, 1867, 1.

24. Erika Rappaport, *A Thirst for Empire: How Tea Shaped the Modern World* (Princeton, NJ: Princeton University Press, 2017), 166–77.

25. "Extract of True Mexican Vanilla," *Boston Evening Transcript*, December 31, 1858, 2.

26. KSLA, Chauvet papers, MS E59, 3:24, entry for February 1869.

27. Ai Hisano, *Visualizing Taste: How Business Changed the Look of What You Eat* (Cambridge, MA: Harvard University Press, 2019), 78; *About Vanilla* (Boston: Joseph Burnett Company, 1900), 16.

28. Ad for Dreier's, *News-Sentinel* (Fort Wayne, IN), July 22, 1921, 13.

29. "La vanille à la Réunion: Entre agriculture et patrimoine," *Agreste* 77 (April 2012): 1; Lucas, *La Réunion île de vanille*, 75, 79; Kourí, *Pueblo Divided*, 298; Prosper Eve, *Histoire d'une renommée: L'aventure du caféier à Bourbon / La Réunion des années 1710 à nos jours* (Saint-Denis: CRESOI, 2006), 327; Tim Ecott, *Vanilla: Travels in Search of the Ice Cream Orchid* (New York: Grove Press, 2005), 135.

30. Claude Bavoux, "Les Réunionnais de Madagascar de 1880 à 1925" (PhD diss., University of Paris VII, 1997), 7.

31. ANOM, MIS 67, Paul Dussert mission to Réunion and the Comoros. Dussert had previously owned and operated a vanilla farm in Mexico and now served as a consultant on Indian Ocean vanilla for the French Ministry of the Colonies. Another source made the same point about Réunion *vanillons* some years later; see "La production de la vanille," 232.

32. ANF, F12/7213, monthly export figures from Réunion, 1885–92.

33. David McCreery, "Indigo Commodity Chains in the Spanish and British Empires," in Steven Topik, Carlos Marichal, and Zephyr Frank, eds., *Commodity Chains in Theory and in Latin American History* (Durham, NC: Duke University Press, 2006), 63.

34. "Docu: Trois générations photographient La Réunion de 1891 à 2004," *Franceinfo*, September 24, 2021, https://la1ere.francetvinfo.fr/docu-trois-generations-photographient-la-reunion-de-1891-a-2004-1111000.html. A 1934 British book about raffia suggested that the very finest came from Madagascar; see Annie Begg, *Raffia* (London: Pitman, 1934), 1.

35. Nancy Green, *Ready-to-Wear and Ready-to-Work: A Century of Industry and Immigration in Paris and New York* (Durham, NC: Duke University Press, 1997), 37; Judith Coffin, *The Politics of Women's Work: The Paris Garment Trades, 1750–1915* (Princeton, NJ: Princeton University Press, 1996), 3, 9, 14; Clare Haru Crowston, *Fabricating Women: The Seamstress of Old Régime France, 1675–1791* (Durham, NC: Duke University Press, 2001), 400.

36. ANF, F12/7213, monthly exports from Réunion, 1885–92.

37. Chambre de Commerce de Marseille, *Situation commerciale*, 1899–1900, 226–27.

38. "Chronique maritime," *Le Matin derniers télégrammes de la nuit* (Paris), March 6, 1889, 4.

39. Bavoux, "Les Réunionnais," 565n1. For an example of the clamoring, see ADGIR, 8M 14, "Transports à l'Ile Bourbon."

40. ADE, 48J 241.

41. ADR, 6M1367, "Vaille que vaille sur la vanille."

42. ANOM, 100 APOM 400.

43. Gabriel Sinke, "A Tribute to the Oldest American Flavor and Fragrance House," *Perfumer and Flavorist* 17 (January–February 1992): 37–39.

44. "La vanille," *Le Journal de l'Île de la Réunion*, May 15, 1906, 1.

45. "Comice agricole," *Moniteur de l'Ile Bourbon*, December 6, 1841, 1.

46. ADR, 2Q 46, "Note: Intervention du Domaine."

47. ADR, 2Q 46, letter to M. de Tourris, December 3, 1874. For the evidence on Ranguin Livambarom's ownership commencing in 1871, see ADR, 2Q 46, "Note: Intervention du Domaine."

48. ADR, 2Q 46, "Note: Intervention du Domaine."

49. ADR, 2Q 46, report to the Director of the Interior, December 8, 1876, and Bureau des Domaines to the Director, February 16, 1876.

50. ADR, 2Q 46, report to the Director of the Interior, December 8, 1876

51. ADR, 2Q 46, letter to M. de Tourris, December 3, 1874.

52. ADR, 2Q 46, table of the letter from the Bureau des Domaines to the Director, February 16, 1876.

53. ADR, 2Q 46, Bureau des Domaines to the Director, February 16, 1876.

54. ADR, 2Q 46, recap letter of August 17, 1882. Thanks to Owen White for the fungal comparisons he drew in his April 14, 2023, paper presented at the University of Toronto, "A Different Kind of Colonist: Phylloxera in Algeria." On the contrary phenomenon of mold as a colonial instrument, see Gerard Sasges, "Mold's Dominion: Science, Empire and Capitalism in a Globalizing World," *American Historical Review*, March 2021, 82–108.

55. Pierre-Eric Fageol, "Les normes d'enseignement et leur adaptation en situation coloniale et post-coloniale à La Réunion, 1870–1970," unpublished *habilitation à diriger des recherches*, University of Paris I, 2024, 209.

56. ADR, 4M64, Saint-Joseph report for July 1877.

57. ANOM, 100 APOM 400.

58. ANM, D 98.

59. "Les préparateurs de vanille à Madagascar," *La Patrie créole*, July 18, 1901, 1.

60. ADR, 6M1367, "Vaille que vaille sur la vanille."

61. ANOM, 174 APOM 1.

62. ADR, 6M1367, document signed Léonce Panon, February 13, 1941.

63. ANF, 72AJ/434, Rapport sur le marché de la vanille aux Etats-Unis, February 15, 1945.

64. ADR, 6M1367, Governor Aubert to the heads of the Chambers of Commerce and Agriculture, January 31, 1941.

65. ADR, 6M1367, Admiral Platon to Réunion, November 20, 1940.

66. ADR, 6M1367, Joseph Volsan to the president of the Chamber of Commerce, February 11, 1941.

67. ADR, 6M1367, Raphaël Sangany to the president of the Chamber of Commerce, February 18, 1941.

68. ADR, 6M1367, E. Sauger to the president of the Chamber of Commerce, March 17, 1941, and to Alexis De Villeneuve, February 7, 1941.

69. ADR, 6M1367, Laboratoire d'analyses report, Saint-Denis, February 14, 1941.

70. ADR, 6M1367, Boyer to the president of Réunion's Chamber of Agriculture, May 27, 1946.

71. ADR, 6M1369, September 10, 1941, note for the secretary general.

72. ADR, 6M1369, May 29, 1944, vanilla planters' petition and agriculture report, June 12, 1943.

73. ANF, 20120067, programme sectoriel, vanille; ADR, 318 W28, note sur la vanille October 4, 1966.

74. Khalid Khan, Chi-Wei Su, Adnan Khurshid, and Muhammad Umar, "Are There Bubbles in the Vanilla Price?," *Agricultural and Food Economics* 10 (2022): http://www.doi.org/10.1186/s40100-022-00213-y.

75. ANF, 20120067, filière vanille.

76. Bertrand Côme, discussion with author, Grand Hazier, May 7, 2022.

77. "La vanille à La Réunion, entre agriculture et patrimoine," *Agreste* 77 (April 2012): 1–7.

78. ANF, 20120067, programme sectoriel, vanille.

79. "Vanille Bleue, la vanille qui se mange entièrement," Escale Bleue, accessed November 4, 2024, http://escale-bleue.fr/quest-ce-que-la-vanille-bleue; Philippe Stéphant, "Nicole Leichnig fait briller La Réunion avec sa Vanille Bleue," *L'Eco austral*, no. 312 (September 2016): https://escale-bleue.fr/wp-content/uploads/2016/10/eco_austral_312_final_regionale_lr-short-version.pdf.

80. ANOM, 196 APOM 102, Univanille, June 1968.

FIVE. MADAGASCAR'S MR. VANILLA

1. Louis Lacaille, *Importance et nécessité de coloniser l'île de Madagascar* (Paris: Au dépôt, rue du Four Saint-Germain, 1848), 28.

2. On views of Madagascar as an Eden, see Eric Jennings, *Perspectives on French Colonial Madagascar* (New York: Palgrave, 2017), 16–17.

3. Solofo Randrianja and Stephen Ellis, *Madagascar: A Short History* (Chicago: University of Chicago Press, 2009), 123–35 (quote on 127). On the London Missionary Society and the Merina monarchy's shared centralizing ethos, see Françoise Raison-Jourde, "Mission LMS et Mission jésuite face aux communautés villageoises Merina," *Africa: Journal of the International African Institute* 53, no. 2 (1983): 70.

4. Faranirina V. Rajaonah and Phares Mukasa Mutibwa, "Madagascar, 1800–1880," in J.F. Ade Ajayi, ed., *Histoire générale de l'Afrique* (Paris, UNESCO, 1997), 6:233. Regarding Malagasy youngsters who traveled to the UK and Mauritius, see Gwyn Campbell, *The Madagascar Youths: British Alliances and Military Expansion in the Indian Ocean Region* (Cambridge: Cambridge University Press, 2022). On the census, see Stephen Ellis, *The Rising*

of the Red Shawls: A Revolt in Madagascar, 1895-1899 (Cambridge: Cambridge University Press, 1985), 13.

5. Gwyn Campbell, An Economic History of Imperial Madagascar, 1750-1895 (Cambridge: Cambridge University Press, 2005), 181-97.

6. Randrianja and Ellis, Madagascar, 123-39; Solofo Randrianja, Société et luttes anticoloniales à Madagascar, 1896-1946 (Paris: Karthala, 2001), 113-18; Gwyn Campbell, "Gold Mining and the French Takeover of Madagascar, 1883-1914," African Economic History 17 (1988): 103-4.

7. Randrianja and Ellis, Madagascar, 105-6; Ellis, Rising of the Red Shawls, 26; David Graeber, Pirate Enlightenment or the Real Libertalia (London: Penguin Books, 2023); Monique Djisitera, "La représentation du colon réunionnais à travers des récits receuillis dans la région de Vatomandry," Revue historique de l'océan Indien 1 (2005): 235-36. Concerning the 1947 revolt, see Jennifer Cole, Forget Colonialism? Sacrifice and the Art of Memory in Madagascar (Berkeley: University of California Press, 2001).

8. Jeffrey Kaufman, "Recoloring the Red Island," Ethnohistory 48, no. 1-2 (Winter-Spring 2001): 3-4.

9. SHDM, BB4 435, 1822, 11:2, L'Espérance.

10. "La production de la vanille," Bulletin de l'Office colonial, 1914, 227-28.

11. MNHN, Bibliothèque de Botanique, Per K G 26 (call number), Voyage de Louis-Hyacinthe Boivin, 29.

12. ANOM, 54APC1, Commandant Alphonse Seignac-Lesseps's records.

13. ANOM, GGM 2D 178, report to Governor Joseph Gallieni.

14. "Juillet," Madagascar, notes, reconnaissances, explorations 3 (1898): 955.

15. Revue de Madagascar, July-December 1901, 813.

16. Samuel Sanchez, "Le long XIXe siècle de Nosy Be et de la baie d'Ampasindava: Dynamiques malgaches et mondialisations dans un comptoir du sud-ouest de l'océan Indien" (PhD diss., Université de Paris VII, 2013), 571-74, 626-28.

17. ANOM, SG Madagascar 290.

18. Renseignements Commerciaux, Bibliothèque de la Chambre de Commerce de Paris, March 11, 1894, 6; Journal officiel de Madagascar et dépendances, December 2, 1899, 3824-25.

19. Manassé Esoavelomandroso, La province maritime orientale du Royaume de Madagascar à la fin du XIXe siècle (Antananarivo: FTM, 1979), 176-178; Journal officiel de Madagascar, no. 156 (October 17, 1901): 512. Not only did French customs officials double as entrepreneurs, but they also began training Malagasy customs agents in 1886. See SHDL, 4C[8] 9 (call number), note dated May 26, 1886.

20. Jean Fremigacci, Etat, économie et société coloniale à Madagascar (Paris: Karthala, 2014), 445.

21. "From Madagascar, Tamatave May 26, 1876," Essex County Mercury and Weekly Salem (MA) Gazette, August 9, 1876, 2.

22. Louis Catat, Voyage à Madagascar, 1889-1890 (Paris: Hachette, 1895), 16.

23. ANOM, 4Z 111, exportations, 1881.

24. Samuel Sanchez, "L'Etat et les matières premières à Madagascar," Afrique contemporaine 251 (2014): 161; Rajaonah and Mutibwa, "Madagascar," 230, 236.

— 261 —

25. KSLA, Chauvet papers, MS E59, 4:72–73. Regarding Betsimisaraka women's motivations for marrying outsiders, see Dominique Bois, "Tamatave, la cité des femmes," *Clio: Femmes, Genre, Histoire* 6 (1997): 61–86 (note 12 for chief status). Concerning William W. Robinson, see Liliana Mosca, "The Merina Kingdom in the Late 1870s as Reported in the Despatches of Colonel William W. Robinson," *Omaly Sy Anio* 37–38 (1995): 109–40.

26. KSLA, Chauvet papers, MS E59, 4:75.

27. KSLA, Chauvet papers, MS E59, 4:75, 82, 83, 89, 93. For the local varietals, see Michel Grisoni, "Mission d'expertise en génétique des vanilliers dans la SAVA," CIRAD, November 30, 2009, https://agritrop.cirad.fr/554839/1/document_554839.pdf.

28. KSLA, Chauvet papers, MS E59, 4:75.

29. On predatory practices in the rubber and timber sectors in Madagascar, see Samuel Sanchez, "L'Etat et les matières premières," 163–64.

30. KSLA, Chauvet papers, MS E59, 4:82–83.

31. Samuel Sanchez, "La valeur du bain royal (fandroana): Echanges tributaries et souveraineté dans le Royaume de Madagascar du XIXe siècle," *Revue d'histoire du XIXe siècle* 52 (2019): 71–94.

32. KSLA, Chauvet papers, MS E59, 4:76, 78, 80, 81, 82 88 89, 92, 94.

33. KSLA, Chauvet papers, MS E59, 4:89.

34. KSLA, Chauvet papers, MS E59, 4:93–94.

35. Campbell, *Economic History*, 312. Not all Mauritian planters struck it rich. In July 1883, the governor of Mauritius agreed to send a steamer to Tamatave to repatriate "inhabitants of Mauritius [. . .] desirous of leaving Madagascar, who are unable to quit the country for want of funds or other reasons." SHDL, 4 C^5 62, letter to Admiral Pierre, July 4, 1883.

36. TNA, FO 403, 41, Further Correspondence Concerning the Affairs of Madagascar, January–June 1884, 156. After the war in 1885, the Malagasy crown was forced to pay an indemnity for "all damages related to the conflict, caused to individual foreigners." See Pierre-Eric Fageol and Frédéric Garan, *La Réunion-Madagascar: Une histoire connectée dans l'océan Indien* (Saint-Denis: Presses universitaires Indianocéaniques, 2022), 63. The Mauritian Talbot family were notables in late nineteenth-century Madagascar. They appear in 1885 port archives as well as 1884 police records. See SHDL, 4C8 20, and 48C 23. See also Bois, "Tamatave, la cité."

37. CHETOM, 18H 36, Fonds Cointet.

38. Gouvernement Général de Madagascar, *Guide de l'immigrant à Madagascar* (Paris: A. Colin, 1899), 82.

39. Jean Paulhan, *Lettres de Madagascar, 1907–1910* (Bassac: Claire Paulhan, 2007), 71.

40. ANM, L794, syndicat des planteurs de vanille.

41. ANM, L794, syndicat des planteurs de vanille; ANOM, OCEA 159, relevé des exportations (for consumption in 1913).

42. AGCSE, 2D180.1.1, letters dated January 22, 1906, October 31, 1906, and August 1, 1907.

43. Gilliam Feeley-Harnik, *A Green Estate: Restoring Independence in Madagascar* (Washington, DC: Smithsonian Institution Press, 1991), 271–72.

44. AGCSE, 2D180.1.1, letters dated May 2, 1907, and October 2, 1907.

45. AGCSE, 2D180.1.1, letters dated August 31, 1909, and October 22, 1910. On child labor on coffee plantations, see Steven Topik and William Gervase Clarence-Smith, "Conclusion," in William Gervase Clarence-Smith and Steven Topik, eds., *The Global Coffee Economy in Africa, Asia and Latin America, 1500–1989* (Cambridge: Cambridge University Press, 2003), 395.

46. AGCSE, 2D 62.2a4, response to Raimbault dated November 22, 1927.

47. Gwyn Campbell, "Slavery and Fanompoana: The Structure of Forced Labor in Imerina, 1790–1861," *Journal of African History* 29, no. 3 (1988): 463–85 (480–81 for the discussion of eastern coast plantations); Campbell, *Madagascar Youths*, 167–70.

48. ANM, D 361.

49. AGCSE, 2D180.1.1, letters dated August 20, 1910 (but date has been crossed out), October 21, 1911, and November 15, 1913.

50. AGCSE, 2D180.1.1, letters dated October 3, 1910, September 1, 1911, and October 22, 1915.

51. AGCSE, 2D180.1.1, letter dated July 9, 1920.

52. AGCSE, 2D180.2.1, letter to his brother Joseph, November 21, 1924.

53. AGCSE, 2D 62.2a4, Statistique des plantations.

54. AGCSE, 2D180.2.1–2, letter to his brother Joseph, November 10, 1930.

55. ANOM, GGM 2D 222, table 4, 1898.

56. Paul Joanne of Cinq Frères vanilla estate, personal communication with author, Antalaha, May 15, 2022.

57. ANOM, GGM 2D 154, 1909 report for Maroantsetra province district.

58. Randrianja, *Société et luttes*, 65; Raymond Decary, "La vanille de Madagascar," *Encyclopédie mensuelle d'outre-mer* 65 (January 1956): 32.

59. ANOM, GGM 2D 45, reports on the Antalaha region, 1928–30.

60. ANOM, GGM 2D 223, tables.

61. ANOM, GGM 2D 223, Moriceau report, 1899.

62. ANOM, GGM 2D 223, Moriceau report, 1899.

63. "Vanillard," *L'Echo de Tananarive*, October 11, 1924, 1.

64. Cole, *Forget Colonialism?*, 163.

65. ANOM, GGM 2D 178, December 31, 1906.

66. ANOM, GGM 3D 274.

67. ANOM, GGM 2D 154.

68. "L'agriculture à Maroantsetra," *Journal officiel de Madagascar et dépendances*, June 26, 1902, 1059–60. Dupavillon obtained French citizenship in 1940 when his status as a British subject from Mauritius became problematic, following the sinking of part of the French fleet at Mers-el-Kébir by Britain and the establishment of an anti-British regime at Vichy. For the date of his citizenship, see Philippe Nun, "La migration des Mauriciens à Madagascar, 1863–1947" (PhD diss., University of Réunion, 2007), 691. Regarding sartorial and power parallels with rubber, see Stephen Harp, *A World History of Rubber: Empire, Industry and the Everyday* (London: Wiley Blackwell, 2016), 21–28.

69. Gregory Mann, "What Was the Indigénat? The 'Empire of Law' in French West Africa," *Journal of African History* 50 (2009): 331–53; Isabelle Merle, "Retour sur le régime de l'Indigénat: Genèse et contradictions des principes répressifs dans l'empire français,"

French Politics, Culture and Society 20, no. 2 (2002): 77–97; Sylvie Thénault, "L'indigénat dans l'Empire français: Algérie/Cochinchine, une double matrice" *Monde(s)* 2, no. 12 (2017): 21–40. On the Indigénat in Madagascar specifically, see Jean Frémigacci, "Le code de l'indigénat à Madagascar," *Outre-mers, revue d'histoire* 378–79 (2013): 251–69.

70. "L'indégénat devient un instrument d'oppression et de tyrannie," *L'Opinion de Diego-Suarez*, August 25, 1928.

71. "Comment on fait fortune dans la culture à Madagascar," *Le Madécasse* (Antananarivo), November 19, 1923.

72. ANOM, GGM 6 (8) D 6; Mouhssini Hassani-el-Barwane, *La Société coloniale de Bambao Comores (1893-1975)* (Moroni: KomEDIT Editions, 2015), 29.

73. Jean-Pierre Domenichini, "Jean Ralaimongo et l'origine du mouvement national malgache," unpublished typewritten manuscript (ANOM BIB AOM 20381), 89, 113, 121–29; Jean-Pierre Domenichini, "Jean Ralaimongo (1884-1943) ou Madagascar au seuil du nationalisme," *Revue française d'histoire d'outre-mer* 56, no. 204 (1969): 255.

74. By 1939, Ralaimongo had retired to Sava to become a vanilla planter himself. *Ny Rariny, La Justice* (Antananarivo), June 1, 1939, 2.

75. ACFDT, 6P3 Madagascar, vanilla imports to the United States; "Le commerce extérieur de Madagascar en 1944," *La revue de Madagascar* 21 (January 1945): 28.

76. ANOM, GGM, 3B 184, Governor of Madagascar to the Ministry of the Colonies, December 15, 1945.

77. Abandoned archives of the Ambohitsara vanilla research station, 138 Iv/Ge, "Etude botanique du vanillier hybride Planifolia X Humblotii," document shared by Michel Grisoni.

78. Abandoned archives of the Ambohitsara vanilla research station, 138 Iv/Ge, Annual report for 1959, document shared by Michel Grisoni.

79. ANM, Présidence, 468–69, Activités économiques, 1969. For Paris's ongoing influence, see Randrianja and Ellis, *Madagascar*, 181–82.

80. André Saura, *Philibert Tsiranana, premier Président de la République de Madagascar* (Paris: L'Harmattan, 2006), 1:149, 191.

81. ANOM, 196 APOM 102.

82. CADN, 673PO/1, note to the French ambassador, July 20, 1972.

83. "Le nouvel accord commercial sovieto-malgache," *Gazety Ekonomika* (Antananarivo), November 1975, 52.

84. Pierre Lepidi, "Vanille de Madagascar: le goût amer de la spéculation," *Le Monde* (Paris), January 6, 2017, 2.

85. Annah Zhu, "Hot Money, Cold Beer: Navigating the Vanilla and Rosewood Export Economies in Northeastern Madagascar," *American Ethnologist* 45, no. 2 (2018): 253–67; Tim Ecott, *Vanilla: Travels in Search of the Ice Cream Orchid* (New York: Grove Press, 2005), 201; Andrew Walsh, *Made in Madagascar: Sapphires, Ecotourism and the Global Bazaar* (Toronto: University of Toronto Press, 2012); Lepidi, "Vanille de Madagascar," 2. On boom-and-bust cycles just south of the Sava region, see Genese Sodikoff, *Forest and Labor in Madagascar* (Bloomington: Indiana University Press, 2012), 120.

SIX. TAHITI'S BLACK GOLD

1. Eugène Hänni, *Tahiti, Rurutu, îles sous-le-vent, 1894–1896*, ed. Roland Kaehr (Papeete: Haere Pō, 2015), 319, 359; Roland Kaehr, "L'assassinat du 'Père Vanille,'" *Bulletin de la Société des études océaniennes* 334 (January–April 2015): 118; ad in *L'Impartial* (Chaux-de-Fonds, Switzerland), January 5, 1905, 1.

2. APPP, CB 43.40 N 326, main courante.

3. "Qui étrangla le père vanille?," *Le Matin* (Paris), March 3, 1908, 2; "L'assassinat du marchand de vanille," *La Liberté* (Paris), April 26, 1908, 2; "L'assassinat du père vanille: L'accusé bénéficie d'un acquittement," *Le Parisien*, January 1, 1909, 2.

4. Christel Brunschwig, François-Xavier Collard, Sandra Lepers-Andrzejewski, and Phila Raharivelomanana, "Tahitian Vanilla (Vanilla ×tahitensis): A Vanilla Species with Unique Features," in Hany A. El-Shemy, ed., *Active Ingredients from Aromatic and Medicinal Plants* (Rijeka: InTech, 2017), 29–47; "Achat Vanille," Epices Rœllinger, accessed November 21, 2022, https://www.epices-roellinger.com/fr/taxons/vanilles.

5. Kenneth M. Cameron, "Vanilla Phylogeny and Classification," in Daphna Havkin-Frenkel and Faith C. Belanger, eds., *Handbook of Vanilla Science and Technology* (London: Wiley Blackwell, 2019), 388.

6. Pesach Lubinsky, Gustavo A. Romero-González, Sylvia M. Heredia, and Stephanie Zabel, "Origins and Patterns of Vanilla Cultivation in Tropical America (1500–1900): No Support for an Independent Domestication of Vanilla in South America," in Havkin-Frenkel and Belanger, *Handbook of Vanilla Science and Technology*, 135.

7. Colin Newbury, *Tahiti Nui: Change and Survival in French Polynesia, 1767–1945* (Honolulu: University Press of Hawaii, 1980), 2–4 (quote on 2); Neil Gunson, "Pomare II of Tahiti and Polynesian Imperialism," *Journal of Pacific History* 4, no. 1 (January 1969): 65–82; Douglas L. Oliver, *Ancient Tahitian* Society (Honolulu: University of Hawaii Press, 1974), 3:1171–72.

8. Newbury, *Tahiti Nui*, 102–22 (quotes on 102 and 109); Bruno Saura, *Histoire et mémoire des temps coloniaux en Polynésie française* (Pirae, Au vent des Iles, 2015), 186; Claire Laux, *Le Pacifique au XVIIIe et XIXe siècles: Une confrontation franco-britannique* (Paris: Karthala, 2011), 72–77.

9. "Tahiti," *Le Courrier du Havre*, December 2, 1846; Newbury, *Tahiti Nui*, 164–65.

10. ANOM, OCEA 9, Lavaud report, October 14, 1847.

11. Tim Ecott, *Vanilla: Travels in Search of the Ice Cream Orchid* (New York: Grove Press, 2005), 168; Pierre-Yves Toullelan, *Tahiti colonial, 1860–1914* (Paris: Publications de la Sorbonne, 1984), 153. There is one outlier: Patricia Rain has Admiral Hamelin introducing vanilla in 1786. See Rain, *Vanilla: The Cultural History of the World's Most Popular Flavor and Fragrance* (New York: Jeremy Tarcher / Penguin, 2004), 168. She may have confused Hamelins. The uncle, Jacques Félix Emmanuel Hamelin, was a rear admiral who lived from 1768 to 1839. His nephew, Ferdinand, lived from 1796 to 1864.

12. ANOM, OCEA 56, document signed Lieutenant Petit, November 1, 1849.

13. ANOM, OCEA 56, "produits divers," 5.

14. ANOM, OCEA 56.

15. "Tahiti," *Le Courrier du Havre*, December 2, 1846. For the naval records, see SHDM, 1M 981.

16. Ecott, *Vanilla*, 168.

17. Alan Chambers et al., "Genotyping-by-Sequencing Diversity Analysis of International Vanilla Collections Uncovers Hidden Diversity and Enables Plant Improvement," *Plant Science* 311 (2021): 10. On the 1856 hybrid, see Joseph Arditti, "An History of Orchid Hybridization, Seed Germination and Tissue Culture," *Botanical Journal of the Linnean Society* 89 (1984): 367.

18. ANOM, OCEA 56, document signed Lieutenant Petit, November 1, 1849; part of the report was then printed in *La Revue coloniale* 6 (January–June 1851): 261.

19. ANOM, OCEA 56, document signed Pancher or Panche, November 18, 1850.

20. ANOM, OCEA 56, Navy, August 6, 1843.

21. ANOM, OCEA 56, letter from Lieutenant Petit to the Naval Ministry, June 30, 1845.

22. *Le Messager de Tahiti* (Papeete), December 18, 1859, 1-2.

23. AAT, H2-10, response of the Ministry of the Navy to Jaussen, December 1860.

24. AGSSCC, TAH 57-M, Bonnes mesures à prendre.

25. Eugène Pelletier and Auguste Pelletier in *Le thé et le chocolat dans l'alimentation publique* (Paris: Compagnie française des chocolats et des thés, 1861), 64, described "Micentella" as the best Mexican vanilla to use for folding into chocolate. The spelling is rare enough to suggest that Jaussen might have drawn from this source.

26. AAT, B22-34 and B22-35.

27. AAT, H2-10, Governor to Jaussen, September 18, 1864.

28. AGSSCC, 47-2-C, Rogatien Martin letter, February 4, 1885. On the alliance born of necessity, see J. P. Daughton, *An Empire Divided: Religion, Republicanism and the Making of French Colonialism, 1880-1914* (Oxford: Oxford University Press, 2006), 126-27.

29. "Avis au public," *Océanie française* (Papeete), December 31, 1854.

30. Julien Constantin and Désiré Bois, "Sur trois types de vanilles commerciales de Tahiti," *Académie des Sciences*, August 1915, 196n2.

31. ANOM, OCEA 56, customs form for 1864.

32. AAT, B22-30; *Le Messager de Tahiti*, January 21, 1865, 12; David de Floris, *Notice sur la culture du vanillier* (Paris: S. Raçon, 1860).

33. "The Vanilla Trade at Bordeaux," *Reports from the Consuls of the United States* 96 (August 1888): 207.

34. Toullelan, *Tahiti colonial*, 142-43; "Cultivation of Vanilla in Tahiti," *Bulletin of Miscellaneous Information (Royal Botanic Gardens, Kew)* 91 (July 1894): 208.

35. *Le Messager de Tahiti*, August 24, 1862, 133-36; Toullelan, *Tahiti colonial*, 122, 154-55.

36. "Cultivation of Vanilla in Tahiti," 206.

37. Jennifer Newell, *Trading Nature: Tahitians, Europeans, and Ecological Exchange* (Honolulu: University of Hawaii Press, 2010), 195.

38. Tati Salmon, *Lettres de Tahiti*, ed. and trans. Pierre Lagayette, (Papeete: Editions du Pacifique, 1980), 9-21, 40; Claus Gossler, "The Social and Economic Fall of the Salmon/Brander Clan of Tahiti," *Journal of Pacific History* 40, no. 2 (September 2005): 198-200.

39. Salmon, *Lettres de Tahiti*, January 14, 1899, 162.

40. Salmon, *Lettres de Tahiti*, June 28, 1894, 101; July 2, 1893, 68. Vanilla was just one of many commodities for Hamburg companies, as they had already taken control of a third of Guatemala's coffee production before the Great War. See Michael Miller, *Europe and the Maritime World: A Twentieth Century History* (Cambridge: Cambridge University Press, 2012), 142.

41. Salmon, *Lettres de Tahiti*, August 6, 1894, 106-7.

42. SAH, 621-1/29-5, band 3, and 621-1/29-5, band 4, doc. 116; Newbury, *Tahiti Nui*, 243-52; Gossler, "Social and Economic Fall," 198-99 (quotes on 198 and 208).

43. Salmon, *Lettres de Tahiti*, October 12, 1895, 114; February 26, 1902, 170; September 28, 1904, 185.

44. Matt K. Matsuda, *Pacific Worlds: A History of Seas, Peoples and Cultures* (Cambridge: Cambridge University Press, 2012), 135.

45. Devika Ponnambalam, "Gauguin's 'Child-Wife': In Search of the Muse Who Inspired a Masterpiece," *Guardian*, March 18, 2023.

46. *Lettres de Paul Gauguin à Georges-Daniel de Monfreid* (Paris: Editions Georges Crès, 1918), 174, 184; B. Danielsson and P. O'Reilly, *Gauguin journaliste à Tahiti et ses articles des "Guêpes"* (Paris: Société des Océanistes, 1966), 46.

47. Robert Louis Stevenson, *Sophia Scarlet, and Other Pacific Writings*, ed. Robert Hoskins) (Auckland: AUT Media, 2008), 130-34 (quote 134).

48. Robert Louis Stevenson, *Vailima Letters: Being Correspondence Addressed by Robert Louis Stevenson to Sidney Colvin, November 1890-October 1894* (New York: Charles Scribners, 1896), 137.

49. Stevenson, *Vailima Letters*, 137.

50. C. Kinloch Cooke, "Europe in the Pacific," *Nineteenth Century,* November 1886, 747-48.

51. Paul Gauguin, *Lettres de Gauguin à sa femme et à ses amis*, ed. Maurice Malingue (Paris: Grasset, 1946), 274-75.

52. *Le Messager de Tahiti*, January 31, 1863, 17.

53. *L'Année coloniale* (Paris), January 1, 1899, 326.

54. Toullelan, *Tahiti colonial*, 122; "Le movement commercial en 1918," *L'Océanie française* (Papeete), January 1, 1919, 92.

55. AMBAC, Fonds Bouge, III C 10 C, report from Rikitea, February 1929.

56. Désiré Teivao, "De la vanille made in Gambiers," *Tahiti Infos*, August 5, 2019, https://www.tahiti-infos.com/De-la-vanille-made-in-Gambier_a183832.html.

57. ANOM, GGM 2D 154, table for 1910-11.

58. "Comité d'agriculture et de commerce," *Le Messager de Tahiti*, January 3, 1879, 2.

59. "La vanille de Tahiti," *Bulletin de la société de géographie commerciale*, August 20, 1883, 482.

60. "Correspondance particulière de l'Océanie française," *L'Océanie française*, July 10, 1883, 113-14.

61. Giorgio Riello, "Les consommateurs britanniques et la qualité des produits à la fin du XIXe siècle," *Revue d'histoire moderne et contemporaine* 67, no. 3 (2020): 65.

62. There are parallels with other French colonial goods that experienced smear campaigns, such as Algerian wine. See Owen White, *The Blood of the Colony: Wine and the Rise and Fall of French Algeria* (Cambridge, MA: Harvard University Press, 2021), 69.

63. Direction de l'Intérieur, Etablissements français de l'Océanie, *Notice sur la vanille* (Papeete: Imprimerie du Gouvernement, 1895).

64. L. G. Seurat, *Tahiti et les établissements français de l'Océanie* (Paris: Augustin Challamel, 1906), 51.

65. Henry N. Ridley, *Spices* (London: Macmillan, 1912), 91.

66. Constantin and Bois, "Sur trois types de vanilles commerciales de Tahiti," 196–200.

67. Désiré Bois, "La vanille de Tahiti," *Bulletin de la Société nationale d'acclimation de France*, 1916, 174.

68. Pharmacien-Major Lespinasse, *Etude sur la vanille de Tahiti* (Bordeaux: Institut colonial, 1920), 2.

69. ANOM, MIS 63 bis, Chalot; ANOM, OCEA 159, Inspection of Agriculture, October 15, 1908, and report from the head of the Jardin Colonial. On the Jardin Colonial, see Christophe Bonneuil, *Des savants pour l'empire: La structuration des recherches scientifiques coloniales au temps de la "mise en valeur des colonies françaises," 1917-1945* (Paris: ORSTOM, 1991), 30; and Dominique Pinon, "Naissance d'une institution au bois de Vincennes," in Isabelle-Levêque, Dominique Pinion, and Michel Griffon, eds., *Le Jardin d'agronomie tropicale: De l'agriculture coloniale au développement durable* (Arles: Actes Sud, 2005), 48–58.

70. *Journal officiel des Etablissements français de l'Océanie*, May 4, 1911, 175.

71. ANOM, OCEA 159, Director of the Union coloniale to the Minister of the Colonies, May 11, 1911.

72. ANOM, OCEA 159, Governor Bonhoure to the Minister of the Colonies, January 21, 1911.

73. ANOM, OCEA 159, Pellet to the Ministry of the Colonies, January 10, 1911.

74. ANOM, OCEA 159, procès-verbal de la chambre de commerce, November 7, 1912. For the 1905 British source, see TNA, AY4/1053, October 4, 1905.

75. NARA, RG 59, decimal file 851M.61336, Winship report, 1911.

76. Frederick O'Brien, *Mystic Isles of the South Seas* (New York: Century Company, 1921).

77. Anne-Christine Trémon, *Chinois en Polynésie française: Migration, métissage, diaspora* (Paris: Société d'ethnologie, 2010), 56–57, 66–67, 121–22; Bruno Saura, *Tinito: La communauté chinoise de Tahiti* (Papeete: Au vent des îles, 2022), 88, 94.

78. ANOM, OCEA 125, Vigiollas letter and response from Governor H. Gery, 1937.

79. M. Rivière, "Composition chimique de la vanille de Tahiti," *Annales d'hygiène et de médecine coloniales* 15 (1912): 839–42 (quote on 841).

80. ANOM, OCEA 159, "La question de la vanille à Tahiti," 1913.

81. "La vanille française et les maîtres d'hôtels allemands," *La conserve alimentaire* 11, no. 22 (October 1913): 337.

82. ANOM, OCEA 159; ANOM, 9 Affeco 9.

83. ANOM, 1 Affeco 890, Etablissements Jean-Marie Vial to the Ministry of the Colonies, July 10, 1933.

84. "Informations," *Bulletin de la chambre d'agriculture et d'élevage de Polynésie française*, January–February 1960, 26; SAPF, B 41:44 (357), D. Drakni, "Approche du marché de la vanille," 1982, 5. There are rare instances of the United States importing vanilla from Vichy colonies until November 1942, when relations were severed. In November 1940, Philadelphia-based Zink and Triest sought to purchase vanilla from Ralph Monplaisir in Martinique. See NARA, RG 84, box 1, 861.33.

85. Mario Samper K., "The Historical Construction of Quality and Competitiveness," in William Gervase Clarence-Smith and Steven Topik, eds., *The Global Coffee Economy in Africa, Asia and Latin America, 1500–1989* (Cambridge: Cambridge University Press, 2003), 126.

86. SAPF, B 41:44 (357), D. Drakni, "Approche du marché de la vanille," 1982, 11, 15, 16.

87. "Tahaa: 300 kilos de vanille dérobés à Joël Hahe, 3 millions cfp de manque à gagner," *Franceinfo*, June 2, 2022, https://la1ere.francetvinfo.fr/polynesie/tahiti/polynesie-francaise/tahaa-300-kilos-de-vanille-derobes-a-joel-hahe-3-millions-cfp-de-manque-a-gagner-1290308.html.

88. Daniel Sherman, "Paradis à vendre: Tourisme et imitation en Polynésie française, 1958–1971," *Terrain* 44 (March 2005): 46.

89. Information provided by Taha'a's Vanille de Tahiti EPIC (Établissement public à caractère industriel et commercial) office, August 2022.

90. Charlie Réné, "À Raiatea, deux hectares de vanille sous des serres photovoltaïques," *Radio1 Tahiti*, January 14, 2021, https://www.radio1.pf/a-raiatea-deux-hectares-de-vanille-sous-des-serres-photovoltaiques; Jean-Tenahe Faatau, "Polynésie: Sur l'île de Raiatea, deux hectares de vanille sous des serres photovoltaïques," *Outremers360*, January 15, 2021, https://outremers360.com/energies/polynesie-sur-lile-de-raiatea-deux-hectares-de-vanille-sous-des-serres-photovoltaiques.

SEVEN. VANILLAMANIA

1. ADML, 5 E 8/374, Abraham succession, December 9, 1805; Sylvain Bertoldi, "Les débuts du chocolat," *Vivre à Angers*, no. 412 (2017–18), archived April 22, 2021, at https://web.archive.org/web/20210422135644/https://www.angers.fr/fileadmin/plugin/tx_dcddownloads/vaa-412.pdf; David Audibert, "Epiciers de l'ouest, Le Mans, Angers, Nantes, au XVIIIe siècle; étude comparative" (PhD diss., Université du Maine, 2003), 476.

2. Thirty years prior, a French source had already described Veracruz as the "headquarters" of yellow fever among Central and South American port cities. *Le Journal des débats politiques et littéraires*, January 19, 1839, 2.

3. NARA, RG 59, despatches of the US consuls to Veracruz, reel 11, 1869–73, letter to Mrs. Saulnier, July 13, 1869.

4. Kourí, *Pueblo Divided*, 298.

5. Ludovic Chambon, *Un Gascon au Mexique* (Paris: Paul Dupont, 1892), 213.

6. Henry Bruman, "The Culture History of Mexican Vanilla," *Hispanic American Historical Review* 28, no. 3 (August 1948): 372.

7. David Skerritt, "A Negotiated Ethnic Identity: San Rafael, a French Community on the Mexican Gulf Coast, 1833–1930," *Cahiers des sciences humaines* 30, no. 3 (1994): 461.

8. Kourí, *Pueblo Divided*, 89–90, 100–101.

9. Skerritt, "Negotiated Ethnic Identity," 460.

10. CADN, 725 PO/1/9, French cultural agent in Jicáltepec and San Rafael, September 12, 1906.

11. "A Thriving Colony," *Two Republics* (Mexico City), February 8, 1899, 6.

12. Skerritt, "Negotiated Ethnic Identity," 460.

13. Delvaille and Attias had also reestablished an outlet in San Sebastian at this juncture. See Jean-Pierre Léon, "Le retour en Espagne des Juifs de Bayonne," *GenAmi*, no. 27 (March 2004): http://www.genami.org/culture/fr_retour-espagne.php.

14. Jean-Christophe Demard, *Jicáltepec, Chronique d'un village français au Mexique* (Paris: Porte-Glaive, 1987), 110–11; Jean-Christophe Demard, *Une colonie française au Mexique, 1833–1926* (Langres: Dominique Guéniot, 2000), 293. On the vanilla prize at Briançon, see P.-Ch. Joubert, *Exposition universelle de Besançon, compte-rendu* (Paris: La propriété industrielle, 1861), 281.

15. CADN, 725 PO/1/5, letter to the French consul in Veracruz, May 21, 189; David Todd, *A Velvet Empire: French Informal Imperialism in the Nineteenth Century* (Princeton, NJ: Princeton University Press, 2021); J. P. Daughton, "When Argentina Was 'French': Rethinking Cultural Politics and European Imperialism in Belle-Epoque Buenos Aires," *Journal of Modern History* 80, no. 4 (December 2008): 831–64; Edward Shawcross, *France, Mexico and Informal Empire in Latin America, 1820–1867* (London: Palgrave, 2018).

16. CADN, 725 PO/1/8, "Culture de la vanille planifolia ou sylvestre." For Lavoignet and Mahé, see Demard, *Une colonie française*, 341.

17. Chambon, *Un Gascon*, 211–212.

18. Kourí, *Pueblo Divided*, 119.

19. "The Cultivation of Vanilla," *Two Republics* (Mexico City), issues of July 20, July 22, July 25, July 26, and July 27, 1893. On *poscoyon*, see Kourí, *Pueblo Divided*, 33.

20. Jason Mason Hart, *Empire and Revolution: The Americans in Mexico Since the Civil War* (Berkeley: University of California Press, 2002), 207.

21. AGN, Fomento, Industrias Nuevas, caja 19, exp. 4.

22. BANC, MSS M-B 3, vol. 112, letters dated May 25, 1890, to Alberto Schaar; May 27 1890, to Struller, Meyer, and Schuacher; June 13, 1890, to Schaar; June 24, 1890, to Struller, Meyer, and Schuacher; June 27, 1890, to Schaar; July 1, 1890, to Charles Boucher; July 1, 1890, to Loustau; July 5, 1890, to Alfred Lefebvre; July 11, 1890, to Alfred Lefebvre; July 15, 1890, to Alfred Lefebvre; July 11, 1890, to Alfred Lefebvre.

23. *Archives de la commission scientifique du Mexique* (Paris: Imprimerie impériale, 1865), 1:344–45.

24. M. H. de Vriese, "Histoire des Plantes Utiles: Histoire de la Vanille," trans. Edouard Morren, *La Belgique horticole* 6 (1856): 370–71.

25. S. Kalff, "Lets over Vanielje," *De Natuur*, March 15, 1905, 87.

26. NAN, NL-HaNA, Cie Cultures Ned-Ind inv. 272, correspondence from Mexico, May 4, 1852.

27. De Vriese, "Histoire des Plantes Utiles," 371. The Dutch on Java were manually pollinating oil palms at this same time. See Jonathan E. Robins, *Oil Palm: A Global History* (Chapel Hill: University of North Carolina Press, 2021), 166.

28. Karl Scherzer, *Narrative of the Circumnavigation of the Globe by the Austrian Frigate Novara Undertaken by Order of the Imperial Government in the Years 1857–1858 and 1859* (London: Saunders, Otley, and Company, 1862), 2:205–6.

29. NADGM, Mauritius Blue Books: 1858, 464–65; 1870, T 173–74; 1888, 610, 650. See also "Port-Louis, 4 octobre 1865," *Commercial Gazette* (Mauritius), October 5, 1865, 2. For the 1900 data, see TNA, AY4/1057.

30. NADGM, RA Series box 250, year 1903, vanilla committee, March 31, 1903.

31. James Morris to L. Bouton, *Commercial Gazette* (Mauritius), May 6, 1865, 2; "Report on the Contributions of Mauritius to the International Exhibition at Dublin in 1865, by James Morris, Commissioner for the Colony," *Commercial Gazette* (Mauritius), April 18, 1866, 2.

32. NADGM, Mauritius Blue Book 1888, 610, 650.

33. John Uri Lloyd, *Vanilla Planifolia* (Cincinnati: Western Druggist, 1897), 15.

34. "The Vanilla Industry," *Merchants and Planters Gazette* (Mauritius), September 22, 1887, 2.

35. *Colonial Reports: Seychelles*, 1901, 18.

36. "Vanilla in Seychelles," *Bulletin of Miscellaneous Information (Royal Botanic Gardens, Kew)* 136–37 (April–May 1898): 93–95.

37. *Colonial Reports: Seychelles*, 1901, 17.

38. TNA, AY4/1053, W. Davidson to Professor Dunstan, February 3, 1906; S. J. Galbraith, *Vanilla Culture as Practiced in the Seychelles Islands*, bulletin 21 (Washington, DC: US Department of Agriculture, Division of Botany, 1898), 7–11.

39. TNA, AY4/1054, entire file, but esp. Caley and Son to the Imperial Institute, May 12, 1909.

40. L. J., "Vanilles," *La Dépêche coloniale*, January 29, 1912.

41. *Colonial Reports: Seychelles*, 1905, 15 (1904 data); *Colonial Reports: Seychelles*, 1913, 10 (manuring); *Colonial Reports: Seychelles*, 1919, 4 (1919 figures and disease). Use of manure is also mentioned in Galbraith, *Vanilla Culture*, 9–10, 21.

42. James Edward O'Connor, *Vanilla: Its Cultivation in India* (Delhi: Office of the Superintendent of Government Print, 1881), 5.

43. Dr. R. Mahendran, personal communication with author, July 5, 2023.

44. T. B. McClelland, *Vanilla: A Promising New Crop for Porto Rico*, Bulletin (Porto Rico Agricultural Experiment Station) 26 (Puerto Rico: Agricultural Experiment Station, 1919), 1–5.

45. ANF, F12/7291, Nanès Texas file.

46. NARA, RG 59, M179, Land of Sunshine Company, August 16, 1894.

47. Ryan Ballogg, "Vanilla Could Spice Up Florida's Agriculture," *AP News*, September 16, 2018, https://apnews.com/article/006bc75b2d30435e8b810a2cc1618561; Alan Chambers, Pamela Moon, Vovener Edmond, and Elias Bassil, "Vanilla Cultivation in Southern Florida," Horticultural Sciences Department, UF/IFAS Extension, November 2019, HS1348.

48. Mark Peattie, *Nan'yo: The Rise and Fall of the Japanese in Micronesia, 1885–1945* (Honolulu: University of Hawaii Press, 1988), 135.

49. Michael Osborne, "The System of Colonial Gardens and the Exploitation of French Algeria, 1830–1852," *Proceedings of the Meetings of the French Colonial Historical Society* 8 (1985): 160–64.

50. AGCSE, 3J1.4a3, letter to Father Stoffet, January 6, 1892; "La production de la vanille," *Bulletin de l'Office colonial*, 1914, 219–21; ADN, 77J 1691, Afrique équatoriale française, 1930.

51. "Exposition agricole," *L'indépendant politique littéraire et artistique* (Pondichéry), March 5, 1899, 19; ACCM, MP 3.1.9., F. Dumas to the head of Marseille's chamber of commerce, April 2, 1900.

52. "La production de la vanille," 243.

53. VNA2, Goucoch 30753, head of Binh Dinh province, August 15, 1887, and letter from the head of the jardin d'acclimatation, October 6, 1887.

54. VNA2, Goucoch 31361, 1922 report on Le Guidec's plantation; Henri Le Guidec, "La culture du vanillier en Cochinchine," *L'Eveil économique de l'Indochine*, June 18, 1922.

55. A. Garnier, "Vanille de Hon-Quan," *Annales de l'Institut colonial de Bordeaux*, 1924, 55.

56. "Les entreprises coloniales françaises: Inde et Indochine," accessed December 13, 2022, https://www.entreprises-coloniales.fr/inde-et-indochine.html.

57. Demard, *Une colonie française*, 189–90; Kourí, *Pueblo Divided*, 105.

58. Genese Sodikoff, *Forest and Labor in Madagascar* (Bloomington: Indiana University Press, 2012), 123.

59. ANOM, 1Affeco 890, "La vanille aux Antilles"; the export data is drawn from "La production de la vanille," 215–16. On the 1928 hurricane, see ADG, 1P 19.

60. ADM, 99J10, "Exploitation vanille, Note N 5," August 1938.

61. "Les vols à Flacq," *La Sentinelle de Maurice* (Port-Louis), May 3, 1873, 1.

62. "Vanille," *Le Cernéen, journal de l'Île Maurice* (Port-Louis), June 22, 1874, 1; "Nouvelles des districts," *La Sentinelle de Maurice* (Port-Louis), September 1, 1874, 2; "Des moyens de protéger la culture de la vanille," *Le Cernéen, journal de l'Île Maurice* (Port-Louis), June 30, 1874, 1.

63. "Vanille," *Le Cernéen, journal de l'Île Maurice* (Port-Louis), November 5, 1874, 1; "Encore des vols de vanille," *Le Cernéen, journal de l'Île Maurice* (Port-Louis), December 8, 1874; "Plus de vols de vanille!," *Commercial Gazette* (Mauritius), May 19, 1875, 1; "Marquage de la vanille" *La Sentinelle de Maurice* (Port-Louis), May 20, 1875, 1.

64. "La nécessité d'une enquête," *Le Journal de Maurice* (Port-Louis), September 2, 1885, 2.

65. NADGM, RA Series box 250, year 1902, projet d'ordonnance, 1902–3. Segrais's portrait is drawn from "Paul Jean 'Léonce' LE JUGE de SEGRAIS," Geneanet, accessed October 7, 2024, https://gw.geneanet.org/balco?lang=fr&iz=0&p=paul+jean+leonce&n=le+juge+de+segrais.

66. Cerveau Kotoson, "Ces gens-là... Zama Marcellin et sa femme, planteurs de vanille," *La Tribune de Diego-Suarez*, November 24, 2015.

67. NADGM, RA Series box 250, year 1902, meeting of April 16, 1902. The ripeness argument was already raised by other complainants in 1886. "A propos des vols de vanille," *Mercantile Record and Commercial Gazette* (Mauritius), August 13, 1886, 2.

68. NADGM, RA Series, box 250, year 1902, meeting of December 11, 1902.

69. NADGM, RA Series, box 250, year 1902, report of the vanilla committee, 1902.

70. NADGM, RA Series, box 250, year 1902, dissenting opinion, 1902; and box 250, year 1903, dissent formulated at Pamplemousses, March 18, 1903.

71. "Seychelles Affairs," *Planters and Commercial Gazette* (Mauritius), January 12, 1888, 11.

72. TNA, AY4/1066.

73. "Le commerce," *Le Figaro* (Paris), January 29, 1863, 5. Of course, contraband was nearly universal. For the example of eighteenth-century French Guadeloupe, see Laurent Dubois, *A Colony of Citizens* (Chapel Hill: University of North Carolina Press, 2004), 48–50.

74. ANMT, 9AQ 352, Compagnie générale transatlantique, April 15, 1884.

75. Kourí, *Pueblo Divided*, 111.

76. Kourí, *Pueblo Divided*, 294–97.

77. A. Massinot, "La vanille," *Bulletin de la chambre d'agriculture et d'élevage de Polynésie française*, January 1960, 38.

78. ACCM, MP 3.1.9 "la vanille."

79. ANOM, 1 Affeco 890, "débouchés australiens pour la vanille."

80. *La Vanille* (Paris: Syndicat des exportateurs français d'Indochine, 1945), 25.

81. Jeffrey Pilcher, *Food in World History* (New York: Routledge, 2006), 35; on enduring gaps between rural and Parisian food in nineteenth-century France, see Theodore Zeldin, *France, 1848-1945: Taste and Corruption* (Oxford: Oxford University Press, 1980), 378–82.

82. Léon Brisse, *Le calendrier gastronomique pour l'année 1867: Les 365 menus du Baron Brisse (un menu par jour)* (Paris: Bureaux de la Liberté, 1867). Julia Child's copy is available at SLRIHU. On pork in Brisse's menus, see Zeldin, *France*, 405. There is a parallel here with the shortcut that was curry powder. See Lizzie Collingham, *Curry: A Tale of Cooks and Conquerors* (New York: Oxford University Press, 2006), 141.

83. Pilcher, *Food in World History*, 36. On the reduction of spices in late seventeenth- and early eighteenth-century French cuisine, see Susan Pinkard, *A Revolution in Taste: The Rise of French Cuisine* (Cambridge: Cambridge University Press, 2009), 124. On the enduring influence of the French nobility, see David Higgs, *Nobles in Nineteenth-Century France: The Practice of Inegalitarianism* (Baltimore: Johns Hopkins University Press, 1987).

84. Özge Samanci, *La Cuisine d'Istanbul au XIXe siècle* (Tours: Presses universitaires François-Rabelais, 2022), 61; Özge Samanci, "A la table du Sultan Abdülhamid, 1876–1908," in Nathalie Clayer and Erdal Kaynar, eds., *Penser, agir et vivre dans l'Empire Ottoman et en Turquie* (Paris: Peeters, 2013), 345–51; Menu kindly transmitted by Nicholas de la Bretèche, author of *A la table des Tsars: La fabuleuse ascension de Pierre Cubat à la cour des empereurs russesi* (La Varenne Saint-Hilaire: Macha, 2019).

85. Pellegrino Artusi, *Science in the Kitchen and the Art of Eating Well*, ed. and trans. Stephen Sartarelli and Murtha Baca (Toronto: University of Toronto Press, 2003), 392–93, 399–411, 421, 427–63, 465–78, 481, 486, 488–89, 495, 499, 501, 503, 506, 511–12, 516, 519, 545, 548, 553–54; August Oetker, *Grundlehren der Kochkunst* (1895; Project Gutenberg, 2010), 70, https://www.gutenberg.org/ebooks/31537.

86. ADM, 99J10 Motta Panettoni to Syndicat des Planteurs de Vanille, Milan, December 16, 1938. On the conveyor belt, see "A Culinary History of Panettone, the Italian and South American Christmas Treat," *Smithsonian Magazine*, accessed December 30, 2022, https://www.smithsonianmag.com/arts-culture/culinary-history-panettone-180971058.

87. "Pays basque, un gâteau fourré de tradition," *Sud-Ouest*, July 13, 2017; Philippe Maffre, "De l'origine et de l'usage des cannelés de Bordeaux," *Le Festin* 25 (February 1998): 110.

88. Frédéric Duhart, "Le poids des innovations récentes dans la constitution de l'identité culturelle alimentaire actuelle du sud-ouest de la France," in Alain Drouard and Jean-Pierre

Williot, eds., *Histoire des innovations alimentaires, XIXe et XXe siècles* (Paris: L'Harmattan, 2007), 243–50.

89. Mark Pendergrast, *For God, Country, and Coca-Cola* (New York: Basic Books, 2013), 489–91.

90. NARA, RG 21 (279263), argument and brief, *Coca-Cola v. Henry Rucker*, May 14, 1902, 11; NARA, RG 21 (279254), "Brief for the Coca-Cola Company."

91. Frederick Allen, *Secret Formula: The Inside Story of How Coca-Cola Became the Best-Known Brand in the World* (New York: HarperCollins, 1984), 27–28.

92. Carole Sugarman, "Express Lane: Coke, Madagascar, and Vanilla Beans," *Washington Post*, July 28, 1985.

93. S. T. Rorer, *Dainty Dishes for All the Year Round. Recipes for Ice Creams, Water Ices, Sherbets, and Other Frozen Desserts* (Philadelphia: North Brothers, 1915), 20–31, 34 45, 48, 50–51, 58.

94. Kourí, *Pueblo Divided*, 29; Susanne Freidberg, *Fresh: A Perishable History* (Cambridge, MA: Harvard University Press, 2009), 39.

95. Helen Zoe Veit, *Modern Food, Moral Food: Self-Control, Science and the Rise of Modern American Eating in the Early Twentieth Century* (Chapel Hill: University of North Carolina Press, 2013), 127–29; Camille Bégin, *Taste of the Nation: The New Deal Search for America's Food* (Champaign: University of Illinois Press, 2016), 140.

96. "Millón de recetas" section of *La Patria* (Mexico City), February 4, 1902, 3; February 22, 1902, 3; May 23, 1902, 3.

97. Nicholas Tselementes, *Greek Cookery* (New York: D. C. Divry, 1950). Vanilla imported from Cádiz was already used in small quantities in Ottoman-era Greece. In late colonial Madagascar, a Greek community of some 850 members maintained contact with its homeland at the very time that Tselementes published. See Georges Condominas, "Introduction à une étude sur l'émigration grecque à Madagascar," in Jean G. Peristiany, ed., *Contribution to Mediterranean Sociology: Mediterranean rural communities and social changes* (Paris: Mouton, 1968), 215–43.

98. Olivier Fruneau-Maigret, *Lu, une marque à l'avant-garde* (Rennes: PUR, 2020), 84, 110.

99. TNA, COL 318/297, 116–21.

100. "Fine French Cordials," *Japan Times* (Yokohama), September 8, 1865, 1; Request for Additional Shipment of Articles Including German Sausages, August 19, 1904, Japan Center for Asian Historical Records, Tokyo, ref. C07082316000, fig. 3; "Envois d'échantillons de vanille par la poste," *Journal officiel de Madagascar et dépendances*, October 13, 1906, 14020.

101. "Morinaga's Vanilla Chocolate on Sale," *Asahi Shimbun* (Osaka), August 20, 1919, 1, and *Asahi Shimbun* (Osaka), August 13, 1919, 6.

102. TNA, FO 262/1645, 356–62, British Embassy Tokyo, August 26, 1925.

103. *La Vanille*, 24.

104. SAPF, B 41:44 (357), D. Drakni, "Approche du marché de la vanille," 1982, 7; ADR, 28 W 56, direction des douanes; CADN, 674 PO/1, exportations de Madagascar de vanille en gousse en 1971.

105. "Amusements: Ball in Aid of the Shanghai Masonic Charity Fund," *North China Herald* (Shanghai), March 21, 1882, 316; "New Things Every Woman Ought to Know," *China*

Press (Shanghai), October 7, 1917, 6; "Shanghai Shopping with Dorothy," *Shanghai Gazette*, January 13, 1920, 5.

EIGHT. REVENGE OF THE ORCHID

1. "558 Americans Took Vanilla!," *Life*, August 21, 1944, 97; Matt Siegel, "How Ice Cream Helped America at War," *Atlantic*, August 6, 2017; Rosa Abreu-Runkel, *Vanilla: A Global History* (London: Reaktion Books, 2020), 66.

2. Siegel, "How Ice Cream Helped America."

3. ANF, 72AJ 434, rapport sur le marché aux Etats-Unis, 3.

4. Stephen Harp, *A World History of Rubber: Empire, Industry and the Everyday* (London: Wiley Blackwell, 2016), 101-3.

5. David Goodman, Bernardo Sorj, and John Wilkinson, *From Farming to Biotechnology: A Theory of Agro-Industrial Development* (New York: Basil Blackwell, 1987).

6. Nadia Berenstein, "Making a Global Sensation: Vanilla Flavor, Synthetic Chemistry, and the Meanings of Purity," *History of Science* 54, no. 4 (2016): 408.

7. Théodore-Nicolas Gobley, *Sur le principe odorant de la vanille* (Paris: E. Thunot, 1858).

8. Berenstein, "Making a Global Sensation," 405-8, 423; Paulina S. Gennermann, "Becoming Natural: The Naturalization of Synthetic Flavors in the Twentieth Century and the Introduction of *Konsumstoff*," *Berichte zur Wissenschaftsgeschichte* 46 (2023): 306-8.

9. Louis-François Raban, *Plus de Fraude: les Falsificateurs dévoilés* (Paris, 1859), 84-85; "Vanille au verre pilé," *Le Rappel*, August 23, 1895, 1; J. Moroy, "Les poudres de vanille," *Annales des Falsifications et des Fraudes* 217 (January 1927): 21-25.

10. *Le Catholique des Pays-Bas*, July 9, 1828, 3; "Courrier de Vienne," *L'Europe politique, scientifique, commerciale* (Frankfurt), July 16, 1863, 2; "Poison Ice Cream Epidemic," *Detroit Free Press*, July 29, 1866, 4; "Gleanings from Exchanges," *American Journal of Homeopathic Medica and Record of Medical Science*, March 1, 1873, 249; "Poisoning by Vanilla-Ices," *New Remedies*, January 1, 1874, 65; Edward Geist, "When Ice Cream Was Poisonous: Adulteration, Ptomaines and Bacteriology in the United States, 1850-1900," *Bulletin of the History of Medicine* 86, no. 3 (Fall 2012): 333-60. On milk poisonings, see Susanne Freidberg, *Fresh: A Perishable History* (Cambridge, MA: Harvard University Press, 2009), 208-10.

11. "Artificial Vanillin and Vanilla Flavors," *Scientific American* 89, no. 12 (September 17, 1898): 188.

12. Charles-Albert Vibert, *Précis de toxicology clinique et medico-légale* (Paris: Librairie J. B. Baillière, 1907), 918.

13. Berenstein, "Making a Global Sensation," 412-16; "Taxe de consomation sur la vanille," *Bulletin de la Chambre de commerce de Paris*, April 15, 1911, 676.

14. Berenstein, "Making a Global Sensation," 412.

15. ADGIR, 21 J 99, "Congrès colonial," August 1907.

16. W. W. Green, Imperial Institute, n.d.; Imperial Institute, March 10, 1906; Fry and Sons, March 13, 1906, all in TNA, AY 4/1053.

17. SLRIHU, MC 693, folder 9.5, Rindlaub proposal to Burnett foods, March 16, 1934.

18. General Mills, *Betty Crocker's Picture Cook Book* (New York: McGraw-Hill, 1950).

19. Marjorie Shaffer, *Pepper: A History of the World's Most Influential* Spice (New York: Thomas Dunne Books, 2013), 13.

20. US National Library of Medicine, interview with Mr. Gilbert S. Goldhammer (online oral histories, interview conducted by James Harvey Young, August 26, 1968), http://resource.nlm.nih.gov/2935141R.

21. TNA, AY4/1148, August 1939 report.

22. BUA, RG 75-12, box 2, folder 28, internal correspondence and 1979 document from Monsanto (*Chemical Marketing Reporter*, July 23, 1979). For the dates, see BUA, RG 75-12, box 3, folder 19; RG 75-12, box 5, folder 3; and RG 75-12 box 5, folder 16. For the "gunk" story, which turned out to be sulfur dust, see "Residents Complain to Council of Sulphur Dust from Factory," *St. Catharines Standard*, June 9, 1959. Regarding Hibbert's research, see MCG 3076, C 3, 122, and C 4, 138, for the 1937 correspondence with the Flavoring Extract Association. The two files also show that Swedish inventor N. B. E. Rang already patented a method for extracting vanillin from lignin in 1934 and that two Leipzig-based chemists patented another in 1940. Concerning the *Tribune*, see Michael Stamm, "The Flavor of News," *American Journalism* 32, no. 2 (2015): 210, 216.

23. All-China Federation of Industry and Commerce Bakery Association, eds., *Chinese Baked Food Dictionary: Products and Processes* (Beijing: China Light Industry Press, 2009), 244–45.

24. BUA RG 75-12, box 5, folder 20, media releases, 30.

25. CADN, 674 PO/1, report from the French commercial attaché to Madagascar, July 20, 1972, and "Vanille, 350 tonnes en 1967 pour la CEE."

26. Berenstein, "Making a Global Sensation."

27. ANOM, 196 APOM 102, documentation Univanille, June 1968.

28. ACCM, MP 30131, file 7; Raymond Decary, "La vanille de Madagascar," *Encyclopédie mensuelle d'outre-mer* 65 (January 1956): 34.

29. Kolleen M. Guy, "Food Representations," in Martin Bruegel, ed., *A Cultural History of Food in the Age of Empire* (London: Bloomsbury, 2016), 196.

30. ADR, 28 W 56.

31. ADR, 28 W 56.

32. ANOM, 196 APOM 102, situation aux Etats-Unis.

33. ANOM, 196 APOM 102, letter from the Groupement national interprofessionnel de la vanille to the Vanilla Bean Association of America, August 25, 1967; ANOM, 196 APOM 102, réunion de la commission des affaires professionnelles, April 23, 1968.

34. *The Oxford Dictionary of Difficult Words*, ed. Archie Hobson (Oxford: Oxford University Press, 2004), 61.

35. ADN, 673PO 1, PMB/FR/134, February 3, 1966, and the January 28, 1966, protocol.

36. ANOM, 196 APOM 102, communiqué conjoint des pays producteurs de vanille de l'océan Indien.

37. ADIL, 906 W 22, Vanille Malilé.

38. ANOM, 196 APOM 102, compte-rendu de la réunion sur les problèmes de commercialisation de la vanille, Ambassade de Madagascar en France, December 8, 1966.

39. CADN, 674 PO/1, February 9, 1967, note from Antananarivo to Réunion.

40. ANM, Présidence, 418-19, service des renseignements généraux, January 2, 1967.

41. Another energy cartel bringing together France and some of its former colonies was created as a reaction to a 1971 US embargo on uranium. See Gabrielle Hecht, *Being Nuclear: Africans and the Global Uranium Trade* (Cambridge, MA: MIT Press, 2012).

42. "Nous ferons la publicité dans les pays acheteurs, décident les producteur de vanille de l'océan Indien," *Le Courrier de Madagascar* (Antananarivo), January 17, 1968, 1.

43. ANOM, 196 APOM 102, Hautant correspondance, letter dated October 14, 1968.

44. *Plantation Crops: A Review of Production, Trade, Consumption, Stocks and Prices Relating to Coffee, Cocoa, Tea, Sugar, Spices, Tobacco and Rubber* (London: Commonwealth Secretariat, 1973), 220.

45. ANOM, 196 APOM 102, Univanille documentation, June 1968.

46. ANOM, 196 APOM 102 Univanille, January 31, 1968, meeting.

47. Alessandro Stanziani, "Municipal Laboratories and the Analysis of Foodstuffs in France Under the Third Republic: A Case Study of the Paris Municipal Laboratory, 1878–1907," in Peter Atkins, Peter Lummel, and Derek Oddy, eds., *Food and the City in Europe Since 1800* (Aldershot: Ashgate, 2007), 105–16.

48. ANOM, 196 APOM 102, Univanille, Hautant interview, February 13, 1968.

49. CADN, 674 PO/1, Protection de l'appellation "vanille naturelle."

50. ANOM, 196 APOM 102, Univanille documentation, June 1968.

51. ANOM, 196 APOM 102, Univanille report, October 10, 1968.

52. ANOM, 196 APOM 102, Plan de promotion et de propagande, February 14, 1968, and Salon international de l'alimentation.

53. Victoria de Grazia and Ellen Furlough, eds., *The Sex of Things: Gender and Consumption in Historical Perspective* (Berkeley: University of California Press, 1996), 104, 361.

54. ANOM, 196 APOM 102, Univanille, April 1968 report.

55. ANOM, 196 APOM 102, Essor, Univanille: Etude de motivation et sondage national, August 1968.

56. ANOM, 196 APOM 102, Univanille, October 9, 1968, meeting; Roland Barthes, *Mythologies* (Paris: Le Seuil, 1957), 128–30.

57. "Univanille, le mot vanille sur l'étiquette," INA, Paris, November 16, 1972, https://www.ina.fr/ina-eclaire-actu/publicite/pub3212568084/univanille-le-mot-vanille-sur-l-etiquette. On the mass consumption of yogurts in 1960s France, see Catherine Lecomte and Nathalie Claret, "Analyse historique de l'évolution des technologies, des produits-emballages et des organisations dans l'industrie des laits fermentés," in Alain Drouard and Jean-Pierre Williot, eds., *Histoire des innovations alimentaires, XIXe et XXe siècles* (Paris: L'Harmattan, 2007), 140.

58. ANOM, 196 APOM 102, ESSOR, Univanille: Etude de motivation et sondage national, August 1968.

59. ANOM, 196 APOM 102; "La leçon de la vanille," Université de Limoges, Service Commun de la Documentation, Fonds d'Histoire de l'Education.

60. ANOM, 196 APOM 102.

61. CADN, 674 PO/1, Univanille to the French ambassador to Madagascar, July 17, 1970.

62. ANOM, 196 APOM 102, Univanille, CEDUS letter, July 1968, and April 1968 Univanille report.

63. ANOM, 196 APOM 102, CEDUS, press.

64. ANOM, 196 APOM 102, ESSOR, Univanille: Etude de motivation et sondage national, August 1968.

65. ANOM, 196 APOM 102, ESSOR, Univanille: Etude de motivation et sondage national, August 1968.

66. ANOM, 196 APOM 102, Univanille, October 9, 1968, meeting.

67. ANOM, 196 APOM 102, "Salon international de l'alimentation"; Mario Samper K., "The Historical Construction of Quality and Competitiveness," in William Gervase Clarence-Smith and Steven Topik, eds., *The Global Coffee Economy in Africa, Asia and Latin America, 1500-1989* (Cambridge: Cambridge University Press, 2003), 135.

68. ANOM, 196 APOM 102, Essor, Univanille: National poll, August 1968.

69. Guadeloupe reached a first production peak in 1925, with 31,400 tons, then a second in 1945-46 thanks to pent-up US wartime demand. See ADG, INC 107 (for 1946); and *La Vanille* (Paris: Syndicat des exportateurs français d'Indochine, 1945), 21 (for 1925).

70. ANOM, 196 APOM 102, Essor, Univanille: national poll, August 1968; David Ciarlo, *Advertising Empire: Race and Visual Culture in Imperial Germany* (Cambridge, MA: Harvard University Press, 2011), 151.

71. ANOM, 196 APOM 102.

72. ANOM, 196 APOM 102.

73. ANOM, 196 APOM 102.

74. ANOM, 196 APOM 102. The notion of vanilla being geriatric was not new. In Fyodor Dostoevsky's 1880 *The Brothers Karamazov*, one character picks out a chocolate, exclaiming, "I'd like one with vanilla [...] they're for old folks, sir. Hee hee!" Fyodor Dostoevsky, *The Brothers Karamazov*, trans. Richard Pevear and Larissa Volokhonsky (New York: Vintage Books, 1991), 436.

75. Amanda Fortini, "The White Stuff: How Vanilla Became Shorthand for Bland," *Slate*, August 10, 2005.

76. ANOM, 196 APOM 102, Univanille October 10, 1968, report.

77. ANOM, 196 APOM 102, Inquiry into the distribution of vanilla, July 1968.

78. ANOM, 196 APOM 102, Essor, Univanille: national poll, August 1968. On food packaging, see Freidberg, *Fresh*, 181-96.

79. Willem Scheire, "'Bring Joy to Your Home with the Real Frigidaire': Advertising the Refrigerator to Belgian Female Consumers, 1950-1965," *Food and Foodways* 23 (2015): 57-79.

80. ADM, 99J 6, Lemerle, March 14, 1932.

81. ANOM, 196 APOM 102, Essor, Univanille: national poll, August 1968.

82. ANOM, 196 APOM 102, Stephen Manheimer, "Pourquoi une campagne de publicité?," February 25, 1969.

83. ANOM, 196 APOM 102, Stephen Manheimer, "Pourquoi une campagne de publicité?," February 25, 1969; Library of Congress LOT 13145 (H) [P&P].

84. ANOM, 196 APOM 102, Stephen Manheimer, "Pourquoi une campagne de publicité?," February 25, 1969.

85. CADN, 674 PO/1, producing nations.

86. CADN, 674 PO/1, seventeenth export plan, March 20, 1978.

87. ANOM, 196 APOM 102, Zink and Triest data, May 28, 1968; Khalid Khan, Chi-Wei Su, Adnan Khurshid, and Muhammad Umar, "Are There Bubbles in the Vanilla Price?," *Agricultural and Food Economics* 10 (2022): http://www.doi.org/10.1186/s40100-022-00213-y.

88. ADN, 673PO 1, Jean Dupont to the French embassy in Moroni, April 27, 1984.

89. Michel Manceau, "Vanilla Market Volatility and Speculation," paper presented at the Fifth International Vanilla Congress, Réunion, June 6, 2024.

NINE. TOWARD BLAND AND WHITE?

1. Gabriela Zapolska, "Pawilony Kolonii," in *Publicystyka: Część 1* (1889–95; repr., Wrocław: Zakład Narodowy Imienia Ossolińskich, 1958), 104–5.

2. Mark Smith, *A Sensory History Manifesto* (University Park: Pennsylvania State University Press, 2021), 79.

3. Marie Ranjanoro, *Feux, fièvres, forêts* (Paris: Laterit, 2023), 9–10.

4. A 1947 set of ethnographic recordings features Carlioto Oyarzun mimicking the sounds of a local man selling vanilla at Bayonne's market. See ADPA, 5NUM 1/247.

5. Jonathan Reinarz, *Past Scents: Historical Perspectives on Smell* (Bloomington: University of Indiana Press, 2014), 209–10. Robert Muchembled claims that this deodorization trend has been overstated for most contexts, except for the United States. See Muchembled, *La civilisation des odeurs* (Paris: Les Belles Lettres, 2017), 244.

6. "Revue dramatique," *Le Charivari*, March 15, 1852.

7. Emile Zola, *Nana* (1880; repr., Paris: Garnier-Flammarion 1968), 207.

8. Emile Zola, *La Curée* (1871; repr., Paris: Garnier-Flammarion, 1970), 75, 201–2; Sarah Maza, *The Myth of the French Bourgeoisie: An Essay on the Social Imaginary, 1750-1850* (Cambridge, MA: Havard University Press, 2003), 5, 52.

9. *Schenectady (NY) Reflector*, May 15, 1846, 3.

10. "Woman's Pet Tipple," *Fort Worth (TX) Daily Gazette*, August 31, 1887, 8; "History of the Idiomatic Usage of Vanilla," English Language and Usage Stack Exchange, accessed January 29, 2023, https://english.stackexchange.com/questions/451476/history-of-the-idiomatic-usage-of-vanilla.

11. Yvonne Kapp, *Time Will Tell: Memoirs* (London: Verso, 2003), 7.

12. "Pauvre proviseur!," *Le Monde illustré*, September 5, 1874, 157.

13. Alain Corbin, *The Foul and the Fragrant: Odor and the French Social Imagination* (Cambridge, MA: Harvard University Press, 1986), 170, 179 (quote on 179); Georges Vigarello, *Le propre et le sale* (Paris: Le Seuil, 1985), 146.

14. Mathilde Cocoual, "La famille Chiris: Des industriels en politique, une politique d'industriels?," *Cahiers de la Méditerranée* 92 (2016): 177–91.

15. Noël Ilari, *Secrets tahitiens: Journal d'un Popaa Farani, 1934-1963* (Paris: Nouvelles éditions Debresse, 1965), 13.

16. ANOM, 151 AQ3, 205.

17. On perfume circulations from France to Russia, see Reinarz, *Past Scents*, 72.

18. "La place de la vanille dans les parfums," *Le Parisien*, archived February 27, 2024, at https://web.archive.org/web/20240227174024/http://pratique.leparisien.fr/beaute/parfum/histoire-parfum/la-place-de-la-vanille-dans-les-parfums-1500008600; Clara Muller, "La

Vanille: Epice aux mille visages," *Auparfum*, August 8, 2015, https://auparfum.bynez.com/LA-VANILLE-EPICE-AUX-MILLE-VISAGES,2424.

19. Marius and Ary Leblond, *L'Île enchantée: La Réunion* (Paris: Librairie de la revue française, 1931), quoted in François Berthier, *Histoire des plantes à parfum de l'île de La Réunion* (Grasse: Somedex, 2017), 240.

20. Jean-Marie Le Clézio, *Révolutions* (Paris: Gallimard, 2003), 27; Anna Lowenhaupt Tsing, *The Mushroom at the End of the World: On the Possibility of Life in Capitalist Ruins* (Princeton, NJ: Princeton University Press, 2015), 48.

21. ADR, 318 W28, Etude du marché de la vanille (December 1963), 15, and annex 8.

22. Pascal Tréguer, "'Plain Vanilla' | 'Vanilla Sex': Early Occurrences," *Word Histories*, April 30, 2020, https://wordhistories.net/2020/04/30/plain-vanilla-vanilla-sex.

23. Anna Iovine, "When It Comes to 'Vanilla Sex,' No Two People Taste the Same Flavor," *Vice*, February 14, 2019, https://www.vice.com/en/article/vbw3bj/when-it-comes-to-vanilla-sex-kink-no-two-people-taste-the-same-flavor; Cheryl de la Rey and Michelle Friedman, "Sex, Sexuality, and Gender: Let's Talk About It," *Agenda: Empowering Women for Gender Equity* 28 (1996): 43; Margot Weiss, "Working at Play: BDSM Sexuality in the San Francisco Bay Area," *Anthropologica* 48, no. 2 (2006): 233.

24. Camille Vernin, "Sexe vanille: faut-il culpabiliser d'être ennuyeux au lit?," *Elle*, January 24, 2023.

25. Harryette Mullen, quoted in Kat Chow, "When Vanilla Was Brown and How We Came to See It as White," *Code Switch*, March 23, 2014.

26. Olivier Fruneau-Maigret, *Lu, une marque à l'avant-garde* (Rennes: PUR, 2020), 126–30.

27. "Newly Produced Vanilla Oshiroi," *Yomiuri Shimbun*, September 17, 1905, 8.

28. Audre Lorde, quoted in Michael W. Twitty, "Black People Were Denied Vanilla Ice Cream in the Jim Crow South," *Guardian*, July 4, 2014.

29. James Bernard, "Why the World Is After Vanilla Ice," *New York Times*, February 3, 1991.

30. On colonial themes in French marketing, see Dana Hale, "French Images of Race on Product Trademarks During the Third Republic," in Sue Peabody and Tyler Stovall, eds., *The Color of Liberty: Histories of Race in France* (Durham, NC: Duke University Press, 2003), 144.

31. Molly Kruse, "The Colonial, Racist Legacy of Danish Supermarkets," *Scandinavia Standard*, March 21, 2021, https://www.scandinaviastandard.com/the-colonial-racist-legacy-of-danish-supermarkets.

32. Adam Karremans, "On the Identity Crisis of 'Mexican Vanilla,'" paper presented at the Fifth International Vanilla Conference, Saint-Pierre, Réunion, June 4, 2024.

33. On innate and acquired odors, see Rachel S. Herz, "I Know What I Like: Understanding Odor Preferences," in Jim Drobnick, ed., *The Smell Culture Reader* (Oxford: Berg, 2006), 194–95.

34. Artin Arshamian et al., "The Perception of Odor Pleasantness Is Shared Across Cultures," *Current Biology* 32 (May 9, 2022): 2061–66.

CONCLUSION

1. "Défendons nos vanilles," *Le Madécasse* (Antananarivo), March 1, 1930, 1.

2. Lauren James, *Colonial Food in Interwar Paris: The Taste of Empire* (London: Bloomsbury, 2016), 147–49.

3. More troublingly, one can also trace the route that colonized people took to be displayed at Vincennes. See Catherine Hodeir, "Decentering the Gaze at French Colonial Exhibitions," in Paul Landau and Deborah Kaspin, eds., *Images and Empires: Visuality in Colonial and Postcolonial Africa* (Berkeley: University of California Press, 2002), 233–52; and Philippe David, "Les Malgaches à l'exposition coloniale de Paris en 1931," *Tsingy* 13 (2011): 32–42.

4. ADR, 8M 102, Exposition coloniale internationale, 1931.

5. ADR, 8M 102, Exposition coloniale internationale, 1931.

6. Michel Grisoni insists on preparation as the difference-maker between "good" and "bad" vanilla. See Florence Merlen, "Les artisans de la vanille," *Casemagazine* 44 (August 1, 2012): 38.

7. "Israël/Innovation: Une startup fait pousser une vanille aux saveurs uniques grâce aux nouvelles technologies," *i24NEWS*, July 25, 2022, https://www.i24news.tv/fr/actu/israel/1658740568-innovation-une-startup-israelienne-fait-pousser-une-vanille-aux-saveurs-uniques.

8. Celina Ribeiro, "Anything but Plain: Inside the Australian Push to Grow Vanilla Outside the Tropics," *Guardian*, September 1, 2022.

9. Laurence Caramel, "Crise de la vanille à Madagascar," *Le Monde* (Paris), April 19, 2023.

Acknowledgments

I am grateful to the Social Sciences and Humanities Research Council of Canada, the Jackman Humanities Institute, Victoria College, and the University of Toronto, without which this project could not have been researched and written. I further benefited from a global web of librarians, archivists, informants, translators, friends, colleagues, and research assistants—with many of the following people fitting more than one category.

Among my paid research assistants, I extend thanks to Juan Carlos Mezo-Gonzáles for his excellent work in Mexico City. In Seville, I am grateful to Esther González for her painstaking digging in the "Indias" archives, and to Geoffrey Parker for having recommended her. From Kansas, Matthew Dunn sent digitized copies of the Chauvet diaries. Bako Narahintsoa helped prepare my archival visit to Antananarivo. Sunny Le Galloudec conducted research for me in Vietnam. In France, Abdelhakim Belhacel sent photos of archival gems I had missed, concerning vanilla's first arrival on Madagascar's satellite islands. Mathilde Cocoual scanned a file in Réunion before I got there. Joseph Stollenwerk consulted the Staatsarchiv in Hamburg. Ursula Carmichael undertook extensive online research. Benjamin Holt scoured American newspapers. Jacob Harvey compiled relevant statistics. Gregory Fewster scanned sources in Oslo.

Others contributed to this project through translations. Adriaan den Hartog translated from Dutch, working by my side in Leiden and The Hague. Jiaying Shen provided translations from Japanese; Chaoran Ma did the same with Chinese materials. Tom Frydel translated a passage from Polish, Gaëlle Esso another from Mauritian Creole. Astrid Klee translated tricky German-language material, and Philip Lekmanov undertook research in and translations from Russian.

A host of archivists and librarians went well beyond the call of duty. My ongoing gratitude extends to Isabelle Dion, head of the French colonial archives. In Rome, Father Eric Hernout generously scanned relevant dossiers. In the Loire Valley, archivists Sylvain Bertoldi and Sylvette Robson shared a mortuary inventory. At the Schlesinger Library, Sarah Hutcheon

ACKNOWLEDGMENTS

photographed material from the Rindlaub papers. In Belgium, I am grateful to Laurent Gohy for his welcome at Liège in 2018, and to Olivier Damme for digitizing files at the Académie de Bruxelles during the global lockdown. The Collectivité Territoriale de Martinique kindly authorized me to reproduce figure 14. At Kew Gardens, Rachael Gardner and Kat Harrington scanned Morren-related material. At the Thomas Fisher Rare Books Library, David Fernandez and Elizabeth Ridolfo introduced me to unique culinary sources. Julien Durup shared his findings on Seychellois vanilla. Guy Marion sent sources relating to Edmond Albius.

A warm thank you to the Jackman Humanities circle of fellows for 2022–23, including Ruby Lal, Seth Bernard, Urvashi Chakravarty, Emily Nacol, Dale Turner, Khanh Vo, Jaclyn Rohel, Lucy Stark, Fatema Mullan, and our directors Alison Keith and Elizabeth Legge. Other colleagues in Toronto provided assistance and advice at every turn, especially Deborah Neill, Margaret Schotte, and Gillian McGillivray at York University; Geoffrey Pilcher, James Retallack, Paul Cohen, William Nelson, Kevin Coleman, Andreas Motsch, Adrienne Hood, Sean Mills, Piotr Wróbel, Yvon Wang, Marga Vicedo, Mark Solovey, Alison Smith, and the late Natalie Zemon Davis at the University of Toronto; Jacqueline Solway at Trent University; as well as Camille Bégin.

My thanks to Pierre-Eric Fageol and Cathy Vidalou for their hospitality on Réunion Island. *Merci* as well to the head of the local archives, Damien Vaïsse. Pascale Moignoux kindly provided digitized copies of her uncle Father Raimbault's papers. (The originals are at Chevilly-Larue.) A community of Indian Ocean specialists contributed leads for this project, including Claude Bavoux, Sarah Fee, Faranirina Rajaonah, Samuel Sanchez, Frédéric Garan, Gilles Gauvin, Solofo Randrianja, Annah Zhu, Jennifer Cole, Violaine Tisseau, Sue Peabody, Helihanta Rajaonarison, Albert Jauze, Genese Sodikoff, Michael Lambek, Andrew Walsh, Marie-Clémence Andriamonta-Paes, Marie Boulaire, Gwyn Campbell, and the late Pier Larson.

Other colleagues, friends, and family helped shape the project. Emilio Kourí was magnanimous with early feedback. David Skerritt, to whom he introduced me, helped me better understand San Rafael's French communities. Michel Grisoni patiently answered my questions about vanilla science and became an invaluable interlocutor, introducing me to other key vanilla scientists, including Adam Karremans and Alan Chambers. Isabelle Merle and Robert Aldrich recommended Polynesian sources. Rikke Andreassen led

ACKNOWLEDGMENTS

me to a Danish visual. Franck Michelin guided me toward material on the Japanese introduction of vanilla to Micronesia in the 1920s. Roland Kaehr put me on the trail of Eugène Hänni. Nicolas de la Bretèche shared the menu of Czar Nicholas II. Erick Noël sent material on vanilla in the Caribbean. Arnauld Bartolomei helped determine the usefulness of the Roux papers.

Hélène Blais, a fellow traveler in the history of colonial plants, invited me to the Ecole normale supérieure in Paris, where this project germinated. So did Len Smith at Oberlin, Andrew Jainchill at Queen's University, Samuel Sanchez at Paris-Condorcet, Glenn Penny at UCLA, and Yun Kyoung Kwon at Seoul National University—I received useful feedback at each campus, including from Lynn Hunt and Ghislaine Lydon at UCLA. As always, Alice Conklin, Owen White, J. P. Daughton, Michaël Ferrier, Derek Penslar, Charles Keith, Anne Perrotin-Dumon, Marie-Pierre Ulloa, Ruth Ginio, Christopher Goscha, Pierre Singaravélou, Olivier Wievorka, and Yerri Urban provided excellent advice. Scott Prudham carefully read an entire early draft, greatly improving it. Anonymous readers for Yale University Press produced constructive reports that bettered the book. Thanks to my editor Jaya Aninda Chatterjee and my agent Suzy Evans, who believed in this project from the start. Thanks to Amanda Gerstenfeld and Nicholas Taylor for their editorial work, to Isabelle Lewis for cartography, and to Celia Braves for the index.

On location, owners of vanilla groves invited me in and shared their knowledge. Thanks to Cédric Coutellier and Marion Cassu in Guadeloupe, Bertrand Côme in Réunion, Paul Joanne at Cinq Frères near Antalaha, and contacts on Taha'a, provided by Marereva Aumeran, through Carine Charron: Murielle Pollock and her circle, including Cristiano, Naomi, and Rodrigo. Thanks finally to Dr. Mahendran in Pollachi, India, for discussing Indian production. Each of their explanations, demonstrations, and tastings helped flavor this book.

Portions of chapter 8 were previously published in French as "Cartels et lobbies de la vraie vanille: Marketing, genre, nostalgie et réseaux postcoloniaux," *Revue d'histoire moderne et contemporaine*, 2019/3 (n° 66–3), pp. 128–155. © Éditions Belin / Humensis, 2019, and are translated here with the journal's permission.

Last but not least, the inner pod. My parents, Chantal Bertrand-Jennings and Lawrence Jennings, provided consistently helpful feedback, as did my spouse, Tina Freris. Our daughters, Alexandra and Sophie, served up literary leads and turns of phrase. I am deeply indebted to all of them.

Index

Page numbers in italics refer to figures.

abolition, 71, 77-79, 84, 87, 99
Abraham, Jacob-Denis, 159
Abreu-Runkel, Rosa, 237n17
acclimatization, 59, 64, 66, 68, 140, 250n91
advertising, 29, 49, 191, 216, 223; for coffee, 209-10; for ice cream, 94, 186, 209; for natural vanilla, 194-95, 198-206; for vanilla wafers, 183-84, 221, *222*
Aeta, Don Martín de, 27
agricultural fairs: Briançon, 162; Brussels, 52-53, 58, 217; Dublin, 168
agroforests, 6
Albany, André, 95, *96*
Albius, Edmond, 160-61, 163, 167; about, 68-70, 72-74; artificial pollination discovery, 7, 13, 16, 63, 74-78, *75*, 106, 143, 232; challengers to his discovery, 80-83, 256n77; choice of surname, 78-80, 255n64, 255n68; Morren's influence on, 61, 250n95; representation and recognition of, 84-88, *85*
Albrand, Fortuné, 111
Album de la Réunion (1863), 84, *85*
Algeria, 172, 268n62
American Banking Company, 103-4
Angelou, Maya, 16, 223
Antalaha (Madagascar), 122, 123, 128, 132; vanilla laboratory, 129-30
Antananarivo, 108, 110, 113, 117, 125, 131, 204
aphrodisiacs, 10, 12, 15, 30, 232
Aramburu, André de, 21
artificial pollination. *See* manual pollination
artificial vanillin. *See* synthetic vanillin
Artur, Jacques François, 32

Artusi, Pellegrino, 180-81
Austria, 16, 55; Vienna, 30, 188-89
Avendaño, Andrés de, 20
Aztecs, 17, 18-20, 159, 224

Baartman, Sarah, 47
Bach, Robert, 98
Backus, William Vernon, 164
Balzac, Honoré de, 93
bananas, 6, 184, 231
Barrère, Pierre, 244n61
Barthes, Roland, 201
Basque borderlands, 181
Bassana, Marie Pauline, 73, 87
Bayonne (France), 69, 162
Beaumord, Madeleine, 203
Beauperthuy, Louis-Daniel, 255n73
Beckert, Sven, 4
bees, 1, 7, 17, 229; *Vanilla planifolia* pollinators, 13, 24, 37, 61; *Vanilla pompona* pollinators, 34, 35
Belgium, 121, 195; agricultural fairs, 52-53, 58, 217; Antwerp, 39-40, 44; colonial power, 59, 60; free trade, 56; history and industrialization, 40-41; Royal Academy, 43, 49-50, 245n13. *See also* Liège
Belin, Pierre, 162
Bellier-Beaumont, Ferréol, 74-76, 78, 81-86, 256n77
Bellier-Beaumont estate, 73-74
Berenstein, Nadia, 187, 190
Bernard L. Lewis Inc., 194-95
Bernier, Joseph, 82

— 287 —

INDEX

Betsimisaraka people, 109–10, 113; vanilla cultivators, 16, 122, 124–25, 128, 132
biscuit makers, 183–84, 221, *222*
Blackness, 78, 223–24
Blancke, John, 79
blandness: masculinity and, 202; vanilla sex and, 15, 215, 219–21; vanilla's resistance and shift to, 214–19, 224–25
"blue vanilla," 106
Bois, Dominique, 113
Boivin, Louis-Hyacinthe, 111
Bojer, Wenceslas, 80–81
Bonhoure, Adrien, 152
Bora-Bora, *136*, 137, 148–49, 157
Bordeaux, 143, 190; cuisine, 181; Mexican vanilla imports, 89–90, 97, 162
botanical gardens: Bourbon, 64–65, 66, 68, 82, 83; Buitenzorg (Bogor Gardens), 167–68; Calcutta, 170; Kew Gardens, 51, 170; Liège, 43, 44–45, 51, 55, 61; Miami, 171; Paris, 63, 65, 68, 83, 160; Pondicherry, 173; Saigon, 173. *See also* greenhouses
botanists, 44, 64, 151; British, 51, 61, 170, 246n26; Dominican missionary, 35; Dutch, 166–67; French, 36, 48, 57, 172–73, 244n61, 245n67; Swiss, 65–67; women, 51–53. *See also* Morren, Charles-François Antoine
Bourbon, 65; botanical garden and introduction of vanilla, 64–68, 160; climate disasters and sugar production, 71–72; enslaved people, 68–71, 72–73; famine and epidemics, 71; renaming to Réunion, 78, 93. *See also* Réunion
"Bourbon vanilla": consumed in Milan, 181; label, 8, 63, 95, 187; Madagascar vanilla as, 94, 101, 106, 187, 195
bourgeoisie, 11, 27, 179–80, 215, 221
Boyer, Joseph Suzony, 104
Brisse, Léon, 179–80, 181, 215
British empire, 9, 60, 94, 135; Belgian industry and, 41, 43–44; chocolate manufacturers, 170, 184, 191; Madagascar and, 108, 109, 116, 129; occupation of Bourbon, 71; vanilla imports and consumption, 155, 179; vanilla production in India and, 170–71, 173; vessels, 25. *See also* Mauritius; Seychelles Islands
Brown, Robert, 246n26
Bruman, Henry, 160–61
Brussels, 40, 41, 55; agricultural fair, 52–53, 58, 217
Bunschoten, Claire, 10

cacao, 6, 18, 29–30, 33, 35, 173, 184; grown on Bourbon, 63, 72; supply chain, 91. *See also* chocolate drinks; chocolatiers and chocolate manufacturers
Cadbury, 170, 191
Cádiz, 27, 39, 274n97; French consul, 9, 23; port of trade, 18, 23–26, 38
caffeine, 30
Canada, 15, 192–93, 194, 195, 210
capitalism: "Champagne," 11; global, 5, 132
Carême, Marie-Antoine, 28
cartels: energy, 197, 277n41; Indian Ocean vanilla, 105, 195, 197–98, 210–11
Casa de Contratación, 22–23, 24, 38
Catat, Louis, 112
caviar, 11
Cayenne. *See* French Guiana
CEDAL (Centre de documentation de l'alimentation), 202, 204
CEDUS (Centre d'études et de documentation du sucre), 203
Céré, Jean-Nicolas de, 251n6
Chalot, Charles, 151
Chambers, Alan, 139
Chambon, Ludovic, 160
Chauvet, Eugène, 92, 94, 113–15, 116
Child, Julia, 180
child labor, 120, 125, 126, 227
China, 185, 193, 232; laborers, 66, 67, 70, 147, 152; merchants, 3, 16, 112, 151–54
Chiris, Georges, 217–18

— 288 —

INDEX

chocolate drinks, 14, 27–30, 182, 232; Aztec *chocolatl*, 17, 18–19, 224

chocolatiers and chocolate manufacturers, 30, 155, 215; Belgian, 39, 50, 63, 247n48; British, 170, 184, 191; Californian, 149–50; Parisian, 28–29; use of synthetic vanillin, 190–91

Ciarlo, David, 205

cinnamon, 28, 32, 33, 64, 111, 159, 225

Clement XIV, Pope, 25

climate, 2, 34, 59–60, 62; Algeria's, 172–73; Bourbon's, 64, 69; frost, 172; global warming, 233; Madagascar's, 115; natural disasters, 71–72, 91, 169, 174; Nosy Be's, 121; vanilla varieties and, 130

cloves, 33, 64, 72, 77, 159, 207; Portugal's monopoly over, 21; vanillin derived from, 3, 15, 188, 192, 194, 213, 230

Coca-Cola, 16, 182

cochineal, 5, 9, 37; Spanish monopoly over, 18, 22, 23, 25, 36

Cockerill, John, 44

Coe, Sophie, 17

coffee, 5, 12, 60, 111, 156, 267n40; geographical region and, 204; Juan Valdez character, 209, 211; plantations, 113, 114, 119, 120, 145, 147; production on Bourbon, 71, 72, 73; *vazaha* planters, 122

Cointet, Emile Edmond de, 116

Colbert, Jean-Baptiste, 33

Cold War, 131, 193

Colombia, 20, 26, 31, 37, 139, 209–10

colonial clichés, 204–6, *206*

commodity chains, 5, 91, 96, 227; middlemen, 134

Comoros Islands, 98, 102, 104, 106, 128, 218; pod exports to the US, 195–98, 210; *Vanilla humblotii* variety, 129–30

consumption, vanilla: advertisers and female, 200–204; democratization of, 107; European trends, 28–30, 210, 232; geographic origin preferences and, 56–57; global trends, 10–12, 14, 20, 160, 179; in India, 171; in Italy, 181; in New Spain, 27–28; realistic amounts of, 39; of real *vs.* synthetic vanilla, 179, 220, 233; in the United States, 12, 14, 190, 209, 220; vanilla madness and, 131–32. *See also* cookbooks; ice cream; recipes

contraband. *See* smuggling

cookbooks, 203; Betty Crocker, 191; Brisse's menu-a-day, 179–80, 215; Italian, 28, 180–81; Mexican, 28

cooperatives, 171; Madagascar, 128–29; Réunion's Grand Hazier and Provanille, 105

Corbin, Alain, 217

corvées, 108, 110, 125

Côte d'Ivoire, 91

cotton, 4, 5, 21, 41, 72, 144, 147–48

Courtois, Richard-Joseph, 43, 45

COVID-19 pandemic, 225, 233

Creoles, 84, 88, 99, 102, 176, 219; enslavement, 70, 71; women, 113, 205

crime, 133–34, 153, 173–74; sabotage, 128. *See also* smuggling; theft

customs duties, 30, 163, 169, 241n16; officials, 112, 178, 261n19; reduction of, 83, 89, 171

Cuzent, Georges, 138

dairy producers, 171, 186, 199

Dampier, William, 9

Darwin, Charles, 52, 61–62

Davis, Natalie Zemon, 31, 52

debt, 101, 109, 133, 144–45

deforestation, 64, 86, 123

Delvaille and Attias firm, 162, 270n13

Demard, Jean-Christophe, 162

democratization, 11, 15, 27, 107, 160, 242n31; of sugar, 60

deodorization trend, 214, 217, 279n5

Desbassayns, Joseph, 76, 80

Deutsche-Östafrikanische Gessellschaft (DOAG), 112, 117–18

— 289 —

INDEX

disease, 71, 76, 112, 117, 157; fungal, 101, 169–70, 233; malaria, 43, 115; resistance, 130; yellow fever, 159, 255n73, 269n2
Dodge and Olcott, 98
Dor, Alfred, 97
Dupuy, Pierre-Sébastien, 81, 255n73
Dupuy-Compton, 200, 202, 204, 207
Dussert, Paul, 258n31
Dutch East Indies. *See* Indonesia
duties. *See* customs duties

Ecott, Tim, 237n17, 257n86
elite, 20, 27, 28, 123, 232; botany and, 52, 256n77; cuisine, 10, 106, 179–80; Franco-Mauritian, 176; Tahitian, 135, 145. *See also* bourgeoisie; *vazaha* settlers
Elle magazine, 220
empowerment, 3, 4, 6, 110, 131, 132, 179
Encyclopédie (Diderot and d'Alembert), 37
enslaved people: abolition, 71, 77–78, 84, 87, 99; of Bourbon, 68–71, 72–73; of Madagascar, 69–70, 109; medical-botanical knowledge of, 76–78; "specialized," 72–73; sugar plantations and, 32, 33; surnames, 78–79. *See also* Albius, Edmond; indentured labor
ESSOR, 200–206, 208–9
European Union, 105–6, 195, 204
Eve, Prosper, 72
exoticism, 204–6, 206, 210, 217, 224
exports: from Gabon, 173; global trends, 14, 130, 149, 159, 227; from India, 171; from Italy, 25; from Madagascar, 109, 113, 115, 129, 130–32, 193, 210; from Martinique, 81; from Mauritius and Seychelles Islands, 169–70; from New Spain / Mexico, 12, 21–26, 38, 39, 89–90, 95, 160; from Nosy Be, 112; from Réunion, 90, 95, 97, 103–4, 210; from Sainte-Marie, 111; SCO's control over, 144–45; from Tahiti, 142–43, 144, 155–56; vanilla preparation and, 104, 155

famine, 71, 72
Férolles, Pierre-Eléonore de La Ville de, 32–35, 36
Fertile Crescent, 17
fertilizers, 72, 170
flavor/flavoring. *See* synthetic vanillin; vanilla flavor
Florentine Codex (1570s), 20, *21*
Florida, 172
Floris, David de, 76, 83, 84, 89, 90; article on vanilla, 86, 142–43, 256n82
Fontaine, Alexandre, 93
Fontecilla, Agapito, 163–64
food regulation, 20, 104, 152, 189–90; testing, 196, 198; US FDA, 192, 195, 199
food tampering, 29, 152, 188–89, 196
forced labor, 5, 87, 109, 120, 125–28, 137
forest vanilla, 6, 114, 123, 157, 161
fragrance. *See* perfume; scent
France, 40, 88, 197, 203; abolition, 71, 73, 78; Brittany, 27; cuisine, 181, 183, 184, 206; decline of colonial power, 65–66, 71–72; luxury goods, 11–12; Napoleon's defeat, 64–66; navy, 24, 36, 135–40, 148, 157; paid holidays, 103; settlers in Mexico, 3, 94, 160–63, 164–67; smuggling, 178–79; synthetic vanillin laws, 189–90, 196, 199; Univanille campaign and, 199–200; vanilla consumption, 28–30, 190; vanilla imports, 9, 26, 33, 90, 95, 97, 151–52, 243n53; Versailles, 33–36. *See also* Paris; Vichy regime
Franco-Mexicans, 3, 161–64
fraud, 20, 21, 24, 86, 188, 192
French Antilles. *See* Guadeloupe; Martinique
French Congo, 173
French Guiana, 32–34, 243n53, 251n9; Bourbon vanilla and, 66, 67, 68, 95, 243n53; vanilla varieties, 30–31, 57, 243n61
French Indochina, 160, 173–74

INDEX

French Polynesia, 133–35, *136*, 143–45, 227, 228; Chinese merchants, 154; diffusion of vanilla, 148–49; global warming and, 233; shade house growing technique, 156–58; vanilla exports, 130, 156, 159. *See also* Tahiti
fusarium fungus, 101, 169–70, 233
Fusée-Aublet, Jean-Baptiste Christophe, 57, 250n3, 251n6

Gabon, 151, 173
Gacon-Dufour, Marie Armande Jeanne, 36
Gaëde, Henri, 43, 45
Gambiers, 149
Gauguin, Paul, 145–47, *146*
Genève, Auguste, 80–81
Gennermann, Paulina, 187
Germany, 117, 152, 155, 179, 195; synthetic vanillin and, 187, 193, 220; World War II and, 186. *See also* Hamburg trading companies
Giorgi, Jean, 173–74
givre (vanilla frost), 53, 57, 188, 231; artificially inducing, 152; vanilla quality and, 28, 58, 229, 230
globalization, 2–3, 5, 8, 10, 12, 232
Gobley, Théodore-Nicolas, 187
gold, 109
Goldhammer, Gilbert, 191
Goodness Vanilla, 171
Graeber, David, 109
Great Depression, 12, 156, 179, 229
Greenfield, Amy Butler, 36
greenhouses, 215; Dutch, 58–59; Kew Gardens, 51, 170; Liège, 13, 44–53, 54, 55–56, 59, 62; for orchids, 45; Raiatea, 158
green vanilla (unprepared), 100, 101–2, 151, 158, 229; Nosy Be planters and, 111, 117; stamping or marking, 175; theft and quality of, 177
Grisoni, Michel, 130, 281n6

Groéme, E., 175, 177
Groissaint, Claude, 162
Guadeloupe, 9, 35, 143, 166, 205; theft and natural disasters, 174; vanilla production, 149, 155, 205
Guatemala, 18, 20, 21, 23, 67, 135, 267n40
Guénot, Joseph Lucien Edouard, 112
Guénot, Stéphane, 161
Guenther, Ernest, 98
Guerlinade, term usage, 218–19
Guermantes Way, The (Proust), 79–80, 255nn67–68
gum arabic, 5
Guy, Kolleen, 194
Guyénot, Marcel, 194

Haarmann, Wilhelm, 187
Haiti. *See* Saint-Domingue
Hamburg trading companies, 112, 117–18, 130, 144–45, 154, 267n40
Hamelin, Ferdinand, 138–39, 141, 265n11
Hänni, Eugène, 133–34, 141, 156
Haquin, Hyacinthe, 52, 53
Hardye, Félicité Anne, 159
health chocolate (*chocolat de santé*), 29
Henderson, George, 170–71
Hernández, Francisco, 20
Hibbert, Harold, 192, 276n22
Hoshino Shūtarō, 172
host trees, 1, 6, 9, 114, 126, 143; avocado trees, 172; Canary Islands dragon trees, 45, *46*; coconut trees, 35; Japanese lilacs (*Melia azedarach*), 173; in Madagascar, 124; old-growth trees, 34; shade houses (*ombrières*) and, 156–57; trellises and, 139
household science, 202, 203
housewives, 200–201, 203, 204, 208, 209
Howard Smith Chemicals Ltd., 192
Hubert, Joseph, 68, 77, 78, 251n6
Hugo, Victor, 44
Humboldt, Alexander von, 22

INDEX

Huntley and Palmers, 183
hybridization, 124, 129–30, 231, 233; *Vanilla tahitensis* and, 134–35, 138–39

ice cream, 2, 49, 79, 171, 220, 221; consumption in China, 185; consumption in the US, 10, 179, 186, 193–94, 197; French dairy producers and, 199; hand-cranked, 182–83; Italian, 180; made with Bourbon vanilla, 94; made with synthetic vanillin, 15–16, 213; made with vanilla extract, 191; poisonings from, 188–89; racist banning of, 223; Soviet, 131, 193; World War II and, 186–87, 193–94
Iceland, 16, 240n44
Île Bourbon. *See* Bourbon
Île Sainte-Marie, 71
indentured labor, 3, 70, 99–101, 120, 177
India, 170–71, 173; laborers, 70, 99, 177
Indigenous people, 76; exploitation and coercion of, 20–21; harvesting and trade, 22, 31–32, 33; uses of vanilla, 17–20; vanilla knowledge and, 31–32, 36, 161
indigo, 3–4, 5, 23, 25, 95, 239n33
Indonesia, 14, 44, 67, 105, 130, 210
industrialization, 40–41, 43–44, 49, 96
instructional documents, 142–43, 150, 162–64, *163*, 167
insurance, 165–66, 175
"internalized ecology," 8
International Colonial Exhibition (1931), 224, *225*, 227–29, *228*, 281n3
inventory, 25, 26, 159, 231
Isle of France, 65, 137, 251n6; enslaved people, 69, 74, 77; plant varieties, 64, 65, 77. *See also* Mauritius
Israel, 17, 231, 232
Italy, 179, 195, 199, 220; cuisine, 28, 180–81; Genoa, 25

Japan, 15, 172, 186, 193, 211, 223; vanilla consumption, 184–85, 231
Jaume, J., 175, 177
Jaussen, Florentin-Etienne, 140–42, 143, 266n25
Java, 67, 149, 172, 174, 270n27; Dutch introduction of vanilla, 56, 166–68
Jefferson, Thomas, 10, 11
Jews, 31, 36, 162, 216
Jicáltepec / San Rafael (Mexico), 141, 160–62, 165–66, 167
Jones, Colin, 27
Joseph Burnett Company, 94
J. S. Fry and Sons, 191
Jussieu, Antoine Laurent de, 111

Kapp, Yvonne, 216–17
Karremans, Adam, 7, 256n77
Klein, Judith, 6
knowledge sharing, 9, 57, 166; of enslaved people, 72–73, 75–77; of Indigenous peoples, 31–32, 76, 161; instructional manuals and documentation, 142–43, 150, 162–64, *163*; local populations and, 126, 132; Morren's, 51, 60–61; of Tahitian vanilla experiments, 140; transmission and, 80–81, 149
kola nuts, 182
Kourí, Emilio, 6, 8, 17, 48, 163, 237n17
Kwass, Michael, 27

Labat, Jean-Baptiste, 35–36
labels: artificial vanillin, 189–91, 195, 196, 199, 203, 211, 224, 230; "Bourbon vanilla," 63, 95, 187; dishonesty of, 15, 209–10; geographical origin and, 204; vanillin vs. vanilla, 191, 207
labor recruitment, 66, 102–3, 119–20, 122, 125–26, 132; of *corvées*, 108, 110, 125. *See also* indentured labor
Lacaille, Louis, 107–8, 114, 125
Lacroix, César-Jacques de, 244n61
land dispossession, 6, 122, 147

— 292 —

INDEX

Langenier, Lucet, 88
Langlois, Nemours, 177, 178
larceny. *See* theft
Latour, Bruno, 7–8
Lavaud, Charles, 137
Leblond, Marius and Ary, 219
Le Clézio, Jean-Marie, 219
Leeward Islands, 135, *136*, 137; vanilla producers, 133, 148–49, 154, 156–58
Lefebvre, Alfred and André, 164–66
Lefèvre-Utile (LU), 183–84, 221, *222*
Legras, Paul, 117
Le Guidec, Henri, 173–74
Leissle, Kristy, 247n48
Le Monde, 217, *218*
Leopold II, King, 55, 56
Lépervanche, Mézières, 64–65, 74
Liebig, Julius von, 184
Liège, 121; greenhouse vanilla, 13, 44–53, *54*, 55–56, 59, 62; industry, 40–41, 43–44
Life magazine, 186, 216
lignin, 15, 192, 213, 276n22
Limbour, Georges, 86–87
Lindley, John, 51, 52
Linnaeus, Carl, 77
literacy, 73
Livambarom, Ranguin, 99–101
Lloyd, John Uri, 169
locomotion, 76, 254n53
L'Opinion de Diego-Suarez (1928), 126–27
Lorde, Audre, 223
Louis XIV, King, 23, 32, 228
Loupy, Ernest, 91
luxury goods, 9, 60, 121, 141, 188, 228; historical trends, 4–5, 11–12; spices, 64

Madagascar, 65, 87, 233, 274n97; American and Mauritian planters, 113–16, 262n35; campaign for natural vanilla, 194–98, 209, 210; Chinese immigrants, 3, 123; colonial officials as vanilla producers, 123–25; competition with Réunion, 102, 104–6; enslaved people, 69–70; exoticism, 204–5; introduction of vanilla, 111–14; Malagasy vanilla producers, 102, 122–23; monarchs and French conquest, 108–10, 116–17, 262n36; post-colonial vanilla production and exports, 130–32, 149, 185, 193–96, 210–11; reptiles and mythical beasts, 114–15; Réunionese planters, 13–14, 102–3, 107; scientific laboratories, 129–30; similarities with Tahiti, 135; unpaid labor and colonial abuses, 108, 110, 120, 126–28, *127*; World Wars I and II and, 129, 155, 156, 186. *See also* Nosy Be; Sainte-Marie
Magellan, Ferdinand, 21
Mahendran, R., 171
Malilé, 196
Manheimer, Stephen, 209–10
manual pollination, 2, 3, 7, 8, 14, 38; Albius's discovery and challengers, 7, 13, 16, 63, 74–78, *75*, 80–84, 232; child and forced labor for, 120, 125–26, 227; Dupuy's technique, 81, 255n73; female labor for, 126, 163, 203; fictionalized writing on, 86–87; importance of timing, 1, 236n1; instructional materials on, 142–43, 162–64, *163*; labor intensity of, 91, 119–20; in Madagascar, 115, *119*, 124; in Mexico, 160–61; Morren's achievement of, 13, 45–49, 55–58, 62; Neumann's technique, 48, 83, 247n42, 256n77
manumission. *See* abolition
margarine, 3, 187
marieuses, 1, 90
Maroantsetra (Madagascar), 126, *127*
maroons, 70, 76, 77
Marseille, 26, 97, 98, 112, 173, 229
Martinique, 35–36, 81, 166, 224, *225*
Mascarenes, 63, 69, 77, 80, 109, 122
masculinity, 202
Massieu de Clerva, Auguste Samuel, 111

INDEX

Mauritius, 3, *65*, 108, 251n7; British colonial, 80, 111, 115–16, 175; Dupavillon of, 126, *127*, 263n68; manual pollination claims, 80–81; settlers in Madagascar, 115–16, 262n35; theft, 175–76; vanilla production and exports, 14, 149, 168–69. *See also* Isle of France

May, D. W., 171

Maya people, 18, 20, 21, 141

Maza, Sarah, 215

McClelland, T. B., 171

medicinal uses, 30, 76–77, 182, 184

Menonville, Nicolas-Joseph Thiéry de, 36–37

Merian, Maria Sibylla, 52

Merina monarchs, 108, 109–10, 260n3; *fandroana* festival, 114

Messageries Maritimes, 175

Mexico. *See* New Spain / Mexico

Meyjes, M. C., 169

Micronesia, 162, 172

Milli Vanilli, 223

Ministry of the Navy and the Colonies, 66, 83, 89, 123, 154, 258n31; Tahitian vanilla cultivation and, 139, 142, 151, 156

Misantla (Mexico), 22, 141, 165

missionaries, 31, 73, 109, 118–21; botanist, 35, 173; Polynesian, 136, 137, 141–42, 145

monoculture, 72, 122, 123, 168

monopolies, 166, 198, 211; coffee, 5; Indian Ocean-produced vanilla, 93, 95, 210–11; New Spain / Mexico's vanilla, 2, 21–25, 30–32, 38, 227–28; Portugal's clove, 21; SCO's, 144–45

Monsanto, 192

Montoia, Alonso de, 27–28

Moriceau, René Jules Edouard, 123–24, 129–30

Moroy, J., 188

Morren, Charles-François Antoine: achievement of manual pollination, 13, 45–49, 82–83, 167; education and interests, 41–43; posting at University of Liège, 43; promotion and failure of vanilla ventures, 49–50, 53, 55–62, 94; translation of his work, 49–53

Morren, Marie-Henriette-Caroline, 13, 42, 50–53, 57–58

Morris, James, 168

Moutien, Virapin, 99–101

"Mrs. Washington Potts" (Leslie), 10–11, 213

Mucha, Alphonse, 184, 221, *222*

Napoleon III, 147, 166

natural pollination, 2, 7, 17, 61; surrealist bestiary and, 86–87. *See also* bees

Naudé, Pierre/Pedro, 162–63

Netherlands, 155, 179, 193, 220; Belgium and, 40, 41, 42; Dutch traders, 33; greenhouse vanilla failure, 58–59; vanilla consumption, 195. *See also* Java

Neumann, Joseph, 48, 83, 247n42, 256n77

Newberry, Colin, 135

New Spain / Mexico, 8, *18*, 169, 178; American entrepreneurs, 163–64; competition with Réunion, 89–90, 93–95; French settlers and traders, 3, 160–62, 164–67, 172; incidents of fraud and coercion, 20–21; Indigenous uses of vanilla, 17–20; near monopoly, 2, 9, 18, 30, 227–28; origin of Tahitian vanilla and, 138–39, 141; superiority of vanilla, 94, 149, 150, 151; vanilla exports, 12, 89–90, 130, 160; vanilla preparation methods, 22–27, 89

New York, 89, 98, 103, 183, 194–95; shipping companies, 165–66

non-natives species, introduction of, 64

Norton, Marcy, 27

nostalgia, 16, 200, 214, 225; childhood memories, 203–4, 205; scent and, 214, 217, 219

Nosy Be, 98, 102, 108; ethnic groups, 109; *fatidra* bond, 119–20; vanilla producers and laborers, 111–12, 117–22, 125–26

nutmeg, 64, 71, 72, 77, 98, 250n3

— 294 —

INDEX

Oaxaca, 18, 25, 37; *alcaldes mayores*, 21
O'Brien, Frederick, 153
Oetker, Dr. August, 180
Office de la recherche scientifique et technique outre-mer (ORSTOM), 129–30
Ontario Paper Company, 192–93
orchids and orchidology, 2, 45, 51, 61. *See also* vanilla orchid
Osterhoudt, Sarah, 6
Ozoux, Raoul, 229–30

packaging, 23–24, 103–4, 150; blister packs, 208; bundling, 95–97, *96*, 169, 229; of catalog seeds, 63–64; cedar cases, 165; glass tubes, 133, 207–9; to prevent theft, 175; tin boxes, 34, 90, 92, 104, 115
palm oil, 6, 17, 251n7, 270n27
Papantla (Mexico), 17, 18, 164, 171, 212, 237n17
Papeete (Tahiti), 138, 139, 140, 143, 153, 155
Paris, 12, 133–34, 136, 144, 165–66; botanical garden, 63, 65, 68, 83, 160; chocolatiers, 28–29; consumption of chocolate drinks, 29–30; differences with provinces, 200–201, 207–8; food protests, 11; horticultural society, 139; International Colonial Exhibition (1931), 224, *225*, 227–29, *228*, 281n3; Madagascar embassy, 196, 198
Pauffret, Claude-François, 162
Peabody, Sue, 70
perfume: essences, 97; plants used for making, 118, 121, 170; vanilla-scented, 9, 98, 217–19, *218*
permits, 175, 177–78
Perrottet, Guerard Samuel, 65–68, 256n77
Petit, Valentin, 139–40
Philibert, Pierre-Henri, 65–68, 95
Philippines, 23, 67–68, 135, 137, 138
Pilcher, Jeffrey, 180
piracy, 2, 9, 25, 36, 38, 188, 232; "biopiracy," 24, 37; fending off, 23
"plain vanilla," 216, 219–21

plant agency, 7
plantations, 99, 100, 162; in Bourbon / Réunion, 73–74, 90; coffee, 72, 113, 114, 120; Comoros Islands' Bambao estates, 128; Dominica, 184; Edmond Albius's tour of, 76, 80; in Madagascar, 102, 112–16, 122–25, 126–28, *127*; in Mauritius, 80–81, 168, 176–77; in Nosy Be, 112, 118–20, 125–26; in Papantla, 164; sugar, 32–33; Tahiti's Eugénie estate, 147; *vazaha*-owned, 122, 124–25, 128
plant trade, 63–68
pods: acts of sabotage to, 128; awards for, 162, 168, 229; cooking with, 28, 180, 181, 182, 203; curing or drying, 9, 91–92, 150, 161, 164, 167, 173; genetic manipulation, 231; gestation and maturation, 46; glass tubes for, 133, 207–9; illustration, 53, 54; Indigenous uses, 18–20; samples, 133; scent, 20, 129, 214, 244n61; shipping, 23–26, 38, 95, 115, 165; size, 95, 169, 244n61; stamping or marking, 175–77; Tahitian, 134, 140, 149–50, 158; theft, 9, 92–93, 174–78; water content, 1, 91, 104, 155. *See also givre* (vanilla frost); packaging; preparation and processing
poisoning, 76, 188–89, 223
Poivre, Pierre, 64, 77, 245n67, 250n3
Pollan, Michael, 7, 237n14
pollination. *See* manual pollination
Pomare IV, Queen, 136–37
Pomeroon, 31
Portugal, 21, 31, 34–35, 186
poscoyon (oven), 164
preparation and processing, 7, 14, 171, 231; climate and, 59; curing or drying, 1–2, 91–92, 164, 167; Guianese methods, 57; household science teaching and, 202; knowledge and secrecy, 31–32, 36, 51, 101, 167; labor intensity of, 91, 164, 203, 229–30; lack of mechanization, 3, 96; laws, 151, 154, 177–78, 189–90; Mexican

— 295 —

INDEX

preparation and processing (*continued*)
  expertise, 89, 167, 169; mold prevention, 103–4; Morren's, 46–47, 57, 58; sizing and bundling, 95–97, 96, 169, 229; skill, 102–3; synthetic vanillin, 192–94; of Tahitian vanilla, 149–53
preservation techniques, 104, 121, 150, 155, 208
price, 6, 14–15, 39, 124; decline in, 93–94, 105, 121, 149, 233; demand and, 26, 145, 171, 210; gradations, 95; greenhouse production and, 50, 56, 59; of ice cream, 197; of Mexican vs. Bourbon vanilla, 94; overproduction and, 131, 194; in Paris compared to the provinces, 200–201, 207–8; of shipping rates, 165–66; synthetic vanillin and, 185, 193, 209, 232; of Tahitian vanilla, 151, 153, 155, 156; of unprepared vanilla, 100
prison labor, 126
property ownership, 99–101, 113, 116, 122, 158
protectionism, 60, 72, 169
Proust, Marcel, 79–80, 87, 219, 255nn67–68
public relations, 202–3
Puerto Rico, 14, 160, 166, 171
pulp paper, 192–93, 194, 232

quality: of French Indochinese vanilla, 173; *givre* and, 28, 58, 188, 229, 230; gradations, 26, 95, 165, 169; of Liège vanilla, 56; of Mexican vs. Bourbon vanilla, 89–90, 94–95; middlemen as guarantors of, 194; of small-scale vanilla production, 230–31; of synthetic vanillin, 192; of Tahitian vanilla, 149–53; theft and, 177

race, 16, 24, 47, 86, 153–54; identity and, 84, 88; sexualization and, 47–48; surnames and, 78–79, 255n68; whiteness, 221, 222, 223–24. *See also* exoticism
Radama I, King, 108–9, 110
Raffeneau-Delile, Alire, 48–49

Raiatea, 136, 137, 148–49, 156, 158
Raimbault, Father Clément, 118–22, 125, 144
Rain, Patricia, 237n17, 265n11
Ralaimongo, Jean, 127, 128
Rama, Charles, 77
Rang, N. B. E., 276n22
Ranjanoro, Marie, 214
Ratsiraka, Didier, 131, 193
recipes, 10, 16, 28, 179–81, 191, 240n44; that promote natural vanilla, 201, 202, 203
registers of goods, 25, 178
Reinarz, Jonathan, 214–15, 217
reptiles, 114
retailers, 200, 205, 206, 207
Réunion, 3, 6, 167, 172, 219; competition with Madagascar, 102, 104–6; competition with Mexico, 89–91, 93–95; expansion into international markets, 98–99, 185; hurricanes, 91, 105; laborers on Madagascar, 13–14, 102–3, 107; Paris's botanical garden and, 83, 256n77; pod preparation techniques, 91–92, 95–97, 96, 151, 229–30; production and exports, 90, 95, 97, 143, 149, 195–98, 210; quality complaints, 103–4; recognition of Edmond Albius, 84, 87–88; renaming, 78, 93; small-scale producers and cooperatives, 105–6, 229; South Asia immigrants, 99–101; speculation and buyers, 101–2; theft, 92–93. *See also* Bourbon
rice farming, 6, 250n91
Richard, Claude, 82, 84
Ridley, Henry, 150
Rindlaub, Jean Wade, 191
Rivière, M., 155
Robinson, Solon, 10
Robinson, William, 113–15
Roche, Salomon de la, 31, 32
Roellinger, Olivier, 134
Roman Catholic Church, 41, 136, 140–42
Rorer, Sarah Tyson, 182–83
Roussin, Antoine, 84–86, 85, 87, 88

— 296 —

INDEX

Roux brothers (French merchants), 26
Rowntree and Company, 170, 184, 191
rubber, 5, 6, 109, 114, 122, 164, 187
Russia / Soviet Union, 53, 55, 99, 130, 131, 193

Sade, Marquis de, 15
Sahagún, Bernardino de, 20
Saint-Cyr, Claude Carra, 66, 251n9
Saint-Domingue (Haiti), 36–37, 59, 71, 245n67
Sainte-Marie, 108, 111, 117, 143
Sainte-Suzanne (Réunion), 70, 79, 88, 99; Bellier-Beaumont estate, 69, 73–74, 84; climate disasters and famine, 71; plantations, 76, 80, 87, 105
Saint-Hilaire, Geoffroy, 251n9
Saint-Joseph (Réunion), 101, 219
Saint Pern, Léon de, 177
Sakalava people, 109, 112, 119, 124, 132
Salmon, Tati, 144–45
San Francisco, 144, 145, 149, 150, 151, 227
Saulnier, E. H., 159–60
Sava region (Madagascar), 109, 174, 193, 212, 214, 233; post-colonial vanilla production, 130, 131, 132; rise of vanilla, 7, 122, 123–25
scent, 30, 204, 212–13; global popularity of vanilla, 225–26; intensity, 58, 217, 218; regional differences, 230; of vanilla pods, 20, 36, 129, 149, 229; of vanillin, 187–88. *See also* perfume
Schaar, Alberto, 165
seed exchanges, 63–64
Segrais, Paul Léonce Le Juge de, 176–78
Seville, 18, 22–23
sexualization, 86–87, 215; of vanilla as female, 47–48, 217, 221, 222
Seychelles Islands, 14, 72, 97, 149, 169–70, 178, 190
shade houses (*ombrières*), 156–58
Sherzer, Karl, 167–68

shipping companies, 165–66, 175
shipping routes: Bourbon-to-Asia, 66–68; to California, 144, 151; duration of transport, 151–52; Jicáltepec-to-Veracruz, 165–66; from Madagascar, 109, 115, 132, 227; from Martinique, 81; Mexico-to-Bordeaux, 89–90; from Nosy Be, 112, 121; from Réunion, 97–99, 103–4; smuggling and, 178–79; from Tahiti, 136–37, 155–56; Veracruz-to-Cádiz, 23–26, 38
slave trade. *See* enslaved people
smear campaigns, 150–55, 268n62
smuggling, 9–10, 24, 178–79, 181, 241n21
social mobility, 116, 125, 147
Société Commerciale de l'Océanie (SCO), 144–45, 154
Society Islands, 135, *136*, 148
Sodikoff, Genese, 174
Solana, Ana Crespo, 23
Sophia Scarlet (Stevenson), 147–48
soundscapes, 214
South Asian immigrants, 3, 70, 99–101, 120, 123, 177
Soviet Union. *See* Russia / Soviet Union
Spain: clergymen, 20, 27–28; expulsion of Jews, 162; pod monopoly, 2, 21–23; Veracruz-to-Cádiz shipping route, 18, 23–26, 38
Spang, Rebecca, 27
Spary, Emma, 29
spices, 4, 64, 77, 98, 180
Sprengel, Christian, 246n26
stamping device, 175–77
Stassart, Goswin de, 41, 43, 49–50, 245n13
Stevenson, Robert Louis, 144, 147–48
Stewart, William, 148
substitutionism, 3–4, 187, 199, 213, 219, 232; lemon and, 10, 180; for real vanilla, 191–92; vanilla price and, 93–94. *See also* synthetic vanillin
Suez Canal, 97, 112, 229

— 297 —

INDEX

sugar, 5, 11, 29, 70, 111, 113; beet vs. cane, 59–60; French Guiana, 32–33; lobby, 203; prices, 95, 145; processing, 91; production in Bourbon, 71–72; in syrup, 182; vanilla or vanillin, 180–81, 188, 196, 203, 206, 208

Suriname, 30, 31, 32, 76

surrealism, 86–87

sustainability, 4, 6, 158, 179, 209

synthetic vanillin, 3, 155, 185; consumption trends, 179, 209, 220; flavor and scent, 213; ice cream and, 15–16, 213; labels and legislation, 189–91, 195, 196, 199, 203, 211; machinery for detecting, 198; in perfumes, 219; producers, 192–93; real vanilla vs., 193–200, 230, 232–33; rise of, 8, 15, 187–89, 230, 276n22

Taha'a, 136, 137, 148–49, 156–58, 174

Tahiti, 4, 16, 61, 90, 124, 136; Chinese immigrants, 3, 153–54; competition with Réunion, 102; cultural objects, 97; French colonization, 14, 135–37; Gauguin's stay, 145–47, 146; landholders, 144–45; natural disasters and, 99; origin and introduction of vanilla, 9, 134–35, 137–43, 149, 265n11; referenced in Stevenson's writings, 147–48; reputation for inferior vanilla, 149–53; vanilla production and exports, 142–44, 149, 155–58, 185, 227

Talbot, Antoine Joseph, 116, 262n36

Tamatave (Madagascar), 109, 112–13, 115–16, 122, 123, 262n35

Tananarive. *See* Antananarivo

tariffs. *See* customs duties

tea, 6, 94, 182, 219

Teijsmann, Johannes, 167–68

terroir, 12, 57, 94, 230, 231

textile industry, 41

theft, 9, 20, 37, 59, 161, 174–78, 232; on Réunion, 92–93, 100

Thiers, Adolphe, 10

Tiemann, Ferdinand, 187

tlilxochitl (black flower), 19, 19–20

Tørsleffs, 224

Totonac people, 16, 17, 18, 161, 164, 174

tourism, 106, 157

trade secrets: of manual pollination, 43, 46, 56, 75; rose varieties and, 52; of vanilla preparation, 1, 31–32, 36, 92, 101, 164

Trastour, Honoré, 140

Tréguier, Pascal, 220

Tromelin (Île de Sable), 69, 70

tropicality, 59

truffles, 12

Tselementes, Nicholas, 183, 274n97

Tsiranana, Philibert, 130

unions, 117–18, 198

United States, 144; consumption trends, 12, 14, 190, 209, 220; Food and Drug Administration (FDA), 192, 195, 199; Mexico's vanilla sector and, 163–64, 227; obsession with ice cream, 10, 179, 186, 193–94, 197; Pure Food and Drug Act (1906), 189–90; vanilla cultivation, 171–72; vanilla imports, 97, 98, 103–4, 115, 129, 169, 171, 195, 210; in World Wars I and II, 103, 155, 156, 186, 269n84

Univanille / Provanille, 196–204, 207–10, 224

Valentin Petit, François, 138

van Breda, Jacob Gijsbertus Samuël, 41, 42

vanilla, definition and term usage, 14, 15, 27, 37, 232

Vanilla Bean Association of America (VBA), 209

vanilla beans. *See* pods

vanilla extract, 94, 170, 192, 216; in capsule form, 191; factories, 164; standardization of, 189–90; in syrups, 182; in vanilla biscuits, 183–84

INDEX

vanilla flavor: of "blue vanilla," 106; in Coca-Cola, 182; descent into blandness, 4, 15, 16, 207, 213–17, 219–21, 224; for enhancing chocolate, 8, 18–19, 28–29, 159, 170, 184, 266n25; enjoyed in Japan, 184–85; genetic manipulation and, 231; intensity of, 217–19; as perceived for elderly people, 207, 278n74; in recipes, 2, 28, 179–84, 183, 191, 203; of Tahitian beans, 134, 149–50, 156; as unpleasant tasting, 204; varietal differences, 30, 134, 154–55, 232. *See also* ice cream

Vanilla Ice, 223–24

vanilla orchid, 16, 17, *19*, 224; bloom time, 1; color, 19–20; lack of scent, 20, 36; in Liège greenhouses, 13, 45–49

Vanilla planifolia, 8–9, 12, 13, 37, 154, 187; cultivated in Liège, 44–53; cultivated in Madagascar, 110, 114; cultivated in Puerto Rico, 171; hybrid varieties, 124, 129–30, 134–35, 138–39; instructional documentation on, 162–63, *163*; introduced to Bourbon, 63, 68, 95; introduced to Java, 166–68; New Spain / Mexico origin, 17–18, 95; preparation methods, 231

Vanilla pompona, 9, 18, 20, 26, 150, 231; Guianese, 30–35, 57, 67, 68, 243n61, 245n67; medicinal qualities of, 30; pollinators, 13, 35

vanilla powder, 16, 180, 183, 188, 208, 223

"vanilla sex," 15, 215, 219–21

Vanilla tahitensis, 9, 154–56, 158, 187, 231; origin, 134–35, 138–39, 141

vanillin, 106, 154, 187, 213, 215, 232–33; description, 15, 28; infused sugar, 206–7. *See also* synthetic vanillin

vanillons, term usage, 95, 258n31

varieties, 8–9, 13, 114; flavor differences, 232; hybrid, 124, 129–30, 134–35, 138–39, 233; indigenous to Madagascar, 114; indigenous to Martinique, 35; inedible, 36, 46, 110–11, 244n61; "Micentella," 141, 266n25; in Saint-Domingue, 36, 37; *Vanilla aromatica*, 138; *vanille musquée*, 244n61; vanillin levels and, 154, 187

Vaughan, Megan, 74–75

Vaughan, Victor, 189

vazaha settlers, 122, 124–25, 128, 132

Veracruz, 18, 23–26, 38, 160, 162; US consul, 159, 269n2

Vergès, Paul, 88

Vermond, Henri, 250n95

vessels, 39–40, 97, 112; *Adèle*, 81; *Beadle*, 115; *Durance*, 66; *El Fuerte* or *Fort de Nantes*, 25; *La Boussole*, 156; *L'Aube*, 148; *Lexington*, 186; *Rhône*, 66; *Santiago*, 23; shipping rates, 165–66; *Sydney*, 97; *Thisbé*, 138; *Utile*, 69; *Virginie*, 138

Vichy regime, 103–4, 129, 156, 263n68, 269n84

Vietnam. *See* French Indochina

Villeneuve, Alexis de, 104

vines, 1, 6, 9, 17, 34, 149; depicted in *Florentine Codex*, 20, *21*; destroyed by salt, 121; fungal disease, 100–101, 169–70; Gauguin's drawing of, 145, *146*; ideal height, 163; Liège greenhouse cultivation, 45, 46, 49, 56, 57, 83; on Madagascar plantations, 114, 117, 124, 126, 132; Mexican growing system, 169; on Nosy Be plantations, 112; Polynesian growing techniques, 139, 143; shade houses (*ombrières*) and, 156–57. *See also* host trees

vola mafana (hot money sprees), 131–32

Volsy-Focard, Eugène, 82–83, 85

Vries, Jan de, 39

Vries, M. H. de, 166–67

wafers, vanilla, 183–84, 221, *222*

wages, 102, 105, 106, 118, 120, 145, 210

— 299 —

INDEX

Westwood, John, 61, 62
whales, 42, 136
whiteness, 16, 221, *222*, 223–24
Winship, North, 153
women: in advertisements, 221, *222*; Betsimisaraka chiefs, 113; botanists, 51–53; hand pollination by, 126, 163, 203, 229; racialization of, 196; vanilla consumption and marketing to, 200–202, 203, 207; vanilla retailers, 205, *206*
World War I, 102, 118, 121, 154, 155, 161

World War II, 11, 103, 129, 156; ice cream consumption and, 186–87, 193–94, 209

yogurt, 201, 203, 211, 224, 232

Zafy, Cécile, 131, 132
Zama, Marcellin, 236n1
Zapolska, Gabriela, 212–13
Zhu, Annah, 131–32
Zink and Triest, 210, 269n84
Zola, Emile, 215